opus signed

23.00

Best wishes

[signature]

Best wishes for new ideas.
to Jim Flanders.

Walter Crease

PLANNING CITIES: LEGACY AND PORTENT

William Houghton-Evans

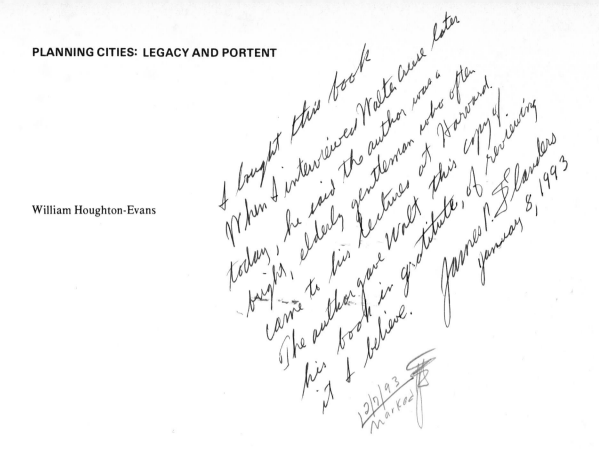

*I bought this book
When I interviewed Walter Creese later
today, he said the author was a
bright, elderly gentleman who often
came to his lectures at Harvard.
The author gave Walt this copy of
his book in gratitude, of reviewing
it I believe.*

James R. Flanders
January 8, 1993

12/7/93
Marked

Lawrence and Wishart Ltd, 46 Bedford Row, London

To those whose courage will always keep open the road to Utopia

IBSN   0-85315-319-1

Production and process work under the supervision of the Head of THE UNIVERSITY PHOTOGRAPHY SERVICE, University of
Leeds: typeset by DESA TYPESETTING, Nottingham: printed by SOLAPRINT of LEEDS LTD.

CONTENTS

Preface

page 5	Chapter 1	Britain and the urban heritage
6	2	A survey of cities
24	3	Town planning: the rise and fall of a tradition
34	4	Utopia
47	5	The ideal industrial town
52	6	A town planning movement
55	7	Communications and the city
59	8	The modern movement
65	9	Political revolution
72	10	Cataclysmic technology
80	11	Organic growth
88	12	Theories and practice 1936-1950
93	13	New town and neighbourhood
99	14	The plan from MARS
103	15	Cumbernauld and Hook
113	16	Traffic in towns
122	17	Critical re-appraisal
126	18	Linear new towns
141	19	The resurrection of the gridiron
149	20	Two tales of one city
157	21	Lessons from the 'sixties
162	22	Developing practice and theory
175	23	Folk and place
182	24	Work

References

Acknowledgements

Index

I am grateful to my colleagues at the University of Leeds who allowed me sabbatical leave to prepare this book; to Professor Arnold Noach who (although in no way responsible for what I have written) has over many years helped me with scholarly advice; to my son Michael who deciphered my manuscript, and to Christine Bestington who typed it; to Mr. Ford and his colleagues at DESA who set the type; to the University of Leeds Director of Photographic Services, Mr. Hewitt, and his staff, who did the photo-litho work, and especially Patricia Appleton, who set the pages; to J. Skelley, Maurice Cornforth and the staff at Lawrence & Wishart who guided things through the shoals of publication; to Sheila Wheeler for help and criticism; and above all to my wife, who not only assisted at every stage, but unobtrusively maintained the serene atmosphere without which surely no book could be written.

PREFACE

To the Reader

I wrote this book because, at this time of uncertainty and crisis, there seemed to me to be a need for a coherent appraisal of town planning, out of which we might hope to discover some principles to guide us in the future.

I hope it will be useful to the practitioner, the student, the politician and the ordinary citizen who wishes to be well-informed. Those familiar with the subject will find nothing new in the opening chapters, and they will recognise my sources in such worthy authorities as Lavedan, Mumford, Hiorns, Korn and the many others whose work has sunk so deep into my memory that I am not always aware from whom I have borrowed.

I am by training an architect: a professional planner, and merely a latter-day academic. As a historian, I claim no more than amateur status, but I trust I have not sinned too greatly by way of omission, over-simplification or downright distortion of the facts.

I hope I have needlessly offended no-one — especially not my fellow practitioners. I know today I have the easier task of merely picking over what they are doing. I know their motives, methods and conclusions are more complicated than I have given credit for, and that they work within the limits they are given. I hope they will allow that one cannot resist every opportunity that presents itself for pointing up a contrast or turning a paradox. Such things are intended to leaven the dough, not poison it.

It is not possible (or, it seems to me, desirable) to write about town planning without airing one's views. I have tried neither to allow opinion to interfere with fact, nor to over-state my case. But selection is inevitable, and some emphasis is needed if error is to be refuted. I see no point in nailing my colours to the mast before we sail: they will be unfurled as we proceed, and you will judge them, I hope, on their merits as I have presented them.

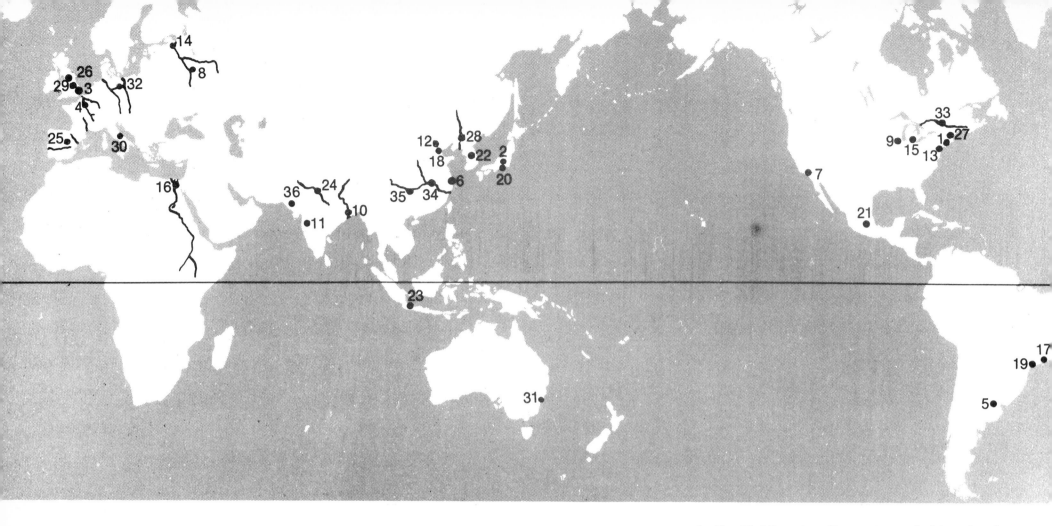

1 The World's metropolitan centres ranked in order of their size.

RANK	NAME	POPULATION	RANK	NAME	POPULATION	RANK	NAME	POPULATION	RANK	NAME	POPULATION
1	NEW YORK	14,114,927	10	CALCUTTA	4,518,655	19	SAO PAULO	3,164,804	28	SHENYANG (MUKDEN)	2,411,000
2	TOKYO	10,177,000	11	BOMBAY	4,422,165	20	OSAKA	3,151,000	29	BIRMINGHAM	2,377,230
3	LONDON	8,176,810	12	PEKING	4,010,000	21	MEXICO CITY	3,050,723	30	ROME	2,278,882
4	PARIS	7,369,387	13	PHILADELPHIA	3,635,228	22	SEOUL	2,983,324	31	SYDNEY	2,215,970
5	BUENOS AIRES	7,000,000	14	LENINGRAD	3,552,000	23	DJAKARTA	2,906,533	32	WEST BERLIN	2,176,612
6	SHANGHAI	6,900,000	15	DETROIT	3,537,309	24	DELHI	2,549,162	33	MONTREAL	2,156,000
7	LOS ANGELES	6,488,791	16	CAIRO	3,418,400	25	MADRID	2,443,152	34	WUHAN	2,146,000
8	MOSCOW	6,354,000	17	RIO DE JANEIRO	3,223,408	26	MANCHESTER	2,442,090	35	CHUNGKING	2,121,000
9	CHICAGO	5,959,213	18	TIENTSIN	3,220,000	27	BOSTON	2,413,236	36	KARACHI	2,060,000

There have been men for at least a quarter of a million years. Until a few thousand years B.C. — the length of time is disputed and is unimportant to us here — there were no cities. Anthropologists tell us that groups over five hundred strong are exceptional before civilisation began.[1] By the time of Christ, it is possible that there were about twelve settlements of 100,000 or so each, around the Mediterranean, but cities of this size have been exceptional until recent times. Carthage is said once to have numbered 700,000, and Classical Rome may have approached a million. From Marco Polo's accounts, we learn that China already in his day boasted large cities, but the record generally is obscure and unsure. In counting heads — an infrequent exercise until modern times — a not uncommon failing was to reckon only 'freemen', taxpayers, or heads of households as being alone worthy of enumeration. There is confusion also concerning what at various times has been meant by 'city', 'town' or 'village'. The earliest civilisations would include within a city not only its urban nucleus, but also the rural hinterland over which it ruled. From medieval times, we still inherit degrees of rank which exalt small chartered 'cities' above upstart manufacturing 'towns'. For our purposes, we may perhaps best accept that 'town' or 'city' implies, in contradistinction to 'village' or 'hamlet', the settlement of a community not mainly themselves engaged in agriculture.

About 1600 A.D., at the height of their power, a handful of Italian, Spanish and Dutch cities had six-figure populations, but as recently as 1700, London was the only settlement in the British Isles with a population in excess of 30,000. At that time, England's population (probably less than 5 million in all) was split at least five-to-one in favour of the countryside: a circumstance still today not untypical of many lands. Since then, however, Great Britain has charted a course in urban development that sees her still among the leaders in the field, and with the whole world now seemingly hell-bent on overtaking her.

From 1801 to 1901, the population of Great Britain quadrupled: from about 10 million to nearly 40 million. During the same time, the rural/urban split was reversed in favour of the town. London in 1800, alone among the world's cities, had already reached the million mark, and by 1900, Greater London was approaching 7 million. In 1950, England was the most urbanised country in the world, with 80% of her population living in places with 2,000 or more inhabitants.[2] Over half of her population lived on one-fifth of her land area — a belt extending from Kent to Cheshire. Today, nearly one-quarter live within daily 'commuting' distance of London alone. And today, London is not unique. She is no longer even the biggest. Tokyo and New York now number over 13 million each, and are among several metropolitan 'world-cities' with multi-million populations.[3] A recent report reveals that Sao Paulo in Brazil has grown from 600,000 in 1935 to 8,500,000 today, and that she continues to receive immigrants at the rate of 150 per hour.[4]

With this experience behind her, and with no less pressing problems still to be met, it is not surprising that for modern times the art of town planning has enjoyed in Great Britain a unique development. No history of the subject, no textbook or learned review, no matter in what language, will today fail to discuss the growth of the British nineteenth century industrial town, the English Garden City Movement, and the British New Towns. Other lands and other times have also much from which we can learn, but Britain's experience as the first in the field, still gives a unique authority to those of her theorists and practitioners who, for nearly two centuries, have tried to make sense of and control the industrial city. It needs no more than the evidence of everyday life in Britain to confirm how small has been their success. And it will surprise no-one that an economic system dedicated to private fortune-hunting is not the most favourable for community planning and endeavour. But planning and endeavour there have been, and among the general failure, there has been some progress. The most significant achievement, however, is in the realm of theory, and this, as it has developed and is still developing, and defective though it undoubtedly is in many ways, will repay investigation.

Modern town planning theory does not come out of a vacuum, however. Although largely forgotten and neglected, there was available to the planners of Victorian Britain a not inconsiderable body of theory, accumulated since the days of Greece and Rome. Archaeology and research have added much in recent years, and it is only in the last few decades that town planning has again become a major field of study. But an understanding of what is at issue must begin with some acquaintance with the city itself in its historical evolution.

Pre-historic settlements can be known only from the investigations of anthropology and archaeology, and being, strictly speaking, closer to the village than the town, might be excluded from our consideration. But there is much that town planning still seeks to learn from village life, and primitive societies have many virtues we may yet recover. The earliest societies were probably nomadic, and such settlements as they created were temporary encampments. With settled agriculture inevitably come permanent settlements, and some of these, either as relics or as they still exist in various parts of the world, have been studied.

The pitching of a tent (as every schoolboy knows) requires considerable forethought. Shelter, the lie of the land, the prevailing wind, access, water supply, a place for a fire, sunshine, safety from attack by bull or farmer — these and much beside figure in an experienced camper's calculations. Multiply these factors several times to embrace a tribal encampment; add to them the grim struggle for survival in a fickle and potentially hostile environment; compound them with folk-lore, traditions and taboos relating to the whole complexity of social and economic life; and we have some idea of the motives and methods of primitive men. A recent comparative study of early village planning reveals wide variety in formal arrangements which, it is asserted,

'indicate a correlation between the level of economic development and the complexity of the planning schemes evolved. The simplest societies, such as those of the Pygmies and Bushmen, retain a maximum of design flexibility, just as their economic and social systems insist upon physical mobility and relatively free interpersonal relationships. The more sedentary groups become, the greater their emphasis on land and property and the more inclined they are toward fixed spatial organisation. In still more complex groups, an economic surplus combined with increasingly hieratic

social and political distinctions frequently prompts the priveleged placement of meetinghouse, market place, or important chief's dwelling.

'Social relationships rather than geometric order appear to be the major determinant in the placement of buildings . . .'

but the Cheyenne camped in a circle, and other examples exhibit formal arrangements of a most complex kind. *'The concept of the center'* is widespread, and *'military and political factors apparently gain importance . . . with the growth in wealth . . .'*[5]

Precedent, primitive science and custom, enshrined in religious ritual, have an influence which survives to Roman times. Roman writers themselves attributed much of the practice associated with the planning of a new town to rites inherited from their predecessors — the Etruscans. A modern scholar tells us:

'These customs belong to the fields of religion, agrarian land settlement and war. All three exhibit the same principle, the division of a definite space by two straight lines crossing at right angles at its centre, and (if need be) the further division of such space by other lines parallel to the two main lines. The roman Augur who asked the will of Heaven, marked off a square piece of sky or earth — his templum — into four quarters; in them he sought for his signs. The Roman general who encamped his troops, laid out their tents on a rectangular pattern governed by the same idea. The commissioners who assigned farming-plots on the public domains to emigrant citizens of Rome planned their plots on the same rectangular scheme. In their original character these customs were probably secular rather than religious. They took their rise as methods proved by primitive practice to be good methods for laying out land for farming or for

encamping armies. But in early communities all customs that touched the state were quasi-religious; to ensure their due performance, they were carried out by religious officials . . . We possess certainly no such clear evidence with respect to towns as with divisions agrarian or military. But the town plans . . . show very much the same outlines as those of the camp or of the farm-plots. They are based on the same essential element of two straight lines crossing at the centre of a (usually) square or oblong plot . . . We need not hesitate to put town and camp side by side, and to accept the statement that the Roman camp was a city in arms.'[6]

While much of what is attributed to Roman town planning cannot always be taken at face value, it is also known that tradition required that the site of a town (or at least of its consecrated nucleus) should be delimited by an antique ceremony in which a furrow was cut and turned to form, as it were, a rudimentary fortifying ditch and wall.* The Lord Mayor who turns the first sod with his silver-plated shovel, today stands last in the line of a time-hallowed tradition.

The rectilinearity of the Roman town is not however characteristic of pre-historic settlements. Curved forms both in buildings and in their grouping are more typical, although examples employing straight lines and the more rectangular shapes which characterise later periods, do occasionally occur.

A basic requirement of agriculture is storage, and primitive communities, whether or not they needed shelter for their comfort had to provide it for their grain. A granary has to be sited with an eye to defence against natural hazard and pillage by covetous enemies, and from it some authorities trace the treasuries, citadels and temples of history. Of greatest importance also were the burial grounds and ritual places, and when the Copper Age village is replaced by the Bronze Age town, we shall find these things live on in the minds and practices of the community.

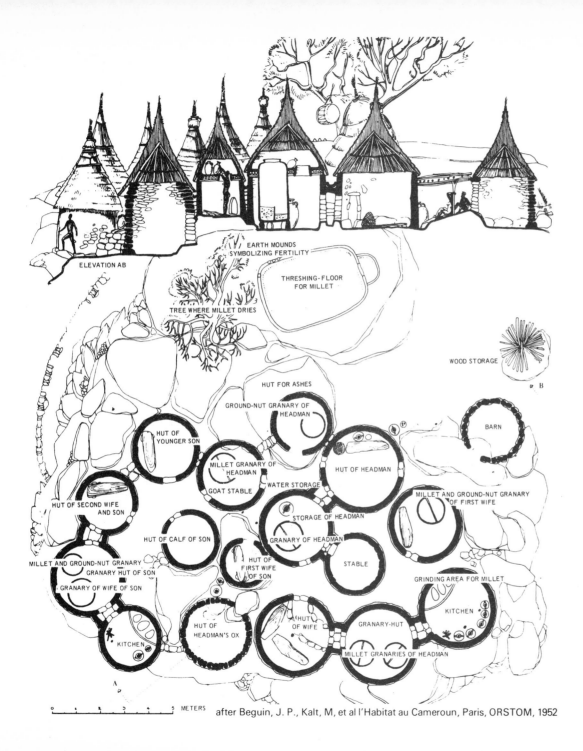

2 Homestead,
Cameroun,
Africa:

ELEVATION AB

EARTH MOUNDS
SYMBOLIZING FERTILITY

THRESHING-FLOOR
FOR MILLET

TREE WHERE MILLET DRIES

WOOD STORAGE

HUT FOR ASHES

GROUND-NUT GRANARY OF
HEADMAN

BARN

HUT OF
YOUNGER SON

MILLET GRANARY OF
HEADMAN

HUT OF HEADMAN

GOAT STABLE

WATER STORAGE

MILLET AND GROUND-NUT GRANARY
OF FIRST WIFE

HUT OF SECOND WIFE
AND SON

STORAGE OF HEADMAN

HUT OF CALF OF SON

GRANARY OF HEADMAN

STABLE

MILLET AND GROUND-NUT GRANARY
GRANARY HUT OF SON

HUT OF
FIRST WIFE
OF SON

GRINDING AREA FOR MILLET

GRANARY OF WIFE OF SON

KITCHEN

HUT OF HEADMAN'S OX

HUT
OF WIFE

GRANARY-HUT

KITCHEN

MILLET GRANARIES OF HEADMAN

0   1   2   3   4   5   METERS

after Beguin, J. P., Kalt, M, et al l'Habitat au Cameroun, Paris, ORSTOM, 1952

Hundreds of thousands of years of mankind's existence elapsed before copper was alloyed with other metals to produce more serviceable bronze tools and weapons. The ensuing technical advances gradually facilitated more efficient production which in favourable locations produced a regular surplus above that required for subsistence. The same advances encouraged the emergence of specialists, including not only smiths and other craftsmen, but also a literate class responsible for the elaborate budgeting and planning of resources now necessary. All of these new specialists dwelt in cities which dominated the countryside around them. New forms of social organisation arise, based on the rule of a propertied élite over a subjugated peasantry and enslaved labouring class. War for conquest and pillage becomes a normal state, as a result of the economic advantages to be gained from the concentration of wealth and slave labour for ambitious building, irrigation and drainage works. Dynasties of monarchs, whose position was combined with a priestly or military role, headed powerful aristocracies. A literary culture develops, as does science and mathematics — especially geometry.

Bronze Age civilisation dates from before 4000 B.C. and it is in the valleys of the Nile, the Tigris and Euphrates, the Indus and the Hwang Ho that the first cities appear. The most successful foundations may have been the result of collaboration between village communities to drain and control the rivers themselves,[7] thus making riverside settlement with its attendant advantages possible. † In Egypt, the chief remains are of tombs such as the Pyramids, there having been apparently little effort to make anything like such durable provision for the living. In Mesopotamia, however there was no such natural defence as the desert afforded Egypt, and defensive building works were of prime importance and can still be detected. Of the Egyptian cities, Memphis and Thebes are the best known, and of the Mesopotamian, Ur, Nineveh and Babylon. The ruins of Harappa and Mohenjo-Daro, built by the early Dravidian civilisation in India, have only recently been studied and still less is known of the beginnings of Chinese civilisation which has developed unbroken to the present day.

† Jane Jacobs in her 'Economy of Cities' (London, 1970) contests this on the basis of recent archaeological evidence. She argues that the city necessarily precedes agriculture, and is not a consequence of it.

* For a full discussion *see* Rykwert, J., 'The Idea of a Town' in *Forum Lectura Architectonica*, Hilversum (n.d.).

There is evidence that the defensive walls of some Mesopotamian towns were built to a circular plan, but the most striking new characteristic which, in spite of considerable differences in detail, persisted throughout the millenia during which Bronze Age civilisation flourished, is the dominance of rectilinear forms. Many influences combined to produce this result. In the plans necessary to the founding or rebuilding of a city, the orderliness of the straight line may be expected to supplant the haphazard 'organic' curves of primitive building. The division of land into separately owned plots of known area is most easily achieved using *'square measure'* — an early discovery in geometry, which (as Herotodus reminds us) derives from surveying. Technical innovation was no doubt a contributory factor. The introduction of the right angle is sometimes held to be a consequence of the use of bricks, a standardised, prefabricated and mass-produced substitute for the stone not readily to hand in alluvial river valleys.[8] The rectangle has many advantages in bulk handling and assemblage — whether of bricks in a wall or buildings in a town, and the straight line is probably as 'natural' to directed large-scale works as is the curved to individual craftmanship.

However rectilinearity may have originated, there is no doubt that in due course it came to be exploited for its own sake, even when its use ran counter to convenience. For instance, in Ancient Egypt, wide straight streets were sometimes formed, although fully exposed to torrid noonday heat.[9] Geometrical regularity emphasised an atmosphere of purposeful discipline. Principal monumental works would stand out 'four-square' above surrounding buildings, which would also often be grouped in subordinate arrangements to add to the effect of dominance. This *monumentality* of temple, palace or tomb persists to a greater or lesser extent throughout history, as does the *processional way* along which it is approached. Its purest form is *axial symmetry*, in which a dominant climax is centrally placed and flanked by lesser elements which are mirrored left and right in a balanced and complementary composition.

In Egypt, little remains apart from tombs, and the cities of the living have in large measure to be reconstructed from evidence found in the cities of the dead. Herodotus records that in Egypt the land was parcelled out into rectangular fields. At Kahun, near one of the Pyramids, a workers' settlement was built in about 2000 B.C. and its remains reveal a walled compound rigidly rectilinear in its layout. Five centuries or so later, a similar settlement was built at Amarna. Here,

'geometry reigns supreme. The village is a perfect square, enclosed with walls. It is divided by streets running north-south at equal intervals and joined only at their extremities. All the houses save one (apparently that of the foreman) have the same surface area and arrangement. The unit of measurement is a 10m. square for two houses.'[10]

The persistence over five centuries of a stereotyped plan amply demonstrates the extreme conservatism of Egyptian culture, and suggests that such layouts had been widely used. At Amarna also are the remains of a grand processional way 60m. wide with streets joining at right angles. But we know that the term 'city' was used in antiquity to embrace an entire settled area, including much cultivated land and lowly building associated with the nucleus of an extensive royal court with its residences, temples and official apartments. It is recorded that Memphis was 5km. long and Thebes had a perimeter of 25km., but these in reality were probably groups of settlements with a common name. They had, as well as a monumental architecture and formal processional routes, a loose semi-rural and irregular total form. Diodorus writes of five-storey houses, but his evidence is not first hand and it is unlikely that three storeys were exceeded as a rule.[11]

Mesopotamia never enjoyed over long periods the political stability of ancient Egypt. Her towns were fortified settlements and her rulers war-lords rather than priests. Herotodus visited Babylon later in its history (in about 450 B.C.) and describes an area 14 miles (22.5 km.) square enclosed with a wall 340 ft. (104 m.) high and nearly 90ft (27.5 m.) thick. Excavations tend to confirm the arrangement he describes, but not the gigantic dimensions. Haverfield[12] suggests a square nearer to 4 than 14 miles. It is likely however that some cities embraced an agricultural hinterland not only politically as in Egypt, but to some extent physically also, within a protective enclosing wall. But other cities were of much more modest size.

Childe[13] records that Lagash, a smaller city of the Sumerian period (2000 B.C.) held 36,000 people — but this may have accounted for adult males only. Excavation has also revealed in Babylon, Asshur and Nineveh evidence of straight processional routes and some indication of streets crossing at right angles in a 'gridiron' or 'chessboard' fashion. Fortifications, royal palaces, astronomical observatories (ziggurats) and temples, rather than tombs, are characteristic of the remains of Mesopotamian civilisation, and brickwork is used in place of stone, which was difficult to obtain.

3 A reconstruction of an ancient Egyptian processional way. Geometrical regularity emphasises an atmosphere of purposeful discipline: a device which persists throughout history.

Remains of ancient cities have also been investigated in Crete (at Knossos) and in the Indus valley (at Harappa and Mohenjo Daro), where there is evidence that over 3,500 years ago such civilised 'luxuries' as water closets, sewage systems, paved streets and windows were known. From the archaeologist's evidence, we can safely assume that the later cities of Greece and Rome inherited much from the now largely forgotten millenia of Bronze Age civilisation.

Iron was first worked by barbarian tribes outside the first civilisations, and its superiority over bronze provided the technical means which facilitated the eventual transformation of Bronze Age civilisation into the classical cultures of Greece and Rome. Iron tools and ploughs made possible more efficient and widespread agriculture, and iron weapons ensured success in war. Trade increased in significance, accompanied by imperial conquest and colonisation. Bronze Age forms of social organisation survive, and slavery persists. But the increasing division of labour results in the appearance of more numerous 'middle' classes of officials, merchants and craftsmen. Governmental forms to some extent retain traces of the consultative assemblies of primitive tribal practice, as well as those taken over from the early civilisations. In addition also to carrying forward the previous cultural achievements, advances are made in science and technique — especially in hydraulics, warfare and navigation.

Iron Age civilisation dates from after 2000 B.C. and reaches maturity in the Greek city states. Stock-rearing and sea-borne trade free the city from the plains of the great rivers, and the sites of most Greek cities are chosen with an eye to natural defence; a harbour; pasturage; and a spring, stream or well for water supply.

The first settlements had as their core a stronghold, generally elevated and fortified, which originally would serve as a refuge and a place for the safe-keeping of the community's valuables. Around this *acropolis* would be huddled the citizens' unsubstantial houses and, among them, an open space (survival of the village meeting-ground) used variously for trade and public assembly: the *agora*. As commerce increased in significance, the agora would be duplicated or resited nearer to the harbour and quayside.

4 Workers' compound, Amarna, Egypt: 2nd millenium B.C.

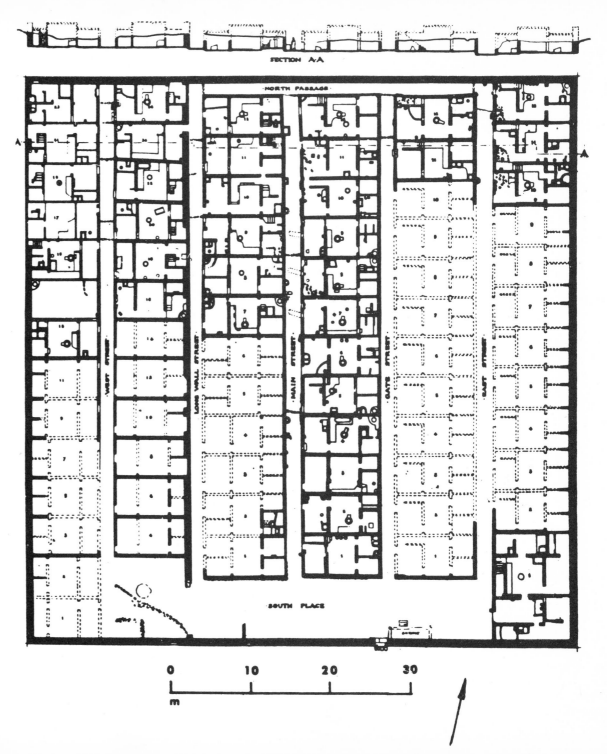

Most later Greek cities were colonies, and with them is firmly established and widespread a pattern which has characterised colonial towns throughout history: the gridiron or chessboard plan. The agora is still there — now a formal 'square', with perhaps one or more colonnaded *stoa* alongside. As in some respects a religious descendant of the 'treasure house', a *temple* would still often stand on an elevated dominant acropolis. In imitation of Athens, the sloping ground below the acropolis might serve as a natural site for the *theatre*, which with the *gymnasium*, the *bouleterion* or town hall, and scores of roughly built houses would complete the whole. On the vulnerable approaches there might be built a protecting wall, and beyond the city's limits would lie burial grounds and rubbish dumps.

With few exceptions, whether they evolved from primitive beginnings or were planted as colonies, Greek cities provide (by today's standards) a mean setting for so great a civilisation. The Greek street was *'made for the pedestrian, not for carriages, for conversation rather than traffic'*[14] and few of them apparently exceeded 4 to 5 metres in width, and in many cases, were little more than 1m. wide. One major route, about 8m. wide, might serve for community festivities and processions, but only in Alexandria is there evidence of a processional way approaching 20m. in width. Much would be unpaved and drainage of any sort was of the crudest.

It would however be surprising if a people whose buildings have justly been held up for succeeding ages to admire, had not in some instances produced, on the wider canvas of civic design, some evidence of their architectural skill. The Acropolis at Athens itself is by many admired as an example of informal (and apparently accidental) grouping, as impressive in its subtlety as is the Royal Road at Amarna in its monumental formality. And there is no doubt that Pergamom (developed in the centuries after 300 B.C.) displays a mastery in the exploitation of its site rarely — if ever — equalled since. Here,

'. . . The dominant idea was that of a semi-circle of great edifices, crowning the crest and inner slopes of a high crescent-shaped ridge. Near the northern and highest end of this ridge stood the palace . . . Next, to the south was the library . . . The middle of the crescent held the statues of Athena, Goddess of Pergamom, and beside it the Altar of Zeus the Saviour, gigantic in size, splendid with sculpture, itself the equal of an Acropolis. Lastly, the southern or lower end of the ridge bore a temple of

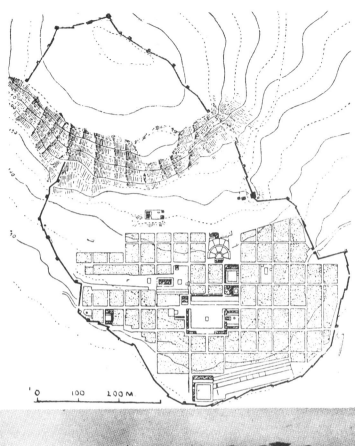

5 Priene: a 'gridiron' Greek colony.

6 Priene: a reconstruction showing the Agora.

7 *Pergamom: A sketch of the ruined city which once displayed a rare mastery in the exploitation of its site.*

Dionysus and an agora for assemblies.

> *'These buildings ringed the hill-top in stately semi-circle; below them, a theatre was hewn out of the slopes and a terrace 250 yards long was held up by buttresses against precipitous cliffs. Lower yet, beneath the agora, the town of common men covered the lower hillside in such order or disorder as steepness allowed.'*[15]

The Greeks founded numerous colonies around the Mediterranean. At the same time, other peoples — Phoenicians, Carthaginians and Etruscans — were developing their own urban cultures. Great empires in Egypt and Persia still persisted, and for a time the Macedonians under Alexander consolidated old and new in a vast Greek Empire. The achievement of stable political unity in the classical world did not come, however, until Rome became dominant towards the end of the pre-Christian era.

Rome, like Athens, did not in herself clearly display the characteristics peculiar to Roman town planning. For these, as with Greece, we have to turn to the colonies she founded in even greater numbers. Here, as with most things Roman, we find forms and practices deriving from the Greek. The gridiron layout persists. In place of the *agora* we find the *forum;* in place of the *bouleterion,* the magistrates' court or *basilica.* Streets do not always cross at right angles, however, and the trapezoidal *insulae* occasionally found (as at Pompeii) have been held to betray the influence of earlier Italian settlers.[16]

We have seen how primitive traditions sanctified rectilinear forms. The *'two straight lines crossing at right angles in the centre'* — the principal streets of the Roman camp or colony — were known technically to the *Gromatici* or surveyors as the *Decumanus* and the *Cardo*, and they *'appear to follow some method of orientation connected with inaugural science'*.[17] There is, indeed, little doubt that the intention was that the Decumanus and Cardo should be set with regard to the sun, linking the principal entrances into the town through its defensive wall. In the course of several centuries the demands of tradition were tempered however by experience and common sense.

Roman colonisation differed from Greek in many ways. The objective was not to found politically independent cities, but to plant new outposts of civilisation, often peopled by discharged soldiers, linked politically and physically with Metropolitan Rome. More efficient agriculture made possible the founding of some towns inland, no longer tied to navigation. These depended for water supply, drainage and communications on technical innovations such as the aqueducts, sewers and roads which have earned the Romans their reputation as the greatest engineers of antiquity. Colonisation, especially that associated with military pioneering, encourages the adoption of standard procedures and techniques, adaptable to a variety of local conditions and capable of execution by the semi-skilled under expert direction. Thus, for instance, since timber or stone beams are not everywhere available, the Romans made use of the voussoir arch which employs small stone or brick to bridge a stream or roof a public building. Rules abounded: often with the force of law. At one time, for instance, streets were required to be not less than a minimum width: the *via* (for vehicles) 8 Roman feet: the *actus* (for beasts) 4 feet and the *iter* (for pedestrians) 2 feet.[18] In Rome itself the height of buildings was limited by Augustus to 70 feet, and by Trajan to 60 feet on street frontages. It was an offence to dump refuse in streets and frontagers had some responsibility for their upkeep.

At the time of the Caesars, Rome possibly had about 1,000,000 inhabitants at a probable density of 520 persons per hectare[19] (about 200 persons per acre.) But this was exceptional. Most towns were much smaller. Roman London covered 325 acres (132 hectares) and Timgad (a typical colony founded in A.D. 100), was planned as a square only 1,000 x 1,000 feet. It is however interesting to remember that, because of her great size, Imperial Rome experienced, no less than any modern city, congestion and traffic chaos so great that the circulation of carriages was at one time forbidden (except for some 'public' vehicles) during daylight.

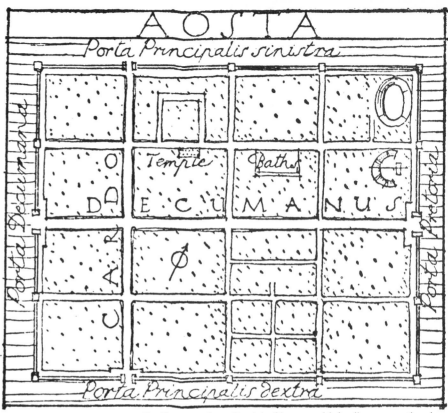

8   Roman plan: Patrick Abercrombie's diagrammatic plan of a Roman colony.

9   The Pont-du-Gard, Nimes: 1st century A.D.
The Romans brought water to their cities on aqueducts and used standard techniques as in the semi-circular voussoir arch.

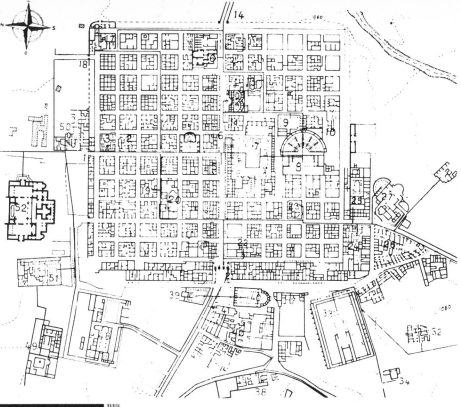

The street blocks or *insulae* between the roads vary in dimensions and area. At Timgad they were squares of about 70 x 70 Roman feet and contained 1-4 dwellings. At Carthage (for several centuries after Augustus, a Roman town) they were oblongs 130 x 500 feet, arranged lengthways on ground rising steeply from the coast, and thus better accommodating changes in floor level. Some authorities suggest that *insulae* are related in dimension to the Roman unit of land measurement — the *jugerum* (an area of 120' x 240'), but the evidence is not conclusive.

In some towns, the more substantial methods used for house building by the Romans have left sufficient evidence for reconstruction. At Pompeii, excavation has revealed houses almost intact. A marked characteristic (still common in Mediterranean lands) is that of building up to the plot boundary and relying mainly on internal courtyards for natural light and ventilation.* To the public buildings of 11 Greece are added the *basilica* (or law courts) and *thermae* (baths). There are signs also of a more widespread concern for civic dignity in the arrangement of principal streets which were sometimes paved, flanked by raised and colonnaded walkways and spanned by triumphal arches. Below them would run well-built sewers.

The Romans continued the later Hellenic practice of providing separately for markets and for public assembly, and the *forum civilia* or *judiciaria* would most often stand at the crossing of *decumanus* and *cardo*, and be surrounded by colonnaded public buildings. As the Roman town was designed with an eye to the defence of the whole, an acropolis is not part of the typical plan.

The Romans extended civilisation throughout Europe, and many towns still flourishing have a Roman foundation. As is well known, however, the empire in the west declined. Byzantium (founded in 276 A.D.) by the fifth century exceeded Rome in size and importance. Civilisation retreated from the outposts of empire, and the succeeding Dark Ages saw the destruction or decay through neglect of numerous Roman settlements. Rome herself shrank to a fraction of her imperial size. In Byzantium, however, and around the Mediterranean and in Asia Minor generally, civilisation endured. Classical culture survived in the religious establishments of the west, and long before the sack of Constantinople in 1453, it had passed safely into the hands of Arabs and others, whence it again entered Europe, enriched from Indian and Chinese sources.

10   Timgad: A Roman colony of the 1st century A.D. The Romans developed the discipline of the right angle to define the form of the town as a whole.

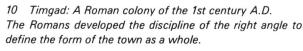

11   Pompeii: the house of the Vetii.

* To some extent also for circulation. The narrowness of streets in some towns is today still acceptable because vehicles can turn and park in courtyards.

The typical products of Feudalism are to be found in the countryside and, as may be expected of an economic and political system based initially on agriculture and local self-sufficiency, the town may be seen as existing in spite of, rather than because of it. This existence itself is varied. War and pillage did not prevent the survival, in more or less continuous occupation, of some Roman cities. From time to time attempts were made by rulers to rebuild the glory that was Rome. Theodoric (c.445-526) earned himself the title 'Restorer of Cities', and the Empire of Charlemagne (c.742-814) endured over 300 years. The Ottoman Empire, with its new capital Baghdad, re-established civilisation in the Near and Middle East. Thus, by the time political stability in Europe favoured the growth of new cities, there was much that still survived from classical times to serve as a model and
12 foundation. The Decumanus and Cardo still persist in some of our most ancient cities, although changes have in most instances obliterated chessboard layouts and forum.

Where, in the later Middle Ages, new towns were founded by a deliberate act to settle discharged soldiers, to police a province, or to develop agriculturally unproductive land, they owed much to classical precedent. Best known are the
13 *bastides* which in France, Wales and England still display the rectilinear layouts throughout history favoured by the pioneer and the military man. Generally their fortified enclosure was rectangular also. But for the towns which display most strikingly the forms peculiar to the Middle Ages, we look to the innumerable settlements which took as their point of departure the village, the castle or the church.

With local agriculture as its basis, the medieval village developed initially with mutual protection as a dominating condition. In a Europe politically fragmented and open to pillage from warrior bands, defence of the community and its livestock was essential. Choice of site at first therefore owes less to navigable waterways or overland routes than in previous ages, and the naturally defensible terrain (often less easy of access) is preferred. A characteristic is a space enclosed by dwellings which provide shelter for livestock, and (together with such fortifications as might be contrived) protection against an attacker. The importance of secure fortification, however, favoured those villages associated with a feudal stronghold, and it was these that first began to deserve the name of towns. Eventually, ecclesiastical settlements came to exert a similar influence, relying not only upon their physical defences, but also upon the protection they claimed as places of refuge, exempt on religious grounds from attack.

12 Chichester: the Decumanus and the Cardo still persist in some surviving Roman cities.

13 Aigues Mortes: a mediaeval 'Bastide'. Where in the later Middle Ages new towns were founded, they owed much to classical precedent.

14 Fountains Abbey, Yorks. A 12th century monastic colony.

Settlements would most often develop alongside and around the principal route into the stronghold, forming before its gate a sheltered space used now more for trade than for pasturage. When attacked, the *Seigneur* might well at first destroy the hovels and booths in the interests of defence. The advantage brought by trade and manufacture would however in time lead to his agreeing to the enclosure of the *faubourg* outside his gate with defences of its own.

In the later days of Rome, the *villa* had developed throughout the empire as a form of settlement detached from the town. Within, a landowner had gathered a considerable household whose work in his surrounding farmlands and vineyard had provided sufficient resources for patrician luxury. Similar, in form at least, were the monasteries which colonised Europe from the 10th century onwards, and it was in them especially that industry began to grow. The high level of efficiency eventually attained can be judged from the account of the Cistercian Clairvaux Abbey in Migne:

"The river enters the abbey as much as the wall acting as a check allows. It gushes first into the corn-mill, where it is very actively employed in grinding the grain under the weight of the wheels and in shaking the fine sieve which separates flour from bran. Thence it flows into the next building and fills the boiler in which it is heated to prepare beer for the monks' drinking, should the vine's fruitfulness not reward the vintner's labour. But the river has not yet finished its work, for it is now drawn into the fulling-machines following the corn-mill. In the mill it has prepared the brothers' food and its duty is now to serve in making their clothing . . . Thus it raises and alternately lowers the heavy hammers and mallets . . . of the fulling-machines . . . Now the river enters the tannery where it devotes much care and labour to preparing the necessary materials for the monks' footwear; then it divides into many small branches and, in its busy course, passes through various departments, seeking for those who require its services for any purpose whatsoever, whether for cooking, rotating, crushing, watering, washing, or grinding . . . At last, to earn full thanks and to leave nothing undone, it carries away the refuse and leaves all clean.'[20]

Monasteries such as this, often little less than small towns in themselves, understandably encouraged urban growth, and the arts of manufacture they developed eventually found their place also in the feudal manor and castle.[21] Their *collegiate form*, with its open garths enclosed by buildings

and cloisters, persists also in the arrangement of some medieval towns where (as at Richmond, Yorkshire), systems of linked 'squares' largely replace the corridor street.

The advantage to be gained from trade became a powerful argument in the hands of the medieval townsman in his struggle to establish his place in feudal society. Organised in craft and merchant guilds, he was eventually able to secure from both his temporal and his spiritual lords the right to own urban land, to employ labour, to fortify his town, to bear arms in its defence, to hold his market on appointed days and to welcome to it whom he wished without let or hindrance. In the pursuit of these aims, he became in countries such as England a powerful champion of a national monarchy, able to overrule the arbitrary power of local rulers and better organised to promote widespread trade and the defence of the whole realm against attack. Elsewhere (as in Northern Italy) he established powerful independent city states under the leadership of princes who were themselves merchants.

Relative political stability from the eleventh century onwards led to the establishment throughout Europe of numerous towns. The opening up of the continent for settlement in the ensuing three hundred years has been compared to the opening up of North America between the seventeenth and twentieth centuries; and the doubling of population in the English counties, in the two centuries after the Domesday census, is quoted as evidence of the population growth which must have preceded such vigorous town building as occurred, for example, in eastern Germany between 1100 and 1400 A.D.

It is not possible to discuss the towns bequeathed to us by the Middle Ages (or indeed, those of any age) as being of one uniform type. We can distinguish the *market town,* with its nucleus of castle, cathedral or abbey church; the *university town;* the *merchant city* based on a port or navigable waterway; and the *planted town* or colony, built to settle virgin land or to police a province. Each of these will have characteristics as diverse as may be found among towns today. But we shall find some features which may be regarded as typically medieval.

The first (in all but the last type) is an *irregular form* in which buildings and open spaces adapt themselves to a terrain, chosen and exploited to assist defence, to provide shelter, to ease ascent and to promote natural drainage. The result is today justly admired as having a charm born of intimacy and variety, in which the natural and the man-made blend into an harmonious whole. The medieval town is an outstanding example of *organic design* which adapts and utilises the given circumstances of materials and site, rather than imposing ruthlessly upon them the orderliness of the right angle and processional way.

A second characteristic is an enclosing *defensive wall* — again contrived to exploit natural advantages such as water courses and commanding slopes. This is a powerful unifying feature, both to the morale and the form of a town. To view from afar the profile of a city married to the natural features of the site, encircled with a wall and dominated by a spire, tower or castle keep is still an impressive and stimulating experience. A wall also inevitably imposes *planning* upon a community. This will especially be so when growth and overcrowding demand expansion and the establishment of new defences to enclose a larger area.

While new open spaces for trade and congregation might arise at the city gate or elsewhere within the town, that originally below the citadel or at the cathedral door would often retain its role as *market place:* the characteristic focal point of the medieval town. This place itself would rarely be at the physical centre, neither would it be regular in form. But to it all incoming routes would inevitably lead, and within it the community could find for assembly and commerce the same shelter as the village green had earlier provided for grazing and defence.

The converging routes and the later roads marking the lines of successive city walls, together may produce a plan resembling a spider's web, and it is to the Middle Ages that some authorities ascribe the first use of the *radial-concentric* plan still typical of many European cities.

By the fourteenth century, urban populations numbering tens of thousands were not uncommon, and one or two exceeded 100,000. Stone paving was used in some streets and water courses were controlled to assist surface drainage. Foul drainage to cesspit or river was not unknown, but the dung cart and compost heap were in the main relied on. Where a town was on a river, this was the principal source of drinking water, but many relied on other sources. As still today in many a village, a spring or well might stand in the market-place — a focus not only of domesticity but also of urban social life. Much has been written to suggest that the medieval town was overcrowded and insanitary, and this undoubtedly they from time to time became. But there is evidence to suggest that within them ample open space — especially garden plots and orchards — was usually sufficient to offset the lack of efficient sewerage and refuse disposal.[22]

16 *A sketch of 16th century Nuremburg.*

15 *Laufenburg on the Rhine: a town shaped by its site.*

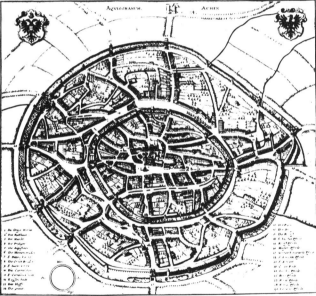

18 *Aachen in 1649: a radial-concentric plan still typical of many European cities.*

17 *Cordes: a French fortified town of the 13th century.*

* Beresford in his 'New Towns of the Middle Ages' records that to avoid conflict with established privileges, territory near to the edge of an existing rural parish was preferred for a new town site.

Except in the Bastides and other 'planned' towns, streets and alleys were irregular in width and direction. They were primarily intended for pedestrians and pack animals, and still-remaining examples remind us of the shelter afforded by closely-spaced buildings, sometimes with overhanging upper storeys. The buildings themselves — often of timber with rush and plaster, occasionally of brick or stone — would serve a variety of purposes. Shop, workshop, store and dwelling for a household of many families and classes would all be combined on one site. But within the town as a whole there are instances of the 'zoning' with which we are today familiar. Commerce naturally sites itself near and around the market, and there is a tendency for similar trades to group themselves. Noxious industries like tanning and butchery are excluded from crowded quarters. Communities of 'foreigners', in some of the larger merchant cities, establish distinct 'quarters' (imitating perhaps an Islamic practice). Universities, which begin to appear in the late Middle Ages, tend also to establish for themselves a distinct precinct.

Of public buildings, the church undoubtedly dominated, and as a city grew it became divided into parishes,* each with its own church. Castle and abbey remain to some extent aloof and never really become part of the town, even when outgrown in size and importance. Within or by the market place, a *moot hall* might in time appear, below which business could be done in foul weather, and wherein court or council could deliberate. With the granting of a charter, a town hall or mansion house might be built, and guilds might eventually erect their own halls for conference and ceremony. Almshouses, hospitals and foundling homes are, in the more prosperous medieval towns, also to be found.

Trade at first was largely local, and the market served in the main as a point of exchange for food and goods produced at no greater distance than could be reached by a man or beast making the return journey within one day. Those towns which established themselves at key points on national and international routes became in time, however, centres of trade on a much wider basis. As in antiquity, towns having a natural harbour or a navigable river prospered. Of greater significance was also the town sited at a nodal point on routes — especially those with a harbour or at a river crossing. Here goods were transferred from water and many roads would probably converge. Many of our towns have continued successfully to exploit the benefits of such a site, and in some, the quayside or bridge with its attendant wharves, warehouses and markets still forms the commercial nucleus.

After the fourteenth century, civilisation was re-established throughout the territory of the classical empires, and the development of capitalist society and its characteristic urban forms can be traced from this time. Three principal stages may be distinguished. The first is typified by the merchant principalities of Renaissance Italy, the second by powerful national monarchies such as pre-revolutionary France, and the third by England after the Industrial Revolution. The complexities of modern history prevent more than the most cursory discussion here of some of the salient influences and characteristics.

As in classical times, the growth of trade and a market economy, added to the age-old rivalry between town and country, that between town and town. New techniques of warfare replaced the less highly organised practices of the Middle Ages. In place of the armed citizenry there emerges the standing army of mercenaries and conscripts, and in place of the battering ram and bow-and-arrow, gunpowder and siege artillery. The four-square wall and moat is replaced 19 by elaborate fortifications designed to deflect gunfire, with outworks encircling the city at a sufficient distance to keep the enemy's guns out of range, and having salients and redoubts from which a defending army could out-gun and out-manoeuvre an attacking force.

Developing technical complexity in defence and other matters calls forth the professional designer able to plan and supervise the construction of large scale works. He, like every other artist of the period, developed not only the practice but also the theory of his profession, searching among the relics of classical buildings and writings for the rational precedents he expected to find. In building, as is well-known, medieval forms were abandoned in favour of the 'orders' and the Roman arch. In town planning we shall find similar attempts to replace 'barbaric Gothic' practices with more rational arrangements conforming with the 'eternal truths' of mathematics and philosophy.

20 Town planning in the early Renaissance:
Florence, the square of SS. Annunziata with the Ospedale, designed by Brunelleschi in 1419.
21 Sixtus' plan for Rome:
Bordino's engraving of 1588 explains the essence of the Pope's plan to make Rome a centre of pilgrimage by linking principal shrines with a Baroque system of avenues and vistas.

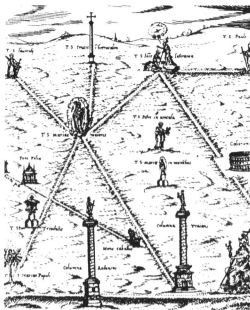

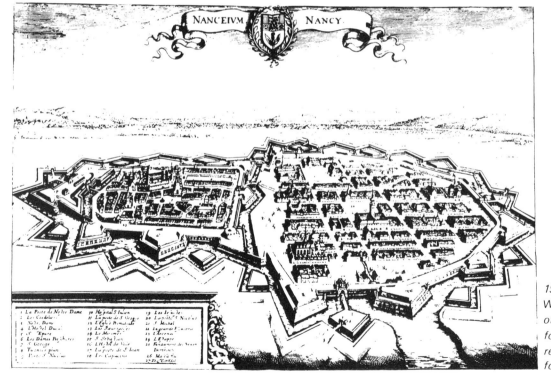

19 Nancy, 1645. With new techniques of warfare, the foursquare wall is replaced by elaborate fortifications.

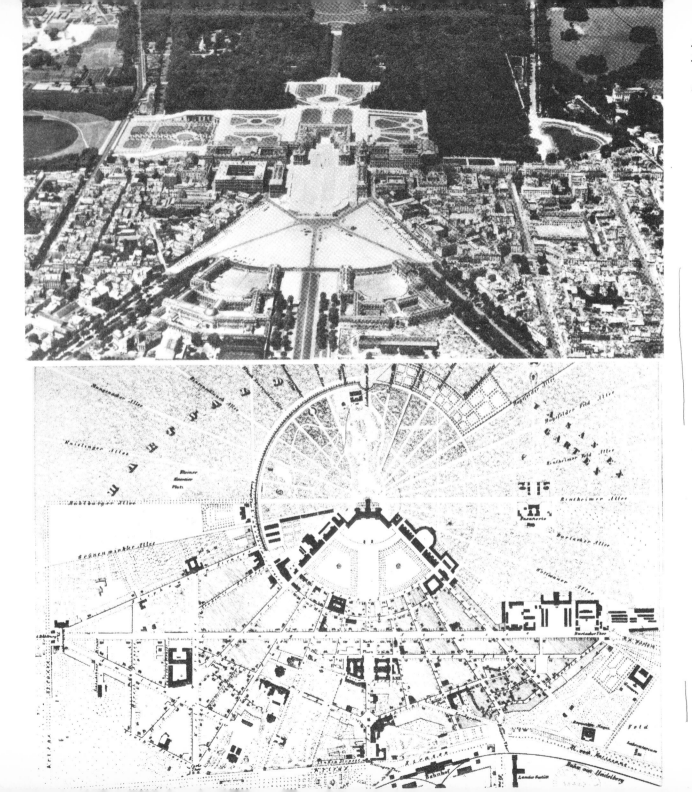

22 *Versailles: the egocentric order of absolute monarchy.*
23 *Karlsruhe, founded 1715: the 'grand manner' of Versailles became the pattern for princelings throughout Europe.*

Apart from fortifications, the new town planning of the early Renaissance achieved little on the grand scale it had to attempt if it wished to fulfil its ambitions, and it is in terms of its theory that we shall later discuss it. By the seventeenth century, however, its ideas had influenced the whole of civilised Europe, and, in the form of the *Baroque*, were re-shaping her towns. The formal *place* was carefully proportioned with a unified facade 'building-up' to a dominating climax of palace, church or civic building; the palace or cathedral was set at the focus of radiating routes; the street itself was disciplined to provide unified facades flanking a grand processional route; the whole plan of a town became a network composed as a disciplined whole, in which important focal points (market, cathedral, palace, stock exchange, fortress, bridge) would stand as nodes in an open-space system embracing avenues, crescents, circuses and squares. But as in so much town planning before and since, some of the finest visions remained unfulfilled.

With the development of our modern national states, we can begin to discern variations as between one country and another. Pope Sixtus V drove new avenues through the medieval slums of Rome to link the key places of pilgrimage and assembly, setting a fashion for 'improvement' with which today we are only too familiar. The France of Louis XIV developed military art to a high level and, under the leadership of the celebrated Marshal Sébastien le Prestre de Vauban (1633-1707), military engineering and the design of fortifications reached unprecedented sophistication. The 'Grand Manner' of Paris and Versailles eventually became the pattern for ambitious princelings throughout Europe, one which, with seemingly boundless perspective, at times sought to discipline the entire surrounding countryside as if it were an extension of the town. England, relying on her naval protection, gradually abandoned the practice of circumvallation, and after the Restoration, the destruction of city walls in general was ordered as a precaution against further urban insurrection.

20

21

22

23

The conquest of new territories overseas by the European powers led, especially in the New World, to the founding of numerous new towns. An almost invariable characteristic of

24 these is their 'gridiron' plan. Wars between the colonial powers resulted in the adoption in many instances of elaborate defensive works here also. With more settled political conditions in the eighteenth and nineteenth centuries, the colonisation of America provided an opportunity for pioneering experiments, but however radical the political intentions of the colonists, their settlements clung to rectangular sub-division almost as inflexibly as the architecture of the period clung to the classical orders. One interesting variant does however eventually appear, with

25 cities such as Washington (designed under the supervision of Jefferson by the French architect and military engineer l'Enfant), where the imposition of a Baroque pattern of radiating avenues on a gridiron plan attempts to combine the advantages of rational subdivision with the focal point, the vista, and the rapid cross-town route.

The new spirit of enquiry brought in by the Renaissance was to bear fruit in a rapidly-developing industrial economy based on more rational methods of production. Towns increased in number and size. At first their growth overtakes primitive sanitary arrangements, little changed from medieval practice, and plague such as that which struck London in the mid-seventeenth century was not uncommon. Water courses were cleaned to improve natural drainage, and new *leets* sometimes cut to bring in supplies of drinking water.

Florence, in the hundred years up to 1450, had doubled her population, and by then numbered about 200,000 inhabitants. Few other cities at that time boasted half that

24 Philadelphia: the American colonists almost invariably use the 'gridiron'.

25 Washington: the marriage of a Baroque pattern of radiating avenues to a gridiron plan: L'Enfant's plan of 1791.

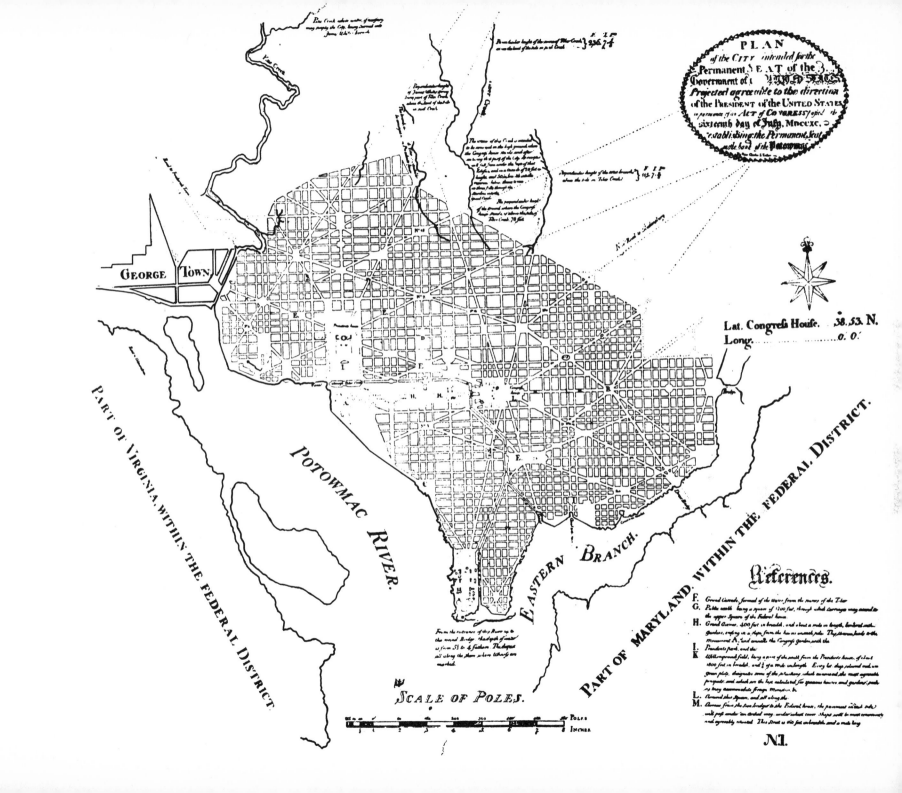

number: London had about 40,000 citizens. By 1600, a small group of capital cities and major ports — Amsterdam, Rome, Lisbon, Antwerp, Seville, Palermo — had populations exceeding 100,000. Naples, Milan, Paris and London each had 200,000 or more. The rise of centralised monarchies and of transatlantic trade tended to concentrate growth around the royal court as the seat of government, or the port as the focus of trade. Growing populations were absorbed both by intensifying the use of the existing built-up area, and by planned extensions — often associated with the construction of new defensive works. While many smaller settlements throughout Europe grew at a lesser rate, the founding of new towns (except in the new worlds beyond the seas) was confined in the main to fortified outposts intended primarily as garrison towns. One great exception is Peter the Great's new capital on the Baltic, St. Petersburg, which in spite of siege and battery, today as Leningrad remains one of the finest examples of Baroque town planning.

English towns began their marked expansion in the eighteenth century. Although by no means free from slums, the period of growth up to 1820 or so produced the Georgian and Regency housing, elegantly grouped in terrace, crescent, circus and square, still admired as among the finest domestic urban planning in the world. Manufacture still relied upon 'cottage industry', and small family workshops within town and village. To this day 'weaving lofts' can be seen over the older houses in some of our towns. The introduction of more elaborate machinery, powered by a watermill, was accompanied by the universal adoption of the factory system which first developed apace in mills sited by fast-flowing streams such as are to be found in the Pennine foothills. Subsequently, steam was to give to towns sited over coalfields an advantage they have only recently begun to lose.

The growth of urban population consequent upon the enclosures, agricultural reform and the development of manufacturing industry, found towns sadly unprepared for their new role as industrial centres. In the hundred years after 1780, city populations multiplied ninefold: a growth of towns unprecedented in history. Even more startling is the increase after 1800. We have already noted the growth of London. In 40 years, Manchester grew tenfold from 35,000 to 353,000; Leeds from 53,000 to 152,000; Birmingham from 23,000 to 181,000; and Sheffield from 46,000 to 111,000. Mankind was at the beginning of an era of urban expansion which still proceeds — now on a world-wide scale and at an even faster rate.

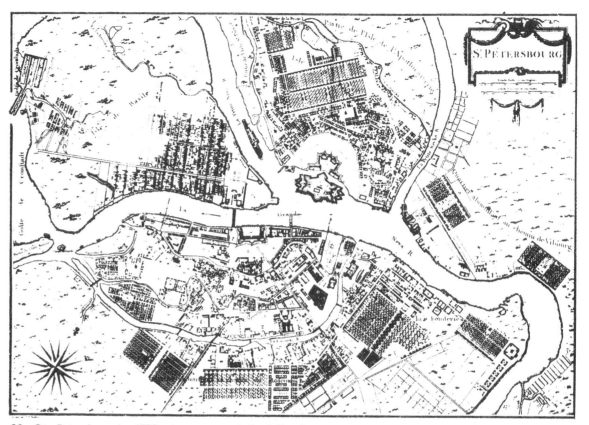

26 St. Petersburg in 1753: the new capital of Russia founded in 1703 by Peter the Great.

27 *Regency housing in Lodon.*
28 *Bath: middle-class elegance.*
29 *Bye-law housing typical of the 19th
century industrial town in England.*

The squalor and degradation of urban life during the nineteenth century is well-known. Sporadic attempts to curb the worst excesses of speculative builders, and to improve sanitation, drainage and water supply, reached a decisive stage with the passing, after 1840, of a series of Public Health Acts. As a result of a report prepared by Chadwick, a lawyer appointed by Parliament to look into the state of the cities, the sewering of towns and their provision with clean drinking water was eventually brought under public control and the supervision of properly trained Borough Surveyors. Later acts introduced building byelaws which forbade the more insanitary practices of greedy landlords. The precise terms in which minimum standards were specified, however, encouraged during the remainder of the nineteenth century the development throughout Britain of acres of barrack-like housing, arranged to conform to the letter of the law, with no thought for any values beyond those of the maximum return on the money invested.

29

The industrial revolution produced, along with new divisions of labour and an elaborately stratified urban society, a division among towns themselves into those that specialised in one product or another; those that served as administrative centres; or as holiday resorts; or remained as market towns serving the countryside around them. It established fashionable spas in which elegant 'Society' continued to enjoy town life without its squalor. Within every town was set aside for the use of the 'well-to-do' a 'West End', in which stately mansions stood in ample grounds. Less grand but still elegant town houses would provide for those slightly lower in the social scale, and successively meaner terraces kept each class in its appointed quarter. Civic pride to some extent developed along with commercial prosperity, and is evinced in the grandiose town halls, art galleries, museums and office blocks which still embellish the civic centres of our towns. Large-scale factory production resulted in the establishment also of areas devoted almost exclusively to industry, with their attendant acres of open space for storage, transport, and the dumping of waste. By the dawn of the twentieth century, the modern industrial town as we still know it was well-established with its population in the hundreds of thousands, its sprawling suburbs, its fragmented structure, transport chaos, soot and grime. By this time, it had inevitably called forth a growing demand for reform and for town planning according to more enlightened principles. Aspirations and ideals now begin to play an important role in the development of cities, and an understanding of these, and of their sources in political and architectural theory, is now necessary.

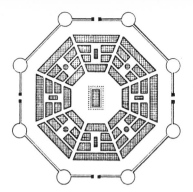

30
Vitruvius' town plan reconstructed from his description.

Town planning, no doubt, has a history as long as that of the town itself, but since here we have to rely mainly on the written record, it is to Greece that we look for the first account.

Plato is more concerned with government than with physical form, and has little to say of relevance to us here beyond the opinion that temples should be near the public place, all houses should be similar, and the city built in a circle on an elevated site. Aristotle, basing himself on realities rather than ideals, discerns three necessities for a town: hygiene, defence, and circulation. He sees some conflict between the last two which leads him to favour a combination of a 'gridiron' layout with irregularities likely to aid a defending force. Like Plato, he would have temples with the agora, and this should be central. The market place should, however, be separately sited on the outskirts. He acknowledges also the difficulty of putting theory into practice, and advocates ingenuity to gain a maximum advantage from site conditions, Of lasting significance is Aristotle's opinion on the size of a city:

'Ten men are too few . . . a hundred thousand too many . . . A man is not a man unless he is a citizen. Men come together in cities in order to live; they remain together in order to live the 'good' life — a common life for noble ends . . . the polis population should be self-sufficient for living the good life as a realisable community, but not so large that a sense of conscious unity is lost . . .' [23]

We know of two architects concerned with Greek town planning: Hippodamos (5th cent. B.C.) and Dinocrates (4th cent. B.C.). Aristotle credits the former with having invented the 'gridiron' layout, and his reputation was such, that cities centuries apart in their origin were attributed to him as

designer. He appears to have subscribed to Pythagorean 'number-magic', and is probably the butt of Aristophanes' parody of a town-planner in his play *The Birds*. Dinocrates was Alexander's architect, and designer of his great new city in Egypt. From Vitruvius we have a legendary account of his exploits and character, but otherwise we know little.

It is indeed from Vitruvius himself, the Roman architect of the first century A.D., that we have the only reasonably full account of classical theory. His ten books *de Architectura* range over the whole field of Roman technology, but give pride of place to town planning as the primary subject of design. He discusses the selection of a site with an eye especially to defence and the avoidance of an unhealthy climate. Of detailed design, his concern is largely with constituent elements. But he does describe at some length an ideal plan, remarkable in that its clear-cut radial form is unlike what we know of classical practice, and came to have significance mainly in its influence upon the architects of the Renaissance.

Vitruvius explains his plan as deriving from the directions 30 of the prevailing winds, which he describes as coming from the cardinal points of the compass. Radiating streets are aligned in such a way that the wind does not blow directly up them. At the end of each radial street is a defensive tower in the city wall. Behind the wall itself is an open space which facilitates defence. From a central open space the assembled defenders can be quickly deployed as needed. The town's gateways are disposed north, south, east and west, in such a way that they and all the walls can be commanded from the towers. Parallel with the enclosing walls there are additional streets, The principal temple is in the central place, others being distributed one to each of the eight sub-divisions formed by the radial roads. [24]

Virtually nothing survives of the theory which must have guided the builders of cities from the fall of Rome to the

fifteenth century. We have instructions from Theodoric to his minister Cassiodorus in which is displayed a lively interest in town planning. We know the arts of civilisation flourished long in Byzantium and among the Arabs. Edward I commissioned 24 *bastidors* to '*devise, order and array*' new 31 towns for '*the greatest profit of ourselves and merchants*'. [25] But from the Middle Ages in northern Europe little remains apart from the material evidence to remind us of their undoubted understanding. Roman commentaries like those of Vitruvius were certainly known and read, and from them contemporary scholars would have developed their own ideas of design.

From the period leading up to the Renaissance, we have fragments of notebooks in which medieval craftsmen-designers recorded some of the mysteries they knew and practised. Especially significant is their interest in military engineering, which throughout history has never been far removed from town planning. After 1400 A.D., with the dawn of the Renaissance, we find this tradition very much alive, and among the most significant works of the period are those of the Sienese, Francesco di Giorgio Martini (born 1439), and 32 the German, Albecht Durer (1471-1528), both of whom wrote treatises concerned, among other things, with fortifications.

The first work of the Renaissance which especially concerns us here, is that of Leone Batista Alberti (1404-1472), the Florentine *uomo universale*, whose *de re Aedificatoria* [26] still stands as the greatest treatise on architecture ever written. He bases himself largely on Vitruvius, whom he follows in giving town planning foremost place. But he does not uncritically accept all that the Roman had written. Alberti was a man of a new age, imbued with the confidence that with science and understanding, perfection was

+ In hot climates best to have the breeze blow.

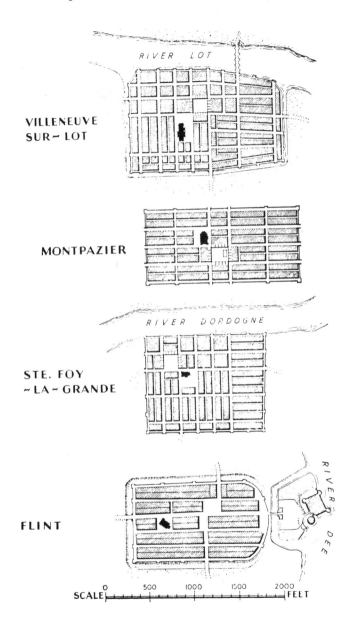

31 Plans of some of the Bastides founded in the late Middle Ages.

VILLENEUVE
SUR ~ LOT

MONTPAZIER

STE. FOY
~ LA ~ GRANDE

FLINT

SCALE 0 500 1000 1500 2000 FEET

* See also: Aristotle, *Politics*, vii 11.

attainable in all things. Although a fashionable enthusiasm for the Greek and Roman coloured his taste, his respect for the craftsman's experience and his thirst for new knowledge gives a value to his judgement from which we can still profit today.

Alberti likens the city to a house. He discusses its siting with an eye to health, economy and defence. The internal arrangement must inevitably vary, but he tells us that *'of all cities, the most capacious is the round one; and the most secure, that which is encompassed with walls broken here and there into angles by bastions jutting out . . .'*

He has something to say in detail about the design of defensive walls, and advises that the town plan should allow for a possible increase in population.

He distinguishes between highways *'by which we go into the provinces, with our armies and their baggage; for which reason the highways ought to be much broader than the others';* and *'private ways'* which *'leaving the public ones, lead us to some town or castle, or else into some other highway, as lanes in cities, and cross-roads in the country.'*

Another kind of public way *'which may not improperly be called High Streets'* leads to the public places in the town.

'If the city is noble and powerful, the streets should be strait and broad, which carries an air of greatness and dignity; but if it is only a small town or fortification it will be better, and as safe, not for the streets to run strait to the gates; but to have them wind about . . . For this besides that by appearing so much the longer, they will add to the idea of the greatness of the town, they will likewise conduce very much to beauty and convenience, and be a great security against all accidents and emergencies. Moreover, this winding of the streets will make the passenger at every step discover a new structure, and the front and door of every house will directly face the middle of the street . . . it will be both healthy and pleasant to have such an open view from every house by means of the turn of the street . . . In our winding streets there will be no house but what, in some part of the day will enjoy some sun; nor will they ever be without gentle breezes . . . and yet they will not be molested by stormy blasts, because such will be broken by the turning of the streets. Add to all these advantages, that if the enemy gets into the town, he will be in danger on every side . . .'

He allows, however, that *'private streets'* might be built straight to *'answer better to the corners of the buildings'*. He

considers the bridge the *'main part of the street'* and advises it should be in the town centre where all can use it.

Alberti regards drains as a necessity in a healthy city.

Without them

'the town not only stinks every night and morning, when people throw their nastiness out of the windows, but even in the day time . . .'

The overall layout of a city will be influenced by its form of government:

'A good king takes care to have his city strongly fortified in those parts which are liable to be assaulted by a foreign enemy: a tyrant, having no less danger to fear from his own subjects than from strangers, must fortify his city no less against his own people, and one part of his people against the others.'

He is aware of the advantages of 'divide and rule', and advises subdivision of the city, preferably into an 'inner circle' for *'cooks, victuallers and other such trades'* surrounded by a more spacious zone for *'the richer sort'*. Defensive walls between zones and other fortifications should be built so that *'every place which in any way commands the town, should be in the hands of the Prince . . .'* He consequently advises that *'a town in a plain is most convenient for a free people; but one upon a hill, the safest for a Tyrant.'** While both king and tyrant should have a watch-tower in their houses from which they could see *'any commotion in the city'*, the king's palace

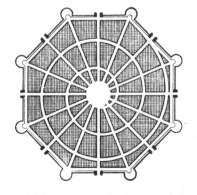

32 A design for a fortified hill-top town, having a spiral street leading uphill to the centre, by Francesco di Giorgio.

25

'should stand in the heart of a city, it should be easy of access, beautifully adorned, and rather delicate and polite than proud or stately. But a Tyrant should have rather a castle than a palace, and it should stand in a manner out of the city and in it at the same time . . . entirely separated from all the other buildings . . .

'We should not omit one contrivance very convenient for a Tyrant, which is to have some private pipes concealed within the body of the wall, by which he may secretly hear everything that is said either by strangers or servants.'

Alberti describes the design of a fortress or citadel, conceived primarily as a tyrannical stronghold and not as a refuge for the citizenry.

He then turns to the design of a republican city, wherein the temples and private houses are of greater significance. Great men should site their houses apart from those of commoners and the principal temple should stand *'where it may appear with the most majesty and reverence.'* He discusses cloisters, monasteries, nunneries, and their siting. The schools *'where the learned may meet and converse'* should be away from the noise and smell of industry. He wants hospitals to be in the most healthy places, and the lawcourts and senate house to be with the temple in a central place.

'The entrance into the Senate House ought to be made no less strong than handsome . . . particularly to the intent that no foolish headstrong rabble, at the instigation of any ringleader, may be able at any time to attack and insult the Senators . . .'

There is much more by way of detail. Alberti's whole work is devoted to prescriptions for all manner of buildings and public works in town and country. He approves the Roman practice of burial and cremation outside the city proper, but does not presume *'to blame the present practice of burying our dead within the city'* although *'the custom of burning the dead was much more convenient.'* He has much historically on the width of streets, and advises that the gate or harbour, as the *'principal head or boundary of all highways'* should be adorned. He approves of some uniformity of facades, and likes an archway where a street enters a square. As to 'squares' themselves, he gives this advice for their proportions: the length should be twice the breadth; the height of the surrounding buildings should be one-sixth to one-third of the breadth.

With Alberti there begins a tradition in architectural theorising that extends to modern times. Like Alberti's own work in his lifetime, much remains in manuscript and was at best privately circulated. His contemporary Antonio Averlino (1416-1470), better known as 'il Filarete', wrote his *Trattato d'Architettura* in which he uses a fictional narrative concerning the imaginary city of *Sforzinda* as a framework in 33 which to fit prescriptions for the design of buildings. He, like Francesco di Giorgio, has much on fortifications. He includes a design for a labyrinth, carrying to a formalised extreme the arguments both Aristotle and Alberti had used favouring the winding street. As an appendage to his ideal city, Averlino also adds a port: *Plusiapolis*. Throughout he epitomises the renewed interest of the times in classical learning, attempting to combine the precepts of Vitruvius with those of a contemporary neo-Platonism which sought perfection in regular geometrical forms. A characteristic of this attitude, which infuses the architecture of the Renaissance, is the conception of a building or a city as a *perfect whole*, which is then elaborated by sub-division. Throughout the whole of architecture, this conception is paralleled by its opposite (found, for instance, in much medieval work) which proceeds by adding part to part. We shall find both tendencies very much alive today.

Leonardo da Vinci (1452-1519) comes close to Francesco di Giorgio in his interest in machines and fortifications. For much of his life he was employed more as a military engineer than artist, and in his notebooks are sketches for schemes of 'regional planning' involving new canals, irrigation and drainage works. He advocated the building of 'overspill' towns, each of 30,000 population, to reduce congestion in Milan. In one sketch, he has a prophetic proposal for a multi-level building with pedestrian areas above carriageways. 34

Within a century of Alberti's death, the introduction of printing — and especially of engraved illustration — led to a steady growth in the number of architectural treatises circulating throughout Europe, written not only in Latin (as Alberti's had been) but now mainly in Italian, and translated into French, Flemish, English and the other tongues of sixteenth century Europe. Typical of those which dealt especially with town planning is Scamozzi's *Idea dell' Architettura Universale* published in Venice in 1615. This 35 includes an ideal city plan owing much to Vitruvius and to a generation which from the time of Filarete had experimented with his ideas. In Palma Nova, a Venetian frontier town, 36 Scamozzi was able to realise his ideals.

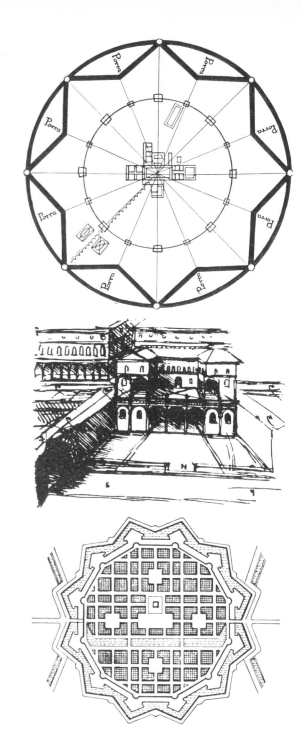

33 *Sforzinda: an ideal town designed in 1457 combining the precepts of Vitruvius with Renaissance concepts of geometrical perfection.*

36 *Palma Nova: an early 17th century Venetian frontier town designed by Scamozzi.*

34 *Leonardo's prophetic proposal for the segregation of pedestrian and vehicular traffic onto separate levels.*

35 *An ideal town of 1615 by Scamozzi.*

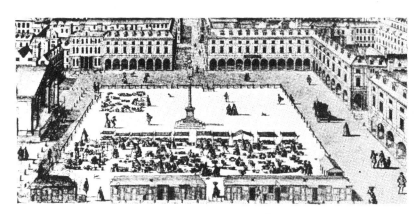

38   Covent Garden: an early 18th century print shewing Inigo Jones' design.

37   The recreation of part of the glory that was Rome: the Palazzo del Senatore.

39   St. Peter's Piazza, Rome.

From these examples it can be seen how Renaissance theory and practice tried to reconcile, into disciplined compositions, the classical tradition and the contemporary requirements of military science and of society generally. It is a measure of the confidence of the age, that it should set out even to dream of cities perfected in forms totally unlike any that had been seen. For the most part, these aspirations remain on paper, and the greatest achievements of the Renaissance in civic design lie in individual buildings and more modest schemes to bring order into sections of the town.

After its first flowering in 15th century Florence, Renaissance art developed to its most adventurous stage: the Baroque. Here, all the devices known to art are exploited to the full in the pursuit of the desired effect. While still employing classical motifs, architects found a freedom of expression unequalled to this day. Of particular significance is the use of curving, flowing forms which, in their restless rejection of the static perspective of earlier work, reflect the restlessness of an expansive age. Significant also, is the development (in step with the consolidation of powerful monarchies) of the *Grand Manner*, in which the principal streets and spaces of a city become an impressive 'set' for the acting out of pageant, procession and courtly life, no less than a necessity for growing commerce. The men of the time were eager to establish architecture and the design of cities as having considerable social significance. In an unpublished treatise, Christopher Wren, the great English exponent of the Baroque, wrote:

'Architecture has its political use; public buildings being the ornament of a country; it establishes a nation, draws people and commerce, makes the people love their native country, which passion is the original of all great actions in a Commonwealth.'[27]

37
38
39
40
41
42

40 Rome: the Spanish Steps.

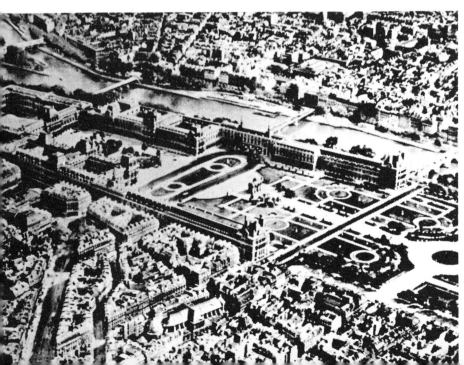

41 The grand manner in central Paris.

The inquiring spirit of the Renaissance resulted not only in new ideas about the beauty and form of cities. From it directly springs the science of our modern age, and new industry based on the use of machines and the harnessing of natural power. The first impact of these developments upon urban life comes with improvements in firearms and artillery, which at first (especially on the European mainland) largely subordinated civic design to the design of fortifications. Palma Nova may be said to sum up the sixteenth century ideal. Thenceforward, fortifications with salients and fortified outposts became ever more elaborate, reaching a 43 climax with Vauban, whose fortified towns rest on principles derived in equal measure from classical precept and contemporary military science.

The revolution in social production which ushers in our modern age had, by the eighteenth century, laid the foundations necessary to the subsequent development of the modern industrial town. But from that vital formative period, we know of only one attempt by an architect to design an 44 industrial town. This was *Saline de Chaux*, designed in 1773 by the French architect C. N. Ledoux, and described in great pictorial detail by him in his *Architecture*, published in 1804. The town (half of which was built) was intended to exploit salt production. It is conceived in the regular geometrical form prescribed by the Renaissance. Originally the architect proposed an octagon enclosed in a square, but the final proposal is circular. Ledoux' scheme remains unique as the only ideal industrial settlement to have placed the factory right at the heart of the town.

Modern industry, as we have seen, grows first under the influence of water power, later on the basis of coal. The construction works associated with it are undertaken in the main by designers drawn from the ranks of millwrights, smiths and other craftsmen, who increasingly come to be identified by the name of 'engineer'. Vitruvius, Alberti, and all other writers on architecture up to that time, had emphasised the bond which for them necessarily united the requirements of strength, usefulness and beauty. Henceforward, the growing preoccupation of architecture with matters of form, and its neglect of developing constructional science, accelerates a process which, in distinguishing between those whose concern was beauty, and those whose concern was economical strength, often failed to achieve either, and left usefulness — especially in matters of town planning — largely to take care of itself. Developing individualism in any case saw the destruction of those aristocratic values which previously had sustained some sense of social responsibility in matters of civic well-being, and at first the unprecedently rapid development of the modern industrial town was undertaken with little guidance from theory or design. Eventually, as we have seen, Victorian utilitarianism gave over to the lawyer and the sanitary engineer the role of defining a framework wherein speculative building and commercial enterprise could safely operate.

In matters of town planning, doctrine leaned heavily upon prevailing medical theory, which, having established that

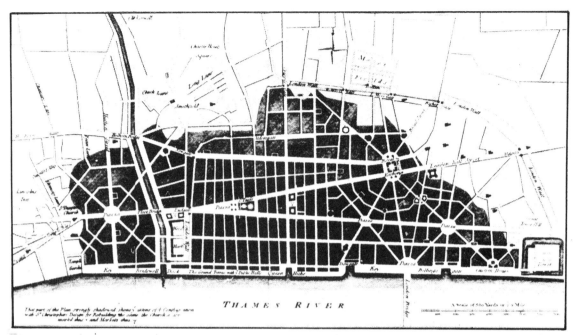

42 Wren's unfulfilled plan for London after the fire: the whole composed around a network of routes linking important focal points.

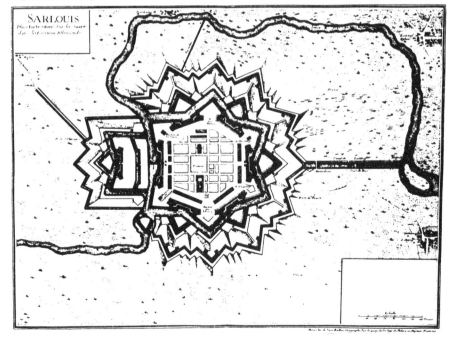

43 Saarlouis: a town designed by Vauban and established in 1687 on the Franco/German frontier.

44 *Saline de Chaux: a model industrial town designed by Ledoux in 1773.*

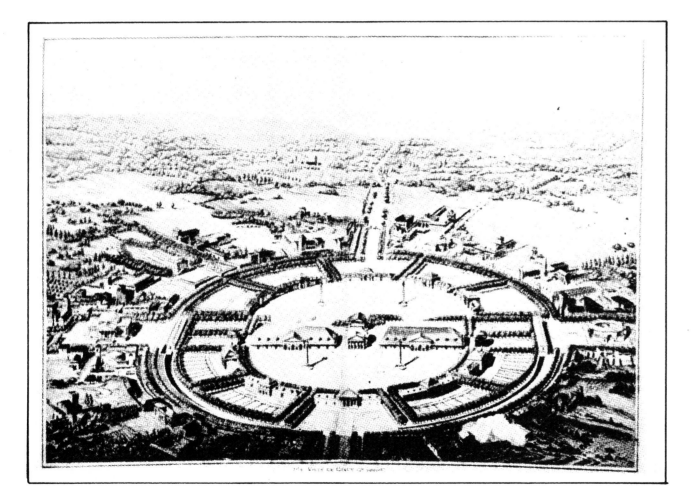

contagious disease was spread by infected water-supply and overcrowding, set about establishing minimum standards of hygiene and public health. An outstanding campaigner in these matters was a Dr. Southwood Smith who

'was early convinced that the fever epidemics which so constantly swept over the poorer parts of London were due to the insanitary conditions in which the poor lived. This proposition, to us so self-evident, aroused storms of protest. Those who were making money out of bad houses, those in authority in local government who feared that they might be forced to do something, all became vocal in their belief that fever epidemics were the Act of God, and that, in any case, the poor liked to live in insanitary squalor, and in the name of liberty must be allowed to do so . . .' [28]

Smith's crusading work prompted official enquiries, and as we have seen, the introduction of legislation. This effectively defined the sizes of houses, the space around them, their sanitary equipment and form of construction. Municipal authorities were charged with the provision of a safe supply of drinking water, and with the disposal of sewage and wastes. To these duties in time were added the responsibility for other 'municipal engineering services': street lighting, public transport, gas and electric power supply. New statutory powers were administered by officials trained in those skills most required to interpret standards defined in legal enactments and their technical appendices. Thus they became in effect the overseers of the transformation of town and village into industrial city, and during the nineteenth century few were concerned to develop a theory of town planning adequate to the unprecedented challenge of the age.

In new colonial towns, in fashionable 'watering places', in the High Street and the West End there persisted, of course, the long-established practices of Renaissance civic design — increasingly adapted to the coarser values of the successful businessman. From the high achievement of Jefferson and l'Enfant in the creation of Washington, town planning in the United States degenerated into the speculative parcelling out of territory as building lots. The wholesome urbanity of Portland Place and Bath declined to the level of 45 Middlesbrough. Where the great merchants of the Middle Ages had vied with each other in creating stupendous parish churches as monuments to their prosperity, the pinchbeck municipal worthies of Victorian Britain, even when persuaded that a new town hall would be a fitting symbol for their corporate self-esteem, would haggle over the price.

Rarely, except in their own secluded suburbs, a comfortable carriage-ride from 'the works', did they create original civic design of lasting value. 'Where there's muck, there's brass' was their slogan, and however notable an occasional achievement, it is bye-law housing, the factory and the slum, thrown together with little thought save for a quick return on investment, which typify the nineteenth century industrial town.

Here and there, usually when faced with the problem of providing homes as well as workplaces, something approaching comprehensive planning inevitably forced itself upon the factory owners:

'It is obvious that every capitalist who is tied down to a particular rural locality by the conditions of his industry — water power, the location of coal mines, iron-ore deposits and other mines, etc. — must build dwellings for his workers if none are available.' [29]

Planning on the grand scale, however, occurs only when in the interests of commerce, new roads and railway lines are ruthlessly cut through built-up areas, removing thousands from their homes. This practice has come to be identified with the name of Haussmann, Napoleon III's Prefect of Paris, who broke *'long, straight and broad streets right through the closely built workers' quarters'* and lined them *'with big luxurious buildings'*, the intention there being to make barricade fighting more difficult and to turn Paris *'into a luxury city pure and simple.'* [30] On a more modest scale, industrialists here and there established model 'colonies' combining, in one planned undertaking, factory, houses and some public buildings. Outstanding in England, is Saltaire, now virtually a suburb of Bradford, its name compounded from that of its founder — Sir Titus Salt — and that of the river beside which it stands. Later examples such as Port Sunlight (Unilever), New Earswick (Rowntree) and Bournville (Cadbury) in increasing measure mix philanthropy with commercial shrewdness. Of the philanthropy, one writer wryly remarks the case of Akroyd (creator of Akroyden, Halifax) who

'loved his workers, and in particular his female employees, to such an extent that his less philanthropic competitors in Yorkshire used to say of him that he ran his factories exclusively with his own children.' [31]

45   Cumberland Terrace, Regent's Park, London, designed by John Nash.

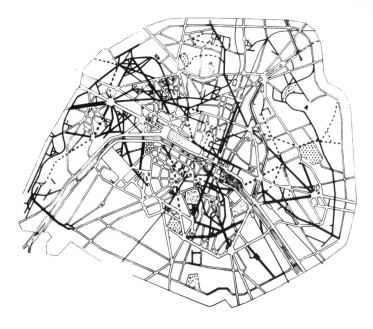

47   Haussmann's plan for Paris: new roads ruthlessly cut through built up areas.

46   Part of 19th century Leeds.

49   *Saltaire: beside the railway, looking east.*

50   *Saltaire: looking north towards the church and the Aire valley beyond.*

48   *Saltaire, Yorks.*
An outstanding example of an industrialist's new town.

Of the commercial shrewdness, he writes:
. . . the English capitalists . . . realised that for factory production in the rural districts expenditure on workers' dwellings was a necessary part of the total investment of capital, and a very profitable one, both directly and indirectly.'
They
'had practical experience of the pressure they can exert on striking workers if they are at the same time the landlords of those workers.' [32]

For the worst example of such pressure, however, the 'model' town of Pullman, Ohio, was subsequently to become notorious. Company excesses in combating a strike by employees of the Pullman Car Company in 1894, led to the intervention of the U.S. Supreme Court, and to half-hearted legislation to moderate the worst excesses inevitably implicit in the 'company town'. [33]

VTOPIAE INSVLAE FIGVRA

51 *The frontispiece to More's 'Utopia'.*

Self-seeking and autocratic benevolence were not the only influences at work, however, in the nineteenth century. From the point of view of modern town planning theory, a much profounder influence begins to develop step by step with the growth of large-scale industry itself. It represents, or attempts to represent, the interests of the common people, and above all the urban working class. From the outset it is identified with socialism, and comes to reflect in time the varying tendencies in working class politics. For town planning, that tendency characterised as *Utopianism* has most obviously a great significance which must now be examined.

At least since the time of Plato, the ideal city has persisted as a vehicle for the exposition of political theory, or to express the aspirations of the deprived or oppressed. The 'New Jerusalem' of the Book of Revelations is the oldest example in Christian literature, and the theme is revived by, among others, St. Augustine. 'Utopia' itself is the name invented by 51 Sir Thomas More in 1516 to describe a mythical country. The name is a play upon Greek words implying both 'healthy place' and 'nowhere'. More's book is mainly a critique of contemporary society, and has little to say that matters to us here.

Of pioneering significance for modern times, however, are 52 the proposals of Robert Owen (1771-1858). In common with all ideal schemes up to about 1850, Owen's projects are conceived in terms of a single factory. This reflects his own experience and the circumstances typical of the time, when (as we have seen) mills were built in the countryside often far removed from established settlement. For this reason, we are with Owen not dealing with towns so much as with industrial villages. 'Village' is indeed the word which he uses to describe his proposals. He envisaged a group of buildings set in open countryside — a form by no means uncommon during the early days of industrialisation in Great Britain. His motivation was outspokenly political. In the years after the

Napoleonic Wars, there was widespread unemployment and poverty. Owen saw this as the result of machinery having displaced the worker, and this his proposal was intended to correct, by building new factories throughout the land together with housing and other necessities for the unemployed and their families. He well understood the problem of overproduction in terms of the market, and hoped to overcome this by means of co-operative ownership and distribution which (although they are chiefly what he is remembered for) are beyond our scope. We should note, however, that his intentions for a socialist commonwealth result in there being little sub-division based on social status, and the total layout he proposes emphasises social unity and identity of interest.

His proposals (which were developed over many years from about 1816 onwards) were first made for Lanarkshire, where he himself was proprietor-manager of weaving mills and where he put some of his ideas into practice. He later extended the concept to have universal applicability and would presumably have been happy to see the whole habitable landscape covered in the manner of his illustration. He writes in terms of a population between a minimum of 300 and a maximum of 2,000 (preferably between 800 and 1,200) with $\frac{1}{2} - 1\frac{1}{2}$ acres per person. Owen describes the total concept thus:

'The drawing exhibits, in the foreground, an establishment, with its appendages and an appropriate quantity of land: and at due distances, other villages of a similar description.

'Squares of buildings are here represented sufficient to accommodate about 1,200 persons each: and surrounded by a quantity of land, from 1,000 to 1,500 acres.

'Within the squares are public buildings, which divide them into parallelograms.

'The central building contains a public kitchen, mess-rooms and all the accommodation necessary to economical and comfortable cooking and eating.

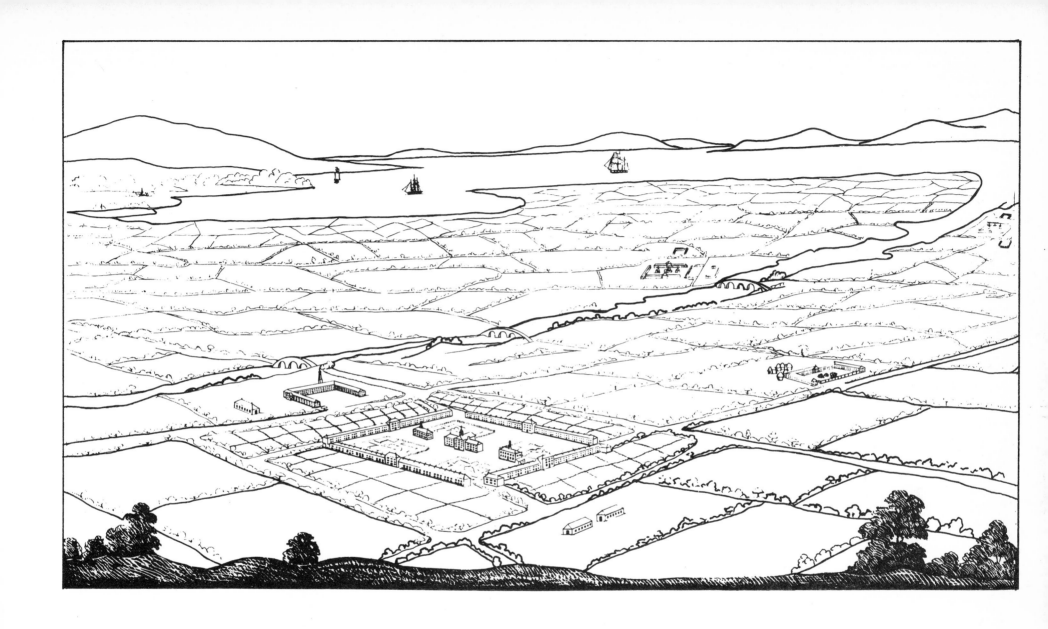

52 Robert Owen's proposal for industrial villages.

'To the right of this is a building, of which the ground-floor will form the infant school, and the other a lecture-room and a place of worship.

'The building to the left contains a school for the elder children, and a committee-room on the ground floor: above, a library and a room for adults.

'In the vacant space between the squares are enclosed grounds for exercise and recreation: these enclosures are supposed to have trees planted in them.

'It is intended that three sides of each square shall be lodging houses, chiefly for the married, consisting of four rooms in each: each room to be sufficiently large to house a man, his wife, and two children. The fourth side is designed for dormitories for all the children exceeding two in a family, or above three years of age.

'In the centre of this side of the square are apartments for those who superintend the dormitories: at one extremity of it the infirmary; and at the other a building for the accommodation of strangers who may come from a distance to see their friends or relatives.

'In the centres of two sides of the squares are apartments for general superintendents, clergymen, schoolmasters, surgeons, etc.; and in the third are store-rooms for all the articles required for the use of the establishment.

'On the outside, and at the back of the houses around the squares, are gardens, bounded by roads.

'Immediately beyond these, on one side, are buildings for mechanical and manufacturing purposes. The slaughter-house, stabling, etc., are to be separated from the establishment by plantations.

'At the other side are offices for washing, bleaching, etc.; and at a still greater distance from the squares, are some of the farming establishments, with conveniences for malting, brewing, and corn-mills, etc.; around these are cultivated enclosures, pasture-land etc., the hedgerows of which are planted with fruit trees . . .

'Each lodging-room within the square is to accommodate a man, his wife and two children under three years of age: and to be such as will permit them to have much more comforts than the dwellings of the poor usually afford.

'It is intended that the children above three years of age should attend the school, eat in the mess-room and sleep in the dormitories; the parents being, of course, permitted to see and converse with them at meals and at all other proper times; — that before they leave school they shall be well instructed in all necessary and useful knowledge: — that every possible means shall be adopted to prevent the acquirement of bad habits from their parents or otherwise; — that no pains shall be spared to impress upon them such habits and dispositions as may be most conducive to their happiness through life, as well as render them useful and valuable members of the community to which they belong.' [34]

Revolutionary as Owen's proposals were, they did not immediately aim at the revolutionary reconstitution of society as a whole, although he occasionally acknowledges that they tended in that direction. He was a practical man opposed to 'closet theorists', and aimed at the solution of real problems which he saw around him. Basically, his point of view was very straightforward, and rested on two propositions: it was better to put the poor and unemployed to useful work than to have them a burden of poor relief; and, since character was a consequence of the material environment, only by making a decent environment could society produce decent people. While some of his establishments might be communally managed, others might be run by capitalists. He clearly preferred the former, and both in England and the United States tried to establish model communist settlements. Later also, he became, of course, more and more directly involved in trade unionism and the political struggles of his time, and it is in these affairs that his influence has been the more lasting and significant.

We cannot leave Owen's project, however, without also noting some of the more general notions which prompted his particular solution. Firstly he unquestioningly assumes the marriage of agriculture and factory production in one establishment, combining the advantages of both. 'Villages of this extent, in the neighbourhood of others of a similar description, at due distances, will be found capable of combining within themselves all the advantages that city and country residences now afford, without any of the numerous inconveniences and evils which necessarily attach to both these modes of society.' [35] Then, there is the further integration of domestic and productive life: homes, schools, canteens, workshops and fields form a compact unity 'combined as in a new machine: a machine it truly is, that will simplify and facilitate, in a very reasonable manner, all the operations of human life . . .' [36] This unity finds rational expression in his chosen architectural form, one which he says: 'affords so many advantages for the comfort of human life, that if great ignorance . . . had not prevailed . . . it must long ago have become universal.' [37] And, perhaps of the greatest significance for us today, he places first among the details to be decided upon, 'the number of persons who can be associated to give the greatest advantages to themselves and to the community'. This, he says, is 'the corner-stone of the whole fabric of human society', and to do justice to it 'would require a work of many volumes'. [38] These we are spared, and Owen advances his own range of preferred population sizes with scant argument in support of them.

It is of technical interest to note that his layout shows considerable sophistication, and betrays so much familiarity with architecture, that, were it not that he lived in the dying years of the great age of the Amateur, we should attribute much to an unknown professional collaborator. It will be seen that the refectory at the focal point, with the schools either side, subdivides the central square into more intimate areas. The road which enters each corner does so in the 'turbine' manner commended nearly a century later as least destructive of enclosure.* The road layout is of interest also in that there is a rudimentary primary and secondary system of a type we have since become accustomed to, so arranged that 'through traffic' is by-passed. The clarity of the total form belongs however only to the residential part and is to some extent achieved by separating out elements considered too disruptive to incorporate in so neat a scheme. The dominance of the more leisurely aspects of community life would have been severely challenged had labour also been placed at the centre of things, and in banishing workplaces beyond tree belts, Owen sets a fashion since invariably adopted on hygienic grounds. It is probable that his reasoning also owed something to the wish to keep noise, smoke and smell out of the way.

In Owen's scheme, therefore, we find political and economic objectives eloquently expressed in architectural form. The community goes out to work, but converges upon a central place for all other activities which can be undertaken in common. The dwelling is little more than a bedroom, family life being largely subsumed into that of the community at large.

* By Camillo Sitte in his Stadtebau.

The next significant contribution comes from Charles Fourier (1772-1837). As a French political theorist he was as sophisticated as the Welshman Owen was naive. His convoluted theories included a history of human progress towards Utopia, to be attained after succeeding stages of future development. This does not inhibit him from spelling out in great detail prescriptions of his ideal settlement, sufficiently precise for elaborate drawings to be made. To an even greater extent than Owen he provided a ready-made panacea for the use of philanthropic enthusiasts and would-be reformers. His influence upon town planning is consequently not inconsiderable, especially as he may be regarded as the father of that school which conceives the town as a single building.

Fourier's proposals were not made specifically in terms of modern factory production, and betray their author's preference for agriculture. His *phalanstère* was to be taken up however by later industrial reformers — most notably by Jean Baptiste Godin (1817-1889), who from 1859-1870 built at Guise in France, the colony which attempted to translate Fourier's ideas into reality.

For Fourier, neither the philosopher's pursuit of reason nor the economist's pursuit of profit were worthy aims for mankind. Worse — they perverted society from the pursuit of its necessary objective: the gratification of the 'passions'. 'Passionate' attraction and repulsion operated within society in conformity with laws analogous to those of Newton. A satisfactory society would therefore be one which brought together in correct proportions a sufficient number of people to cover the full range of passionate personalities, in circumstances which promoted their harmonious interaction in accordance with 'natural law'. Fourier proceeds to calculate from 'first principles' what these numbers would be, and to specify the kind of environment necessary. He lists as the basic elements of his system the basic passions of mankind, combining them in various ways to produce a formidable range of passionate types. He is concerned neither to limit himself to the morally acceptable, nor to eliminate conflict. For him, the suppression of the passions could only lead to perversion, and it was from this that the real ills of society sprang. A healthy society would be one in which all passion could find a 'healthy' outlet. He may thus be regarded as the prophet of much that is still fashionable in psychiatry and 'Hippie' culture.

For town planning theory, Fourier is no less prophetic. The doctrine of the 'well-balanced population', containing within it an adequate number of workers in this or that industry; of members of this or that 'socio-economic group'; of men, women and children of various 'age-groups': this today is very much alive, as we shall see. In spite of what cannot but appear as a 'crankiness' verging on the insane, he foretells much else which has now passed into the mainstream of planning theory and practice, as the following extracts from his writings will show:

'The Establishment of a trial phalanx

'*We will suppose that the trial is made by . . . a powerful company which desires to avoid all tentative measures and proceed directly to the organisation of Full Harmony, . . . I am going to indicate the procedure to follow in this case.*

'*An association of 1500 or 1600 people requires a site comprising at least one square league of land, that is to say a surface area of six million square* toises* . . .

'*A good stream of water should be available; the land should be hilly and suitable for a variety of crops; there should be a forest nearby; and the site should be fairly near a large city but far enough away to avoid unwelcome visitors.*

'*The trial Phalanx will stand alone and it will get no help from neighbouring Phalanxes. As a result of this isolation, . . . it will be particularly important to provide it with the help of a good site fit for a variety of functions. Flat country, . . . would be quite inappropriate . . . It will therefore be necessary to select a diversified region, . . . or at the very least a fine valley provided with a stream and a forest, . . .*

'*The 1500 or 1600 people brought together will be in a state of graduated inequality as to wealth, age, personality, and theoretical and practical knowledge. The group should be as varied as possible; for the greater the variety in the passions and faculties of the members, the easier it will be to harmonize them in a limited amount of time.*

'*All possible types of agricultural work should be represented in this trial community, including that involving hot-houses and conservatories. There should also be at least three types of manufacturing work for winter and for rainy days, as well as diverse types of work in the applied sciences and arts, apart from what is taught in the schools. A passional series will be assigned to each type of work, and it will divide up its members into sub-divisions and groups according to the instruction given earlier.*

---

* 1 toise=6 feet. 6 million sq. toises=2,000 ha. or 5,000 acres.

'At the very outset an evaluation should be made of the capital deposited as shares in the enterprise: land, material, flocks, tools, etc. This matter is one of the first to be dealt with; and I shall discuss it in detail further on . . .

'Let us discuss the composition of the trial Phalanx. At least seven-eighths of its members should be people involved in farming or industry. The remainder will consist of capitalists, savants and artists . . .

'In readying the gardens and workshops of the trial Phalanx one should try to predict and estimate the approximate quantity of attraction which each branch of industry is likely to excite. For example, we know that the plum-tree has less attraction than the pear-tree; and so we we will plant fewer plum-trees than pear-trees. The quantity of attraction will be the sole rule to follow in each branch of agricultural and manufacturing work.

'Economists would follow a different line of reasoning. They would insist that it is necessary to cultivate whatever produced the greatest yield and to produce a large quantity of the most productive objects. The trial Phalanx should avoid this error; its methods should be different from those of the Phalanxes that will follow it. When all regions have embraced Harmony and when they are all organized in combination with each other, then it will no doubt be necessary to adapt farming to the dictates of interest and attraction. But the goal of the experimental community is quite different: it is to get a group of 1500 or 1600 people working out of pure attraction. If one could predict that they would be more actively attracted to work by thistles and thorns than by orchards and flowers, then it would be necessary to give up orchards and flowers and replace them with thistles and thorns in the experimental community.

'In point of fact, as soon as it has attained its two goals, industrial attraction and passional equilibrium, the trial Phalanx will have the means to widen the scope of its labours so as to include any useful tasks which may have been neglected at the outset. Moreover, its strength will be doubled when neighbouring communities organize their own Phalanxes . . .

'The Phalanstery

53   'The edifice occupied by the Phalanx bears no resemblance to our urban or rural buildings; and in the establishment of a full Harmony of 1600 people none of our buildings could be put to use, not even a great palace like Versailles nor a great monastery like Escorial . . .

'The lodgings, gardens and stables of a society run by series of groups must be vastly different from those of our villages and towns, which are perversely organised and meant for families having no societary relations. Instead of the chaos of little houses which rival each other in filth and ugliness in our towns, a Phalanx constructs for itself a building as perfect as the terrain permits. Here is a brief account of the measures to be taken on a favourable site . . .

'The center of the palace or Phalanstery should be a place for quiet activity; it should include the dining rooms, the exchange, meeting rooms, library, studies etc. This central section includes the temple, the tower, the telegraph, the coops for carrier pigeons, the ceremonial chimes, the observatory, and a winter courtyard adorned with resinous plants. The parade grounds are located just behind the central section.

'One of the wings of the Phalanstery should include all the noisy workshops like the carpenter shop and the forge and the other workshops where hammering is done. It should also be the place for all the industrial gatherings involving children, who are generally very noisy at work and even at music. The grouping of these activities will avoid an annoying drawback of our civilized cities where every street has its own hammerer or iron merchant or beginning clarinet player to shatter the ear drums of fifty families in the vicinity.

'The other wing should contain the caravansary with its ballrooms and its halls for meetings with outsiders, who should not be allowed to encumber the center of the palace and to disturb the domestic relations of the Phalanx. This precaution of isolating outsiders and concentrating their meetings in one of the wings will be most important in the trial Phalanx. For the Phalanx will attract thousands of curiosity-seekers whose entry fees will provide a profit that I cannot estimate at less than twenty million . . .

'The PHALANSTERY or manor-house of the Phalanx should contain, in addition to the private apartments, a large number of halls for social relations. These halls will be called Seristeries . . .

'In all social relations it is necessary to have small rooms adjoining the Seristery in order to encourage small group meetings. Accordingly, a Seristery, or the meeting place of a series, is arranged in a compound manner with halls for large collective gatherings and for smaller cabalistic meetings. This system is very different from that employed in our large assemblies where, even in the palaces of kings, everyone is thrown together pell-mell according to the holy

53   Fourier's' Phalanstère'.

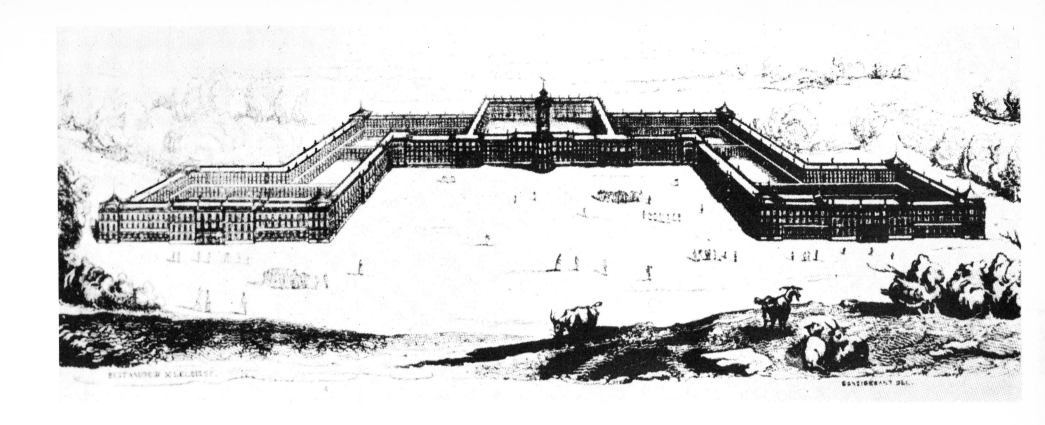

philosophical principle of equality. This principle is completely intolerable in Harmony.

'The stables, granaries and warehouses should be located, if possible, opposite the main edifice. The space between the palace and the stables will serve as a main courtyard or parade-ground and it should be very large. To give some idea of the proper dimensions I estimate that the front of the Phalanstery should have a length of about 600 toises de Paris. The center and the parade grounds will run to about 300 toises and each of the two wings to about 150 . . . The gardens should be placed, insofar as possible, behind the palace and not behind the stables, since large-scale farming should be done in the area near the stables. These plans will of course vary according to local circumstances; we are only talking here about an ideal location . . .

'All the children, both rich and poor, are lodged together on the mezzanine of the Phalanstery. For they should be kept separate from the adolescents, and in general from all those who are capable of making love, at most times and particularly during the late evening and the early morning hours. The reasons for this will be explained later. For the time being let us assume that those who are capable of forming amorous relations will be concentrated on the second floor, while the very young and the very old . . . should have meeting-halls on the ground floor and the mezzanine. They should also be isolated from the street-gallery, which is the most important feature of a Phalanstery and which cannot be conceived of in civilization. . . .

'The street-galleries are a mode of internal communication which would alone be sufficient to inspire disdain for the palaces and great cities of civilization. Once a man has seen the street-galleries of a Phalanx, he will look upon the most elegant civilized palace as a place of exile, a residence worthy of fools who, after three thousand years of architectural studies, have not yet learned how to build themselves healthy and comfortable lodgings. In civilization we can only conceive of luxury in the simple mode; we have no conception of the compound or collective forms of luxury . . .

'The poorest wretch in Harmony, a man who doesn't have a penny to his name, has a well-heated and enclosed portico at his disposal when he gets into a carriage; he goes from the Palace to the stables by means of paved and graveled

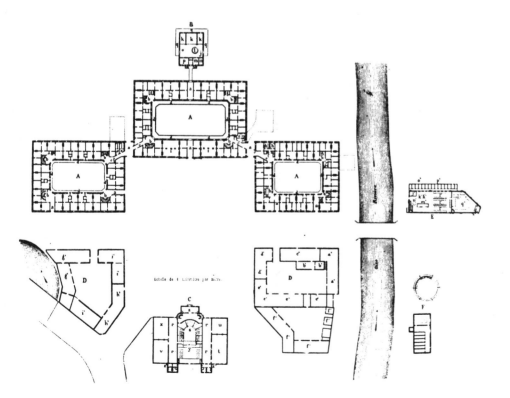

underground passage-ways; he gets from his lodgings to the public halls and workshops by means of street-galleries which are heated in winter and ventilated in summer. In Harmony one can pass through the workshops, stables, shops, ball-rooms, banquet and assembly halls, etc., in January without knowing whether it is rainy or windy, hot or cold. The detailed treatment which I shall give to this subject entitles me to say that if, after three thousand years of study, the civilized have not yet learned how to house themselves, it is no wonder that they have not yet learned how to direct and harmonize their passions. When one fails in the most minute material calculations, one is likely to fail in the great calculations concerning the passions.

'Let us describe the street-galleries which are one of the most charming and precious features of a Palace of Harmony. A Phalanx which may consist of up to 1600 or 1800 people, is actually a small town in itself; the more so in that it has a large number of adjacent rural buildings of the sort that our proprietors and city-dwellers relegate to their country residences.

'The Phalanx has no outside streets or open road-ways exposed to the elements. All the portions of the central edifice can be traversed by means of a wide gallery which runs along the second floor of the whole building. At each extremity of this spacious corridor there are elevated passages, supported by columns, and also attractive underground passages which connect all the parts of the Phalanx and the adjoining buildings. Thus everything is linked by a series of passage-ways which are sheltered, elegant, and comfortable in winter thanks to the help of heaters and ventilators.

'These sheltered passage-ways are particularly necessary in view of the fact that there is a great deal of movement in Harmony. In conformity with the laws . . . the sessions of the various work and recreation groups never last more than one or two hours. If the Harmonians were obliged to go out of doors in moving from one hall to another, from a stable to a workshop, it would take just one week of wintry, damp weather to leave even the most robust of them beset by cold, inflamations and pleurisy. A state of things which requires so much moving about makes sheltered means of communications an absolute necessity.

'The street-gallery or continuous peristyle extends along the second story.* It could not be placed on the ground floor since the lower part of the building will be traversed by carriage entrances. Those who have seen the gallery of the Louvre may take it as a model for the street-gallery in Harmony. It will be taller than the Louvre, however, and the

* i.e. the first floor.

windows will be differently placed.

'The street-galleries of a Phalanx wind along just one side of the central edifice and stretch to the end of each of its wings. All of these wings contain a double row of rooms. Thus one row of rooms looks out upon the fields and gardens and the other looks out upon the street-gallery. The street-gallery, then, will be three stories high with windows on one side. The entrance to all the apartments of the second, third and fourth stories is located in the street-gallery. Flights of stairs are placed at intervals to ascend to the upper stories . . .

'After thirty years, when permanent buildings are constructed, the street-gallery will have a width of six toises *in the central portion of the Palace and four* toises *in the wings. But at the outset, since the present poverty of the globe requires modest structures . . . the street gallery will be only four* toises *wide in the center and three in the wings . . .*

'The main body of the building will have a width of about eight toises, *not including the street-gallery. This will allow room to put alcoves and toilets in all of the apartments . . . The minimum lodging for a member of the poorest class will thus include a room, an alcove and a private toilet . . .*

'The kitchens and some of the public halls will be located on the ground floor. There will also be trap-doors in the floors of the dining rooms on the second story. Thus the tables may be set in the kitchens below and simply raised through the trap-doors when it is time to eat. These trap-doors will be particularly useful during festivities, such as the visits of travelling caravans and legions, when there will be too many people to eat in the ordinary dining rooms. Then double rows of tables will be set in the street-galleries, and the food will be passed up from the kitchen.

'The principal public halls should not be situated on the ground floor. There are two reasons for this. The first is that the patriarchs and children, who have difficulty climbing stairs, should be lodged in the lower parts of the building. The second is that the children should be kept in isolation from the non-industrial activities of the adults . . .

'To spend a winter's day in a Phalanstery, to visit all parts of it without exposure to the elements, to go to the theatre and the opera in light clothes and coloured shoes without worrying about the mud and the cold, would be a charm so novel that it alone would suffice to make our cities and castles seem detestable. If the Phalanstery were to be put to civilized uses, the mere convenience of its sheltered, heated and ventilated passage-ways would make it enormously valuable.' [39]

One of Fourier's objectives is to 'accelerate relations' by building compactly: this is the prime reason for adopting a multi-storey solution, and for the disposition of the 'wings' of the Phalanstery around internal courts crossed at intervals by bridges. More recently, high density multi-storey building has been urged on similar grounds, as has also the separation onto different levels of vehicular and pedestrian circulation. Fourier specifies dimensions throughout, allowing that private apartments would differ in size and be priced accordingly. But he is most careful to insist that no 'class districts' shall be allowed to result from their grouping: an intermingled distribution, specifically designed to promote social interaction, is planned in detail.

Fourier's phalanstery is not, like Owen's village, used to enclose a common ground. It resembles rather a country mansion set in a park: a building in a landscape, outward-looking and proclaiming order and symmetry to the world at large, as much an exercise in propaganda as in philanthropy. The doubling into parallel blocks results in significant internal spaces, but these are conceived in the spirit of light-wells rather than courtyards essential to the design. His parade ground also is poorly defined. Architecturally and in every way Fourier lacks the experience that Owen, a practical man in a burgeoning industrial society, was able to bring to bear. His tiresome precision on points of detail betrays the mind of a prophet *'guided by fondness for his own invention'* — in architecture (according to Alberti), a cardinal sin. But, stripped of their pretensions, there is much of value in his ideas which has, directly or indirectly, seeped into the consciousness of his successors.

Godin modified Fourier's scheme to suit an industrial community. As with Owen, there is a primary division which banished industry, sited across the Oise, and related it to the settlement by a *Rue des Usines* which bisects the site. The *Familistère* then became the generator of the design on the river's left bank. It followed superficially the pattern decreed by Fourier, but was exclusively residential, and the internal courts were entirely glazed over. The apartments were for families, and reflected the standards of the 1860's: two rooms per family being the norm. In the attic there was provision for visitors, and to supplement the lavatory accommodation in each block, a bath house and laundry were sited across the river. Community life was also provided for in separate buildings. Eating and recreation were accommodated in two blocks (one of which combined also pig-styes and a slaughter-house). It was education that took pride of place on the

54

principal axis. A kindergarten block was to be linked centrally to the *Familistère*, and a school and theatre complex to face the principal front. The total scheme thus underlined the emphasis Fourier (like Owen) had placed on education, which with Godin's proposal was already emerging in a form still fostered today.

The scheme as executed, departs in detail but not in principle from what was intended. In 1886 the community consisted of about 400 families united in a form of co-operative enterprise. As the buildings stand today, however, there is little of this unity apparent, and although trees have been planted in an attempt to reinforce the unity of the 'parade ground' between *Familistère* and theatre, the Rue des Usines destroys what little enclosure is achieved. The potential of the roofed courtyards as a community focus is not exploited, and impressive as the achievement is, it would probably have been better for Godin's architecture if Fourier had never lived.

Owen's and Fourier's pioneering visions were followed by others both in Europe and America, but revolutionary *Utopianism*, unable to cope with the political realities of its time, gradually succumbed to the less radical reformism which characterised popular political thought in the latter half of the nineteenth century. Not the reconstitution of society at large, but the gradual amelioration of the lot of the working classes, became the objective even of many who still called themselves socialists, and we find little to match the bold vision of Owen's *New View of Society* for the best part of one hundred years after his publication of that name. Like the Universal Men of the High Renaissance, who, fully conscious of the changed conditions they were helping to initiate, could see beyond their beginnings to their destiny, Owen and those like him fearlessly grasped the potential of the industrial revolution and were not afraid to look beyond it to the new society it could bring about. Owen's industrial villages and Fourier's phalansteries may yet prove no less prophetic than were Leonardo's aeroplanes.

For the record, we may note Cabet's *Icaria*, Pemberton's *Happy Colony*, Richardson's *Hygeia* and Buckingham's *Victoria*. We should note also Pugin, Ruskin and Morris, whose criticism of the debased architectural standards of their time extended to the city. Especially noteworthy is Morris's *News from Nowhere* which unreservedly rejects not only contemporary capitalism and its cities, but looks beyond a transitional 'state socialism' to a communist Britain wherein large cities are done away with, and the drudgery of

55 *The Familistère at Guise today.*

'useless toil' replaced with the joyfulness of 'useful work' essential to the well-being of mankind. Morris's spokesman from the twenty-first century recalls how;

. . . . 'England was once a country of clearings amongst the woods and wastes, with a few towns interspersed, which were fortresses for the feudal army, markets for the folk, gathering places for the craftsmen. It then became a country of huge and foul workshops and fouler gambling-dens, surrounded by an ill-kept, poverty-stricken farm, pillaged by the masters of the workshops. It is now a garden, where nothing is wasted and nothing is spoilt, with the necessary dwellings, sheds and workshops scattered up and down the country, all trim and neat and pretty . . .' Government was based on commune, ward and parish. Steam power was superseded by a new form of 'force' engine. 'All work which would be irksome to do by hand is done by immensely improved machinery, and in all work which it is pleasant to do by hand, machinery is done without.'

Morris's fictional prognostications were part of a growing vogue in socialist propaganda. Shortly before *News from Nowhere*, Edward Bellamy's *Looking Backward* had appeared. It was widely read — among others by a young inventor and adventurer, Ebenezer Howard, whom it inspired to more practical speculations which were to culminate in the British Town Planning Movement and the New Towns built after the Second World War.

56   Inside the Familistère today showing the glazed-over central space.

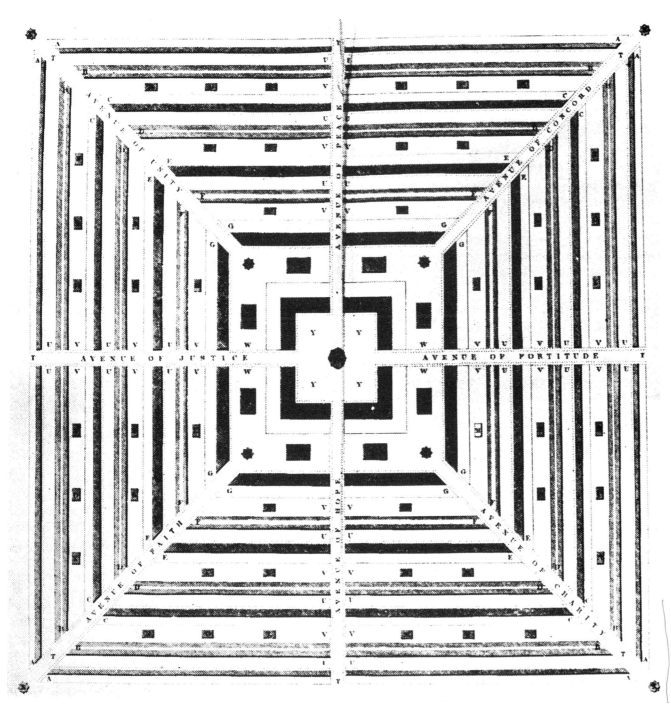

57 The plan of a model town by James Silk Buckingham. 'Squares' of terraced houses and gardens alternate with other 'land uses', the best houses being near the centre, and a 'covered arcade' for workshops near the boundary. Large factories, abbatoirs, cattle markets, a public cemetery, hospital, etc., are outside the town where sites are also reserved for 'suburban villas'.

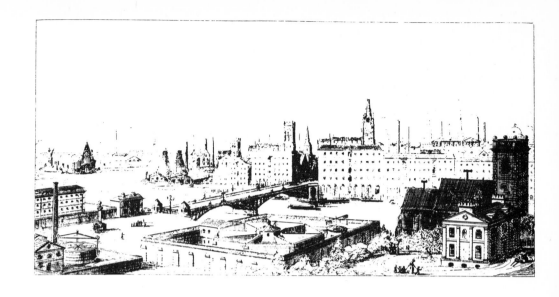

58 A jaundiced view of change as observed by the architect Pugin in 1836.
The lower picture shows a 'Catholic town in 1440', with its Guild Hall and numerous religious establishments; the upper picture, the same town in 1840, with its jail, gasworks, ironworks, non-conformist chapel and 'socialist hall of science'.

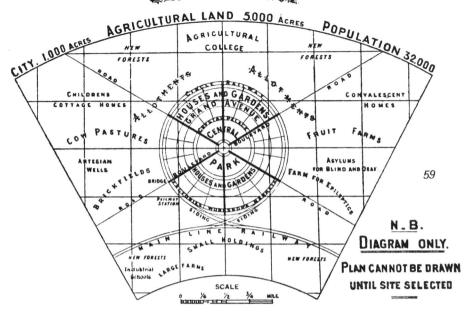

GARDEN-CITY

CITY, 1,000 ACRES — AGRICULTURAL LAND 5,000 ACRES — POPULATION 32,000

AGRICULTURAL COLLEGE

NEW FORESTS

NEW FORESTS

CHILDRENS COTTAGE HOMES

CONVALESCENT HOMES

COW PASTURES

ALLOTMENTS

ALLOTMENTS

FRUIT FARMS

ARTESIAN WELLS

BRICKFIELDS

FARM FOR EPILEPTICS

ASYLUMS FOR BLIND AND DEAF

BRIDGE

RAILWAY STATION

SIDING

SIDING

HOUSES AND GARDENS

GRAND AVENUE

CENTRAL PARK

HOUSES AND GARDENS

MAIN LINE RAILWAY

SMALL HOLDINGS

NEW FORESTS

NEW FORESTS

LARGE FARMS

Industrial Schools

59

N.B.

DIAGRAM ONLY.

PLAN CANNOT BE DRAWN UNTIL SITE SELECTED

SCALE

0   ¼   ½   ¾   MILE

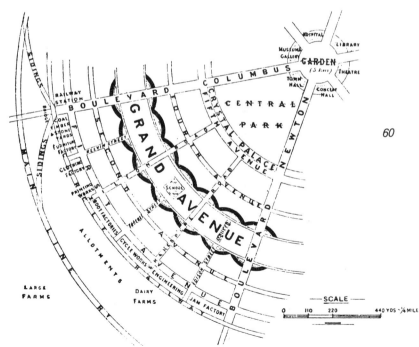

RAILWAY STATION

COAL TIMBER STONE YARDS

FURNITURE FACTORY

CLOTHING FACTORY

PRINTING WORKS

BOOT FACTORIES

CYCLE WORKS or ENGINEERING

JAM FACTORY

KELVIN STREET

GRAND AVENUE

BOULEVARD

COLUMBUS

CRYSTAL PALACE

AVENUE

NEWTON

CENTRAL PARK

MUSEUM GALLERY

HOSPITAL

LIBRARY

GARDEN (5 Acres)

THEATRE

TOWN HALL

CONCERT HALL

SCHOOL

MAIN LINE RAILWAY

SIDINGS

ALLOTMENTS

LARGE FARMS

DAIRY FARMS

60

— SCALE —

0   110   220   440 YDS — ¼ MILE

DIAGRAM

ILLUSTRATING CORRECT PRINCIPLE OF A CITY'S GROWTH — OPEN COUNTRY EVER NEAR AT HAND, AND RAPID COMMUNICATION BETWEEN OFF-SHOOTS.

COUNTRY

GARDEN CITY
POPULATION 32,000

HIGH ROAD

CENTRAL CITY
POPULATION 58,000

INTER-MUNICIPAL RAILWAY

INTER-MUNICIPAL RAILWAY

COUNTRY

COUNTRY

COUNTRY

CONCORD
POPULATION 32,000

INTER-MUNICIPAL RAILWAY

HIGH ROAD

HIGH ROAD

COUNTRY

COUNTRY

61   Howard's entire scheme for a 'cluster of cities'.

46

Howard published in 1898, a book which has become known world-wide as *Garden Cities of Tomorrow.*[42] He deplores urban congestion (especially in London) and rural depopulation, and proceeds in considerable detail to put forward a policy which he claims would provide *'a peaceful path to reform'* for both these evils and, through them of all the ills attending the society of his day. He is above all the apostle of 'gradualism', and, in distinguishing his proposals from his predecessors', points chiefly to the fact that he does not envisage the revolutionary reconstitution of society at large. Instead, he sets out a plan for the acquisition of agricultural land by philanthropic investors, and the building thereon of a new town to be settled by those whom the obvious advantages of low rents and good surroundings would attract from the urban slums. The essential physical ingredients of his proposals are amply illustrated in his diagrams.

59
60   The *'Garden City'* is to have at its core public buildings set in a central park. Surrounding this, is the *'Crystal Palace'* — a shopping arcade overlooking the park. Then come the residential areas, interrupted by a *'Grand Avenue'* — a linear park wherein are placed the schools. There is a hint that as we move outwards, houses may be somewhat meaner than the *'very excellently built houses, each standing in its own ample grounds'* which front onto Fifth Avenue. Beyond First Avenue, and able to take advantage of the Circle Railway, are the factories of the town. The whole stands in the midst of a considerable tract of agricultural land, owned by the municipality which is thus able to retain it as a 'green belt' free from any threat of urban encroachment.

61   The fan shaped form of this green belt will be found to be an enlarged segment of another diagram in which Howard eventually lays bare his entire scheme: the planning and building of *'town clusters'*. His first Garden City (which at first he talks of numbering 30,000) he allows may grow. Having reached 32,000 he envisages the establishment of another city, separated from the first by a buffer zone of open country. He does not allude in his text to the 58,000 population his diagram indicates as presumably the maximum size he considers viable for his *'Central City'*. His city cluster he believes would, once achieved, lead to the depopulation of the congested parts of London, after which slums could be cleared to make room for parks and other amenities.

The essence of his financial proposals is that, having acquired the land at agricultural prices, all 'betterment' due to development should go to the municipality. It would therefore be possible to meet interest charges on the original capital and, after thirty years, clear the debt. He envisages public buildings, roads etc. being developed by the municipality itself, all other development being undertaken by 'private enterprise': apparently by future tenants building for themselves 'on a mortgage'. He claims thus to combine the advantages of 'socialism' with those of 'individualism'.

Howard's ideas, as he himself acknowledges, owe much to others. He had taken over from Owen (via Buckingham, who had retained also Owen's rectangular form) the concept of a central open space surrounding community buildings. But these are no longer canteens, debating chambers and common rooms. In place of an active, involved community the emphasis now is upon provision for passive contemplation, administration and welfare. Schools are sited as the nucleus of 'wards', each conceived as a sufficiently complete segment of the town as a whole, and thus in place of Owen's simple undifferentiated community of 1,000 or so, established at a stroke, we have (in embryo at least) the concept of a city divided into suburbs and capable of growing by stages. As with Owen also, workplaces are sited on the outskirts, but instead of the whole being conceived as one production unit, we have with Howard the first fully worked proposal for an industrial town with numerous industrial establishments grouped in an *industrial zone*.

While Howard abundantly warns his readers not too literally to interpret his diagram, a characteristic of his proposal, which is abundantly epitomised by the form he chooses, is *finiteness*. The circle, the square or any such figure derived from regular geometry, with a central focus and radiating routes, can only expand peripherally, and in doing so cannot maintain its original proportions, since the centre remains fixed in size, and increasingly embedded and remote. The balance aimed at originally is, in the event of expansion, destroyed.* Howard's proposal for town clusters correctly recognises the consequences of this limitation, but his assumption of a hierarchical relationship between 'mother' and 'daughter' cities, betrays a questionable attitude which is still with us. It will be seen how important to his whole scheme is the insistence upon an agricultural zone. Of no less significance for Howard (and of growing significance ever since) was the provision of adequate communications between and within the towns in the cluster. In terms of later circumstances, it is interesting to note that he makes a clear distinction between inter-city *'rapid transit'* (by rail) and short-distance travel (by tramways on the *'high roads'*).

The effects of Howard's proposals, and the attempts to work them out in practice, merge into the whole pattern of recent town planning experience in Britain and abroad, and will be discussed shortly in that context. For the moment, we may note that it was in the further suburban extension of London (in Hampstead Garden Suburb) that his ideas were first embraced in name, if not entirely in spirit; that slum-dwellers were not typical of those who found a home in the first Garden City (Letchworth) or the second (Welwyn); that where slum clearance has been carried out — whether it has followed the creation of new towns or not — it has more often made room for more roads and office blocks than for parks, museums and recreation areas; and that in spite of Howard's financial ingenuity, most of what the Garden City Movement was eventually to achieve, involved extensive legislation for public ownership and building, including an Act of Parliament to rescue Letchworth itself from the hands of property speculators.

The nineteenth century ideal towns were all the brain children of those whose primary interest was political, and professional designers, where they were involved at all, played a subsidiary interpretative role. We have noted that the period also saw the development of municipal engineering, and the divergent growth of the modern professions of architecture, surveying and civil engineering resulted in no profession being in undisputed command in matters of urban design. Roads, railways, drains and other 'utilitarian' works came to be seen as the province of the engineer, and 'beautification' as the role of the architect, and we have seen how such an attitude cannot but violate architectural integrity. The professions themselves — though never completely — acquiesced and played the roles expected of them.

For the engineers especially, design became a purely technical matter — one of finding an appropriate technical solution to a problem already posed by others. But although in this way the modern engineer may be said to have inherited from the obseqious Slave of the Lamp an attitude as well as a name, there were some who paused to reflect upon the problems they were asked to solve. The names of two Spaniards stand out in this regard: Cerda, whose *Teoria General de Urbanizacion* was published in 1867; and Soria y Mata, (1844-1920). Cerda's work attempts to summarise for his own time the 'state of the art', is still little known outside Spain, and need not delay us here. Both he and Soria were primarily concerned with *communications* as a formative element of the city, and Soria was eventually to put forward proposals for a linear city, which he developed after 1882, even to the point of partial realisation in *Ciudad Lineal*, a suburb of Madrid. The essence of his ideas is an infinitely 62 extensible route for public transport and utilities

'whose extremities could be Cadiz and St. Petersbourg, or Peking and Brussels. Put in the centre of this immense belt trains and trams, conduits of water, gas and electricity, reservoirs, gardens and, at intervals, buildings for different municipal services — fire, sanitation, health, police, etc. — and there would be resolved at once almost all the complex problems that are produced by the massive populations of urban life.'[43]

Soria's proposals have recently attracted renewed attention, but for their time they remain unique as the only truly inventive solution to have come from the inventors themselves. Closer acquaintance reveals Soria as untypical of his profession in that he played an active role in politics as a radical republican. This serves to remind us of the visionary potential of technology and political radicalism combined, which, at the beginning of the twentieth century, was more commonly revealed in the fantasies of writers like Wells. In his *Sleeper Awakes*, Wells takes up the theme explored by Bellamy and Morris, and describes a city of the future in which an entirely artificial urban environment is provided by

62   Soria y Mata: Cuidad Lineal, 1894: section and plan.

* It is interesting to note how Howard in his own diagram is obliged with his Central City of 58,000 to enlarge both Central Park and Grand Boulevard in proportion.

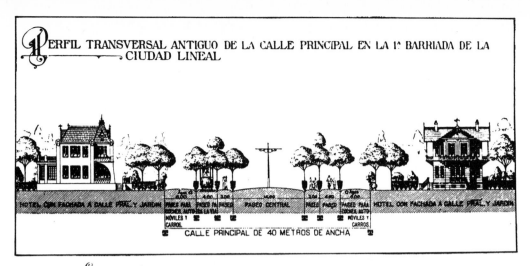

PERFIL TRANSVERSAL ANTIGUO DE LA CALLE PRINCIPAL EN LA 1ª BARRIADA DE LA CIUDAD LINEAL

CALLE PRINCIPAL DE 40 METROS DE ANCHA

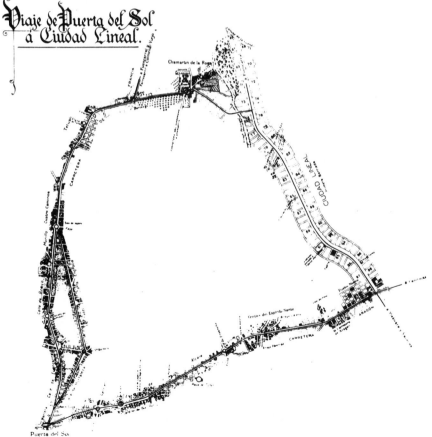

Viaje de Puerta del Sol a Ciudad Lineal.

62

total enclosure. But an atmosphere of pessimism and of technocratic tyranny portentously begins at this time to enter the literature of 'futurism', and has continued down to the science-fiction of our own times.

Even more surprising than the comparative silence of the nineteenth century engineers in matters of town design, is the similar lack of response from the architects. We have remarked the criticism of Pugin and the continued disapproval of others for the urban environment of their day. But the theme of their complaint rested in large measure on a desire to recapture the city or the village of the past. In the light of the enthusiasm of architects before and since for ideal towns, how are we to account for their neglect of the theme throughout the nineteenth century? However vigorous their criticism, they appear in practice to have accepted, like the engineers, the role of mere interpreters of the decisions others saw fit to make. The only positive contributions to planning ideals are in terms of improving the appearance of the city. Here, the outstanding contribution was that of Camillo Sitte, whose *Der Stadtebau* was published in Vienna in 1889. His purpose is to elucidate, on the basis of comparative studies of the best historical examples, guiding 'artistic principles' for the design of streets and urban places. The design of the city as a whole does not concern him, and while in detail there is much of value in his discoveries, they remain outside our present concern.

The rejection of the artistic consequences of industrial capitalism had with Morris led to the rejection of the system itself as injurious to social as well as artistic values, which were in any case seen as inseparable. Morris regarded himself as a communist, and many artists and architects, in their youth at least, have since more or less embraced his views. In his later work, Morris sought himself to come to terms with modern industry, (although never with the society it had produced) and by 1900 there were many who were prepared once more to look with confidence at a future made possible by the rational use of developing technology. Since then, the city has come to occupy a place in modern architecture as fundamental as in the architecture of Vitruvius and Alberti. It is to this that we must now turn our attention.

At the turn of the century, the leading architectural academy of Europe — the *Ecole des Beaux Arts* in Paris — had among its students a group of young radicals who all more-or-less embraced the ideas of socialism.[44] One of their number — Toni Garnier — won the coveted *Prix de Rome*, an honour which carried with it the opportunity to study Classical and Renaissance architecture during prolonged residence in Rome itself. The conditions required that he send back to Paris from time to time drawings illustrating the results of his studies. These were expected to have antiquarian and classical subjects. But Garnier, in spite of professorial opposition, stubbornly perserved at his chosen theme — the *Cité Industrielle*.

63   The result is outstanding, and marks a turning point in the whole development of town planning. It consists mainly of drawings — many of which were added during the period up to 1917 when the whole was first published, and by which time Garnier had become City Architect of Lyons. The text is brief and to the point. The industrial city is accepted as the typical problem of the age. He assumes 35,000 inhabitants. He posits a site having real characteristics. Of three possible factors determining location — proximity of raw materials, an energy source, or good communications — he chooses the second, and sites his town in conjunction with a new hydro-electric scheme. The whole is conceived as part of a wider regional development: the new town is in fact alongside an old town to which it may be regarded as an appendage. He divides the whole into functional zones: residential, industrial, etc., linked by routes between such nodal points as railway station and city centre. Blocks of flats are sited with hotels, secondary schools, administrative offices, markets and other larger buildings around the railway station. The rest of the residential accommodation is disposed as a single

64   unit around a public building complex (which includes numerous meeting-rooms, assembly halls, and amphitheatres for up to 3,000, all approached via a covered promenade) as its focal climax. Above the principal entrance is inscribed a passage from Zola's *Travail* — a novel based upon the teaching of Fourier.

Between the functional zones there are green spaces. The layout is orthogonal, with streets so arranged that sun and air can penetrate to the best advantage. Although most dwellings are 'semi-detached', there are no fences, hedges or other obstructions to pedestrian movement, which is consequently possible independent of the roads. There are no churches, prisons or lawcourts (Garnier envisaged no need for them) but there is ample provision for the infirm. While there is order in the disposition and linking of parts, there is no attempt to impose a rigid total form. On the contrary, each element is so disposed that growth is possible. But growth and change for Garnier does not mean leaving the future to

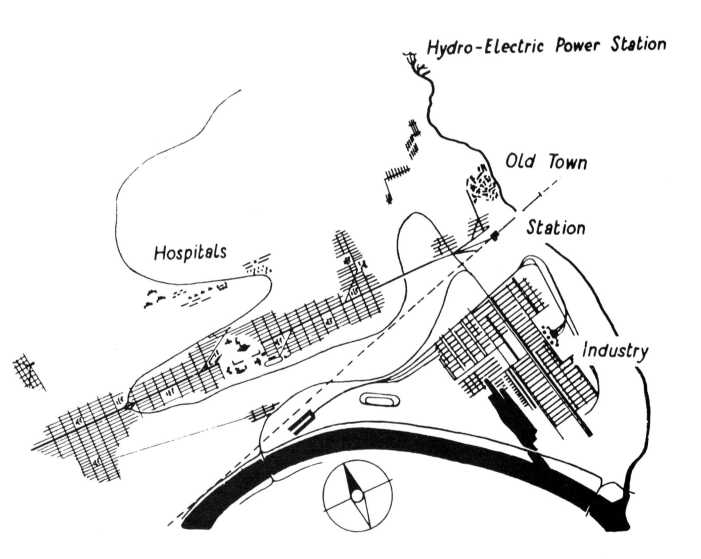

63   Tony Garnier: Cité Industrielle: a turning point in the development of town planning. Schematic plan.

Hydro-Electric Power Station

Old Town

Station

Hospitals

Industry

64 *An aerial view of the Cité Industrielle looking westwards from the city centre.*

65 *The industrial area of the Cité Industrielle.*
Garnier's whole approach asserts the belief that the industrial town, like any other product of mankind is entirely capable of being designed.

take care of itself. He proceeds to design every part in detail, making the maximum use of what he regarded as the most advanced technology of his time. His buildings are of reinforced concrete — in his day a barely-explored novelty. He designs the industrial zone as a single metallurgical complex with a greatly diversified output, in forms which still today would appear *avant garde*. His basic technical theme 65 — a town related to an energy source — he pursues in terms of communications, and of the disposal and utilisation of refuse. While he is abundantly clear that for every site and situation there is a different appropriate solution, his whole approach asserts his professional belief that the industrial town, like any other product of mankind, is entirely capable of being *designed*.[45]

Garnier's work was little known until recently, but its influence upon what later became known as the 'Modern Movement' in architecture is undoubted. Le Corbusier visited Garnier in 1907 and (as will become apparent) learnt much from him. In the period up to the First World War, there were probably others who were beginning to turn from architecture as the design of buildings, to architecture as the design of towns. But we know of only one or two: most notably the Italian Sant'Elia, whose sketches for a 66 mechanised city of the future have survived to inspire the many similar fantasies of our time. Already in the United States, architects and engineers were showing what could be done with sky-scrapers — employing structural steel, lifts and other mechanical services to transform buildings. And the automobile and the aeroplane were both well on their way.

The spirit of the 'New Architecture' to which Garnier and his contemporaries were dedicated, derived much from the belief that *'form follows function'*. For the design of the city this meant that the first requirement was an understanding of the city's purpose, of the essential realities which lay behind its outward forms. Thus we shall find in the development of the Modern Movement — especially after 1917 — a preoccupation with questions of this sort. While many of the architects themselves might have been naive enough to suppose that these realities were self-evident, and could be conjured out of an inventive imagination, many of the most relevant issues had in fact already by 1900 begun to occupy the attention of scholars in various fields.

When Garnier was in his twenties, a congress of French geographers took place in his native town, and discussed the development of the region. His plan suggests that their ideas (like those of the inventors of reinforced concrete and hydro-electric power) were part of the background against which — consciously or unconsciously — Garnier worked.[46] The French geographer Le Play had made already a special study of the characteristics of man's modification of the natural environment. Outstanding among his disciples was the Scot Patrick Geddes, who, as a biologist, sought to apply the principles of Darwinism to the human habitat and society in general. And since he has had the greatest influence upon town planning of those whose approach was analytical rather than assertively creative, his ideas will repay our attention at this point.

Geddes developed his argument over the decades up to the First World War, and in 1915 published his most complete exposition of it in *Cities in Evolution*. His work is to be seen as part of a growing 'town planning movement' which had already some notable achievements to its credit. The first Garden City of Letchworth was commenced in 1903. Raymond Unwin (who, with his partner, Barry Parker, was responsible for its planning) had published his *'Town Planning in Practice'* in 1909, and other publications with similar titles were beginning to appear. The first British legislation specifically to deal with town planning was enacted in 1909. Professional congresses throughout Europe chose town planning as a topic, and in London in 1913 the Town Planning Institute was formed to promote professionalism in the field.

The central theme of this movement was the promotion of planning in general, and there was by no means unanimity among the participants about what that might in practice imply. We have seen how for Howard it meant the establishment in the first place of new towns. Geddes approves of Howard's schemes, but his account makes it clear that for him the main problem was to control the further development of the existing city. To this end, he advocates a new science of 'Civics': one which would, in the spirit of science, concern itself with the detailed study of concrete circumstances as a basis for prognosis. *'Survey before plan'* is the essence of Geddes' teaching. Equally significant is his insistence upon the *'synoptic view'*, by which he meant the comprehension as a whole of the myriad facets of the city. It was necessary to see as the *'elements of a single process'* Le Play's categories of *'place, work and folk — environment, function, and organism'*.[47] He gives *'a general outline'* of the main headings for a survey as follows:

'SITUATION, TOPOGRAPHY, AND NATURAL ADVANTAGES:—

(a) *Geology, Climate, Water Supply, etc.*
(b) *Soils, with Vegetation, Animal Life, etc.*
(c) *River or Sea Fisheries.*
(d) *Access to Nature (Sea Coast, etc.).*

MEANS OF COMMUNICATION, LAND AND WATER:—

(a) *Natural and Historic.*
(b) *Present State.*
(c) *Anticipated Developments.*

INDUSTRIES, MANUFACTURES, AND COMMERCE:—

(a) *Native Industries.*
(b) *Manufactures.*
(c) *Commerce, etc.*
(d) *Anticipated Developments.*

POPULATION:—

(a) *Movement.*
(b) *Occupations.*
(c) *Health.*
(d) *Density.*
(e) *Distribution of Well-being (Family Conditions, etc.).*
(f) *Education and Culture Agencies.*
(g) *Anticipated Requirements.*

→ I should read & apply more here, as my own 3-year old idea about continuously refining HT using research is exactly the same — dynamic.

TOWN CONDITIONS:—

(a)   Historical: Phase by Phase, from Origins onwards. Material Survivals and Associations, etc.

(b)   Recent: Particularly since 1832 Survey, thus indicating Areas, Lines of Growth and Expansion, and Local Changes under Modern Conditions, e.g., of Streets, Open Spaces, Amenity, etc.

(c)   Local Government Areas (Municipal, Parochial, etc.).

(d)   Present: Existing Town Plans, in general and detail. Streets and Boulevards.
   Open Spaces, Parks, etc.
   Internal Communications, etc.
   Water, Drainage, Lighting, Electricity, etc.
   Housing and Sanitation (of localities in detail).
   Existing activities towards Civic Betterment, both Municipal and Private.

TOWN PLANNING: SUGGESTIONS AND DESIGNS:—

(A)   Examples from other Towns and Cities, British and Foreign.

(B)   Contributions and Suggestions towards Town Planning Scheme, as regards:—
   (a)   Areas.
   (b)   Possibilities of Town Expansion (Suburbs, etc.).
   (c)   Possibility of City Improvement and Development.
   (d)   Suggested Treatments of these in detail (alternatives when possible).

The concept of the city as a process required, of course, that planning should be conceived not as once-for-all decision making, but as itself also a continuing process. Neither could the city be conceived in isolation: it was necessary to see it in wider context. It is to Geddes we owe the word 'conurbation' to describe the conglomerate urban environment already in his day established in London, 'Lancaston' (Manchester), West Riding, South Riding (Sheffield), 'Midlanton' (Birmingham), Greater Cardiff, Tyne-Wear-Tees and Clyde-Forth. But beyond this, he was concerned to stress the need for 'regionalism' — for him primarily a matter of natural resources: water supply, drainage, etc. He refuses to advance universal panaceas, advocating instead *'the concrete study . . . of cities as we find them, or rather as we see them grow'.* [48]

This advocacy of scientific detachment did not however imply for Geddes an indifference to the urban conditions of his time. His outspoken condemnation of the industrial town is in the same indignant tones as that which reformers had used throughout the nineteenth century. The whole, irrespective of apparent gradations, he characterises as 'slum'. He divides the development of industrial society into two stages (analogous to those of the Stone Age): *paleotechnic* and *neotechnic*, and optimistically sees the present time as a period of transition. Previous Utopias, he says, were based upon

'the more rational use of the comparatively scanty resources and limited population of the past. But just as our paleotechnic money-wealth and real poverty is associated with the waste and dissipation of the stupendous resources of energy and materials, and power of using them, which the growing knowledge of Nature is ever unlocking for us, so their better neotechnic use brings with it potentialities of wealth and leisure beyond past Utopian dreams'. He instances the development in Norway of hydro-electric power — *'white coal'* — as evidence of the potentialities he has in mind.

Although not overtly socialist, he castigates private greed and approves social endeavour, and *'social costing'.* But he sees little good in party politics, and regrets that the working-men of his day were not only masters of, but mastered by, *'abstract politics'* which had
'long raised them far above sharing the petty local interests of us city improvers or town planners, who occupy our minds and hands with concrete trifles like homes and gardens, and pleasanter streets' [50],

to concern themselves with national affairs. Real politics with Geddes start at the parish pump and he endeavours to show that, from adequate reform at that level, all else could be expected to follow.

For Geddes, the study of concrete circumstances tacitly assumes the primacy of geographical and technical factors. In likening London to a coral formation (a *'man reef'*), in his talk of healthy *'crops of human population'* he betrays his training in biological science. To this as much as to anything else we may perhaps also attribute his treatment of mankind as a more-or-less undifferentiated species, among whom the *'contrast of social ranks'* was *'recent and modern'* which, with *'the incipient domestic order — electric, hygienic, eugenic'* [51] would disappear. Such differences as existed were the result of blindness to the real interests of society as a whole, which would become apparent to all through the study of civics and the local endeavour this would invoke.

To these ends, he advocates instead of the futility of 'politics' on the grand scale, a return to the true politics of the *polis.* The first step is to assemble data relating to the concrete local environment and to put it on permanent exhibition. The citizenry should be involved as much as possible, and should themselves be encouraged to make proposals for the future development of their city. On this basis, and with such technical expertise as could be found, a strategic plan should be evolved, while even without waiting for this, *'modest initiatives'* in cleaning up small eyesores could *'prepare the way for that large measure of municipal reorganisation which the public of our cities will soon desire.'* [52]

Some concrete proposals emerge. He writes:

'Towns must now cease to spread like expanding ink-stains and grease-spots: once in true development, they will repeat the star-like opening of the flower, with green leaves set in alternation with its golden rays.' [53]

In this analogy he envisages urban growth along transport routes, with green wedges between. He also advocates the creation of open spaces within the towns themselves. But his underlying assumption is that what is desirable for the future is implicit in present circumstances, and that out of an adequate survey, the right plan would surely emerge. In spite of some brilliant insights which are today assuming greater significance, and in spite of his own humane intentions, the effect of Geddes' teaching has thus been to provide a theoretical basis for two attitudes which have since developed. The first is *trend planning*, which from a study of present trends predicts an inevitable future, and then plans to accommodate it. The second is *technological determinism* which regards technical innovation as having a logic of its own unaffected by political, economic or other considerations.

But these one-sided interpretations of Geddes were in his own day and for some time to come of less significance than his advocacy of planning as a necessity, armed with technical procedures capable of getting to grips with the real problems of city development as, in the twentieth century, something which could no longer be left to chance and *laisser faire*. Most of the procedures he advocated are now embodied in planning law in the United Kingdom. It is a measure, however, of his underestimation of political realities, that the surveys he advocated are almost entirely undertaken by technical experts; that plans when exhibited are usually well-nigh incomprehensible to the layman; and that planning inquiries, instead of the great democratic free-for-all he envisaged, have become an occasion for developers, their lawyers and others to haggle the technicalities of law and property rights. Even that 'regionalism' which he hoped would lead to the decentralisation of government and the corresponding growth of local democracy, has become in Britain today the banner under which true local government threatens to disappear.

The advocates of town planning in Britain before 1914 not infrequently referred to Germany as the land where those things they advocated were already being practised. Germany, one of the last of the major European powers to embark as a national state fully on the path of modern industry, was able to do so in the light of others' experience. Much of her industry was from the beginning organised on a larger scale, and needed a larger view of all the problems involved — including the provision of workers' housing and the growth of industrial towns. For historical reasons, there also existed in Germany greater civic autonomy and a tradition of civic control of urban growth. In German towns therefore, already by 1900, there had been introduced ordinances controlling development. Especially significant was the 'zoning' of different 'land uses' — industrial, commercial, residential, etc. — and their controlled growth in predetermined areas. These practices were acclaimed by English reformers as worthy of imitation. T. C. Horsfall published in 1904 a work entitled *The Improvement of the Dwellings and Surroundings of the People. The Example of*

Germany. He could equally have referred to the example of Italy, where Town Extension Acts had already been passed in 1865, or to Sweden or Austria-Hungary where similar action had been taken in the '70's. Intelligent provision for town extensions and some control over the form they took was so obviously desirable that legislation to promote these things was inevitable.

The '*Housing, Town Planning, etc. Act*' was passed in 1909. It comes as the culmination of public health legislation which, as we have seen, steadily grew throughout the nineteenth century. It was based on the belief that '*the overcrowding of central areas and its attendant ills would be overcome by wholesale 'sub-urbanisation', as long as the new suburbs, which were by then already mushrooming around the industrial towns, were themselves pleasant and healthy.*'[55]

The powers conferred on local authorities were not obligatory and dealt in the main only with new extensions. Legislation safeguarded the rights of property, and if thenceforth sprawl was to be controlled, care was taken to ensure that it should still be profitable. While in the main, official 'town planning' in countries like Britain has continued to mean little more than control of the worst excesses of speculators and has always accepted the rights of property without question, there were already before the First World War those who refused to accept this as town planning at all.[56] But the war itself cut short further significant legislative developments, which in Britain were not to come until after the depression and yet another war — in 1947.

67 *Nash's Regent Street: a processional way from Regent's Park to Piccadilly.*

The suburban growth with which the 1909 Act was mainly concerned, was itself facilitated by new developments in transport, and since these have in ever increasing measure come to assume for modern town planning a significance at least equal to that which trade, defence and public health have had at various times in the past, it will be well to review them here.

We have distinguished a town or city from lesser or more primitive forms of settlement in that its inhabitants are not, in the main, engaged in agriculture. A city has, therefore, to import its food and raw materials and relies on good external communications: on land, sea and air routes linking it with its rural 'hinterland' along which produce can be carried daily. These same routes will also facilitate other necessary traffic between town and town. Equally, movement within the town itself depends upon good communications — upon footways, roads, canals and railways.

Historically, the significance of communications is readily apparent. Our older towns owe their siting — at least in part — to the relative ease with which they can be approached. As we have seen, the first great cities chose sites on navigable rivers linking them with their main food-growing areas. The towns of ancient Greece relied on seaborne supplies and were usually therefore ports. The Romans developed a road system throughout their empire serving numerous inland towns:

'But the first great road system, originally designed by the Romans as an instrument of conquest, could not enable the cart, and still less the heavy four-wheeled waggon, to compete against the ship. In the time of the Emperor Diocletian the land carriage of a load of hay for thirty miles doubled its cost, whereas the carriage of a shipload of wheat the full length of the Mediterranean added only one quarter to the price. Thus, although roads enabled the power and influence of Rome to spread far beyond the Mediterranean hinterland, it remained true throughout the classical period that civilised life depended mainly upon the ships that followed the path of the Ithican "over the wine dark sea".'[57]

In Europe until the late Middle Ages, overland transport was limited in the main to pack horses: the heavier and bulkier loads were carried as far as possible on water. Only with the 'Turnpike Era' of the late seventeenth and eighteenth centuries did overland transport begin to play a significant role, and only with steam power and the rail-road was the superiority of inland transport by navigable river or canal seriously challenged and finally supplanted. Until modern times, therefore, a large city could not without great difficulty have grown except beside a navigable waterway. The railroad alone made possible the settlement of the American West, and it is not until the coming of the automobile and the aeroplane that the restriction placed by communications upon the siting of towns becomes comparatively less severe.

Given an efficient external system, communications for the town planner become mainly a problem of facilitating movement within the town itself. Hitherto, movement on foot has far exceeded all other, and the forms of towns have in large measure resulted from the organisation of a predominantly pedestrian route system giving access to all buildings. While in some measure this route system would also serve the occasional rider or vehicle, bulk goods movement within towns as well as outside them was mainly water-borne, and along navigable river frontages are still to be found warehouses, commercial premises and factories handling bulky materials. The dependence upon water-borne traffic was often so great that (for instance) to this day, the inadequacy of east-west routes across London, reflects her traditional reliance upon the Thames.

Route systems within towns give rise to readily identifiable plan forms by which towns themselves are sometimes classified. As with most such classifications, the exceptions and complications are manifold, but two principal categories may be discerned: the 'radial', and the 'orthogonal', 'gridiron', 'chessboard' or 'chequerboard'. As we have seen, the radial form most often results from gradual 'organic' growth along routes converging upon a nodal point such as a river crossing, a watering place or shrine. A variant — the so called 'spider's web' or radial-concentric form is the result of organic growth controlled and rationalised by routes circling the town at planned intervals. The 'gridiron' on the other hand, is the form most often associated with 'planned' settlement: the military encampment, the pioneer colonial town.

The history of the town, no less than that of civilisation itself, is intimately bound up with the history of transport. Until the late Middle Ages there was little change from the practices of the earliest civilisations. From about the thirteenth century onwards, however, two changes were of growing significance. Improvements in sea-going vessels made possible the navigation of wide oceans and opened up the Atlantic seaboard of Europe, in time shifting the focus of civilisation away from the Mediterranean. The adoption of the horse-collar and the development of axle and hub bearings, for the first time in European history made it possible for a horse to pull a greater load than he could carry, and this was in time to have profound consequences. But it is in the eighteenth century, with the coming of the factory system, that the modern transport revolution begins in earnest. The concentration of many workers under one roof, and of many factories in one favourable location, quickly leads to an increase in the size of towns and, consequently, of distances within them. The separation of home and work-place accelerates the fragmentation and functional compartmentalisation of the town. The collection of materials and the exchange of products on a world-wide scale creates an unprecedented demand for warehousing and carriage. Rivers and harbours were improved. New canals were dug. Innovations were made in vehicles, both for the carriage of goods and of passengers. The street system of the town was adapted to their use by the improvement of pavings and drainage.

Up to that time only the busiest streets were stone-paved — the 'pavement' sometimes being no more than a strip abutting the flanking buildings, leaving a central no-man's-land of rougher ground. On important thoroughfares and in narrow alleys paving would extend full-width, often sloping to a central open gutter for drainage. From the seventeenth century onwards, we have noted the urban improvements which often took the form of new streets driven through the tangle of insanitary alleyways the older cities had become. During the Regency, Nash drove his celebrated processional way from Regent's Park to Piccadilly, and Haussmann transformed nineteenth century Paris with a system of boulevards. Over the same period, advances were made in pavings themselves, culminating in Britain in the work of Telford and Macadam, who showed that good drainage was necessary for sound paving, and thus made possible the use of less expensive materials. Setts, wood-blocks and flagstones continued to find favour in urban paving, however, until the introduction of asphalt and tarmacadam along with the motor-car and the pneumatic tyre. Increase in vehicular traffic eventually resulted in the adoption generally in towns of the cambered cross-section with flanking gutters, kerbs and footways.

Early in the nineteenth century, steam power was introduced to supplement that of the horse, and its use for the first time made it possible to open up for intensive settlement areas inaccessible to water transport. Some early attempts were made to introduce steam-driven vehicles on to the roads, but the railway proved better suited to exploit the application of steam locomotion, and the horse continued to dominate wheeled traffic within towns until well into the twentieth century. By late Victorian times, however, it was clear that some alternative to horse-drawn traffic would have to be found as the following eye-witness account vividly reminds us:

'The whole of London's crowded wheeled traffic — which in parts of the City was at times dense beyond movement — was dependent on the horse: lorry, wagon, bus, hansom and 'growler', and coaches and carriages and private vehicles of all kinds, were appendages to horses. Meredith refers to the 'anticipatory stench of its cab-stands' on railway approach to London: but the characteristic aroma — for the nose recognised London with gay excitement — was of stables, which were commonly of three or four storeys with inclined ways zigzagging up the faces of them ... middens kept the cast-iron filigree chandeliers that glorified the reception rooms of upper and lower-middle-class homes throughout London encrusted with dead flies and, in late summer, veiled with jiving clouds of them.

'A more assertive mark of the horse was the mud that, despite the activities of a numerous corps of red-jacketed boys who dodged among wheels and hooves with pan and brush in service to iron bins at the pavement-edge, either flooded the streets with churnings of 'pea-soup' that at times

68 *Joseph Cugnot's steam road locomotive, 1770.*

69 *Horse-drawn traffic congestion: London Bridge in Edwardian times.*

collected in pools over-brimming the kerbs, and at others covered the road-surface as with axle grease or bran-laden dust to the distraction of the wayfarer. In the first case, the swift-moving hansom or gig would fling sheets of such soup — where not intercepted by trousers or skirts — completely across the pavement, so that the frontages of the Strand throughout its length had an eighteen-inch plinth of mud-parge thus imposed upon it. The pea-soup condition was met by wheeled 'mud-carts' each attended by two ladlers clothed as for Icelandic seas in thigh boots, oilskins collared to the chin, and sou'westers sealing in the back of the neck. Splash Ho! The foot passenger now gets the mud in his eye! The axle-grease condition was met by horse-mechanised brushes and travellers in the small hours found fire-hoses washing away residues . . .

'And after the mud the noise, which, again endowed by the horse, surged like a mighty heart-beat in the central districts of London's life. It was a thing beyond all imaginings. The streets of workaday London were uniformly paved in 'granite' sets . . . and the hammering of a multitude of iron-shod hairy heels upon [them], the deafening, side-drum tattoo of tyred wheels jarring from the apex of one set to the next like sticks dragging along a fence; the creaking and groaning and chirping and rattling of vehicles light and heavy, thus maltreated; the jangling of chain harness and the clanging or jingling of every other conceivable thing else, augmented by the shrieking and bellowings called for from those of God's creatures who desired to impart information or proffer a request vocally — raised a din that . . . is beyond conception. It was not any such paltry thing as noise. It was an immensity of sound . . .'[58]

Although the railway's intrusion often brutally disrupted urban life, and the siting of passenger stations and goods depots greatly influenced subsequent urban growth, the first significant change in traffic *within* towns came with the electric motor which (after 1890) the tram car and the underground 'tube' were to exploit to the full. Both had the limitations imposed by a rail system and a centralised power source. Later, the development of the pneumatic tyre freed the trolley-bus from rails and by the 1930's mechanically-powered public services carried millions about their daily business.

Of these public services, only railways (surface and underground) continued to develop on their own exclusive route system, and suburban lines encouraged the growth of dormitory satellites around stations and halts in comparatively remote country districts. Further

70

encouragement to this form of suburban growth was given by Parliament itself, which not infrequently insisted that statutory permission to develop a line be subject to the granting by the operators of 'workmen's fares'. Cheap housing and low fares were championed by some as a necessary condition for a plentiful supply of cheap, mobile labour.

By 1914, the electric tram was rapidly replacing the horse-drawn bus as the main urban public passenger transport vehicle, and with its superior performance greatly accelerated the tendency for towns to grow along the main roads which were adapted to their use. With stopping places closely spaced, a linear form of growth resulted, having shops and other community facilities alongside the transport route, backed by housing to a depth limited by acceptable walking distance.

A major limitation of all trains and trams, however, is their confinement to a pre-determined route. The search for the complete *automobile*, independent of both railways and a centralised power-supply — as versatile as the horse, but a hundred times more efficient — was by 1900 effectively complete. The petrol engine and the pneumatic tyre had provided all that was lacking. The first significant changes came with the introduction of the motor bus and the taxi to supplement the tram, the 'shillibeer', and the hackney cab, and of the lorry in place of the horse-drawn dray. In industrial Europe and America, these long continued to supplement the established transport services. In the new and more rapidly developing cities of the western United States, however, they from the outset set the pace in urban transport, and in a country of vast distances and mushrooming towns, Henry Ford was soon to find a ready market for his answer to universal unrestricted mobility — the motor car.

70 Doré's illustration of the impact of the railway on the town.

The 1914-18 War proclaimed for all who wished to see, the triumph of the automobile. Soon after the armistice, the numbers of motor vehicles on the streets of London exceeded those still horse-drawn. The war had also demonstrated the potential of aircraft as a means of transport, and the futurist dreams of Sant' Elia (himself a victim of the war) would appear by no means fantastic to his more fortunate successors. Dreams of the future, moreover, had after 1917, an added dimension derived from revolution and total disillusionment with the 'old regime'. Mere reform was no longer enough. In Russia and throughout most of Europe, political battles were being fought which had as their aim the reconstitution of society at large. The objective was a classless society, wherein private ownership of the means of production was done away with, and production itself was planned and managed by a socialist state.

While in Russia civil war was to continue for some years to postpone reconstruction, and while in the rest of Europe and in the United States demagogues were seeking to 'buy off' revolution with talk of 'homes fit for heroes' and 'an acre and a cow', many young architects (whose interests now lay increasingly in town planning) returned to their drawing boards resolved to effect in the urban environment a revolution no less complete than they expected in the political life around them.

The outstanding figure was Le Corbusier, the Swiss-French architect who was to become the leading propagandist of the Modern Movement in architecture, and the most influential theorist of recent times. He had come to architecture via painting, and published, in the immediate post-war period, articles in an *avant garde* journal, *l'Esprit Nouveau*, which advocated a radical reappraisal of all matters pertaining to architecture and town planning. Much of this material was subsequently published in book form, and has since been translated throughout the world. He achieved little by way of built results, but until his death in 1965, retained an unrivalled authority among modern architects as both form-giver and prophet.

The first book to be specifically devoted to town planning was *Urbanisme*, first published in 1924, (English translation 1929) and subsequently re-issued to include not only his 1922 plan for an ideal 'Contemporary City', but also the application of his proposals to Central Paris in the 1925 *Plan Voisin*.

He eschews political objectives. *'I have been very careful not to depart from the technical side of my problem. I am an architect; no one is going to make a politician of me'* Neither, at a time when reaction against the Russian revolution was mounting, did he wish to be identified with Bolshevism.

'People tax me very readily with being a revolutionary. It is an effective if somewhat flattering way of putting a distance between a society preoccupied with maintaining its present equilibrium and eager minds which are likely to disturb it . . . On the other hand, since the Russian Revolution it has become the charming prerogative of both our own and the Bolshevist Revolutionaries to keep the title of revolutionary to themselves alone. Everything which has not chosen ostensibly to adopt their label they call bourgeois . . .' [59]

Later he was to agree that *'by a strictly professional route I arrive at revolutionary conclusions',* [60] but throughout a public life in which he was forever involved in what are unavoidably political matters, he carefully refused 'ostensibly to adopt' any label. The aim of his work

'has been the unfolding of a clear solution; its value depends on its success in that direction. It has no label, it is not dedicated to our existing Bourgeois-Capitalist Society nor to the Third International. It is a technical work.

'And I do not propose to bear witness in the highways and byways as though I belonged to the Salvation Army.' [61]

This 'middle class' reluctance to take sides was to lead Le Corbusier (like others before and since) to prefer a-political explanations for contemporary problems and to look for purely technical solutions to them. His diagnosis leans heavily upon aesthetics and technics. He dislikes the modern city as an offence against reason. It is disorderly, a muddle, derived from the *'pack-donkey's way'*. Reason demanded the orderliness of geometry, the straight line, the right angle. *'Culture is an orthogonal state of mind'* [62] he asserts, and dismisses contemptuously the fashionable whimsicalities of those who claimed to follow Camillo Sitte. Rationality also leads him towards *standardisation*, both on the grounds that Platonic perfection in anything, once achieved, is universally applicable, and in the interests of mass production. And by the same logic, he arrives in time at *cosmopolitanism* — the belief that what is reasonable for Paris holds good also for Moscow and Buenos Aires.

In the same vein as, in his *'Towards a New Architecture'*, he had declared *'a house is a machine for living in'*, [63] he begins his book on town planning with the assertion that *'a town is a tool'*. We may recall that Owen had likened his Industrial Village to 'a machine', but the difference between his and Le Corbusier's understanding is significant. Owen was referring to the working community, who by their common effort, and in the manner of their co-operation, resembled the complex operations of machinery. Le Corbusier refers merely to the technical equipment — the roads, the buildings, the transport and engineering systems — of the city. His whole exposition pays scant regard to the city as a *community*. He sees it rather (like the country as a whole) as *'composed of millions of individuals'* living in more or less identical cells, going out to work or to play. There are no age groups, no sexes. The

'classification of city dwellers would give us three main divisions of population: the citizens who live in the city; the workers whose lives are passed half in the centre and half in the garden cities, and the great masses of workers who spend their lives between suburban factories and garden cities.' [67]

But it is this conception of the town as a tool which provides the main theme of his detailed diagnosis. He notes that the Paris of his day already had 250,000 motor vehicles and writes:

'Up to 1900 no one had any idea, even the faintest notion, of the phenomenon about to burst on the world.

First came the motor-car; then the airplane. The railroads had already caused certain disturbance, but humanity was fully occupied in providing for the needs of the age. But today, in the very midst of a mechanical age, an age of speed, we are still absorbed in the problem of forming new suburbs with winding avenues pleasant to walk about in. And in the city the competent authorities are demanding a reduction in the authorised height of buildings ..

'And all the time the universal use of machinery continues to produce its consequences.' [65]

The 'tool' was out of date. It could not be modified by half-measures. Nothing less than total re-equipment, exploiting the most advanced techniques, would suffice.

The first task was to clarify objectives. Here, he cannot avoid politics, no matter how 'objectively' formulated. The 'great city' determines the life of a country.

'Great cities are the spiritual workshops in which the work of the world is done. The great city, with its throbbing and its tumult, crushes the weak and raises the strong . . . And these great cities challenge one another, for the mad urge of supremacy is the very law of evolution itself to which we are subjected. We challenge, we quarrel, we go to war. Or else we agree and co-operate. From the great cities, the living cells of the earth, come peace or war, abundance or famine, glory, the triumph of the mind and beauty itself.

'The great city expresses man's power and might; the houses which shelter such an ardour should follow a noteworthy plan. At least, this seems to my mind the logical conclusion of a quite simple reasoning.'

The first problem of town planning lies in the fact that, unable to cope with the demands of modern life, *'the centres of the great cities are like an engine which is seized'* and

'a city which has come to a dead stop means a country which does the same.' . . .

'Therefore, my settled opinion, which is quite a dispassionate one, is that the centres of our great cities must be pulled down and rebuilt, and that the wretched existing belts of suburbs must be abolished and carried farther out . . .' [66]

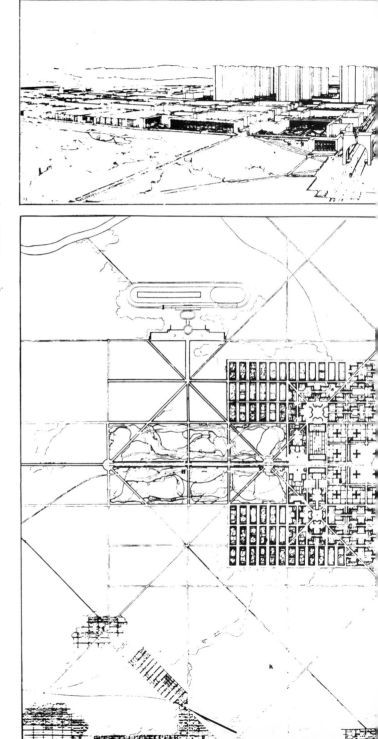

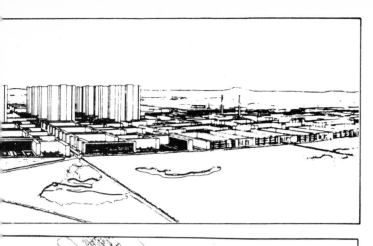

71 *A panoramic view of Le Corbusier's 'Contemporary City' of 1924.*

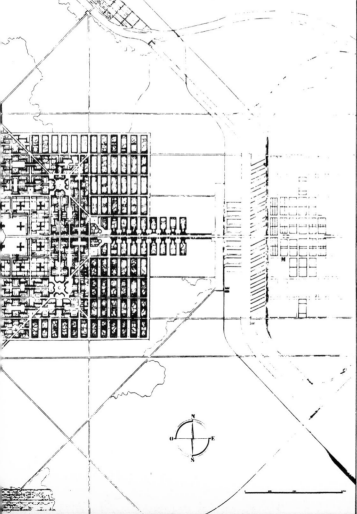

72 *Plan of the Contemporary City.*

* Le Corbusier points out in a footnote this really means a 'basement' level not buried under the earth.

Thus, where others condemned the multi-million city, Le Corbusier embraced it. Where others sought solutions in new towns and garden suburbs, he found the key in the city centre. Where Geddes had urged small beginnings here and there and had avoided total solutions, Le Corbusier resolved to start with rebuilding the middle of Paris itself.

First, however, he wished to devise the main ingredients of his solution, and since for him these could be deduced from a scientific investigation of the technical requirements, and were independent of particular circumstances, he proposes a *'laboratory study'* on an ideal site for a *'contemporary city of* 71 *3,000,000'* in order *'to arrive at the fundamental principles of* 72 *modern town planning'.*[67] We have already noted his classification of population into three groups. Arising from these he proposes a threefold territorial division: the city proper; the industrial City; the Garden Cities. Since *'the more dense the population of a city the less are the distances that have to be covered'* he wants a high density in the centre. Since *'modern toil demands quiet and fresh air'* he also wants abundant space: *'therefore the centre of the city must be constructed vertically'.* Since the *'corridor-street . . . poisons the houses that border on it . . .'* he proposes buildings set back from the roads themselves.

He then classifies traffic:
'(a) Heavy goods traffic:
(b) Lighter goods traffic, i.e. vans, etc., which make short journeys in all directions.
(c) Fast traffic, which covers a large section of the town.'

Three kinds of road are needed, and in superimposed storeys
'(a) Below-ground* there would be the streets for heavy traffic. This storey of the houses would consist merely of concrete piles, and between them large open spaces which would form a sort of clearing-house where heavy goods traffic could load and unload.
(b) At the ground floor level of the buildings there would be the complicated and delicate network of the ordinary street taking traffic in every desired direction.
(c) Running north and south, and east and west, and forming the two great axes of the city, there would be great arterial roads for fast one-way traffic built on immense reinforced concrete bridges 120 to 180 yards in width and approached every half-mile or so by subsidiary roads from ground level. These arterial roads could therefore be joined at any given point, so that even at the highest speeds the town can be traversed and the suburbs reached without having to negotiate any cross-roads . . .'

Eventually, Le Corbusier reaches these conclusions:
'The basic principles we must follow are these:

1. We must de-congest the centres of our cities.
2. We must augment their density.
3. We must increase the means for getting about.
4. We must increase parks and open spaces.

'At the very centre we have the STATION with its landing stage for aero-taxis.
'Running north and south, and east and west, we have the MAIN ARTERIES for fast traffic, forming elevated roadways 120 feet wide.
'At the base of the sky-scrapers and all round them we have a great open space 2,400 yards by 1,500 yards, giving an area of 3,600,000 square yards, and occupied by gardens, parks and avenues. In these parks, at the foot of and round the sky-scrapers, would be the restaurants and cafes, the luxury shops, housed in buildings with receding terraces: here too would be the theatres, halls and so on; and here the parking places or garage shelters.
'The sky-scrapers are designed purely for business purposes. On the left we have the great public buildings, the museums, the municipal and administrative offices. Still further on the left we have the "Park" (which is available for further logical development of the heart of the city).
'On the right, and traversed by one of the arms of the main arterial roads, we have the warehouses, and the industrial quarters with their goods stations.
'All round the city is the protected zone of woods and green fields. Further beyond are the garden cities, forming a wide encircling band.
'Then, right in the midst of all these, we have the Central Station, made up of the following elements:

(a) The landing platform; forming an aerodrome of 200,000 square yards in area.
(b) The entresol or mezzanine; at this level are the raised tracks for fast motor traffic: the only crossing being gyratory.
(c) The ground floor where there are the entrance halls and booking offices for the tubes, suburban, main line and air traffic.
(d) The "basement": here are the tubes which serve the city and the main arteries.
(e) The "sub-basement": here are the suburban lines running on a one-way loop.
(f) The "sub-sub-basement": here are the main lines (going north, south, east and west).

'THE CITY.
'Here we have twenty-four sky-scrapers capable each of housing 10,000 to 50,000 employees; this is the business and hotel section, etc., and accounts for 400,000 to 600,000 inhabitants.
'The residential blocks, of the two main types already mentioned, account for a further 600,000 inhabitants.
'The garden cities give us a further 2,000,000 inhabitants, or more.
'In the great central open space are the cafes, restaurants, luxury shops, halls of various kind, a magnificent forum descending by stages down to the immense parks surrounding it, the whole arrangement providing a spectacle of order and vitality.
'DENSITY OF POPULATION.
'(a) The sky-scraper: 1,200 inhabitants to the acre.
(b) The residential blocks with set-backs: 120 inhabitants to the acre. These are the luxury dwellings.
(c) The residential blocks on the "cellular" system, with a similar number of inhabitants.
'This great density gives us our necessary shortening of distances and ensures rapid intercommunication.
'NOTE. — The average density to the acre of Paris in the heart of the town is 146, and of London 63; and of the overcrowded quarters of Paris 213 and of London 169.
'OPEN SPACES.
'Of the area (a), 95 per cent of the ground is open (squares, restaurants, theatres).
'Of the area (b), 85 per cent of the ground is open (gardens, sports grounds).
'Of the area (c), 48 per cent of the ground is open (gardens, sports grounds).
'EDUCATIONAL AND CIVIC CENTRES. UNIVERSITIES, MUSEUMS OF ART AND INDUSTRY, PUBLIC SERVICES, COUNTY HALL.
'The "Jardin anglais". (The city can extend here, if necessary).
'Sports grounds: Motor racing track, Racecourse, Stadium, Swimming baths, etc.
'THE PROTECTED ZONE (which will be the property of the city), with its AERODROME.
'A zone in which all building would be prohibited; reserved for the growth of the city as laid down by the municipality; it would consist of woods, fields, and sports grounds. The forming of a "protected zone" by continual purchase of small properties in the immediate vicinity of the city is one of the most essential and urgent tasks which a municipality can

pursue. It would eventually represent a tenfold return of the capital invested.
'INDUSTRIAL QUARTERS.
'TYPES OF BUILDINGS EMPLOYED.
'For business: sky-scrapers sixty storeys high with no internal wells or courtyards.
'Residential buildings with "set-backs", of six double storeys; again with no internal wells: the flats looking on either side on to immense parks.
'Residential buildings on the "cellular" principle, with "hanging gardens", looking on to immense parks; again no internal wells. These are "service-flats" of the most modern kind.

'GARDEN CITIES
'THEIR AESTHETIC, ECONOMY, PERFECTION AND MODERN OUTLOOK.

'A simple phrase suffices to express the necessities of tomorrow: WE MUST BUILD IN THE OPEN. The lay-out must be of a purely geometrical kind, with all its many and delicate implications.
'The city of today is a dying thing because it is not geometrical. To build in the open would be to replace our present haphazard arrangements, which are all we have today, by a uniform lay-out. Unless we do this there is no salvation.
'The result of a true geometrical lay-out is repetition.
'The result of a repetition is a standard, the perfect form (i.e. the creation of standard types). A geometrical lay-out means that mathematics play their part. There is no first-rate human production but has geometry at its base. It is of the very essence of Architecture. To introduce uniformity into the building of a city we must industrialize building. Building is the one economic activity which has so far resisted industrialization. It has thus escaped the march of progress, with the result that the cost of building is still abnormally high.
'The architect, from a professional point of view, has become a twisted sort of creature. He has grown to love irregular sites, claiming that they inspire him with original ideas for getting round them. Of course he is wrong. For nowadays the only building that can be undertaken must be either for the rich or built at a loss (as, for instance, in the case of municipal housing schemes), or else by jerry-building and so robbing the inhabitant of all the amenities. A motor-car which is achieved by mass production is a masterpiece of comfort, precision, balance and good taste. A house built to

73 The Voisin Plan for Paris.

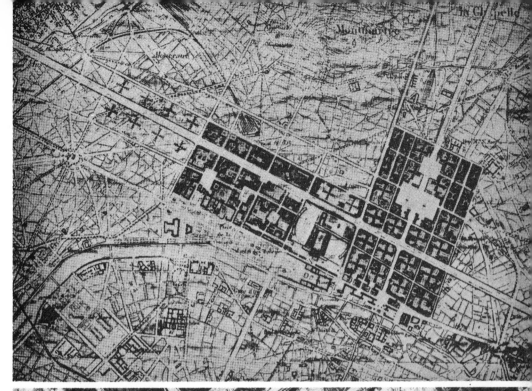

74 Le Corbusier's prophetic vision of central area redevelopment.

order (on an "interesting" site) is a masterpiece of incongruity — a monstrous thing.

'If the builder's yard were reorganized on the lines of standardization and mass production we might have gangs of workmen as keen and intelligent as mechanics.

'The mechanic dates back only twenty years, yet already he forms the highest caste of the working world.

'The mason dates . . . from time immemorial! He bangs away with feet and hammer. He smashes up everything round him, and the plant entrusted to him falls to pieces in a few months. The spirit of the mason must be disciplined by making him part of the severe and exact machinery of the industrialized builder's yard. . . .

'THE CITY AND ITS AESTHETIC

'(The plan of a city which is here presented is a direct consequence of purely geometric considerations).

'A new unit on a large scale (400 yards) inspires everything. Though the gridiron arrangement of the streets every 400 yards (sometimes only 200) is uniform (with a consequent ease in finding one's way about), no two streets are in any way alike. This is where, in a magnificent contrapuntal symphony, the forces of geometry come into play.

'Suppose we are entering the city by way of the Great Park. Our fast car takes the special elevated motor track between the majestic sky-scrapers: as we approach nearer there is seen the repetition against the sky of the twenty-four sky-scrapers: to our left and right on the outskirts of each particular area are the municipal and administrative buildings: and enclosing the space are the museums and university buildings.

'Then suddenly we find ourselves at the feet of the first sky-scrapers. But here we have not the meagre shaft of sunlight which so faintly illumines the dismal streets of New York, but an immensity of space. The whole city is a Park. . . .' [68]

There follows much more by way of discussion and detail. His flat blocks receive considerable attention, and the design of the *Unité d'Habitation* continued to interest him for years to come — even to the point of limited achievement. This was conceived more in terms of the luxury hotel than the block of flats, and would include co-operative arrangements for dining, entertaining, cleaning, etc. *'But . . . it will still always be possible to have a maid or children's nurse of your own, a family servant, should you so wish.'* [69] There would be no markets. Construction for the most part would leave the ground free so that the 'human scale' of landscape could be enjoyed against a back-drop of sky-scrapers and multi-level roads. The 'Voisin' plan for Paris (so-called because, like 73 much speculative town-planning since, it was financed by a motor industry tycoon) did little more than adapt the 'City' to the conditions of central Paris. But with this, as with all of Le Corbusier's projects, the criticism which his extravagant assertion calls forth is silenced by the prophetic vision which in the 'twenties shewed in sketches what now we see around 74 us every day.

Le Corbusier continued to elaborate his ideas, and more mature versions we shall discuss in due course. In detail, much was to be revised. But two decades and another world war later, in 1945, he saw no need to depart from the principles enunciated in 1924.

By 1924, the wars which had cost Russia the lives of millions and had destroyed most of her industry and many of her towns, were effectively at an end. Youthful enthusiasm and inventiveness in the newly formed Soviet Union began to express itself in architectural projects for new towns. In a state committed to Marxism, it was natural that Marx should be consulted to see what guidance could be gained.

From the Marxist classics there was little by way of concrete advice. In Engels' *Condition of the English Working Class*, written in 1845, there was ample description of the degrading conditions of working people in Manchester a century before. In Marx's *Capital*, similar truths were told of other English towns, much of it culled from the reports prepared by Chadwick and others. In *The Housing Question*, published by Engels in 1872, there was advice on how to conduct a political struggle in conditions of capitalism, but little about what workers in a socialist country should do. Marx and Engels would have wholeheartedly agreed with Geddes that concrete proposals should only be advanced on the basis of a concrete analysis of a concrete situation. Rebutting the charge that this concealed an indifference to bad housing as 'an insignificant detail', Engels had written:

'. . . As far as I know, I was the first to describe in German these conditions in their classical form as they exist in England: not . . . because they 'violated my sense of justice' — anyone who insisted on writing books about all the facts which violated his sense of justice would have a lot to do — but, as can be read in the introduction to my book, in order to provide a factual basis, by describing the social conditions created by modern large-scale industry, for German socialism, which was then arising and expending itself in empty phrases. However, it never entered my head to try and settle the so-called housing question *any more than to occupy myself with the details of the still more important* food question. *I am satisfied if I can prove that the production of*

our modern society is sufficient to provide all its members with enough to eat, and that there are houses enough in existence to provide the working masses for the time being with roomy and healthy living accommodation. To speculate on how a future society might organise the distribution of food and dwellings leads directly to utopia.'[70]

And, by their own definition, the socialism of Marx and Engels was 'scientific' and not 'utopian'.

But if little by way of positive advice for the future was offered, Engels had taken good care to 'knock on the head' some of the cherished panaceas we have already encountered. We have noted the close association in recent times of socialism and town planning, and since what Engels writes on the subject of housing comes nearest to what may be taken as the view of Marxism on much of what we have so far discussed, his work will repay our better acquaintance at this point.

First, he notes the *'so-called housing shortage'* is not peculiar to the present:

'On the contrary all oppressed classes in all periods suffered rather uniformly from it . . .

'The period in which a country with an old culture makes . . . a transition from manufacture and small-scale production to large-scale industry . . . is at the same time predominantly a period of 'housing shortage.' On the one hand, masses of rural workers are suddenly drawn into the big towns, which develop into industrial centres; on the other hand, the building arrangement of these old towns does not any longer conform to the conditions of the new large-scale industry and the corresponding traffic; streets are widened and new ones cut through, and railways are run right across them. At the very time when workers are streaming into the towns in masses, workers' dwellings are pulled down on a large scale . . .'[71]

He notes incidentally the difference between those cities like Manchester and Leeds *'which grew up from the very beginning as industrial centres'* where, unlike older towns like London and Paris, *'this housing shortage is as good as unknown',*[72] and describes *'the expansion of the big modern cities'* which

'gives the land in certain sections of them, particularly in those which are centrally situated, an artificial and often enormously increased value; the buildings erected in these areas depress this value, instead of increasing it, because they no longer correspond to the changed circumstances. They are pulled down and replaced by others. This takes place above all with centrally located workers' houses, whose rents, even with the greatest overcrowding, can never, or only very slowly, increase above a certain maximum. They are pulled down and in their stead shops, warehouses and public buildings are erected. Through its Haussmann in Paris, Bonapartism exploited this tendency tremendously for swindling and private enrichment. But the spirit of Haussmann has also been abroad in London, Manchester and Liverpool, and seems to feel itself just as much at home in Berlin and Vienna. The result is that the workers are forced out of the centre of the towns towards the outskirts; that workers' dwellings, and small dwellings in general, become rare and expensive and often altogether unobtainable, for under these circumstances the building industry, which is offered a much better field for speculation by more expensive dwelling houses, builds workers' dwellings only by way of exception.'[73]

The housing shortage

'is a necessary product of the bourgeois social order; . . . it cannot fail to be present in a society in which the great labouring masses are exclusively dependent upon wages, that is to say, upon the quantity of means of subsistence necessary for their existence and for the propagation of their kind; in which improvements of the machinery, etc., continually throw masses of workers out of employment; in which violent and regularly recurring industrial fluctuations determine on the one hand the existence of a large reserve army of unemployed workers, and on the other hand drive the mass of the workers from time to time onto the streets unemployed; in which workers are crowded together in masses in the big towns at a quicker rate than dwellings come into existence . . . in which, therefore, there must always be tenants even for the most infamous pig-sties; and in which finally the house-

owner in his capacity as capitalist has not only the right, but by reason of competition, to a certain extent also the duty of ruthlessly making as much out of his property in house rent as he possibly can. In such a society the housing shortage is no accident; it is a necessary institution and can be abolished together with all its effects on health, etc., only if the whole social order from which it springs is fundamentally refashioned . . .'*[74]

The question does not only affect the working class and the petty bourgeosie however:

'Modern natural science has proved that the so-called 'poor districts', in which the workers are crowded together, are the breeding places of all those epidemics which from time to time afflict our towns . . . and then spread beyond their breeding places into the more airy and healthy parts of the town inhabited by the capitalists. Capitalist rule cannot allow itself the pleasure of generating epidemic diseases among the working class with impunity; the consequences fall back on it and the angel of death rages in its ranks as ruthlessly as in the ranks of the workers.

'As soon as this fact had been scientifically established the philanthropic bourgeois became inflamed with a noble spirit of competition in their solicitude for the health of their workers. Societies were founded, books were written, proposals drawn up, laws debated and passed, in order to stop up the sources of the ever-recurring epidemics. The housing conditions of the workers were investigated and attempts made to remedy the most crying evils. In England particularly, where the largest number of big towns existed and where the bourgeoisie itself was, therefore, running the greatest risk, extensive activity began. Government commissions were appointed to inquire into the hygienic conditions of the working class. Their reports, honourably distinguished from all continental sources by their accuracy, completeness and impartiality, provided the basis for new, more or less thoroughgoing laws. Imperfect as these laws are, they are still infinitely superior to everything that has been done in this direction up to the present (1872) on the Continent. Nevertheless, the capitalist order of society reproduces again and again the evils to be remedied, and does so with such inevitable necessity that even in England the remedying of them has hardly advanced a single step.'[75]

He has little use for bourgeois philanthropy in any form.

We have already quoted his opinion of Akroyd, and he condemns equally Schneider, Krupp, and *'the Workers' City in Mulhausen'* built in the 'seventies. He remarks further that the majority of the English model industrial colonies

'are now no longer in the countryside. The colossal expansion of industry has surrounded most of them with factories and houses to such an extent that they are now situated in the middle of dirty, smoky towns with 20,000, 30,000, or more inhabitants'[76]

He has little use either for 'socialist' schemes to solve the problem by such devices as building societies:

'. . . building societies are not workers' societies, nor is it their main aim to provide workers with their own houses. On the contrary, we shall see that this happens only very exceptionally. The building societies are essentially of a speculative nature, the small ones, which were the original societies, not less so than their big imitators . . . in the end their chief aim is always to provide a more profitable mortgage investment for the savings of the petty bourgeoisie, at a good rate of interest and the prospect of dividends from speculation in real estate.'[77]

He writes at length to refute the notion that all would be well if every worker owned his own dwelling. Complete freedom of movement was of greater advantage than the possession of a house. The possession of a smallholding or kitchen garden merely served to depress the value of labour-power by making the cost of its production cheaper.

'Competition permits the capitalist to deduct from the price of labour power that which the family earns from its own little garden or field. The workers are compelled to accept any piece wages offered them, because otherwise they would get nothing at all and they could not live from the products of their agriculture alone, and because, on the other hand, it is just this agriculture and landownership which chains them to the spot and prevents them looking around for other employment.'[78]

Further:

'In order to create the modern revolutionary class of the proletariat it was absolutely necessary to cut the umbilical

cord which still bound the workers of the past to the land. The hand weaver who had his little house, garden and field along with his loom was a quiet, contented man "godly and honourable" despite all misery and despite all political pressure; he doffed his cap to the rich, to the priest and to the officials of the state and inwardly was altogether a slave. It is precisely modern large-scale industry which has turned the worker, formerly chained to the land into a completely propertyless proletarian, liberated from all traditional fetters, a free outlaw; it is precisely this economic revolution which has created the sole conditions under which the exploitation of the working class in its final form, in capitalist production, can be overthrown.'[79]

Engels' appraisal of such town planning as he had witnessed was as unflattering as anything he had said in condemning the panaceas of would-be reformers: he characterises the bourgeois method of settling the housing question as

'making breaches in the working-class quarters of our big cities, particularly in those which are centrally situated, irrespective of whether this practice is occasioned by considerations of public health and beautification or by the demand for big centrally located business premises or by traffic requirements . . . the result is everywhere the same: the most scandalous alleys and lanes disappear to the accompaniment of lavish self-glorification . . . but — they appear again at once somewhere else, and often in the immediate neighbourhood.'[80]

The burden of the message was not however one of despairing impotence. On the contrary:

'. . . this industrial revolution which has raised the productive power of human labour to such a high level that — for the first time in the history of mankind — the possibility exists, given a rational division of labour among all, of producing not only enough for the plentiful consumption of all members of society and for an abundant reserve fund, but also of leaving each individual sufficient leisure so that what is really worth preserving in historically inherited culture — science, art, forms of intercourse — may not only be preserved but converted from a monopoly of the ruling class into the common property of the whole of society, and may be further developed. And here is the decisive point: as soon as the productive power of human labour has risen to this height,

every excuse disappears for the existence of a ruling class. After all, the ultimate basis on which class differences were defended was always there must be a class which need not plague itself with the production of its daily subsistence, in order that it may have time to look after the intellectual work of society. This talk, which up to now had its great historical justification, has been cut off at the root once and for all by the industrial revolution of the last hundred years. The existence of a ruling class is becoming daily more and more of a hindrance to the development of industrial productive power, and equally so to that of science, art and especially of forms of cultural intercourse. There never were greater boors than our modern bourgeois.'[81]

A political revolution then, had first to establish the basis for the reorganisation of social and economic life. But what of housing? What of the city? 'To speculate . . . leads directly to Utopia.' What, then, of the Utopias we have already discussed?

'. . . these universal social panaceas have always and everywhere been the work of founders of sects who appeared at a time when the proletarian movement was still in its infancy . . . The development of the proletariat soon casts aside these swaddling clothes and engenders in the working class itself the realization that nothing is less practical than these 'practical solutions".[82]

But the 'first modern Utopian Socialists, Owen and Fourier correctly recognised' that

'the housing question can be solved only when society has been sufficiently transformed for a start to be made towards abolishing the contrast between town and country, which has been brought to its extreme point by present-day capitalist society . . . (which) . . . is compelled to intensify it day by day . . . In their model structures the contrast between town and country no longer exists . . .'[83]

Thus, for our would-be builders of socialist towns in the young Soviet Republics, Engels had given something like approval to the ideas of Owen and Fourier. He had also indicated a dislike of the large town: 'To want to solve the housing question while at the same time desiring to maintain the modern big cities is an absurdity.'[84] Both Marx and Engels had however on many occasions insisted that nothing they said should be regarded as inflexible dogma, and their

Russian disciple, Lenin, was equally insistent on this point. But the circumstances which have since had to be faced have not been so far removed from those Engels had been discussing to make what he had to say irrelevant, and town planning which claimed to be Marxist — in the Russia of the 1920's as elsewhere and ever since — has had to reckon with what he had to say.

In one fundamental respect of course, the circumstances for town planning in the Soviet Union were from the beginning different from those in capitalist states: the land and the whole economy were removed from the ownership and control of individuals and private companies and taken over by the state as a whole. While Le Corbusier wrote regretfully of the days when Louis XIV 'was capable of saying "We wish it" or "Such is our pleasure" ' and of having 'conceived immense projects and realized them'[85] his contemporaries in the world's first socialist republics were aware that, provided they could find the way, there was nothing to hinder achievements on a scale that would make those of past despots appear puny. All that was needed, it seemed, was the right policy and the will to carry it out.

Prior to 1914, the urban population of Russia was a small proportion of what was predominantly an agricultural empire of the Czars. Few of the towns had water supply or sewerage. The only architectural tradition was an effete shadow of the greatness that had created St. Petersburg, and town planning was a forgotten art.

But if socialism meant anything, it meant planning. And from the beginning, planning there most certainly was. But priorities dictated that industrialisation, power supply, agricultural reform came first. As had been the case for so many years in Western Europe, the art of civic design was conceived officially as being for the most part a question of housing.

Houses were undoubtedly needed. At the fastest conceivable rate of construction, it would be decades before a bare minimum standard would be available for all. In the old towns, luxury buildings had been requisitioned and used for billetting the homeless as Engels had advised. But in the poorer quarters, wooden shacks and insanitary slum conditions prevailed. Under the same pressure as had accompanied widespread industrialisation in England, the older towns began to grow, and around the new hydro-electric schemes and construction sites, shanty towns developed.

The response of the younger architects — few in number and confined in the main to centres like Moscow and

Leningrad — was a warm-hearted enthusiasm and a sincere desire to place their talent and imagination at the service of the Revolution.

In Russia as elsewhere, however, architecture had for long concerned itself only with the tastes of the aristocracy and the wealthy. How was it now to serve the proletariat — the workers and peasants of the world's first socialist state? What was wanted, it seemed, were power stations and factories: 'engineering', not 'architecture.' Here and there, an architect made a worthwhile contribution to new large-scale construction works. But the essential planned reconstruction of the country's economy was as it had been elsewhere — the work of engineers.

Housing, however, raised essentially architectural problems, and these inevitably bring in train every aspect of town planning. Such housing as had in the past been designed by architects, such town planning as in practice had been done, had never had to concern itself with the revolutionary social changes which socialism was to usher in. But we have seen how, even before the revolution, the nascent Modern Movement had (in the person of Garnier at least,) been tinged with socialism. To the ideas of the Modern Movement, Russia's young architects therefore eagerly subscribed, and before long found themselves expected to 'make the running'.

As a consequence of these circumstances, we find in the first ten years of Soviet rule, a debate concerning every problem in town planning which has been raised since, which if in terms of practical results it proved premature, was fruitful indeed in terms of ideas.

In designing homes, it is possible to make self-sufficient units, each with bathroom, kitchen, childrens' room, etc.; or to separate out some of these facilities with a view to providing them on a communal basis elsewhere. The question where to draw the line can have many answers. Separate houses can be held to promote healthy family life — or the enslavement of women. Communal facilities can be held to promote social well-being — or to lead to an intolerable loss of privacy. The answers for the most part given at the time, tended towards large blocks of flats on the one hand, and dispersed smaller groups of dwellings on the other. Pursued in terms of urban form, these solutions tended to divide Soviet town planners into what have been called the 'urbanists' and the 'de-urbanists'.

'For the former the city was a network of enormous

communal houses with integral collective services; for the latter the problem was to build not communal houses but 'communities of houses': light, prefabricated structures dispersed throughout the countryside'[86]

Both sought to bring the contrast between town and country to an end. The urbanist solution was

'composed of large and even 'immense' communal housing blocks clustered around the plants whose workers they served, it had neither centre nor periphery nor differentiated neighbourhoods. Its maximum size was fixed at forty thousand or fifty thousand inhabitants, and the gradual spread of these communities over the entire land was to realize . . . suppression of the contradictions between city and country, since these centres could be just as easily agricultural as industrial, gathering into 'agrocities' the workers on the collective farms.'[87]

The de-urbanists declared:

'Neither the city nor the village, those two ancient forms of settlement, satisfy the needs of today. They frustrate the rational organization of industry and agriculture, they frustrate the development of new social relations among men.

'The old distinctions between the homes of patriarchal peasant and petty-bourgeois families and the mean quarters of workers and servants are dissolving before our eyes . . .

'The communal or semi-private dormitories that have replaced the old housing, the supposedly modernized workers' barracks built under the deceptive title of 'commune house' — 'commune by name, but barracks by nature' — no longer satisfy the user, that is, the worker, since they are inconvenient, nor the builder, since they are expensive.

'To continue building in the old manner means wasting hundreds of millions or rubles that could be invested . . . in industrialization, means merely adapting the age-old Russian technical and economic backwardness to the new conditions or — what amounts to the same thing — applying the old techniques of production and organization to the new needs . . . the new relations between men.

'We have now arrived at a moment of disenchantment with the so called 'commune' that deprives the worker of living

space in favour of corridors and heated passages. The pseudo-commune that allows the worker to do no more than sleep at home, the pseudo-commune that deprives him of both living space and personal convenience (the lines that form outside bathrooms and cloakrooms and in the canteen) is beginning to provoke mass unrest. The economic impossibility of providing even these simple amenities is now clearly apparent even to the government.

'Meanwhile the need for housing grows more acute. Industry is embroiled with it . . . and the crowding gets worse. 'What should we do? What course must we follow?

'Take the pressure off the city.

'The city is suffocating and while it suffocates it still continues to grow. It is being suffocated by the archaic organisation of industrial and agricultural production. Its growth can be halted only by the reconstruction of the national economy.

'The agricultural areas must become centres not only for producing but also for processing raw materials . . . Long-distance power transmission and a universal network of local power stations . . . will make a reality of Engels's dream of ''putting an end to the big city, whatever the cost.''

'Any other way of relieving urban congestion is mere administrative utopia.

'Reorganize the village.

'So far the builders have ignored the village.

'Rural housing . . . is a prerequisite of production. The growth of agriculture creates new relations between producer and production . . . The transfer of manufacturing industry to the sources of raw materials, the integration of industry and agriculture, is likewise a new condition of residential planning and population distribution. But the new planning raises the problem of cheap housing built of local materials.

'Reorganization of the village means putting an end to isolation, neglect, and the primitiveness and imbecility of village life. This will be possible if we can redispose our new agriculture and industry.

'It is not a question of building urban centres in our endless wastes. Industry must be dispersed as widely as possible. The manufacturing industries must be brought as close as possible to the sources of raw materials in the mining and agricultural areas. Agriculture and mining must form part of the same planning system as manufacturing. We must stop designing piecemeal and start to plan whole complexes, to organize the distribution of production and the territorial distribution of industry and housing over entire economic regions of the Soviet Union . . .

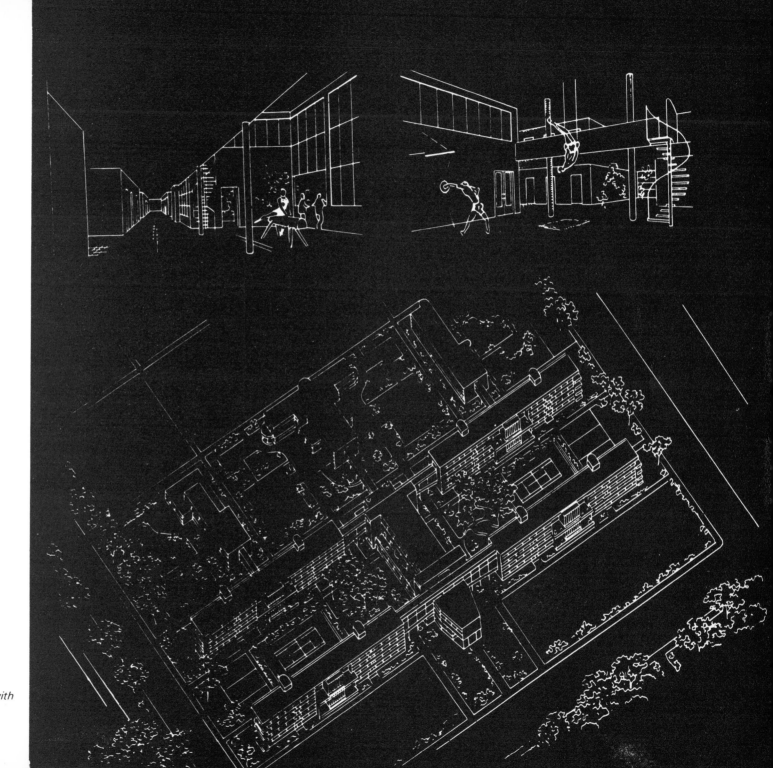

75 An 'urbanist' proposal for flats with integrated collective services.

'. . . In step with the electrification of the country we must convert our transportation system, until we are no longer transporting fuel and raw materials but only finished products. This problem will be solved by long-distance power transmission and the removal of manufacturing industry to the sources of raw materials: at the same time, even the volume of finished products requiring shipment will be enormously reduced . . .

'Replace the old housing with new.

'Replacing the individual domestic economy with a collective economy means better, more appetizing, and more economical meals in public canteens, child care that is better and cheaper than can be provided in the family. It means reducing the worker's expenses, easing his budget, in fact increasing the value of his wages without drawing upon the resources of the state . . . Abolishing the old scheme of things in the home means giving work to all the housewives, not in word but in deed. And that means raising the professional level and the pay of the working woman. It also means that the men will be less preoccupied with domestic matters . . .

'Let us get rid of the notion of a building designed to last, the notion of dimensions . . . fixed once and for all. It is not the man that must adapt to housing, but housing that must adapt to man. It is not for construction to adapt itself to industry, but for industry to adapt itself to construction, to its present and future needs.

'Let us start using cheap, light, local materials.

'Let us start producing standardized elements . . . let us start assembling parts rather than laying bricks . . .

'Instead of demolishing temporary mining and industrial camps let us start disassembling them and transporting them elsewhere . . .'[88]

Something like an intermediate standpoint, and one which received and continues to receive support, was the creation of workers' clubs, palaces of culture, or community centres, as a new up-to-date nucleus for an existing or growing urban area. Within these might be found libraries, debating halls, baths, dining halls, creches, etc. For towns like Moscow, there were optimistic schemes for an inviolable green belt to restrict its further growth and for decongestion of the centre by the removal thence of offices and institutes and industrial establishments. Regrettable as it may now appear, it is not surprising that proposals as unrealistic as this was at that time, were to provide the excuse whereby an effete traditionalism, which had no need to ask questions or to experiment in order to produce acceptable results, was to

eclipse the Modern Movement in Soviet architecture for nearly three decades.

One significant and lasting product of this intellectual ferment was renewed interest in the linear city, as a flexible, extensible form, well-suited to the purposes of the deurbanists. Especially noteworthy is the work of Miliutin, whose plan for inter-war Stalingrad and pronouncements on linear form have since found a growing following throughout the world.

Some of the town planning undertaken in the USSR during the late '20's and early '30's was the responsibility of foreign experts, one of the most notable being the German, Ernst May, who worked on the plan for Magnitogorsk, which, out of many submitted, was chosen for execution. Another to be consulted was Le Corbusier himself. In 1930 he was asked for an opinion concerning the planning of Moscow, and was to use the occasion to elaborate further his ideas about metropolitan planning.

76 Schematic plan for a populated area associated with a major road, planned according to 'de-urbanist' theory. Dwellings of various types are scattered over the countryside within reach of facilities dispersed in a ribbon about 300m wide, each facility occurring with a different frequency.

77 A schematic plan for Stalingrad (Volgograd) exploiting the linear form advocated by Miliutin.

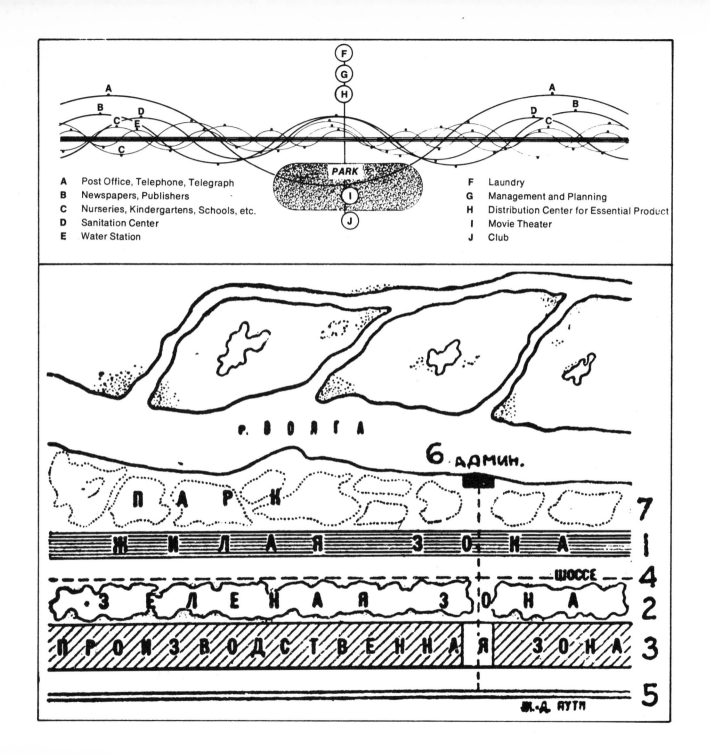

A Post Office, Telephone, Telegraph
B Newspapers, Publishers
C Nurseries, Kindergartens, Schools, etc.
D Sanitation Center
E Water Station

F Laundry
G Management and Planning
H Distribution Center for Essential Product
I Movie Theater
J Club

Modern Architecture throughout Europe had maintained a steady development throughout the 'twenties. *'As a result of the scandal aroused in professional architectural circles by the choice of architects for the Palais des Nations after the international contest in 1927'* — a contest in which Le Corbusier had taken part — the International Congresses for Modern Architecture (CIAM) were inaugurated in 1928. Membership was by invitation, and the intention was *'to formulate the architectural problems of the modern age'* and *'to seek a solution to them'*.[89] The most vociferous participant and outstanding propagandist was Le Corbusier himself. Two themes, seen as closely related, run through the early meetings: prefabrication of housing, and town planning. As work progressed into the 'thirties — the era of depression and Fascism — CIAM became more and more tinged with political radicalism. But, for Le Corbusier at least, the common ground was the desire for an architecture in agreement with the 'new age': new, that is, in technical rather than political terms; the Age of the Machine, rather than of the Common Man, although much was urged in his name. As always with the youthful intelligentsia, there was a tendency to see ageing academics and entrenched officials as the enemy, and although from time to time there were those who succeded in deepening this analysis, CIAM throughout retained something of the character of a student revolt.

At the third Congress, in 1930, Le Corbusier presented his *Ville Radieuse*, and since this represents a high peak in modern town planning theory, it must be examined with care. His studies were undertaken, as we have said, in consequence of an invitation from Moscow, but they are in effect a continuation of his earlier work, coloured especially by the debate that was raging in Russia, abstracted from any particular location and, to his mind, universally applicable. He states the problem of the modern city thus:

'Every day the anxiety and depression of modern life springs up afresh: the city is swelling, the city is filling up. The city simply builds itself anew on top of itself: the old houses towered in a cliff at the edge of the streets; the new houses still tower in new cliffs along the same streets. All the houses are on streets, the street is the basic organ of the city, and the house is the individual, infinitely repeated mold. The street becomes appalling, noisy, dusty, dangerous; automobiles can scarcely do more than crawl along it; the pedestrians, herded together on the sidewalks, get in each other's way, bump into each other, zigzag from side to side; the whole scene is like a glimpse of purgatory. Some of the buildings are office buildings; but how is it possible to work well with so little light and so much noise? Elsewhere, the buildings are residential; but how is it possible to breathe properly in those torrid canyons of summer heat; how can anyone risk bringing up children in that air tainted with dust and soot, in those streets so full of mortal peril? How can anyone achieve the serenity indispensable to life, how can anyone relax, or ever give a cry of joy, or laugh, or breathe, or feel drunk with sunlight? How can anyone live! The houses are cliffs facing one another across the street. Worse still, behind the houses that face the street there are more houses still. They are built around courtyards. Where is the light? What do I see out of my window? Other windows, only six or ten yards away, with people behind them looking back at me. Where is freedom here? There is no freedom for men in this present age, only slavery. A slavery to which they themselves consent, and which is no longer even confined within set limits. To live, to laugh, to be master in one's own home, to open one's eyes to the light of day, to the light of the sun, to look out on green leaves and blue sky. No! Nothing of all that for the man who lives in a city. The man in a city is a lump of coal in a brazier; he is being burned up simply for the energy he produces. Then he fades and crumbles away . . .

'More recently, there has been a reaction, one made possible by the railroad. The labourer, the clerk and the shopgirl have been whisked out of the city along steel rails. Like an exploding shell, the city has shot out in all directions, pushing its tentacles out as far as the eye can see. At dawn, then again in the evening, the laborer, the clerk and the shopgirl sit in their railroad cars and are pulled along the rails. Their little houses are surrounded by greenery, away in the country. What could be nicer? They can really enjoy themselves — every Sunday. That's only one day out of seven, but never mind. So on Sunday, there they are, all alone in their little green nests; their boy friends, their girl friends live on the opposite side of town, in another suburb. So on Sundays, the laborer, the clerk and the shopgirl still tick off the hours without living and without laughter. Or rather, there they are back in their railroad cars riding those steel rails again. Suburbs? Suburbs are broken, dislocated limbs! The city has been torn apart and scattered in meaningless fragments across the countryside. What is the point of life in such places? How are people to live in them?

'Suburban life is a despicable delusion entertained by a society stricken with blindness!

'The problem is to create the Radiant City . . .

'The general characteristics of the plan are as follows: the city (a large city, a capital) is much less spread out than the present one; the distances within it are therefore shorter which means more rest and more energy available for work every day. There are no suburbs or dormitory towns; this means an immediate solution to the transportation crisis that has been forced upon us by the paradox of the city + garden cities.

'The garden city is a pre-machine-age utopia.

'The population density of the new city will be from three to six times greater than the idealistic, ruinous and inoperative figures recommended by urban authorities still imbued with romantic ideology. This new intensification of population density thus becomes the financial justification for our enterprise; it increases the value of the ground.

'The pedestrian never meets a vehicle inside the city. The mechanical transportation network is an entirely new organ, a separate entity. The ground level (the earth) belongs entirely to the pedestrian.

'The "street" as we know it now has disappeared. All the various sporting activities take place directly outside people's homes, in the midst of parks — trees, lawns, lakes. The city is entirely green; it is a Green City. Not one inhabitant occupies a room without sunlight; everyone looks out on trees and sky...'

To those who would protest at the scale of reconstruction, he replied:

'The houses of Europe are centuries old; they are obsolete, antique, rotten. They are about to fall down.'
He stubbornly adhered to his opinion that, in Western Europe at least, new towns were not the solution. Paris, Antwerp, Moscow: regeneration must be *in situ*. *'... all the countries of Europe ought to be reconstructing all their cities...'* [90]

'Home or city, it is all the same thing', he declares, and in his thinking throughout we shall find this emphasis on the individual home. While his calculations are based on family dwellings, his diagram most vividly displays his attitude to what he saw as the fundamental problem in town planning. Homes, houses, housing then became the starting point in his detailed argument.

'... houses must be built inside, in factories ... we must rebuild the country by constructing "prefabricated houses" ... The prefabricated house will provide a different sort of home... A new word, domestic equipment, ... will become a genine source of happiness...'

He calculates the basic dimensions of his dwellings: average 14 sq. m. per person; depth of unit 16 m; number of floors, 12. He arranges them in ribbons *à redents* above a communications network, and calculates the resulting density at over 1,000 persons per hectare. As a consequence, *'for 3 million (which is already an enormous figure, perhaps still far too large) the city need then cover ... a rectangle of only 5 km. x 6 km.'*

Thus he achieves a fundamental objective:
'all problems of distance, dimension, and distribution have to be solved within those precise limits: 24 hours ...

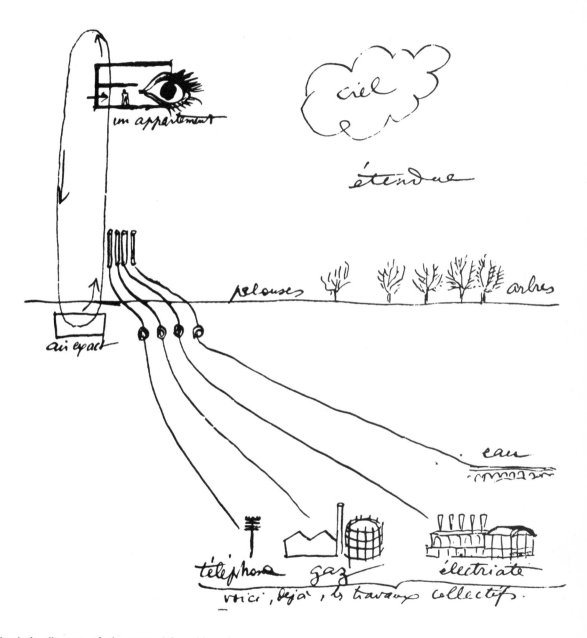

78 Le Corbusier's diagram of the essential problem in town planning as he saw it.

'24 hours! That is the yardstick and rhythm of human life: the unit to which everything must conform.'

With so many on so small an area, the advantages of a vast city could be enjoyed by all without the fatigue of time-consuming travel. Movement would be convenient, safe, enjoyable, with each speed separately catered for.

'We have, of course, eliminated the "corridor-street" — the street that now exists in all the cities of the world. Our living quarters have nothing to do with the streets. More than that, we have deliberately (though not merely for the sake of it) gone against the present tendency to envisage the pedestrians running to and fro on raised walks in the air and the traffic occupying the ground. We have allotted the ENTIRE GROUND SURFACE of the city to the pedestrian. The earth itself will be occupied by lawns, trees, sports and playgrounds. Almost 100 per cent of the ground surface will be used by the inhabitants of the city. And since our apartment houses are all up in the air, raised on pilotis, it will be possible to walk across the city in any direction. In other words: NO PEDESTRIAN WILL EVER MEET AN AUTOMOBILE, EVER! ...

'Thus, the parks, the sports grounds, the entertainment areas, etc., are all around the houses. And under the houses there will be covered playgrounds. The houses will cover 11.4 per cent of the surface of the residential areas. That leaves 88.6 per cent open to the sky. In this way, one of our aims has been attained. SPORTING ACTIVITIES WILL TAKE PLACE DIRECTLY OUTSIDE THE HOUSES. No more courtyards, ever again. Instead, an open view from every window (though there won't be any windows, of course, only walls of glass) ...

'The fundamental calculations are as follows: you take a given city area; you build apartment houses on it that will provide accommodation for a thousand people per hectare and leave your surface area intact — 100 per cent. To that figure you add the 11 per cent surface of the roof gardens. Total: 111 per cent of the surface area of the city brought into use, exploited, producing a maximum yield, reserved for the pedestrian alone, so that he can enjoy himself, walk, run, play, breathe, soak up the air and the sun, revive his body, and even better than that: make his body a thing of magnificence. And as for the speeding traffic, the iron torpedoes that fill our lives with so much anxiety at the moment — he never meets them at all! ...

'The city dweller who owns an automobile will be able to keep it in a garage at the foot of his elevator.

'Anyone who wishes to take a taxi, wherever he may be in the residential district, need never walk more than 100 meters to find one. And when he returns home, whatever the hour of the day or night, he will be taken up to his apartment by specially trained elevator operators.

'From the door of his elevator, the longest distance that he will have to walk to his own front door will be less than 100 meters, along a corridor that will be an indoor street. The outdoor streets of the city (for traffic) will be curtailed to an astonishing degree. As we shall see shortly. Most of the city's streets will now be inside the buildings. There will be 12 or 15 of them one on top of the other, the highest being 47 meters above ground level. The policemen, if he is still needed, will be able to say goodbye forever to his old beat in the heat of the sun or the rain, battered by storms and bustling crowds: he will now be employed on the indoor streets, streets that actually run inside the houses.

'2,700 people will use one front door. Though in fact, if one looks at it another way, the idea of the house will have lost its present form. People will live in apartment houses with no breaks between the units, a ribbon of housing winding in an unbroken pattern across the city. The interior streets will be inside the ribbons, the roads outside. And wherever it is convenient, the roads will cross the lines of apartment buildings. The houses will not form obstructions at ground level because they are built up on pilotis. The ground surface is left entirely free. And, as I have already mentioned, the longest horizontal distance along an inside street from the door of any elevator to the furthest apartment door is 100 meters. Once over the threshold of his apartment, the city dweller will find himself in a self-contained, soundproofed cell. The apartment will be impervious to all outside noise ...

'We shall also be able to build special nurseries for very young children outside the apartment houses, actually in the parks; though they will be directly connected to the apartment unit in which the parents live by a corridor sheltered from the elements. These nurseries will be surrounded by greenery. They will be run by qualified nurses and supervised by doctors — security — selection — scientific child-rearing.

'The schools too will be outside the apartment houses, set in the midst of the parks. For each pair of apartment units (one on each side of a double elevator shaft, each of which will be used by 2,700 people) there will be a kindergarten for children between the ages of 3 and 6, then a primary school nearby for children between the ages of 7 and 14. The schools

will be reached by an avenue running through the park for a distance of from 50 to 100 meters.

'The sports grounds will be at the foot of the apartment houses: soccer, basketball, tennis, playgrounds, etc.... walks, shady avenues and lawns. Each residential unit of 400 by 400 meters will have a swimming pool from 100 to 150 meters in length.

'For rainy days, there are the covered playgrounds extending the whole length of the apartment buildings. Paths and walks everywhere. Limitless opportunities for walking. It will be possible to cross the entire residential area from end to end, in any direction, either entirely in the open air or entirely sheltered from sun and rain. It will be as though the houses have been surrounded by a new Bois de Boulogne.

'And that is still not all: on the roof gardens, there will be sandy beaches for the occupants to sunbathe on in magnificently pure air 50 meters above ground level. And not little beaches either; they will be from 18 to 20 metres wide and several kilometers in length. Spaced out along these beaches there will also be pools and open-air hydrotherapy establishments ...

'Obviously food supplies and consumer goods will have to be brought into the residential areas. So where are the service roads for them? Under the raised highways. How do they reach the buildings? At certain given points where unloading bays are provided for them. These unloading bays occur regularly along the line of buildings, each one under the aegis of a separate catering section. There will be one unloading bay for every 3,000 to 4,000 residents; and a separate catering manager will thus be assured of a very sizeable clientele. And there will be a co-operative organization to see that the profits from this catering business will be used for the benefit of the customers themselves. Each catering section will have at its disposal an area of floorspace 18 meters wide and from 200 to 400 meters in length.

'What functions will these catering departments perform? Primarily, they will see to the storing of incoming food supplies in storage rooms and deep-freeze rooms. These foodstuffs will arrive directly from processing plants or from the country, from the breeder, the hunter, the fisherman, the market gardener, the winegrower. They will be sold at low retail prices reflecting the elimination of the middleman. Adequate refrigeration will assure storage without waste ...' [91]

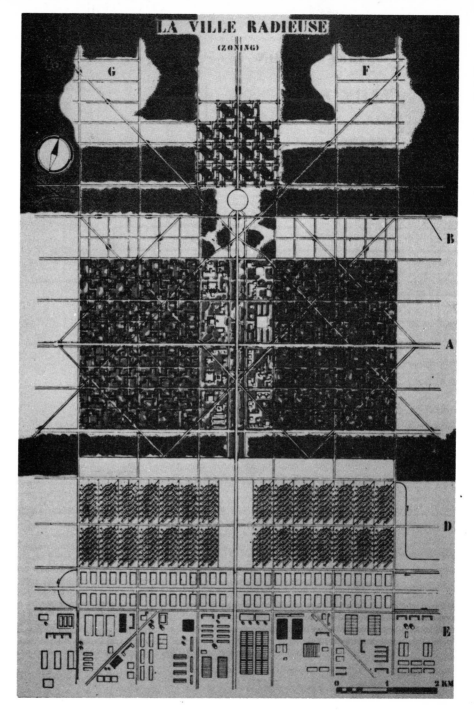

LA VILLE RADIEUSE
(ZONING)

G

F

Satellite cities, e.g.: government buildings or center for social studies, etc.

The business center

Railroad station and air terminal

B   Hotels
     Embassies

A   Housing

D   Factories

Warehouses

E   Heavy industry

79

There would also be laundries and restaurants in each catering section, and it would be possible to arrange for 'home help'.

The greatly augmented density above that now prevailing in cities (he quotes a maximum of 800 p.p.h. in the worst overcrowded districts of Paris) would provide ample finance for his schemes. He answers the charge of monotony with the confidence that local conditions will quite rationally call forth variation, and with his proposal for orientation with reference to an *Axe Heliothermique* (which almost recalls Roman 80 ritual). He touches on questions of female emancipation, 81 increasing leisure and the *'replanning of private property'*.

His principles for traffic are now as follows:

'1° Classification of speeds. Normal biological speeds must never be forced into contact with the high speeds of modern vehicles.

'2° Creation of one-way traffic. No high-speed vehicle should ever be subjected to the possibility of meeting or crossing the path of other moving objects. "One way traffic" should become an automatic element of high-speed locomotion put into universal effect (and should not merely imply innumerable quantities of round signs stuck up on posts with white letters against a red background): crossroads (traffic meeting on the same level) should be eliminated.

'3° High-speed vehicles must all be employed for specifically designated purposes.

'4° The functions of heavy vehicles.

'5° The liberation of pedestrians.'

Pedestrians must retain the human right to the ground itself. So the roads go up into the air: 5 metres above ground. One-way traffic is to be facilitated by 'grade-separated junctions', which he was among the first to propose. Of *'the assignation of specific aims to high-speed vehicles'*, he writes:

'a) To transport loads quickly from the door of one apartment house to the door of another.

'b) To be immediately available for use at all points throughout the city.

'From one door to another. Are there a great many front doors in the city? In the city as it is today, alas yes. One apartment house door with its concierge *provides access to from 6 to 12 apartments containing from 36 to 72 occupants. Given such conditions, the automobile problem is quite intractable: the front doors are all side by side — a door every 10 or 14 meters. The automobile ought to stop right in front of any given door: it ought to be able to stop right in front of all the doors. Which means that the traffic lane must run*

80—81 Le Corbusier's method for orientating each city with reference to sunlight. The 'heliothermic axis' having been determined, flat blocks are optimally aligned. Apartments can then be graded with regard to aspect, from good (white) to bad (black) and the worst ones eliminated, so that all dwellings have adequate sun.

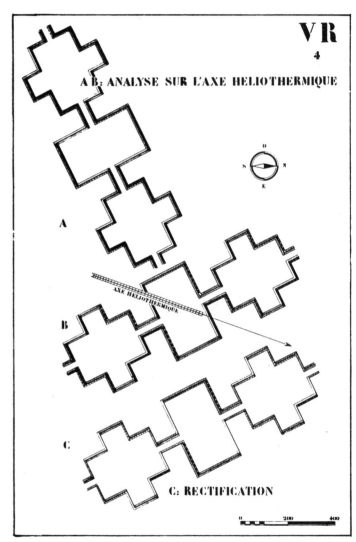

VR
4

A B: ANALYSE SUR L'AXE HELIOTHERMIQUE

A

B

C

AXE HELIOTHERMIQUE

C: RECTIFICATION

0   200   400

82   Traffic movements in the Radiant City.

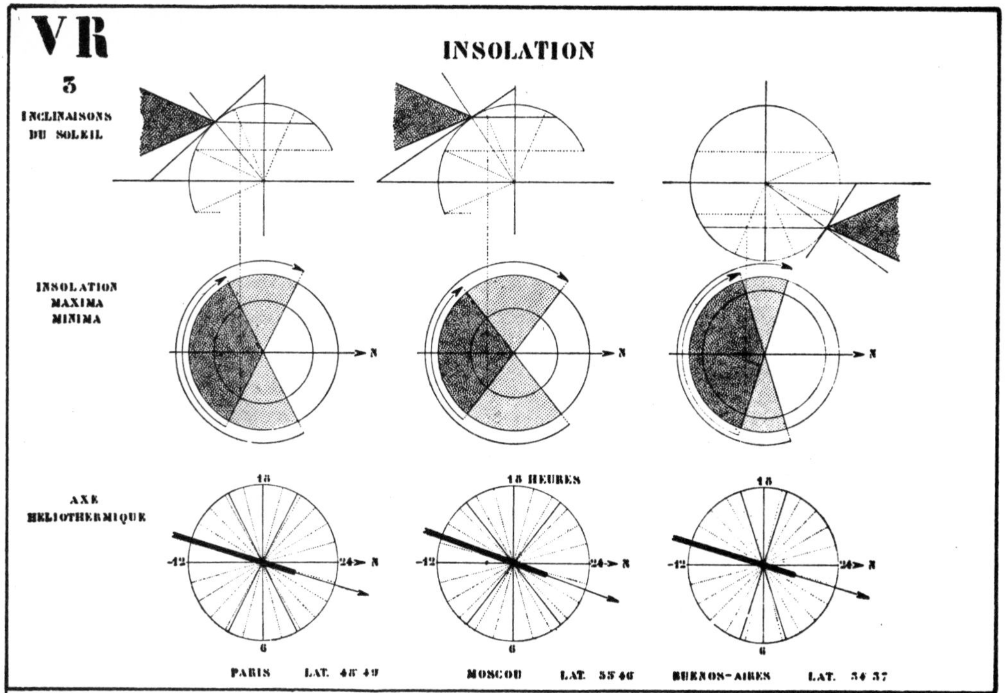

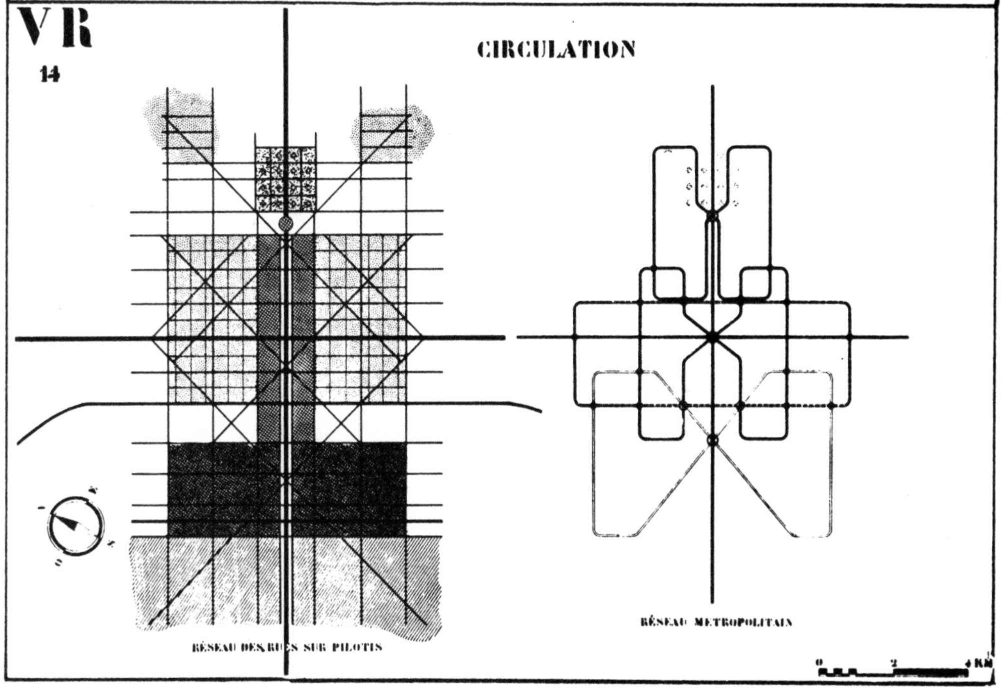

VR

3

INCLINAISONS DU SOLEIL

INSOLATION

INSOLATION MAXIMA MINIMA

AXE HELIOTHERMIQUE

PARIS   LAT. 48 49   MOSCOU   LAT. 55 46   BUENOS-AIRES   LAT. 34 37

VR

14

CIRCULATION

RÉSEAU DES RUES SUR PILOTIS

RÉSEAU MÉTROPOLITAIN

0   2   4 KM

directly alongside all those doors; which means that it is directly beneath the houses; which means that the houses open out onto the traffic lane. *And that is what we can no longer tolerate . . .*

'*In the Radiant City, one door provides access and egress for 2,700 residents. It is not merely a door, therefore, but also a port. A harbor for automobiles to drive into in front of each door. The automobile leaves the main traffic lane (which is a steadily flowing river of vehicles) and enters the appropriate auto-port. Instead of 75 doors opening onto a street, there is* only one door, well away from the street.

'*The street has disappeared in fact. It has been replaced by the highway with its unbroken flow of traffic. No vehicle ever parks on the highway. A motionless vehicle on the side of the traffic lane would create a bottleneck in the flow, paralyze the rest of the traffic. But what possible cause could a vehicle have to stop in this case? None.* The highway is inaccessible on foot. *Pedestrians cannot leave the natural ground level of the city (the parks) except by means of the elevator that will take them up to the auto-port platforms (a maximum walk of 100 meters) on which all vehicles are parked. The pedestrian walks out of the apartment house elevators straight into the automobile parking lot which is outside his front door. And if, by some miracle, there should be no taxi available at that moment, then the catering department, which is directly behind the main door of the building, will immediately order one for him. . . .*

'*In the residential areas, these airborne highways are 12, 16 and 24 meters in width.*

'*Let us take a look at them in cross-section: each highway has two lanes with a thin median wall between the two lanes: jockeying for position, violent and dangerous attempts at overtaking are things of the past. The auto-port, facing the main door used by the 2,700 occupants, is on the same level. Underneath it is the garage for private cars belonging to the residents of the apartment house. Directly beneath the main door into the apartment building there is a similar door opening out onto the parks. This is the entrance for pedestrians into the main hall of the catering section.*

'*Through this lower door for pedestrians only, the occupants of the apartments have access to a direct and yet sinuous network of pedestrian walks criss-crossing diagonally and orthogonally at the same time. Where does this fluid network of paths lead to? Everywhere in the city, by the* shortest route. *The pedestrian is able to take the most direct route to any part of the city, on foot. The paths that make up this fluid network are slightly sinuous, but only slightly: in*

82

83

84

fact, the pedestrians' diagonal and orthogonal networks are direct routes. The sinuousity is there only in order to provide a certain charm, an element of pleasure, a feeling of being out for a stroll.

'We should also note that every 400 meters the pedestrian network passes through an underpass beneath a traffic lane running at ground level — a point that has not been mentioned until now. This new traffic lane is inaccessible to pedestrians because it runs between iron fences rather like those that are used to enclose our present parks . . . These enclosures reserved for the pedestrian, all measuring 400 by 400 meters, are linked together by underground passages as wide as you like, pleasant to walk through, bathed in light. These enclosures are the parks. Within the parks are the schools and the sports grounds. We walk along beside a swimming pool 100 meters in length and designed in the shape of a natural lake; on one side it is bordered by a sandy beach; at one point, curving away from the main body of water and forming a tranquil bay, there is a paddling place for the younger children. Then there are the tennis courts, the running tracks, the soccer fields. From time to time we glimpse the graceful silhouette of a highway amongst the foliage of the trees; the cars are driving along it quite silently (rubber against cement) at whatever speed they choose. No more horns: what would be the point? Along the center of the pedestrian walks there runs a sort of continuous marquise . . .

'There are also large trucks running along underneath the highways. Where are they going? To deliver food and consumer goods to the catering departments. As you see, special bays for them to unload these goods have been provided at intervals all along the length of the apartment buildings, beneath the pilotis. That is where they are heading for. Without disturbing anyone, without getting in each other's way, without interrupting or paralyzing any of the city's functions, they then quietly load or unload their merchandise.

'In the Radiant City, the streetcar has regained its right to existence (whereas in the city as it is today, the streetcar is a critical cause of disturbance). Here, they run on their rails at ground level, to the left and right of the service roads under the highways. There are stops beside every underground passage. At these points, there are breaks in the park fences where shelters for waiting passengers have been provided. The bus will no longer be needed in the Radiant City. For though the bus is the most marvellous and adaptable form of mass transport for cities in chaos (Paris in particular), in an*

83 A housing sector in the Radiant City.

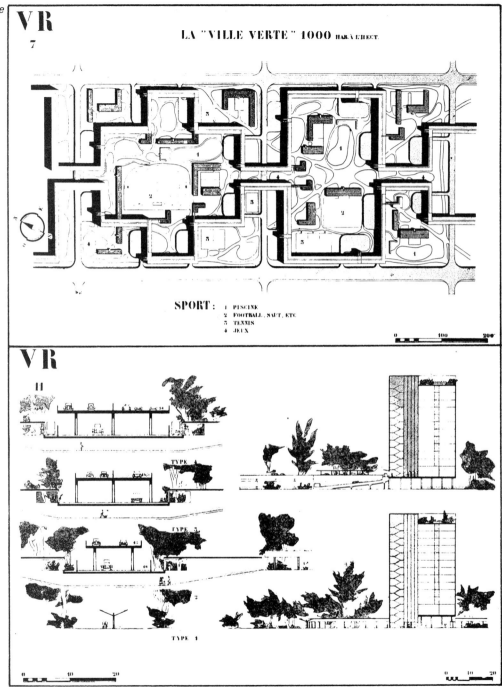

SPORT: 1 PISCINE
2 FOOTBALL, SAUT, ETC
3 TENNIS
4 JEUX

84 Sections of residential blocks roads and footpaths

ordered *city, the streetcar, which is much less costly, will regain its pre-eminence, provided it is subjected to certain improvements. . . .*

'*In the Radiant City, the streetcar (either in its present form or in that of small trains) has been restored to its former eminence (economy and efficiency). The streetcar network does not coincide with the 400 meter by 400 meter highway network; it consists simply of a series of parallel tracks at 400 meter intervals, and therefore includes no intersections. Every 400 meters, the streetcars stop opposite two skyscrapers. There are breaks in the iron fences at these points occupied by sheltered platforms. Simple but functional.*

'*There are wide underground passages, 20 or 30 meters in length, running underneath the streetcar lines and the heavy traffic lanes. (For pedestrians).*

'*Underground: the subway network of the Radiant City will then take the passengers on to particular buildings, the basements of which all include a subway station. The line itself will follow one of the branches of the cross; on either side of it will be the platforms, and beyond the platforms will be located the communal services provided for the personnel working in the building: restaurants, shops, etc.*

'*We do not yet know whether before long, we shall have air-taxis from the Radiant City airport landing on the tops of the business center skyscrapers. . . .*'[91]

The residential area lies athwart a crossroads: the major axes of the city as a whole. In the vertical direction the axis 85 runs through a central park-like strip in which stand the communal facilities — the public buildings of the town. At one end, this axis terminates in the railway station/heliport and 'the City' (i.e. business district). This comprises a group of skyscrapers similar to those in Le Corbusier's earlier ideal plans. At the other end, the vertical axis links across a 'green belt' to successive zones for factories, warehouses, and heavy industry: much of it in multi-storey buildings ('flatted' factories) and abundantly serviced by both road and rail. The other axis links to a stadium (left) and a university (right). But its greatest significance lies in that it is the direction in which future extension is possible. For with *La Ville Radieuse*, Le Corbusier corrects the 'biological defect' he had found in his *Ville à Trois Millions d'Habitants:* it can grow. Like Garnier, from whom he had learned so much, he had combined the *grid* and the *linear* form.

The density is 1,000 persons per hectare (400 persons per acre). Thus there is no subdivision beyond that into 'use-zones'. From the outskirts to the centre of the residential zone is barely 3 km. and one could walk unhindered from one end of the town to the other. For Le Corbusier, the spectator was anathema — participation was what mattered. Hence the liberal provision of sports facilities. And hence, according to some, the impossibility for anyone but a perfect athlete to live in his perfect town.

85   Schematic plan of the Radiant City.

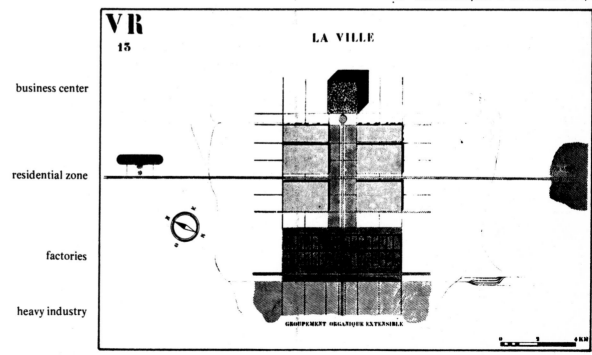

business center

residential zone

factories

heavy industry

Le Corbusier continued his researches throughout the 'thirties. His work breathes an optimistic certainty that sooner or later society will have to accept his solutions, as the only technically feasible answer to today's problem of the city. And in much of what has happened in the more recent past, we can see the influence of his thinking. There were others too, whose work was in the same general direction. Walter Gropius describes in his *The New Architecture and the Bauhaus*, his own investigations into *hochbau* and *flachbau*: flats and houses — a perennial theme in modern times. He was able to show that, for the same density, higher blocks could

'. . . enjoy better isolation, and insure a more rational utilization of the site by providing a greater ratio of green open space per inhabitant'

and concluded that

'Ten to twelve storied tenement-blocks make the ideal of "the City Verdant" a practical possibility.'[92]

To be a young 'modern architect' in the 'thirties, was to be in favour of tall blocks of flats.

In Great Britain the native brand of modernism — that which came via Morris from Pugin, Ruskin and nineteenth century romanticism — continued to express itself, especially in the work executed by architects in the name of the Garden City Movement. In contradistinction to the continental emphasis upon technical innovation, this emphasised the virtues of the 'vernacular'. Gropius also had not been slow to develop the 'Arts and Crafts' preference for 'folk' over 'aristocratic' art:

'There is a widespread heresy that art is just a useless luxury. This is one of our fatal legacies from a generation which arbitrarily elevated some of its branches above the rest as the 'Fine Arts', and in doing so robbed all of their basic identity and common life'[93]

But while for him this implied the development of the new art of the machine, in England the rejection of the 'fine art

mentality' continued to find expression in a predeliction for forms derived from traditional craftsmanship.

In matters of housing this tendency blended happily with the persistent English preference for cottage-and-garden, and a pronounced national suspicion of tenements and 'flats'. In practice it produced the suburbs which, from the turn of the century onwards, public transport facilitated. And its theory was enriched by Raymond Unwin (who, with his partner Barry Parker, was also the outstanding professional in the field) with his account, published in 1909, of *Town Planning in Practice*.

In spite of his own complaint that the English were mere beginners in town planning compared with the Germans and others, what he himself writes about is abundant proof of how much more soundly based in experience Unwin and his compatriots in fact were. His book, some four hundred pages long, for the most part eschews generalisations and abstract theorising, but is full from cover to cover of observations drawn from practical experience, and recommendations concerning such detailed matters as the layout of roads, the design of junctions, and of open spaces. Profound issues like the purpose of the town, its overall size, its location, are hardly, if at all, touched upon. Town planning is conceived as a procedure to secure   *Human needs?*

'the advantage of the land around a growing town being laid out on a plan prepared with forethought and care to provide for the needs of the growing community . . .'[94]

'. . . in town planning the first consideration must be the general convenience of the town, and the arrangement of the main roads. When the main roads have been laid down and the main traffic requirements have been provided for, the spaces left between these roads can be developed . . .'[95]

What a town *is*, is taken for granted, and there are no radical proposals. His prime concern is that what is done shall be done in an orderly way, the elements being arranged so that there is in every detail and in the whole a rational and

purposeful composition. The function of the designer is

'. . . to find artistic expression for the requirements and tendencies of the town, not to impose upon it a preconceived idea of his own . . .'[96]

He approves of Geddes, but doubts if civic surveys can be as thorough as he advocates. He cites historical precedents, and discusses the relative merits of *'formal and informal beauty'*. In the best tradition of compromise and common sense, he explains

'Of this I feel very much convinced, that town planning to be successful must be largely the outgrowth of the circumstances of the site and the requirements of the inhabitants, and going back by way of example, to the point . . . as to whether and to what extent the existing boundaries of properties should be regarded in the making of a new town plan, it would seem to me that, so long as the sense of property means what it does to the owners and occupiers of land, it would be neglecting one of the most important existing conditions if we were to disregard entirely these boundaries: that to try and carry through some symmetrical plan at the expense of upsetting the whole of the properties and destroying all the traditions and sentiment attaching to these properties would be to give to our plan a degree of artificiality which in the result would probably vastly outweigh any advantage which it might gain from a more complete symmetry. On the other hand, it would be attaching undue importance to one only among the many conditions with which a town plan must comply if we were to refuse to the town planner any powers to rearrange properties or boundaries . . .'[97]

Unwin regrets the absence of a defensive wall to define the edges of the modern town, and advocates in its stead some feature within the landscape which marks a sharp division between city and encircling green belt. He approves also the making of some modern equivalent of the city gateway,

illustrating his point with his own partnership's design at
Hampstead Garden Suburb. He has much to say of open
spaces (drawing heavily but critically upon Camillo Sitte's
Stadtebau) and wants his towns to have a central focus in the
best classical and medieval manner. Roads, streets and site
development fill out much of the detailed argument, and it is
to Unwin especially that we owe the English preference for
'12 houses to the acre'. On another occasion he had
demonstrated on financial grounds that there was *nothing to
be gained by overcrowding*,[98] and the low-density cottage
estate has since remained the ideal aimed at in popular town
planning in Britain. Unwin allows that higher densities are
possible: he cites an acceptable example of 20 houses per
acre. Neither had he himself a preference for the detached or
semi-detached form.

The nearest he allows himself to direct political utterance
(thinking no doubt he would be more acceptable in powerful
circles if he muted his undoubted socialist leanings) is in his
stated preference for socially-mixed development, and in a
concluding section arguing the virtues of co-operation. He
discusses the principle only in terms of 'site planning' i.e. the
layout of a residential area, but what he says bears eloquent
testimony to his indebtedness to those Victorian forbears who
had urged the superiority of that lost Golden Age which the
dark satanic mills had destroyed:

*'The fact that our town populations have been too much mere
aggregations of straggling units, having little orderly
relationship one with the other, and little of corporate life,
has naturally expressed itself in our street plans and in the
arrangement of sites. The absence of any attempt to develop
with a view to making the best of the whole site for the benefit
of everybody dwelling on it, and of any unity and harmony in
the total effect produced, are but too evident.*

*'In feudal days there existed a definite relationship
between the different classes and individuals of society, which
expressed itself in the character of the villages and towns in
which dwelt those communities of interdependent people.
The order may have been primitive in its nature, unduly
despotic in character, and detrimental to the development of
the full powers and liberties of the individual, but at least it
was an order. Hitherto the growth of democracy, which has
destroyed the old feudal structure of society, has but left the
individual in the helpless isolation of his freedom. But there is
growing up a new sense of the rights and duties of the
community as distinct from those of the individual. It is
coming to be more and more widely realised that a new order*

*and relationship in society are required to take the place of
the old, that the mere setting free of the individual is only the
commencement of the work of reconstruction, and not the
end . . .*

*'. . . Co-partnership Tenants' Societies are proving the
value of co-operation in the development of the sites
themselves, and in the building of the houses upon them . . .
Consider how different is the position of the site planner
when designing for one of these co-operative societies from
his position when planning an area to be let in plots to
individuals or speculative builders. In the latter case his first
consideration must be the dividing up of the land into well-
marked individual plots, avoiding any joint usage or other
complications — in fact, securing first of all the absolute
separation of each holding from its neighbour. He cannot
well provide sites even for minor public buildings, for these
will be chosen on individual lines and only after the need for
them has arisen. But in working for a co-operative body, such
as the Tenants' Society, where the houses when built remain
the property of the association, the site planner can approach
the problem from a quite different point of view: he at once
begins to think of the good of the whole. Just as in the other
case he was bound to concentrate his attention on making
individual "sell-able" plots, now he can concentrate it on the
creation of a village community; he can consider the needs of
such a community, how far they will be met by outside
opportunities already existing or likely to be developed, and
how far they will need to be met on the area of the site. The
shops, the schools, institutes and places of worship can all be
considered, and the most suitable sites for each reserved.
Some place can be arranged around which many of these
buildings can be grouped and a centre point to the plan be
thus secured. The designer can then proceed to lay out the
buildings as a whole, considering first their main lines and
arrangement, with a view to creating a good total effect, and
to preserve and develop any fine views or other advantages
the site may offer. It is not necessary for him to think of the
absolute isolation of his buildings: this point, instead of being
his first consideration, becomes his last thought. The whole of
the land remaining in one ownership, there is no difficulty in
the common enjoyment of footpaths, greens, or other open
spaces: hence he is able to consider the grouping of his
buildings with much greater freedom. Where, as may often
happen in connection with such co-operative societies, the
architect who plans the site also plans the buildings, a most
complete opportunity is given for making the best of the site.
Only under some such circumstances is it possible to work up*

86   Unwin's equivalent for a city gateway at the entrance
to Hampstead Garden Suburb.

* Here Unwin and Duany-Plater-
Zyberk run afoul of human needs,
because basic needs require a real
physical boundary, both for feeling
secure and avoiding information overload
in an endless environment. The
boundary can actually comprise just
about any marker, but it must
also be potentially defensible,
i.e., able to keep danger out.

the whole scheme in the right order, taking first the big interests and the main lines, following on with the buildings in their masses and their grouping, working down to the individual buildings themselves, and finally to the details of their arrangement, placing the best rooms where it has been planned to give the best aspect and the best outlook; designing bay windows to take advantage of views which have been kept open, giving special attention and care to those elevations which will most prominently come into the picture, and, indeed, welding the plan of the site, the buildings, and the gardens, more and more into one complete whole.

'With a co-operative society it is safe to count also on the common enjoyment of much of the garden space. It is, indeed, possible even where houses are sold to individuals, to arrange some degree of associated use of gardens, as has often been done in the centres of squares; but difficult problems, both legal and practical, are always raised by such schemes, which do not arise where the whole of the site is owned co-operatively. Where this is the case it becomes possible to group the houses around greens, to provide playgrounds for the children, bowling greens, croquet or tennis lawns or ornamental gardens for the elders, or allotment gardens for those who wish for more ground than the individual plot affords. It becomes possible also to carry out some consistent treatment of garden land, such as the creation of an orchard; for by a consistent planting of fruit-trees in an orderly manner in a series of gardens, much of the beauty and effect of an orchard may be produced. In this way it seems possible to hope that with co-operation there may be introduced into our town suburbs and villages that sense of being the outward expression of an orderly community of people, having intimate relations one with the other, which undoubtedly is given in old English villages, and which has been the cause of much of the beauty which we find there.

'The growth of co-operation . . . will lead to a need for something in the way of common rooms, baths, washhouses, recreation-rooms, reading-rooms, and possibly eventually common kitchens and dining-halls. These will give to the architect the opportunity of introducing central features in his cottage group designs, like the dining-halls, chapels, and libraries that we associate with colleges and almshouses.

'However much we may strive to improve the individual cottage, to extend its accommodation, and enlarge its share of garden or public ground, it must for a long time, and probably for ever, remain true that the conveniences and luxuries with which the few rich are able to surround themselves cannot be multiplied so that they can be added to every house. It is possible, however, and indeed easy, by co-operation to provide for all a reasonable share of these same conveniences and luxuries; and if we once overcome the excessive prejudice which shuts up the individual family and all its domestic activities within the precincts of its own cottage, there is hardly any limit to be set to the advantages which co-operation may introduce. Nothing can be more wasteful, alike of first capital cost, cost of maintenance and of labour, than the way in which hundreds and thousands of little inefficient coppers are lit on Monday morning, in small, badly-equipped sculleries, to carry out insignificant quantities of washing. Here, at least, one would think it possible to take a step in the direction of co-operation. Where cottages are built in groups round a quadrangle, how simple it would be to provide one centre where a small, well-arranged laundry could be placed, with proper facilities for heating water, plenty of fixed tubs with taps to fill and empty them, and with properly heated drying-rooms. By two or three hours' use of such a laundry each housewife could carry out her weekly wash more expeditiously and more cheaply than she could do it at home. Perhaps some play-room would need to be attached in which the children could be within reach of their mothers, during the hour or two they would be at work in the laundry. The distance to the laundry from any of the cottages using it must not be too great, and it would be better if it were accessible without passing through the street. In connection with this laundry there might be an arrangement by which, at any time, a hot bath could be obtained at a minimum of charge. Where houses are built in continuous rows it would be easy from such a centre to distribute hot water to all of them, thus effecting a great saving in fuel, boilers, and plumbing systems in the separate houses . . . Cloisters or covered play-places for the children; public rooms of reasonable size, in which the individual may entertain a number of guests, too many for the small accommodation his cottage affords; reading-room, and library at once suggest themselves as obvious and easily managed projects. More difficult, perhaps, is the question of the common kitchen and dining-hall, and yet it is probably quite as uneconomical, in every sense of the word, for forty housewives to heat up forty ovens and cook forty scrappy dinners, as to do the weekly washing in the usual way . . .

'This, however, is carrying us beyond the scope of the present subject. We should need a volume in order adequately to discuss the advantages and the difficulties of co-operative living. Along certain directions it is clearly possible, even with the present prejudices, to secure by co-

Might be a Development option for HT. Laundry is basic. Maybe a business for someone. The whole community? Best they decide

Same option. Food also basic.

operation very great advantages to the individual; but such a form of life can only be developed tentatively, and the subject is considered here mainly as it affects town planning and architecture. One cannot but feel that for successful work to be produced in this there must be some form of social life, some system of social relationships, which must find expression, and may be the means of introducing harmony into the work. We see that in the great periods of architecture there have been definite organizations of society, definite relationships, the interdependence of different, clearly defined classes, and the association of large bodies of people, held together either by a common religion, a common patriotism or by the rules of a common handicraft guild. Many of these uniting forces have been weakened or lost in modern times. One naturally looks around to see in what way the unit members of society, who have secured their freedom from so many of the old restraints and guiding influences, are likely in the future to be drawn and bound together. These units are undoubtedly realising very strongly in the present day how limited is the life which it is possible for them to obtain for themselves under conditions of greater freedom from restraint and organization. They are seeking more and more to procure an extension of opportunities through the State, the municipality, and other existing institutions, and through numberless voluntary unions and associations. It seems, therefore, likely that we may with some confidence predict that co-operation will recover for society some organised form, which will find expression in our architecture and the planning of our towns and cities . . .

'. . .*By the present haphazard system we entrust the satisfaction of the community's needs to the individual, who generally acts only when, and in so far as, that satisfaction falls in with his own inclination, and his own limited view of his personal interest. The real opposition of principle lies between this and the organisation on co-operative lines of the spontaneous ministering of the community to its own requirements. The form in which this associated effort will organise itself is of secondary importance. The essential thing is that it shall be as little artificial as possible, that it shall be a spontaneous growth following the traditional lines of development: for in so far as it is the natural outcome of the past and present life of the community will its foundation be firm and its future assured.*'[99]

It may at first appear paradoxical that of all the architects

of the period who could have discussed from experience the design of the town as a whole, Unwin, the co-designer of Letchworth, should have confined himself almost exclusively to matters of detail and the extension of existing cities. The prime reason no doubt is the purpose of his book, which was to advocate the legal measures that he considered were immediately necessary, and to provide his contemporaries with principles, procedures and models for the tasks he expected them to face. We have noted already how the first fruits of the Garden City were in the very suburban growths it was intended to prevent. (In spite of Howard's grander vision, 'Garden City', by the time Le Corbusier heard of it, meant a dormitory suburb). The re-siting of industry and the scale of co-operative endeavour implied by the building of new towns in the way Howard intended, could hardly have seemed sufficiently likely to make the form typical in the eyes of the practitioner. And since Unwin did not at that time concern himself unduly with the implications of still greater cities, he was content to advocate merely the control of their growth. In practice also, the design of Letchworth itself appears to have posed no problems qualitatively different from those encountered at Hampstead, and Unwin perhaps saw little reason to make much distinction.

In his chapter on the city survey, he does however give some clues to procedure in new town design. Maps shewing all relevant details: topography, geology, climate, history, ownerships, existing buildings and transport facilities having been prepared (for the most part, he thinks, not by the town planner himself) and estimates of future requirements for schools, etc. having been made, the planner should walk over the ground, picturing to himself

'. . . *what would be the natural growth of the town or district if left to spread over the area. He will try to realise the direction which the main lines of traffic will inevitably take, which portions of the ground will be attractive for residences, and which will offer inducements for the development of shops, business premises, or industries. As he tramps along there will arise in his imagination a picture of the future community with its needs and its aims, which will determine for him the most important points: and the main lines of his plan should thus take shape in his mind before ever he comes to put them on paper.*'[100]

This is very much the approach to design which we have already identified as *organic:* the 'marrying into' an existing landscape of new growth, not the imposition upon it of the

uncompromising rationality of the straight line and the rectangle. These contrasting attitudes run through the whole of architecture, and place Unwin and the English vernacular school on the opposite side to Le Corbusier.

* No, here he Unwin fails us. First he says that cooperation in neighborhood tasks reclaims a sense of community, increases efficiency, and fills human needs. I agree, adding that survival as a species may ultimately lie at stake. Second, shunning blatant socialism (A on p. 81), he says that such cooperation must comprise "spontaneous growth." Well, man, if it hasn't happened yet, it ain't a-gonna! Flanders says the solution involves ① laying out defined neighborhoods on a human scale that connote such cooperation as a physical design ② providing a parallel social design that lists out clearly a lot of attractive choices so residents can choose a suitable level of cooperation, and ③ providing the means to accomplish some substantial community tasks, such as a community kitchen, laundry, or teen center. "The means" here includes money (in escrow in HJ), decision-making opportunities by the developer, and an encouraging social design.

83

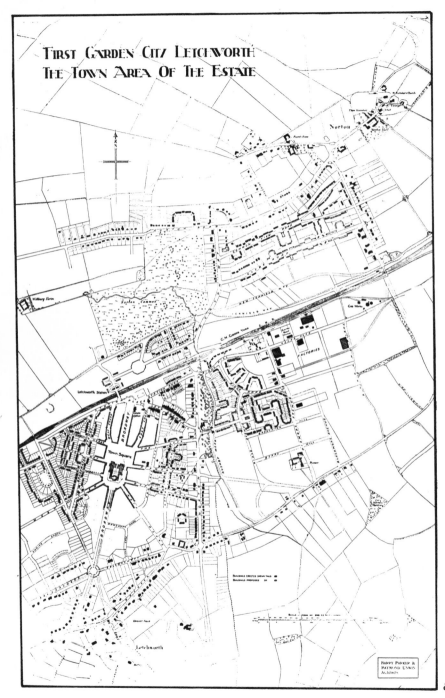

87 Letchworth: Parker and Unwin's plan.

Within the map:

FIRST GARDEN CITY LETCHWORTH
THE TOWN AREA OF THE ESTATE

A study of the plan of Letchworth itself reveals what in practice Unwin intended. (He appends the plan to his book as illustration.) It might be thought that with so definite a diagram as Howard's before them, Parker and Unwin's plan would shew the same general schematic form. But it does not. There is a park near the centre (named after Howard himself) but it is not the focus, neither does it contain the principal public buildings. These are grouped near the railway station, and it is to the 'Broadway' and 'Town Square' that most direct routes tend. There is no 'Crystal Palace', no 'Grand Avenue'. Neither railway station nor the railway itself is peripheral. Rather, it runs through the middle of the town, and there is little doubt that from the limitations imposed by it, much of the plan is derived: the principal roads are aligned with an eye to bridging points — actual or potential — and both industry and the town centre are related to it. A second determinant is the stream running through Norton Common, which becomes the generator of both Howard Park and Norton Way. For the rest, it becomes, in Unwin's own terms, a matter of 'site development', and cul-de-sac or close and lane meander between the more purposefully direct and formal framework of the principal roads.

This presence of the railway line with its associated industrial zone within the heart of the town, results in subdivision of the whole in a manner neither desired nor to any great extent planned for. There was as yet no intention to divide a new town into 'neighbourhoods' and we know that class districts were anathema. But a house backing onto a factory and separated by a tedious walk from the centre of social life, is less desirable than one adjoining the Park. It says much for the pioneering spirit that this is less apparent in Letchworth than might have been feared.

Hampstead Garden Suburb and Letchworth set standards in design that were to sustain a whole epoch of house building between the wars. The Tudor-Walters *Report on the Housing of the Working Classes* was published in 1918 (Unwin himself was a powerful influence in the committee)[101] in response to the popular demand that ex-servicemen should come back to 'a land fit for heroes to live in'. The failure of 'private enterprise' in providing sufficient decent houses at rents working people could afford, and the raised political consciousness of the working class itself, made it impossible for the state any longer to drag its feet in the matter. Local authorities' powers to build housing estates were strengthened, and in the ten years 1920-1929, the London County Council alone built about 35,000 dwellings.[102] Almost all of this was in the form of 'housing estates': new cottage suburbs on agricultural land adjoining all the major cities. In the larger estates, schools and shops, pubs and churches would also be provided. Their planning attempted to imitate the best that Parker, Unwin and a few other public-spirited architects in the London County Council and elsewhere had achieved, but for the most part degenerated into what since came to be lampooned as 'Borough Surveyor's Geometric' or 'Prairie Planning'. With the coming of the depression in the 'thirties, it was also found that only by going hungry could tenants in outlying suburbs find enough money to pay the higher fares and rents their displacement from central area 'slums' entailed.

Town extension is not town planning, however. Letchworth continued to grow slowly, but by the end of the First World War, Howard felt the time ripe for a second Garden City. With the aid of a few wealthy backers and a mortgage, Welwyn Garden City was by 1920 under way. By this time, Unwin was engaged on official work, and the consultant town planner was Louis de Soissons. The railway is again a powerful influence on the design — the main east coast London-to-Edinburgh route runs through the town. Again, the railway station is linked to the town centre. Station, civic centre and central park are here more powerfully organised into a total composition. The severance caused by the railway, however, and the keeping of all industry to a zone on the east, has resulted in a most marked division into those who live on the 'right side,' and those on the 'other side of the tracks'. A fast and convenient rail connection to London has also encouraged the growth of Welwyn as more of a dormitory suburb for London's office workers than Howard might have wished.

Although the Garden City ideal retained its hold in popular esteem, among younger architects its association with a folksy Fabianism encouraged their growing support for the new architecture of Le Corbusier and CIAM. Thus during the inter-war years the 'flats versus houses' controversy tended to range the youthful *avant garde* against the cautious taste of the cottage builders, the philanthropists and mere reformers. Attracted by the glamour of technically more sophisticated solutions, they proclaimed the virtues of the compact town, the preservation of the countryside, and communal living. A notable battle was fought in Leeds during the 'thirties, which culminated in the building of Quarry Hill Flats. These were intended by their enthusiastic designers to embody all that was progressive in social living and building technique, with the retention in the heart of a

88 Part of the Roehampton Estate: an inter-war housing estate by the architects of the London County Council.

WELWYN GARDEN CITY

89 Welwyn Garden
City: Louis de Soissons,
1924.

bustling city of a hitherto deprived population. Deputations visited new workers' flats in Vienna and elsewhere to see how these things might be done. Elaborate plans and a model were made. There were to be tennis courts, playgrounds, swimming pools, laundries and shops. There was to be district heating from a central refuse destructor. Everything was intended to proclaim the superiority of Le Corbusier over Ebenezer Howard. But like all progressive causes of the time, municipal housing was coming under the shadow of advancing reaction, which in Italy and Germany had already established Fascism, and in England the pinch-penny economies of the 'National' Government. Even the minimum standards called for by Tudor-Walters were coming under fire, sustained by such inanities as that which accused rehoused tenants of keeping coal in the bath. The experiment of Quarry Hill, if it were to succeed, would have demanded greater, not less, expenditure. But the cuts were made. Out went the 'frivolities' like swimming pools and district heating. Caught up in the opening years of the Second World War, the project was never given a chance to demonstrate in full the expectations of its designers. Although by no means a total failure, it serves to remind us how the planner's best intentions in a hostile society can pave the way to regions far removed from heaven.

Flats were built elsewhere, too, and the best examples show some attempt to exploit the advantages they were claimed to have. Generally however, they stand not as at Quarry Hill protectively encircling the territory of the community, but as gaunt echoes of the tenements of Victorian philanthropy. Especially where land values were high were they resorted to in order to retrieve maximum rentals. From 1931 to 1937, the London County Council and Liverpool City Council both gradually switched the emphasis away from cottage estates to blocks of flats and maisonettes, and since most of these gave small compensation for loss of garden and a 'foot on the ground', they confirmed, in the minds of the common people at least, their long-established preferences.[103]

Among the leaders of the Modern Movement there was one who shared this popular preference for house-and-garden: the American Frank Lloyd Wright. Older than the other 'moderns' (he was already over thirty at the turn of the century) Wright was before 1914 well established as an architect with a rare talent. His tendency was most firmly in the 'organic' direction — he may indeed have been the first to use the word in an architectural sense. He is best known for the houses he designed for wealthy clients, and he ranks with Le Corbusier as an influential 'form-giver'. Although in his formative years, he was associated with the architects and engineers of the 'Chicago School' who, in addition to some of the world's first skyscrapers, produced grandiose plans for Chicago itself, Wright had little or no first-hand experience of town planning. But in 1932 he started work on one of the few books he was to publish (which saw final completion shortly before his death in 1959, and parts of which were made public at various times after 1935) in which he sets out his proposals for 'Broadacre City'.

Wright's mentors were, *inter alia*, Ruskin, Froebel, Morris, Jefferson, Emerson, and Walt Whitman. Understandably, therefore, his argument is somewhat diffuse and eclectic, in addition to being couched in a Whitmanesque language as irritating, in its own way, as is that of Le Corbusier. Unlike Le Corbusier, however, he was emphatically anti-big-city: *'the old form of city, except as market, has little . . . to give modern civilization . . . except degeneration.'*[104] Putting people into multi-storey flats was *'pig-piling'*. He extols the virtues of the nomad, the pioneer, the wide open spaces, the individual and the family, and quotes Jefferson who considered *'that government best government which governs least'*. The mobility brought by the automobile made dispersal possible, and the widest possible dispersal was what he wanted.

For each family he proposes a lot of one acre, on which would be built a do-it-yourself extensible family home using prefabricated components. There would be no big institutions: universities, factories etc. would be broken down into smaller units sited at strategic points among the houses. He allowed the persistence of *'country seats'* i.e. established towns where banks and official buildings might be sited. The schools (*'40 children would be a very large school'*) would be in beautiful parks, and there would be local industries and artists colonies. He regarded today's *'gasoline stations'* as embryo prototypes for roadside markets, restaurants, theatres and places of entertainment. Most offices would be at home. Golf courses, race tracks, zoos, etc. would be at some *'general centre'* situated *'off some major highway'*. The proposed grid of roads would be of high capacity and new *'humanized'* motor-cars and fast regular public transport would carry us into the new age of *'automobility'*, glass and steel. While Wright's fantasies might be dismissed as the wishful thinking of the petty-bourgeois, the similarity to what he describes of much recent development in America of out-of-town centres, drive-in-cinemas, and dispersed luxury housing should not be overlooked.

90 *Frank Lloyd Wright's Broadacre City.*

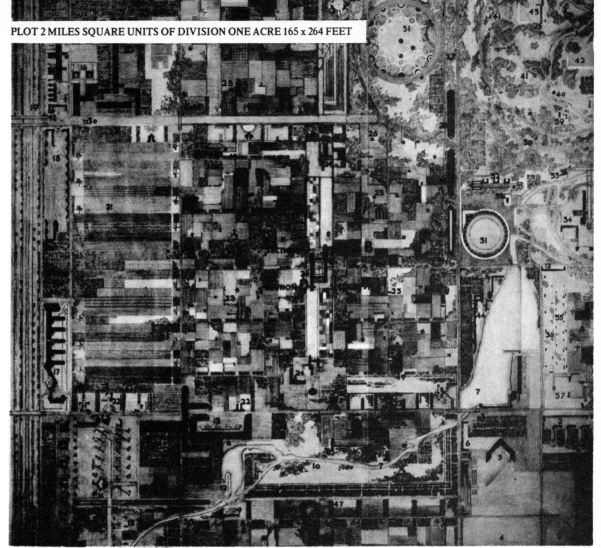

1 County seat
2 Air post port and administration
3 Stables, paddock, and track
4 Polo grounds and other sports fields
5 Baseball
6 Athletic clubs
7 Lake and stream
8 Little farms — fireproof all-purpose units
9 Machine age luxury — House on the Mesa
10 Interior park
11 Music garden
12 Baths and physical culture
13 General merchandising and market
14 Automobile inn
15 Workers' homes
16 Little factories, dwellings above
17 Factory assembly
18 Flight service
19 Main arterial, replacing the present railway
20 Airplane factory
21 Vineyards and orchards
22 Professionals and their private clinics
23 Little homes
24 Schools
25 Universal worship, columbarium, cemetery, nine sectarian temples surrounding a central edifice devoted to universal worship
26 Neighbourhood guest houses
27 Scientific and agricultural research
28 Arboretum
29 Zoo
30 Aquarium
31 Circus — 31A a totem and beacon to the lost tribes of a continent
32 Hotel
33 Country club
34 Sanitarium
35 Little industrial units
36 Little clinics
37 Little apartments
38 Creamery
39 Little school for small children
40 Apartment houses
41 Commodious dwellings
42 Water supply
43 Taliesin equivalent
44 Crafts and county architects
45 Little cinema
46 Forest cabins
47 Larger homes
48 Automobile objective — road system
49 Neighbourhood garage units with little stores
50 Gas stations
51 Educational centre

Wright was working out his schemes in Roosevelt's New Deal America of the 'thirties, and this period saw also America's first attempt at regional planning in the Tennessee Valley. The whole course of a major river and its catchment area was studied. Dams were built to control flooding and irrigation, and to provide electric power. Townships and new farmland were created, under the auspices of a federal government, for once disposed to use the planned and co-ordinated resources of a modern industrial economy in a rational way. The opposition of those whose destructive wrath culminated in the McCarthy witch-hunts against everything and everyone associated with the New Deal, is a just measure of the project's true worth. 'TVA' today signifies to planners everywhere a high point of accomplishment.

The continued growth of cities in the inter-war period — and especially of metropolitan centres — called forth a growing response in many countries. We have already noted the plans for Moscow. Plans were produced, *inter alia*, for Dublin and New York, but the most notable achievement belongs to Holland. The Dutch, whose country was itself in part the planned creation of succeeding generations of statesmen and engineers (it has been said that God made the World, but the Dutch made Holland), had long accepted some measure of town planning as a way of life. The recent growth of Amsterdam itself had been partially planned with the help of the celebrated modern architect Berlage. A research group was set up in 1929, and their investigations when published ran to many volumes, containing detailed information and analysis of the kind that would have warmed Geddes' heart. The influence of CIAM was ensured by the participation of its erstwhile President — van Eesteren — as Chief Architect, and the analysis itself was in accordance with CIAM categories of *housing, work, leisure* and *transport*. The resulting plan envisaged a concentrated city, designed in considerable detail, to take account of prognostications up to the year 2000 AD, but flexible enough to admit continual

revision and change. Submitted in 1933, it was subsequently acclaimed as the *'first instance of a capital city committing itself to a definite plan for its future worked out in detail on the basis of scientific preliminary research'*.[105] But nearly five years were to pass before the plan was officially adopted, and by then other and more pressing matters were overshadowing Holland and the rest of Europe and the World.

The decade 1936 to 1945 was characterised more by the deliberate destruction of cities than by the building of them. But when after 1940 the battle against Fascism was truly joined, there were those whose confidence in victory was already giving rise to plans for a peaceful future free from tyranny and want. Where the wanton destruction of Guernica in 1937 had called forth hatred and embittered comment, the blitz upon Coventry in 1941 resulted in the publication of plans for the city's reconstruction, bolder and more far-reaching than anything attempted before. Patrick Abercrombie — the leading town planner of the day — was commissioned to work on a new plan for London. In besieged Britain and occupied France alike, those adherents of CIAM fortunate enough to be able to pursue professional interests, were looking beyond present destruction to the task of rebuilding ahead, and continuing their researches into the city of the future.

Already before 1939 in the United Kingdom, there had been some moves towards better planning. That there was ample room for improvement, there could be no doubt. The Housing, Town Planning etc. Act of 1909 applied only to land not yet developed for urban purposes, and its ineffectiveness may be gauged from the following:

. . . Not only had a local authority (in England the council of a borough or urban or rural district) to obtain permission from the Local Government Board before it could even begin to prepare a scheme, let alone take any action to implement

it, but it had to give to the owners, lessees and occupiers of all land which it proposed to include in the scheme that it wished to prepare, at least two months' notice of its intention to apply to the Board for permission to prepare the scheme. At every stage further complications were introduced. The result was a labyrinthine procedure in which any scheme might well be lost for ever and which was likely to make town planning appear to all but the most enthusiastic a task involving efforts much more than commensurate with the advantages which it might procure.'[106]

Subsequent measures in 1919 and 1923, mild as they were, met with such resistance from propertied interest, coupled with an indifference from local authorities which amounted to sabotage, that they remained for the most part a dead letter. In spite of the powers they granted to local authorities to initiate town planning schemes controlling future urban growth, from the passage of the 1909 Act to the beginning of 1932, 'only 75,020 acres in all Great Britain were included . . .'[107] By the early 'thirties, however, road accidents, ribbon development, and an economic depression which was putting whole regions out of work, could no longer be ignored. Road Traffic Acts were passed in 1930 and 1934 introducing such elementary controls as driving tests and pedestrian crossings.

A Town and Country Planning Act was passed in 1932 extending limited controls over all kinds of land, and the Restriction of Ribbon Development Act of 1935 was intended as a deterrent to further unplanned sprawl. As a result, by 1939 more than half the country was subject to some kind of planning control over new building. The Barlow Committee was set up to report on matters affecting the *'Distribution of the Industrial Population'*, an issue with obvious implications for both regional and town planning. By 1941, various professional and other bodies concerned, were emboldened to advocate a *'national Planning Basis'* for post-war rebuilding as follows:

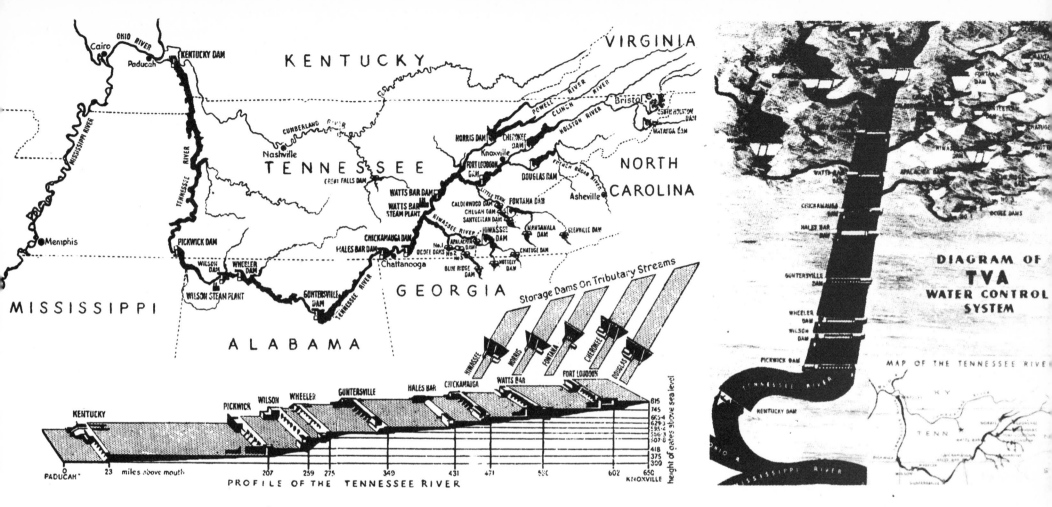

KENTUCKY

VIRGINIA

Cairo   OHIO RIVER
Paducah   KENTUCKY DAM

NORTH
CAROLINA

CUMBERLAND RIVER

Nashville

TENNESSEE

GREAT FALLS DAM

WATTS BAR DAM

WATTS BAR
STEAM PLANT

Memphis

PICKWICK DAM

HALES BAR DAM   CHICKAMAUGA DAM

WILSON
DAM   WHEELER
DAM

Chattanooga

WILSON STEAM PLANT

MISSISSIPPI

GUNTERSVILLE
DAM

GEORGIA

ALABAMA

NORRIS DAM   CHEROKEE
DAM

Knoxville

FORT LOUDOUN
DAM

DOUGLAS DAM

Asheville

POWELL   CLINCH RIVER

HOLSTON RIVER

Bristol

SOUTH HOLSTON
DAM

WATAUGA DAM

FRENCH BROAD RIVER

LITTLE TENN

FONTANA DAM

CALDERWOOD DAM
CHILHOWEE DAM
SANTEETLAH DAM

HIWASSEE RIVER

HIWASSEE
DAM

APALACHIA DAM

OCOEE DAMS No.1

NANTAHALA
DAM   GLENVILLE DAM

CHATUGE DAM

BLUE RIDGE DAM   NOTTELY
DAM

DIAGRAM OF
TVA
WATER CONTROL
SYSTEM

Storage Dams On Tributary Streams

HIWASSEE   NORRIS   FONTANA   FORT LOUDOUN   CHEROKEE   DOUGLAS

KENTUCKY   PICKWICK   WILSON   WHEELER   GUNTERSVILLE   HALES BAR   CHICKAMAUGA   WATTS BAR

815
745
665·4
629·3
595·4
556·8
507·8

418
375
300

height of gates above sea level

0   23   miles above mouth   207   259   275   349   431   471   530   602   650
PADUCAH   KNOXVILLE

PROFILE OF THE TENNESSEE RIVER

MAP OF THE TENNESSEE RIVER

91 TVA: a high point of accomplishment in regional
planning.

'1 A Ministry (advised by a National Planning Council) should be set up to guide future development and redevelopment and the future grouping of industry and population.

2 Distinction should be maintained between Town and Country in all development and sporadic building in rural areas discouraged.

3 Good design and layout of buildings and roads should be an object of policy equally with sound construction, and outdoor advertising limited to approved situations.

4 Residential density should be limited to provide adequate open space, and belts of country preserved round all towns.

5 Any movements of population required should be directed to existing towns or to new towns carefully sited to meet the needs of industry, agriculture and social amenity. New and extending towns should be planned as compact units.

6 The Planning Ministry should have power to prohibit or encourage the settlement of industrial undertakings in particular places.

7 There should be new and improved legislation to deal with compensation and betterment.'[108]

As a result of growing popular pressure, two inquiries were undertaken during the war years themselves: that of the Uthwatt Committee on *Compensation and Betterment*, and of the Scott Committee on *Land Utilization in Rural Areas*. The first of these attempted to grasp those nettles which most stood in the way of any social enterprise affecting property rights. The second reflected the growing concern for urban encroachment upon agricultural land. The subsequent setting up of a Ministry of Town and Country Planning in 1943, and the enactment of measures in successive years up to 1947, provided the most favourable conditions Britain had yet enjoyed for the planning of land utilization and the location of industry. Some of what was achieved has since been whittled away, but since 1947 there has been in Britain complete control over all development in town and country.

SUB-ARTERIAL ROADS...

ROUNDABOUTS.....

TRAFFIC SIGNALS...

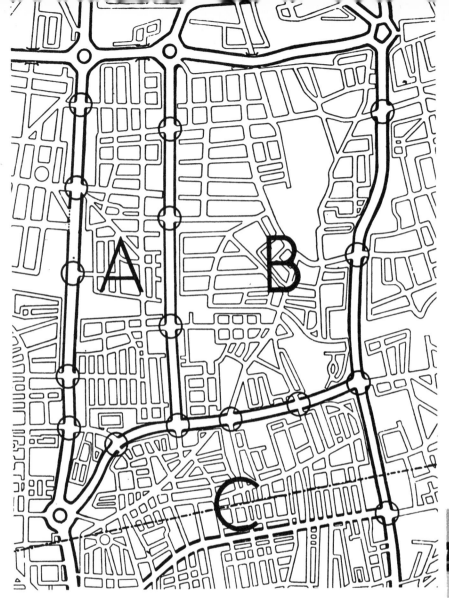

92 Tripp's precincts: *'Daily life is lived in the precincts (three separate precincts A. B and C, are shown); it is there that shops and places of amusements should be located, not on the main roads ... The main traffic routes are treated much as if they were railways ... In the diagram, the upper part has been replanned on safety lines; in the extreme lower part (below the dotted line) the present unplanned condition is retained for purposes of contrast ...'*

94 Rotterdam, the Lijnbaan, a prototype for the pedestrian shopping precinct.

93 *Coventry: the central area showing the pedestrian-only shopping precinct.*

Pedestrian routes ---
Rooftop and multi-level car parks ▨

0 ½ 1 mile
scale

The failure to remove from private ownership the financial gain consequent upon development, however, has consolidated vested interest and prevented much desirable change. The fruits of 'betterment' — often themselves the result of public enterprise — still accrue to the landowner, and the expense of buying out his right to exploit the established use of his property, continues to militate against planning, and towards the perpetuation and intensification of the *status quo*. Especially is this so with industry and commerce. A local authority can only at great expense, extinguish an 'existing user right' attaching to a badly located factory, and there are strong financial incentives against curbing the avarice of the central area office developer. There have from time to time been half-hearted attempts to entice industry away from congested regions to those in need of new employment opportunities, and some public offices have been 'decentralised'. But continued growth where it is not wanted, and continued decline where growth is desired, amply testify to the inadequacies in practice of the existing planning law. These inadequacies have been compounded furthermore by the separate provisions made for roads, transport and other matters intimately involved. To this day, it is not uncommon to find that the intention of a local planning authority is in direct conflict with the policy being operated by another public body responsible for transport or economic affairs.

The 1947 Town and Country Planning Act nonetheless made it possible to prevent the uncontrolled encroachment of the town upon the countryside. It also made it mandatory upon local authorities to plan and to continue planning the area they administered. If the disabilities under which they have worked have militated against positive achievement, at least in a negative sense the total despoliation of the countryside has so far been prevented.

In planning theory also, the wartime years saw considerable progress. First, with regards to traffic planning, we should note the work of Alker Tripp. As a senior police officer he had become aware that something more than mere policing was needed to stop the appalling results in death and injury which the growth in motor traffic was causing. In 1942 he published *'Town Planning and Road Traffic'*: the first work on a topic which, in recent years, has bid fair to eclipse all others in the planning field. He proposed the 92 redevelopment of towns in such a way that a network of arterial roads was created for the exclusive use of motor vehicles, within which would be 'precincts' served by minor

roads. Pedestrians would be excluded from the arterials, and all traffic other than local would be dissuaded from entering the precincts by the closure of all but a few junctions with the arterials. Tripp disliked the 'gridiron plan' as productive of dangerous cross-roads, which he would as far as possible eliminate in favour of the safer 'staggered' T-junctions or, where unavoidable, the 'roundabout'. For the town as a whole he envisaged a spiders-web of 'rings and radials': outer and inner 'ring roads' to bypass unwanted traffic, and 'radials' to give access from suburb to centre. The centre itself would be girdled by its 'inner ring road' and largely free from traffic.

The reader in the United Kingdom will have no difficulty in recognising Tripp's influence in the re-planning which has occurred in most towns. But as his eminent successor notes,[109] his assumption that existing main roads could form the basis of the arterial system presupposes 'turning the town inside out'; and he greatly underestimates the implications for design of the size of roadworks — especially junctions. It is typically only after the impact of these deficiencies has become too apparent in their uncritical application in practice, that they are belatedly gaining official recognition.

The two most notable official plans for existing towns in Britain: that of Abercrombie and others for London and of Gibson and others for Coventry — both embodied ideas, similar in many respects to those of Tripp. The Coventry plan, published almost before the dust of the 'blitz' of 1941 93 had settled, included proposals for complete segregation of pedestrians and vehicles within the central shopping area, setting a fashion which was to be picked up later by the planners of devastated Rotterdam, who were the first to carry 94 it through in practice.*

Coventry had been one of the few English cities outside London to set up an adequate corporation department to deal with matters of architecture — and even then many battles were to be fought before town planning was officially acknowledged as part of its domain. Within London itself there had since the turn of the century been a succession of able professionals who had eschewed the glamour of fashionable practice in order to devote themselves to what they regarded as the more worth-while tasks of rehousing London's poor. Here again administrative anomalies prevented concerted planning, but already before 1939, London had a chief architect — Frederick Hiorns — whose interest in towns and their development was such that he undertook the first major historical survey of the subject to be published in Britain.[110] In 1943, the then Chief Architect to the London County Council — J. H. Forshaw — together with Patrick Abercrombie, produced the County of London Plan.

Abercrombie had already built himself a reputation as a planner. He had written a scholarly essay on the subject,[111] and had produced plans for the expansion and redevelopment of various cities and regions. The *County of London Plan* therefore (and the *Greater London Plan* which supplemented it in 1944) may be regarded as being for its time the summit of his achievement and the epitome of British town planning, at least in so far as it related to the development of the existing city.

Far from setting themselves revolutionary objectives, the authors of the *County of London Plan* declare[112] their aim as being to '*retain the old structure and make it work*'. '*The planning of an existing town should stimulate and correct its natural evolutionary trends*'. They claimed to discover, underneath the seeming chaos, an order which had persisted from an earlier group of separate communities, each with its own local centre, characteristics and loyalties. This they set out to resurrect, with the declared objective of marking more **95** clearly the separate identity of each community and rescuing it from the evils of through traffic.

The trends they wished to correct were reflected in traffic congestion, depressed housing conditions, the inadequate provision of open space, and '*indeterminate zoning*' — by which was chiefly meant the mixing of homes and factories. For metropolitan London proper, they proposed precinctual planning *à la* Tripp, with roads tunnelled underground for drivers who would have to '*become tunnel-minded.*' A system of 'rings and radials' is then proposed for London as a whole, but with arterial routes carefully sited to run (unlike Tripp's) along *new* lines between reconstituted communities. In these communities themselves they envisaged (in sympathy with the egalitarian sentiments of the time) '*a greater mingling of the different groups of London's society*', with people living '*within reasonable distance of their work but not in such close proximity that their living conditions are prejudiced by it.*' Community structure was to be emphasised also by dividing wedges of open space, but not to such an extent that the interdependence of the whole was endangered.

The 'Barlow' recommendations concerning 'decentralisation' were to be implemented by moving out both homes and workplaces from the centre, the strategy being to create for Greater London as a whole, a series of concentric zones: 'inner', 'suburban', 'green belt', and 'outer

country'. Within the residential areas there would be a corresponding diminution of density, from 220 persons per net residential acre nearest the centre, down to 100 in the suburbs: figures which implied a ratio of flats to houses of 55:45 overall. Communities were to be divided into *neighbourhood units* related to elementary schools and having populations between 6,000 and 10,000. The suburbs (described in G. D. H. Cole's words as '*lacking in the spirit of community or in democracy or in any sort of unity save that of mere physical juxtaposition*') were to be made into real communities.

Appropriate existing towns in the home counties were to be augmented to take overspill, and sites were suggested for new towns also. Trading estates were advocated as a major means of industrial dispersal, but office employment only briefly discussed as having significance in this regard. A '*combined operations*' approach to transport was regarded as being of supreme importance.

95 Forshaw and Abercrombie: County of London Plan, 1943, showing reconstituted cellular structure.

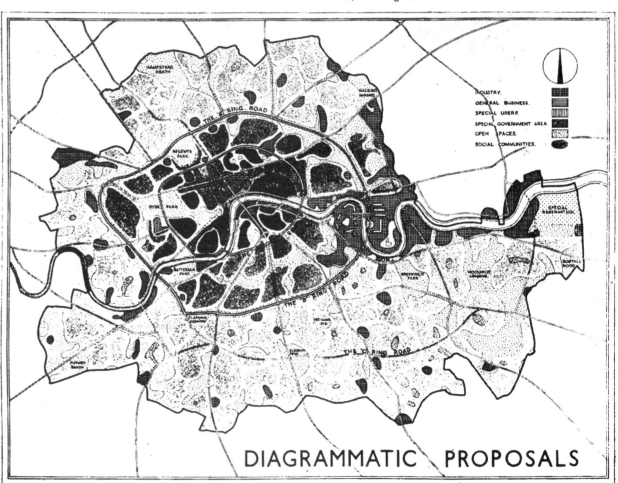

DIAGRAMMATIC PROPOSALS

The Greater London and County of London Plans still remain the basis upon which London is being redeveloped, although many of the assumptions are now questioned and many difficulties have been encountered in trying to put the proposals into effect. Decentralisation of residential population from inter-war London there has certainly been, but the decline in population which Abercrombie and Forshaw envisaged has in fact resulted in a new Greater London, which has extinguished Middlesex completely and now extends its sphere of influence far beyond the Home Counties. Today London still confronts British town planning with its greatest challenge, and poses complex problems which we shall look at in due course. Of present interest are the *New Towns*, which for London were seen as the instrument of 'decentralisation', and elsewhere looked to in order to repair the ravages of depression and war.

A committee was appointed in 1945 (the Reith Committee) to

'consider the general questions of the establishment, development, organisation and administration that will arise in the promotion of New Towns in furtherance of a policy of planned decentralization from congested areas; and in accordance therewith to suggest guiding principles on which such Towns should be established and developed as self-contained and balanced communities for work and living.'[113]

The theoretical position of Howard is apparent in the reference to decentralisation and self-containment, and the occasion was seen as a triumph for the unflagging propaganda which Howard and his followers had maintained. The inclusion of some of these followers on the committee itself, ensured that its report consolidated the Garden City influence. Purchase and tenure were to be by public authorities, but otherwise as Howard intended. There was to be provision for a 'green-belt'. The town proper should have a population generally between 30,000 and 50,000. The peripheral belt should be used for agriculture related to local consumption, and small-holdings should be encouraged.

Desiderata other than those mentioned by Howard are included. There should be variety of employment — an objective prompted by the bad experience of the depression, when some 'one-industry towns' were almost wholly unemployed. A balance of income-groups was desirable, and one-class-districts should be avoided: a wish in keeping with the contemporary democratic spirit we have already noted (sometimes bolstered also by a smug belief that 'middle-class leadership' was required for a flourishing social life). The ring-and-radial road pattern together with the through-traffic-free precinct is approved. An internal bus service should be planned. Shops should be provided at a rate of 1:100-150 persons, and there should be competition in each trade (a notion Howard explicitly disapproves). There is much detail about shopping, and in addition to the city centre shops, there should be groups within half-a-mile of all residents. There are estimates of the amount of land needed for various 'zones', and housing is recommended at an overall gross density of 12 to the acre. Schools, hospitals, health centres, meeting halls, theatres, libraries, museums, restaurants, playing fields, churches and all conceivable details are discussed to some extent, and the final report quickly became a principal reference work for town planning, in both new and existing towns. There were estimates also of cost (at about £700 per head of new town population at 1946 prices), of the labour force required, and of the programming of the work. It is doubtful if before or since there has ever been so comprehensive a 'brief' for the design of towns.

The most significant theoretical advance of lasting importance arises from the discussion of the layout of the town as a whole. Into this is introduced the idea of the 'neighbourhood' as a sub-division of the town, not a closed community in itself, but nonetheless grouped as a distinguishable entity around its own local shops and other public buildings. This 'neighbourhood concept' plays a formative role in subsequent planning policy and must be examined.

During the 'twenties and 'thirties there had grown up in the USA a town planning movement which owed much to the English Garden City movement. Among its leading practitioners were Clarence Stein and Henry Wright, and one of its theorists was Clarence Perry. Stein and Wright, in applying Parker and Unwin's teachings to American conditions, found themselves elaborating the practice of 'super-block planning', designing as a single unit the largest grouping of houses possible under American conditions. Instead of ranging all dwellings alongside the bounding grid of roads, they grouped them around a central pedestrian open space, keeping vehicle access to a system of external cul-de-sacs. They thus not only created the 'Radburn' plan which, in completely segregating vehicle and pedestrian circulation, responded to the high levels of automobile ownership by then already reached in the USA, but they also emphasised the integrity of the 'neighbourhood'. Conceived on a more systematic basis, the 'neighbourhood plan' was advocated by Perry as a logical arrangement for new suburban development, in which houses were grouped in clusters together with such communal services as they demanded.[114] We have seen that Abercombie's County of London Plan had embraced the idea, and upon the basis of the neighbourhood a new concept of urban form was elaborated and eagerly seized upon as a cogently reasoned framework for post-war planning. A good summary of this framework is set out for popular consumption as follows:

'There has been a tendency for the town, which has grown up almost always by the fusion of separate villages, to become more and more an unwieldy, undifferentiated mass, with the different areas of local government just arbitrary divisions on a map with no relation to roads, railways, or other vital elements. Planners want to restore and keep the historically developed localities, where they exist, and to form new ones where they do not. They intend to mark them out and separate them from each other, chiefly by means of the main traffic routes or by open spaces, which will run between them in such a way that the whole town is composed of distinct and living parts, each safely isolated from the busy streams of traffic.

'Let us look at the idea in more detail.

'A "neighbourhood" is formed naturally from the daily occupations of people, the distance it is convenient for a housewife to walk to do her daily shopping and, particularly, the distance it is convenient for a child to walk to school. He should not have a long walk and he should not have to cross

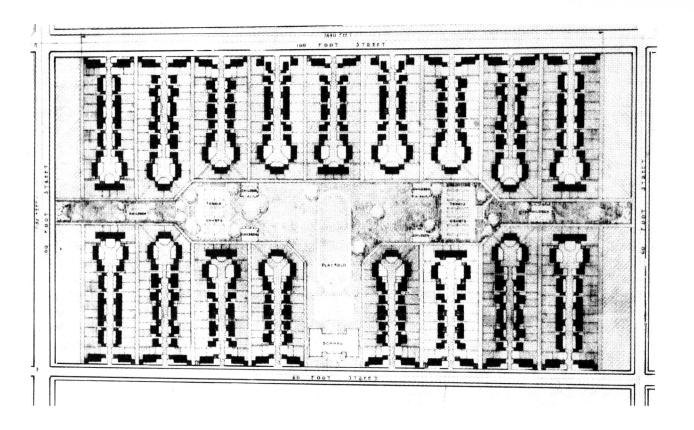

96 *Theoretical study for a 'superblock', 1928.*

* Basildon, Bracknell, Crawley, Harlow, Hatfield, Hemel Hempstead, Stevenage, Welwyn Garden City, Corby, Cwmbran, Newton Aycliffe, Peterlee, East Kilbride, and Glenrothes.

*any main traffic road. The planning of a neighbourhood unit
starts from that. In the proposals of the County of London
Plan the neighbourhood unit is the area that can be served by
one elementary school and it works out at from 6,000 to
10,000 inhabitants. Grouped centrally near the school are the
the local shopping centre and such community buildings as a
clinic, or a communal restaurant. There is no through traffic
in the neighbourhood unit: it skirts it, along one of the main
roads.*

*'Several neighbourhood units together form the
"community", which will be about as big as a small borough.
Sometimes it will correspond to an existing clearly defined
district . . . The community will have one or more secondary
schools and a shopping and civic centre consisting of
larger shops and community buildings, town hall, library, fire
station, health centre, etc. The community will also have
some light industries, not of a kind that needs segregation, so
that work and dwelling can be nearer together and useless
daily travelling reduced.*

*'Roads can be sharply divided into several kinds, each
carrying traffic of a different sort, and the different sorts need
seldom or never mix. The national, long-distance road will
by-pass towns altogether. It will be joined by the main
arterial roads from the towns, which in their turn will be
joined by the main roads of the communities. These roads
will be joined by the minor roads of the communities and
neighbourhood units. Where it is unavoidable for minor
roads to cross major ones the "flyover" and other safe forms
of crossing will be used. Housing and schools will always be
on minor internal roads, sheltered from fast traffic, and the
gain in safety, quietness, and in speed and efficiency of traffic
will be very great.'*[115]

The New Towns designed in the late 'forties and 'fifties all
more-or-less carried these ideas into practice, and with minor
modifications collectively bear witness to the persuasiveness
of a powerful idea. The one exception is Peterlee, which, as
first conceived, retained the unicellular form of the first
garden cities. Welwyn Garden City itself was taken over and
completed as a New Town to the revised formula. Almost
without exception, a continual upward revision of population
targets and a gradual falling in housing and other standards,
has resulted in the first New Towns* shewing, in their
achievement, failings at odds with the intentions of their first
design. But they remain a high-point in town planning and a
testimony to the power of popular enthusiasm for a better
urban environment.

97 *An early example of vehicle/pedestrian segregation in
modern practice.*

LEGEND

BUILDINGS COMPLETED, OR
ABOUT TO BE CONSTRUCTED

GROUPS PROPOSED FOR
FUTURE DEVELOPMENT

SCALE

0   200   400   600   800

RADBURN N.J.
REGISTERED TRADE MARK

PLAN OF NORTHWEST & SOUTHWEST
RESIDENTIAL DISTRICTS
NOVEMBER 1929

CLARENCE S. STEIN & HENRY WRIGHT
ARCHITECTS ASSOCIATED

The application of the new planning formula is epitomised in Gibberd's plan for Harlow. An ascending hierarchy of groupings — neighbourhood, district, town — is married to a hierarchy of roads. Open spaces emphasise this structure. The town is a balanced self-sufficient whole, with clearly defined zones for industry, and the biggest roads are for external traffic. Foot and cycle ways make it safe and easy for what was envisaged as a mainly pedestrian community, living among near-rural surroundings. Everything — or almost everything — in the Garden City was lovely.

98
99

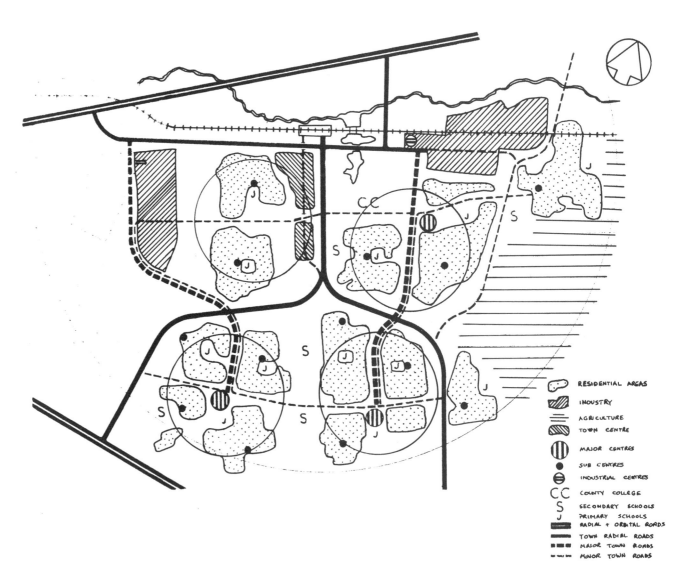

99 *Harlow: the master plan by Frederick Gibberd, 1947: note the formative influence of the existing landscape.*

RESIDENTIAL AREAS
INDUSTRY
AGRICULTURE
TOWN CENTRE
MAJOR CENTRES
SUB CENTRES
INDUSTRIAL CENTRES
COUNTY COLLEGE
SECONDARY SCHOOLS
PRIMARY SCHOOLS
RADIAL + ORBITAL ROADS
TOWN RADIAL ROADS
MAJOR TOWN ROADS
MINOR TOWN ROADS

98 *Harlow, Essex: schematic form in the first new towns with residential 'neighbourhoods', each associated with primary schools, grouped into districts.*

HARLOW NEW TOWN

- TOWN CENTRE BUILDINGS
- SECONDARY SCHOOLS
- PRIMARY SCHOOLS
- SHOPPING CENTRES
- EXISTING BUILDINGS
- INDUSTRY
- BUSINESS CENTRE - INDUSTRIAL AREA
- RESIDENTIAL AREAS
- LAND OUTSIDE THE DESIGNATED AREA

Frederick Gibberd
by Gordon Schoon London W.C.1

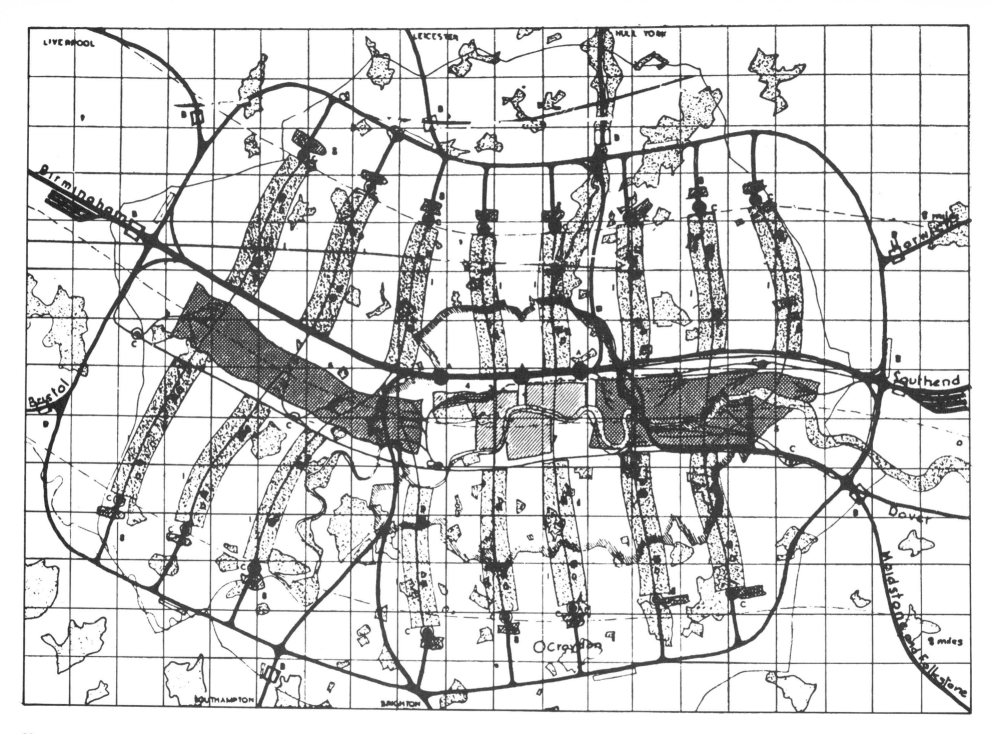

The new town has remained a continuing and vital theme in British town planning up to the present time, but before pursuing it further, it is necessary to record the parallel development of the more radical approach associated with CIAM. Already before the war, in 1937, the British group of CIAM — the *Modern Architectural Research Group* were trying to apply to English conditions the ideas which successive international congresses had elaborated. After the 'blitz' upon London, they took advantage of the consequent popular interest in reconstruction and planning to publish their *Master Plan for London*, which has since become widely known as the *MARS Plan.*[116]

Abercrombie and Forshaw, as we have seen, based their approach on trying *'to retain the old structure and make it work':* not so the young men of CIAM. London was comparable to a factory which was deteriorating to the point where it had to be rebuilt. As it stood, it was technically inefficient — so much so that more than 40% of its labour force was engaged in distribution, a waste analogous to internal friction losses in a machine. It should be possible to replace its present archaic structure with a more efficient one, and the loss in production thus eliminated would be more than enough to pay not only for the rebuilding, but also for the highest standards of housing, cultural and other amenities.

The approach, therefore, became first one of discerning the salient characteristics of the problem — London — as a whole; then of devising *'a master plan, a grid on which the town can be developed';* then of providing *'a schedule by which London can gradually be converted to its new plan'.*

London's essential characteristics were threefold: those of imperial metropolis, financial centre and port. Since *'the final aim of all town planning is to provide the maximum number of amenities for the population'*, and since these were in turn dependent on proper provision for housing, work and transport, it is in terms of housing, work and transport, and

100

100 The MARS plan for London: a linear central area extends westwards from the Port. Residential areas run roughly N-S with open spaces between. The whole is served by elaborate transport networks.

their associated desiderata, that the *'basic grid'* would have to be devised. There should be abundant open space within ten minutes of each dwelling. Industrial pollution should be avoided by segregation. The journey to work *'should be as simple and short as possible, and not underground.'* Density and location should have regard to health and well-being, for which also the provision of hospitals etc. should be adequate.

101 For housing, a hierarchical structure based on the
102 neighbourhood is spelt out in detail in much the same terms as those we have already encountered.

Workplaces are divided into three categories: for *deconcentrated work,* — retail, professional, administrative, domestic, etc. — necessarily spread over the whole town; for work as in docks, etc., which is *tied to its location;* and for *concentrated work* which can be placed anywhere *'according to general town-planning needs'.* An estimated breakdown tabulates about 30% of the working population as 'deconcentrated', and distributes approximately 40% in industrial areas and 20% in an administrative area. The remaining 10% is divided between shopping areas and the 'cultural centre'.

Transport (conceived primarily as *rail* transport) is analysed first into goods and passenger traffic, of which the former is seen as having the greater economic significance: *'GOODS TRAFFIC must be analysed in accordance with its origin and destination:*

1. *Raw materials and semi-manufactures arriving for the local industry; semi-manufactures and manufactures leaving the industry; (industrial goods).*
2. *Transit goods.*
3. *Goods manufactured elsewhere, destined for local consumption (entering the town).*
4. *Goods for consumption (produced inside the town).*
5. *Erratically moving goods.*

*'**Group 1.** The ideal arrangement for these goods is for them to come from an exterior point to a main goods station, thence possibly to a secondary one, and thence to the industry, and vice versa.*

If the passage of these goods is not to interfere with interior traffic, industry must be so located that it is separated from the residential as well as from the administration district. The more compact the grouping of the industry, the smaller the capital outlay and running costs. For reasons given later, main and secondary goods stations have to serve road as well as rail traffic, although for the former the station is merely a clearing point.

*'**Group 2.** Goods in transit should arrive at the main goods stations and depart from there. Most transit goods will either come from, or go to, the Port. A special clearing station is required for these goods. It is essential that this traffic should not pass through the residential industrial or business districts, nor touch even the secondary goods stations.*

*'**Group 3.** Incoming goods for local consumption should arrive at secondary goods stations (by road or rail), each situated in the immediate neighbourhood of the district for which they are destined. From there, the goods must be conveyed to the place of consumption (usually the main shopping street) by the shortest possible route.*

'At present, all suburbs in London could not be provided with a suitable goods station, but in a planned town arrangements could be made by which goods were delivered by rail or road, either at night or (better still) underground. A main shopping centre like the West End of London must have a properly devised goods delivery system.

*'**Group 4.** Goods produced by industry within the town and used in the town itself, would, with small communities, be delivered direct. In a city the size of London it is best to let them pass via the secondary goods station, i.e. by the same route as outgoing traffic for industry and the same as incoming traffic for consumers. The increase in distance involved is more than compensated for by the improved organisation and the complete separation of goods and passenger traffic.*

*'**Group 5.** Erratically moving goods (mainly parcel post) is a comparatively small item (which is already better organised than the rest of the traffic). An underground post collection could easily be combined with the above-mentioned goods delivery.'*

Passenger traffic is then sub-divided as follows:

	Per cent.
'1. Pendulum traffic — comprising traffic of any working member of the community from home to work and back	*60*
2. Point traffic — comprising travel from home to any other points, such as theatres, shops, railway stations, etc	*12*
3. Circle traffic — comprising traffic of any member of the community between several working points, such as commercial travellers .	*20*
4. Local traffic — comprising travel between	

101 MARS plan: a district of 600,000 people.
District Unit
A district unit of 600,000 people is composed of three sub-units of 200,000 each which again is sub-divided into four borough units of 50,000 each. One of these units is indicated by the circle.

102 *MARS plan: a borough of 50,000 people.*

A borough unit contains 50,000 people, being a quarter to half a mile wide with its arterial road on one side and open green on the other. The Civic Centre of the unit opens out into the green with its public buildings.

1. Secondary artery (Station in centre). 2. Shopping street. 3. Town Hall. 4. Cinema. 5. Open-air theatre. 6. Boys' Secondary School. 7. Girls' Secondary School. 8. Hospital. 9. Sports fields. 10. Swimming Bath. 11. Intermediate road for private car traffic.

(All the area to the left of the Secondary School is common and a similar area is arranged on the other side of the artery).

several homes, generally for pleasure or social reasons. 8
The percentages may be altered to a certain extent with the reorganisation of the town.'

Pendulum traffic is the most important, and replanning must aim at making it as simple and rapid as possible. The basic distinction was not between road and rail, but between *'organised'* and *'flexible'*.

'In the general way this coincides with road and rail traffic, but if, for instance, public transport had its own thoroughfares, was absolutely timed to schedule and had no crossings, it would come under organised traffic, although some of the vehicles would run on roads.'

'Flexible transport' is cheaper over short distances and *'organised transport'*, over long: but in England with a density of 766 persons per square mile, circumstances were greatly different from the USA, with only 36 persons per square mile.

Arterial routes unimpeded by frequent junctions are preferred, since even if distances travelled are thereby increased, time — the governing criterion in transport — would be saved. Local traffic is to be segregated onto separate streets. The more closely homes, workplaces, etc. are clustered around an arterial route, the more efficiently it can serve its purposes. But the simplest system — *'one long strip'* — is obviously impossible for London. The ring and radial system is rejected since it makes traffic organisation more difficult, it does not suit the geographical position of London, and does not lend itself to future extension. Instead, a sufficient number of secondary arteries are developed at right-angles to a primary arterial route. Sections through 103 arterial routes indicate the elaboration of their manifold role in handling all manner of organised traffic — goods and passenger; long and shorter distance.

Cyclists and pedestrians are catered for, but motorists are confined to a separate road system. This is in the form of an orthogonal grid: a road runs on both sides of the primary rail artery, and parallel to it; from this, roads branch off at right-angles, midway between the secondary arteries; at right-angles again, roads connect to the residential areas, allowing motorists to leave for what are intended to be mainly recreational trips:

'With an excellently organised public transport system, the number of people going to and from town in private cars will be few, being confined mainly to certain professions. Other private cars would serve mainly for pleasure.'

A ring route for goods traffic, encircling the town at a sufficient distance to permit further growth, and with one diametrical link parallel to the primary artery, completes the preliminary schematic layout.

The whole was found to be remarkably well-suited to London. The primary artery, running E-W beside the Thames, would link successively Port, City, West End and Westminster, passing via industrial concentrations to link with the principal national axis extending towards Liverpool. Mainly residential belts, some 1½ miles wide and up to 8 miles long, would rehouse London's population at densities well within the officially recommended 55 persons per acre. 'Green wedges', extending from outskirts to city centre, would provide sites for recreation, health, and education, and everyone would live within walking distance of both borough centre and open county.

The MARS planners did not claim that they had necessarily come to the right conclusions — the information at their disposal was too thin, and their resources in every way too limited. Nor did they claim originality in all they proposed: borrowings from both Garden City and Le Corbusier are acknowledged. But they did claim to have pioneered, for England at least, new analytical methods which inevitably led to new and different conclusions. They conclude their work with outline proposals for the realisation of their plan over a period of twenty years. Much of London has indeed been rebuilt in the decades since their proposals were first published, and they could with justice claim that, however immature many of their ideas may have been, they could scarcely have produced a worse result than that which now confronts us.

*Somethin' like this may someday be the only way to live outside a city, if energy runs out.

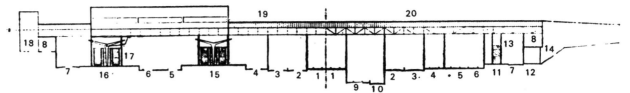

Cross section of secondary artery.

The left-hand part shows a section through the station, the right-hand part between stations. (1) Goods track (secondary goods station to market halls and shopping streets); (2) Goods road for same purpose; (3) Road for fast coaches, stopping only at the the end of secondary and at intersection with main artery; (4) Track for fast trains (same stops); (5) Track for intermediate trains, stopping every third station; (6) Track for trains stopping at every station   (7) Road for buses; (8) Cycle track, raised 8 ft.; (9) Branch of track leading downward to a cross tunnel into a shopping street; (10) Branch of road as track 9; (11) Pedestrian way, connecting platforms 16 for emergency, serves also as intermediate entry to buses; (12) Alternative entry to buses under cycle track; (13) Staircase to pedestrian bridge at intermediate bus stop; (14) Stairway to local street from bus stop; (15) Platform for tracks 4 and 5, every third stop only; (16) Platform for buses and ordinary trains, every mile; (17) Escalators; (18) Cycle lift (where required for difference of level); (19) Access road to station (no through traffic); (20) Intermediate pedestrian bridge (about 300 yards apart).

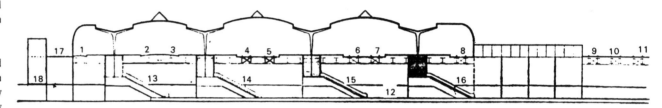

Cross section of main artery.

Only half the centre part (public vehicles) is shown. (1) Fast coaches, stopping at main stations only; (2) Slow coaches, stopping at every arterial crossing; (3) Buses stopping frequently; (4 and 5) Trains stopping at every station; (6 and 7) Trains stopping at crossings only (every 3 miles); (8) Trains stopping at main stations only; (9, 10, 11) Long distance trains; (12) Platform of secondary artery (crossing); (13, 14, 15, 16) Escalators; (17) Centre track; (18) Crossing cycle track and lift.

103   MARS plan: cross-sections of arterial routes

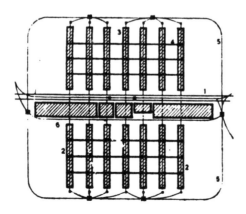

104   MARS plan: transport grid.
Diagrammatic Transport Grid
The main artery is alongside the work area, with local arteries serving the district units of 600,000 and the ring line serving the distribution centres on the outside of the town.

104

106 Brazilia — a new city conceived in sculpturally adventurous forms.

The architectural timidity of the first new towns, together with some deficiencies in their achievement, was, by the mid-'fifties, (in professional circles at least) lending new vigour to those who still hankered after the more radical approach of CIAM. By that time, Le Corbusier's first *Unité d'Habitation* was emerging from its scaffolding at Marseilles. From Holland and Scandinavia came reports of new work more adventurous than the pseudo-village-greens of Harlow and Stevenage. These greens were themselves under attack from the professional press as escapist and destructive of truly urban values. The young men returned from war had had time to assimilate the wartime work of CIAM groups, who throughout Europe had used enforced detachment from practice to improve theory. Outstanding here was the work of the French 'Ascoral' group, which under Le Corbusier's leadership, had continued to develop his ideas. By 1957 two outstanding 'moderns' — Lucia Costa and Oscar Niemeyer — were making known their plans for Brazilia, the brand new capital of Brazil, manifested in forms as sculpturally adventurous as Britain's new town cottages were conventionally restrained.

But above all there was the motor-car. After the immediate post-war austerity, car production had begun to mount, and new vehicles were pouring onto city streets in ever increasing numbers. From America came reports of elevated urban freeways, vast parking lots, grade-separated intersections — and *traffic engineering*.

Faced with an enormous road building programme, and with little guidance from town planning, United States highway engineers had turned their expertise in applied science to an investigation not only of roads and road construction, but of the traffic upon it: its origins and destinations; its physical characteristics of volume, speed, friction, flow — much as they had learnt to deal with a fluid in a pipe system, or particles in a soil. They thus introduced,

into one aspect of town planning, the precision of objectively determined measurement. Since almost every other aspect lacked any such precision, and since it was easy to show that previous estimates relating to the size of road networks were for the most part entirely wrong, traffic engineering quickly came to carry all before it, and at least for a decade after the late 'fifties, in country after country, almost replaced town planning. Nowhere was this more apparent than in the renewal of existing towns, which, during the same period, become more important than the building of new ones. Immediate post-war plans for 'rings and radials', subjected to the tests prescribed by the new science, were hastily modified to try to bring them into line with the mammoth demands foretold for the automobile. High streets were redesignated 'urban freeways', commons became car parks, and roundabouts flyovers. Slowness in execution has in most cases allowed time for more consideration of the consequences, but much has happened to show how disastrous it can be in town planning to lose Geddes' synoptic view and allow one aspect to over-ride all the others.

The first attempts to bring British town planning theory into line with the new discoveries about traffic came with two new towns. One — Cumbernauld — designated in 1955, has been built. The other, Hook, planned by the then London County Council to receive 'overspill' population into Hampshire, was never started. Together they marked a new departure in British planning.

Somewhat surprisingly in view of the outcome, it was not primarily the traffic deficiencies of the first new towns which Cumbernauld set out to correct, but the erroneous *'neighbourhood concept'*, which *'encourages people to look inwards'* to a local centre instead of *'visualising the town as a whole';* and attempted to regulate social life to a fixed pattern. To this end, a compact town was desired, tightly

He's dead wrong.

Le Corbusier's Unité d'Habitation at Marseilles, 1947-52. A suburb for 1600 people in one building.

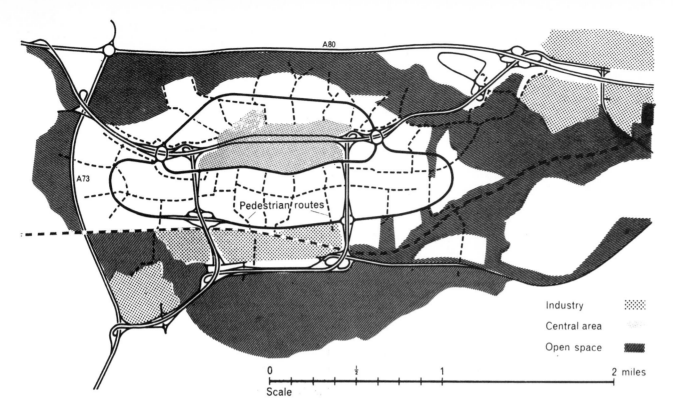

A80

A73

Pedestrian routes

Industry

Central area

Open space

0   ½   1   2 miles

Scale

107   Cumbernauld — basic plan.

clustered around a single centre. Of the three types of road pattern considered possible — radial, gridiron, or linear — the radial was regarded as appropriate to the hill-top site which had been designated for the town. There were to be two ring roads, one around the centre, one on the periphery giving access to 'Radburn' housing. An elongated multi-level centre could avoid central area traffic congestion and be within three-quarters of a mile from all residential areas.

The preliminary planning proposals, published in April 1958[117] had little more to say. Already it was apparent that traffic was posing unfamiliar problems: fifteen paragraphs of the 'Plan' are devoted to roads, in comparison to no more than two on the characteristics of the site. But a compact layout, entirely on the Radburn pattern, having a liberal provision of more-or-less conventional roads, was at that time expected in principle to suffice.

The First Revision of proposals, published in May 1959,[118] reports that a detailed traffic analysis had *'revealed a number of potential problems.'* A special team was researching into the matter, but there was little reliable knowledge from which projections could be made. But they rejected *'despairing suggestions'* that restrictions should be placed upon cars by *'rationing or higher taxation'* and (at least for the time being) *'fantastic schemes'* for moving pavements, monorails, or subsidised transport. The result is made most strikingly apparent in the comparison between the *'master diagram'** published earlier, and the now *'revised basic plan'*. Whereas the former marks in heavy lines the trunk roads *outside* the town, and the new roads within it are conceived as minor by comparison, the latter recognises reality: town roads, if they are to cater primarily for automobiles, are larger by far than their country cousins. Although the later plan retains 107 superficially the features of the first, the differences are overwhelming. The area of land required for roads is increased from 60 to nearly 108 acres, and tree belts are now proposed to separate their vast scale from that of normal life. The second addendum report, published in January 1962, shows no less than *fourteen* 'grade-separated' road junctions. For a total planned population of 70,000, and at a time when scarcely *one* had been built in any city in the Kingdom, this was bold planning indeed!

* The term 'master plan' was by this time dropping out of favour as smacking too much of certainty and dictatorship.

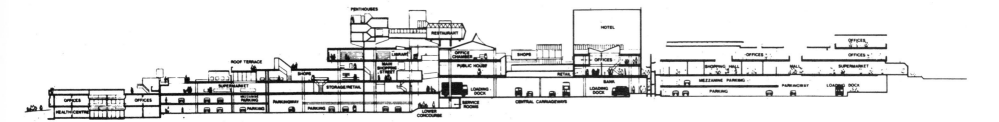

108 *Cumbernauld town centre.*

109 *Cumbernauld town centre — a sketch.*

The feature of Cumbernauld which has attracted most attention is its centre. This is in the form of a single multi-storey complex built immediately over a spine road, and with carparks and service areas linked by stairs and lifts to shops, offices, pubs and dwellings above. This solution to central area problems in the automobile age had been elaborated in detail a few years earlier in an unfulfilled plan for Fort Worth, Texas, designed to rescue its 'downtown' area from outside competition. 'Decks' over traffic areas were appearing on drawing boards everywhere as an answer to 'motorisation'. Planners in Sweden were proposing a similar multi-level centre for Vallingby, a satellite town for Stockholm. Alison and Peter Smithson had put forward a two-level scheme for the whole of central Berlin, and were advocating 'streets-in-the-air' as a panacea. The principle was also adopted for Hook, and since the report on that project elaborates the theoretical premises at some length, it will be well to learn what it has to say.

110 Alison and Peter Smithson, 1958: a pedestrian
network above a road network.

111 Park Hill, Sheffield: a multi-storey development with
'streets in the air'.

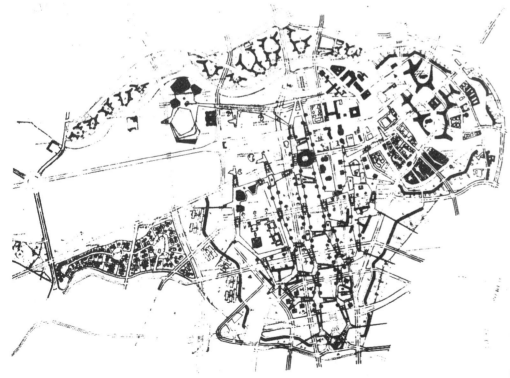

The Planning of a New Town [119] published by the London County Council in 1961, tells how a team of experts in all aspects of town planning had laboured over the preceding years to plan, in the light of all that could be learnt from previous experience, yet another new town to receive London's 'overspill'. The plan was unfulfilled, but they certainly did not labour in vain. Already by 1965 their report had run to five impressions, and was widely known throughout the world. It marks a high point in British town planning, comparable to the work of the Reith Committee, and sets a standard in argument and presentation which every succeeding new town report has tried to emulate. Not content with precedents, it went back to fundamentals, and in order to establish the validity of its proposals, pursued them into the same kind of detail as had Tony Garnier some fifty years before.

The principle aims are stated: to achieve 'urbanity'; to accommodate the motor-car; to maintain an appropriate contrast between town and country; to promote a balanced population, especially in terms of age groups. The first and third of these, result in a preference for compactness and 'hard surfaces' within the town, which should also have a coherent and intelligible structure. Population balance loomed large in view of recent so-called 'teen-age hooliganism' in Stevenage and elsewhere, and it was thought especially necessary to phase the growth of the town in such a way that the lop-sided age structure of the first new towns was avoided. The accommodation of the motor-car was to be on the estimated level of 1 car per household, plus visitor parking at half that rate, but was to be achieved in such a way that the pedestrian still took precedence.

For the given population of 100,000, (note the increase over the earlier new towns) the total area needed for the town could be calculated. This is found to be compounded of two elements: a constant (2,600 acres), which represents non-residential areas; and a variable representing 'residential land use'. The variable ranges from 3,600 acres at 100 persons per acre to 5,100 acres at 40 persons per acre. The total, when combined in a rectangular plan form, demonstrates how greatly residential density can influence distances (and consequently, traffic) within the town, and for this reason the highest possible density is preferred.*

In pursuit of 'coherence' and 'clarity', a strong centre is preferred also, and a schematic form emerges in which an elongated central area runs between residential zones nowhere more than half a mile deep, so that a short walk from the farthest house brings everyone to the central area.

The whole is surrounded by public open space and playing fields in such a way that the town creates its own green belt. Industry is distributed around the town to provide choice of employment, to prevent traffic build-up, and to forestall the creation of a low-class 'industrial side'. Industrial self-sufficiency is not aimed at — the town is conceived as a part of its regional economy — and offices are regarded as necessary to ensure a good social mix.

Vehicle and pedestrian segregation is complete. High capacity roads encircle the town and pass directly through its spine. There are numerous fly-overs and lavish carparks, as calculations showed that even with a town designed to promote pedestrian movement, the road demands of 'one-car-per-family' are high. But by resorting to bridges, decks and underpasses, a system of footpaths allows unimpeded walking from central area to open country in such a way that the footpath, and not the road, becomes the generator of the detailed form.

The neighbourhood concept is faulted on many counts, although lower density (i.e. 'better class') housing neighbourhoods were ultimately added to the outer town. The neighbourhood, it is said, is an over-simplified abstraction at odds with the rich complexity of social life. It does not lend itself to compactness. It is difficult to serve with public transport. Extant examples of 'Radburn' housing are also disapproved, and layouts with gardens onto the pedestrian side proposed as the right solution. The house-and-garden is (perhaps a little grudgingly) accepted as *what the people want* and terraces of mainly 2-storey houses are devised accordingly.

* Another diagram, added almost as a footnote, is honest enough to show that a circular plan is very little influenced in this way.

113

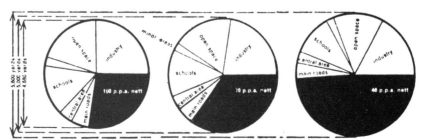

112

housing areas	other land uses	
	1. Industry	900 acres
	2. Open space	730 acres
	3. Main roads	200 acres
	4. Public utility services	50 acres
	5. Hospital	25 acres
	6. Central area	160 acres
	7. Secondary	
	8. Further education	schools 535 acres
	9. Primary	
		2,600 acres

total area of town 3,600 acres

residential area at **100 p.p.a. nett** 1,000 acres

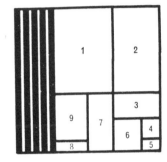

total area of town 4,029 acres

residential area at **70 p.p.a. nett** 1,429 acres

total area of town 5,100 acres

residential area at **40 p.p.a. nett** 2,500 acres

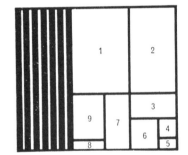
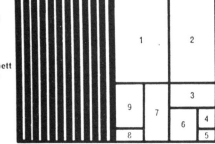

115 *Hook: complete vehicle/pedestrian segregation.*

central area

housing

100 persons per acre

70 persons per acre

40 persons per acre

special housing

industry

secondary schools

primary schools

playing fields

open space

woodland

lakes

cemetery

heliport

hospital

North

114 *Hook: the master plan.*

0   1 mile   2 miles   3 miles

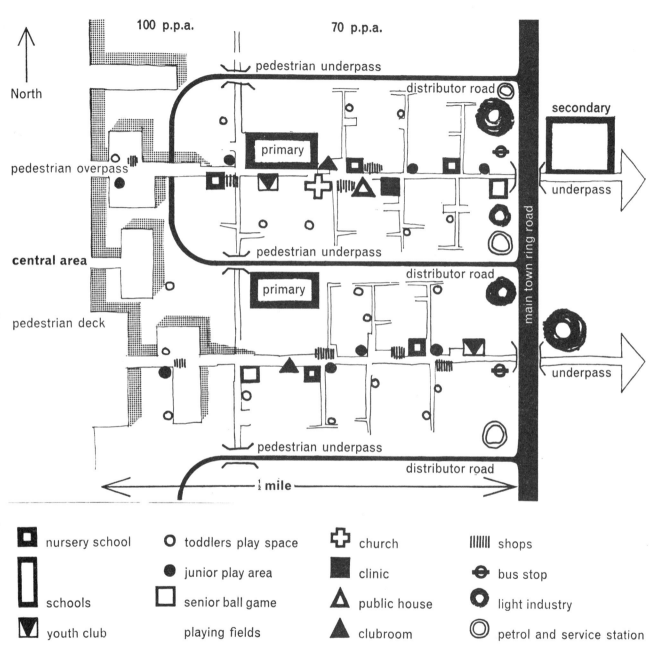

100 p.p.a. 70 p.p.a.

North

pedestrian underpass

distributor road

secondary

primary

pedestrian overpass

underpass

central area

pedestrian underpass

distributor road

primary

pedestrian deck

underpass

main town ring road

pedestrian underpass

distributor road

½ mile

◧	nursery school	○	toddlers play space	✚	church	▥	shops
▯	schools	●	junior play area	■	clinic	☦	bus stop
▼	youth club	☐	senior ball game	△	public house	◉	light industry
			playing fields	▲	clubroom	◎	petrol and service station

*116 Hook: a new form of town street linking central area
to open country.*

117 Hook: pedestrian way with children's play area.

118 Hook: a 70 person-per-acre cul-de-sac group.

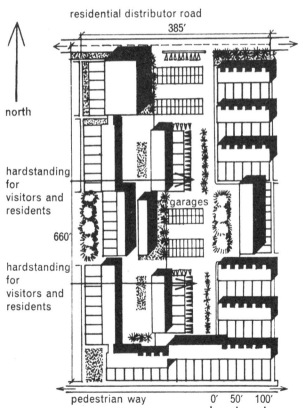

residential distributor road

385'

north

hardstanding
for
visitors and
residents

garages

660'

hardstanding
for
visitors and
residents

pedestrian way

0' 50' 100'

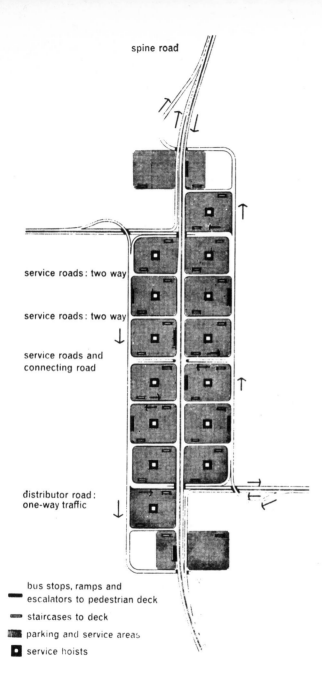

spine road

service roads : two way

service roads : two way

service roads and
connecting road

distributor road :
one-way traffic

▬ bus stops, ramps and
   escalators to pedestrian deck

▬ staircases to deck

▦ parking and service areas

■ service hoists

*121 Hook: the central area. Ground level roads and
service areas.*

122 Hook: the central area from the pedestrian deck.

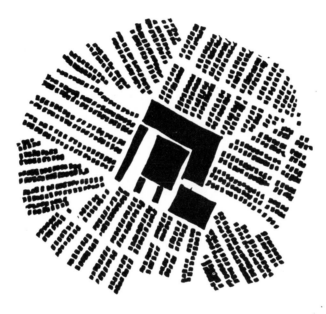

*119 A 'moat of carparks' around an American shopping
centre.*
*120 Hook: section through the central area showing
pedestrian 'decks' over roads and parking areas below.*

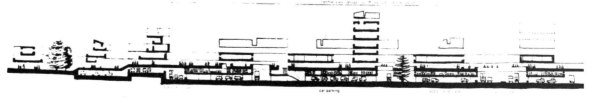

car parking

450 feet

There is to be a hierarchy of open spaces — from garden to open country — and the use of open space as a *'dividing element'* is eschewed. The main pedestrian ways are seen as *'a new form of street'* and, as well as leading directly to the centre, are themselves conceived as a succession of focal points for local community activity. Housing is organised into super-blocks, orientated with regard to sunlight, and dimensioned with reference to desirable walking distances (half-a-mile) and maximum permitted cul-de-sac lengths (600 ft.) The resulting area (80 acres) at 70 persons per acre and an 'occupancy rate' of 0.89, produces a total population of about 5,000 — sufficient to support a 2-form entry primary school. Add back also the local provision of clinics, clubs, corner shops, etc., and we have, somewhat surreptitiously, gone at least halfway to bringing back the neighbourhood.

The Report illustrates what was intended for the centre. An explicit aim was to avoid a *'moat of carparks'* around it, and some 56 acres of carpark, together with service areas, bus stations and a hierarchical grid of roads, is placed underground. At one end, the centre is left free to grow, so that it may keep pace with any unforeseen expansion of the whole.

It is significant that public transport is specifically catered for — both in the central area, and by the provision of stops at each underpass of the peripheral road — not simply as an optional frill, but to cater for the many who even in the coming 'motopia' would be without the use of a car. There is a link with the railway, conceived not so much as a service to industry, as to the 'commuter'.

Although most of the illustration is in terms of Hook, the site in Hampshire chosen for the experiment, most aspects of the basic form were arrived at, in Le Corbusier's fashion, 'on the drawing board' — and only then was the site chosen. Indeed, the report makes clear that a valley running approximately N-S was the most appropriate landform, and the choice fell accordingly. The elaboration of the scheme in situ gave promise of what, had it been achieved, would have been civic and landscape design of the highest quality.

116
117

118

119
120
121
122

208

111

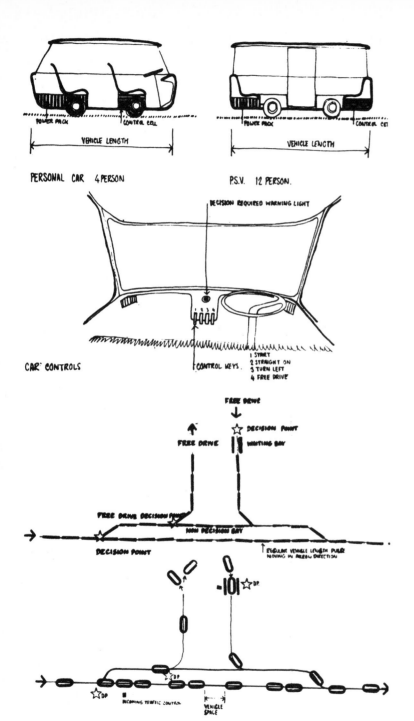

PERSONAL CAR 4 PERSON   P.S.V. 12 PERSON.

DECISION REQUIRED WARNING LIGHT

CAR CONTROLS

CONTROL KEYS.

1 START
2 STRAIGHT ON
3 TURN LEFT
4 FREE DRIVE

FREE DRIVE

DECISION POINT

FREE DRIVE   WAITING BAY

FREE DRIVE DECISION POINT

NON DECISION BAY

DECISION POINT

REGULAR VEHICLE LENGTH PULSE
MOVING IN ARROW DIRECTION

DP.

DP

DP

INCOMING TRAFFIC CONTROL

VEHICLE
SPACE

123—124 *Electronically-guided road vehicles: sketches made by B. Berrett in 1962 showing how such a system could combine the advantages of the automobile with those of the train.*

Whether Hook would have provided all the answers will never be known. The proposal was shelved at a time when new towns were going temporarily out of fashion, and 'urban renewal' coming in. Traffic chaos, and stop-gap measures to meet it, together with the ravages of time and property speculators, were making painfully clear the need for a strategic re-appraisal of our existing towns. The result was the government publication *'Traffic in Towns'*: the epoch-making *'Buchanan Report'* of 1963.[120]

This, the production in its entirety of a group of expert planners, begins by recapitulating those relevant aspects of the 'state of the art' we have already reviewed. Prognosis revealed the likelihood that by the year 2010 A.D. 'saturation' would be reached in motor-car ownership and usage. By that time, a car would be available for everyone wanting to use one (about half the forecast total UK population of 74 millions) and *'nothing would be more dangerous ... than to underestimate ...'* The years up to 1980 would see the most rapid rates of increase, and it would be *'a miscalculation of the mood of the country'* to imagine that car ownership would be deterred by congestion and frustration. While acknowledging that other problems (especially the forecast increase in population) were at least as significant as those directly concerning traffic, they accepted their brief which was *'to study the long-term development of roads and traffic in urban areas and their influence upon the urban environment'*. Acknowledging also the need for further research into methods of transport generally, they believed that the motor-vehicle, or something similar, had an assured future.

'There are so many advantages in a fairly small, independent, self-powered and highly manoeuverable means of getting about at ground level, for both people and goods, that it is unlikely we shall ever wish to abandon it. It may have a different source of motive power so that it is no longer strictly a motor vehicle, it may be quieter and without fumes, it may be styled in some quite different way, it may be produced in smaller forms, it may be guided and controlled in certain streets by electronic means, it may have the ability to perform sideways movement, but for practical purposes it will present most of the problems that are presented by the motor vehicle of today.'

Although

'given its head the motor vehicle would wreck our towns within a decade ... the public can justifiably demand to be fully informed about the possibilities of adapting towns to motor traffic before there is any question of applying restrictive measures.'

With cold reasoning, they proceed to demolish the popular misconceptions about urban traffic. It does 'not come in from the outside'. The larger the city, the larger the proportion of its traffic which begins and ends its journeys within the town. Railways within towns, no matter how intensively used, still leave the final distribution from station or depot to be done by road. Urban journey patterns are extremely complex, and cannot be satisfied by such simplifications as 'rings and radials'. But the problem was susceptible to analysis, it could be investigated and understood. And the solution lay in organising in a rational manner both the layout of buildings, which generated the traffic, and the ways giving access to them. It was essentially a matter of design.

Every architect today is familiar with Le Corbusier's dictum: *'When the problem is clearly stated, the solution is at hand.'* Thus, with commendable clarity, Buchanan proceeds to state the problem. It was

'... no different in its essentials from the circulation problem that arises every day in the design of buildings, where the subject is well understood. The basic principle is the simple one of circulation, and is illustrated by the familiar case of corridors and rooms. Within a large hospital, for example,

there is a complex traffic problem. A great deal of movement is involved — patients arrive at reception, are moved to wards, then perhaps to operating theatres and back to wards. Doctors, consultants, sisters and nurses go their rounds. Food, books, letters, medicines and appliances of many kinds have to be distributed. A good deal of this includes wheeled-traffic. The principle on which it is all contrived is the creation of areas of environment (wards, operating theatres, consulting rooms, laboratories, kitchens, libraries, etc.) which are served by a corridor system for the primary distribution of traffic. This is not to say no movement takes place within the areas of environment, since even in a hospital ward there is a drift of movement up and down the ward, but it is strictly controlled so that the environment does not suffer. If for some reason movement tends to build up beyond the ability of the environment to accept it, then something is quickly done to curtail or divert it. The one thing that is never allowed to happen is for an environmental area to be opened to through traffic — food trolleys being trundled through the operating theatre would indicate a fundamental error in circulation planning.

'There is no principle other than this on which to contemplate the accommodation of motor traffic in towns and cities, whether it is a design for a new town on an open site, or the adaptation of an existing town. There must be areas of good environment — urban rooms — where people can live, work, shop, look about, and move around on foot in reasonable freedom from the hazards of motor traffic. and there must be a complementary network of roads — urban corridors — for effecting the primary distribution of traffic to the environmental areas. These areas are not free of traffic — they cannot be if they are to function — but the design would ensure that their traffic is related in character and volume to the environmental conditions being sought. If this concept is pursued it can easily be seen that it results in the whole of the town taking on a cellular structure consisting of environmental areas set within an interlacing network of distributory highways. It is a simple concept, but without it the whole subject of urban traffic remains confused, vague and without comprehensive objectives. Once it is adopted then everything begins to clarify. It is not by any means a new idea, for Sir Alker Tripp was advocating something on these lines over 20 years ago, and the precincts and neighbourhoods of the County of London Plan reflected the same approach. But in the face of the rapidly increasing number of vehicles it acquires a new urgency: it now requires to be explored and developed from a mere concept into a set of working rules for practical application.

'Some implications of the concept may now be considered. As applied to a whole town, it would produce a series of areas within each of which considerations of environment would predominate. These areas would be tied together by the interlacing network of distributory roads onto which all longer movements would be canalised without choice. As explained previously, in principle it would not be unlike a gigantic building with corridors serving a multitude of rooms. The relationship between the network and the environmental areas would therefore be essentially a service relationship: the function of the network would be to serve the environmental areas and not vice versa. This may seem elementary but in fact it is one of the things which this approach puts into the right perspective, it brings it home that traffic and roads are not ends in themselves, they are services only, the end is the environment for living and working.

'It follows from this that there must be a capacity relationship between the network and the environmental areas. As a rule, in most cases, the network would be designed to suit the capacity of the areas just as a water pipe is designed to suit the cistern it serves. It would be unwise, for instance, to feed in wide roads stimulating much vehicular movement from suburban areas, if the central areas were not capable of accommodating the traffic. Conversely it would not be satisfactory to redevelop a town centre with large office blocks with huge car parks if the network could not deal adequately with the resulting traffic. This second example is one where technical consequences arising from the network. in spite of its service function, exercise a controlling influence over the capacity for traffic of the whole town. The main point, however, is that the concept of a network and areas puts highway capacity, and the capacity of buildings to generate traffic, into an understandable relationship on a calculable basis . . .

'The function of the distributory network is to canalise the longer movements from locality to locality. The links of the network should therefore be designed for swift, efficient movement. This means that they cannot also be used for giving direct access to buildings, nor even to minor roads serving the buildings, because the consequent frequency of the junctions would give rise to traffic dangers and disturb the efficiency of the road. It is therefore necessary to introduce the idea of a 'hierarchy' of distributors, whereby important distributors feed down through distributors of lesser category to the minor roads which give access to the buildings. The system may be likened to the trunk, limbs, branches, and finally the twigs (corresponding to the access roads) of a tree. Basically, however, there are only two kinds of roads — distributors designed for movement, and access roads to serve the buildings.

'The number of stages required in a distributory hierarchy will depend upon the size and arrangement of the town. For the purpose of nomenclature we think it is preferable to refer to the main network of any town as the town or primary network. This may then be broken down into district and local distributor systems as the conditions demand, and in the 'opposite direction' it may have to link to regional or even national networks. Thus a primary network for a town of 10,000 population would be likely to be less powerful in character than in the case of a town of 500,000 population, but in both cases the function would be to effect the primary distribution over the town . . .

'The idea of the network is comparatively easy to understand, but the concept of environmental areas is more difficult. These are the 'rooms' of the town; they are the areas or groups of buildings and other development in which daily life is carried on, and where, as a consequence, it is logical that the maintenance of a good environment is of great importance. The term 'precinct' (a long-standing term in town planning) cannot be used for these areas because it now connotes the idea of a place that is entirely free from motor traffic. It cannot be emphasised too strongly that the environmental areas envisaged here may be busy areas in which there is a considerable amount of traffic, but there is no extraneous traffic, no drifts of traffic filtering through without business in the area. Any kind of development — residential, industrial, commercial, etc. or even mixed uses — can form an environmental area, but naturally the environmental standards will vary according to the kind of area, just as they vary between, say, the kitchen of a house and the bedrooms. Safety will be an overriding consideration in all kinds of area, but, to give an example, much more importance would be attached to freedom from noise in a residential than in an industrial area.

'The maximum size of an environmental area is governed by the need to prevent its own traffic building up to a volume that in effect necessitates sub-division by the insertion of a further distributory link in the network . . . it should be said here that no sociological content is implied by our concept of environmental areas. There is no connection for example with the idea of 'neighbourhoods', the concept is no more and no less than a method of arranging buildings for motor traffic. In fact, a neighbourhood of 10,000 people, which was the unit

Otley
Ilkley

Harrogate

Wetherby

Shipley
Horsforth

Tadcaster

Pudsey
Bradford

Garforth
Selby

Morley
Halifax

Wakefield
Castleford
Barnsley

Dewsbury

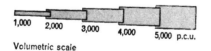

1,000   2,000   3,000   4,000   5,000 p.c.u.

Volumetric scale

External traffic   in
                   out
Internal traffic

**125   Leeds: 'desire lines' for the work-journeys by vehicle
during the peak-hour in 2010 A.D.**

*size postulated in the County of London Plan, would certainly
require subdivision into a number of environmental areas.*

'The idea that within an environmental area the traffic
(using the term of course, to include stationary as well as
moving vehicles . . .) should be subordinated to the environment, carries with it the important implication that any
environmental area must have a maximum acceptable level of
traffic. It must, in other words, have a maximum capacity.
This may be seen by considering the case of an area of
terraced houses in conventional streets with narrow
pavements. The amount of traffic within such an area would
obviously have to be curtailed if reasonable standards of
environment were to be secured. The acceptable amount of
traffic should, in theory, be calculable. In order to ensure that
it is not exceeded it might be sufficient (assuming it is an
environmental area in the making) merely to exclude all
extraneous vehicles, but even then the area's own traffic
might increase beyond the limit as a result, say, of the
conversion of the houses to flats, or as a result of an
unexpectedly high car ownership rate. In this event there
would either have to be a regrettable lowering of the
environmental standards, or a curtailment of the
accessibility. But there would also be the possibility of
making, at a price, physical alterations to the area, for
example by providing garages for cars which would otherwise
be left on the street, or perhaps rearranging the area
altogether by rebuilding.*

'**Three variables.** *So, with respect to any environmental
area, the traffic problem can be approached in terms of three
main variables — the standard of environment, the level of
accessibility and the cost that can be incurred on physical
alterations. These can be related in a rough and ready 'law'.
It is that* within any urban area as it stands the establishment
of environmental standards automatically determines the
accessibility, but the latter can be increased according to the
amount of money that can be spent on physical alterations. *In
plain words this means that if it is indeed desired to have a
great deal of traffic in urban areas in decent conditions it is
likely to cost a great deal of money to make the necessary
alterations. The idea that any urban area, as it stands, has a
definable traffic capacity if the environment is to be secured,
is very important. There is really nothing strange about it. A
factory is designed for so much plant and so many operatives;
a school is designed for so many children; a house will hold so
many occupants and if more are crammed into it, it becomes
a slum. There is some elasticity in capacity, but not much. All*

that is being said here is that exactly the same kind of rule must apply to an area occupied by buildings and the amount of traffic it can decently contain.'[121]

In order to test their ideas in practice, Buchanan and his colleagues then made a series of field studies. For the first they chose Newbury, a Berkshire town with about 30,000 inhabitants and the same number in its dependent hinterland. For the second, they chose Leeds, an industrial city of about 500,000. For the third, Norwich was selected as typical of a town valued on historical and architectural grounds. And finally, they looked at a part of Marylebone, in central London.

It is of interest first to note the method of investigation. The pattern emerges most strongly in the Leeds study. The first step is to establish the locations and general characteristics of the various 'land uses' as they would be in the foreseeable future. Since the journey-to-work generates the maximum movement, the next step is to predict how many will move from each residential zone to each employment zone. Other significant peak-hour movements — goods, business, shopping, etc. — are similarly estimated. This total 'traffic generation' is then translated into numbers of vehicles, having regard to likely future levels of car ownership in each residential area, the numbers likely to walk to work, etc. The resulting 'desire-line diagrams' illustrate the relative volumes of vehicular traffic which in 2010 AD would be moving in the directions plotted if everything could move 'as the crow flies'.

Since ground vehicles are not crows, the next step is to devise in principle an efficient 'primary network' of routes comprising the least number of links which could theoretically satisfy the predicted peak hour movements.

Having thus decided where, if nothing were in the way, the future main roads of the town would lie, it is now necessary to fit these to the realities of the urban environment. The 'environmental areas,' out of which all 'through' traffic is to be excluded must be defined. Special attention is paid here to what might be called the 'social fabric' of the town. Focal points, such as groups of shops and schools and their 'catchment areas' are of special significance, and the city is divided into sections *'possessed of a homogeneity which prima facie should not be cut up by the major distributors'.* The 'primary network' may then be 'bent on', so to speak, to the 'social contours' of the town, and the main essentials of the plan are complete.*

It should be noted that the method is described as it

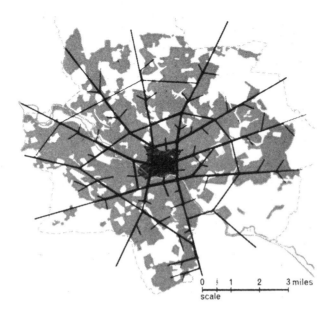

126   *Leeds: a theoretical primary network.*

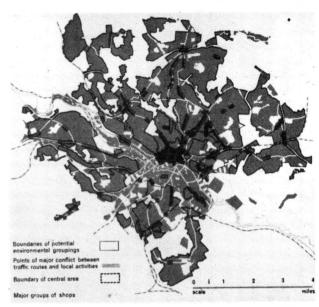

127   *Leeds: defining the areas where extraneous traffic is to be excluded.*

128   *Leeds: the primary network 'bent on' to the social contours of the city.*

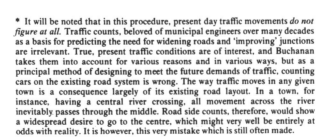

* It will be noted that in this procedure, present day traffic movements *do not figure at all.* Traffic counts, beloved of municipal engineers over many decades as a basis for predicting the need for widening roads and 'improving' junctions are irrelevant. True, present traffic conditions are of interest, and Buchanan takes them into account for various reasons and in various ways, but as a principal method of designing to meet the future demands of traffic, counting cars on the existing road system is wrong. The way traffic moves in any given town is a consequence largely of its existing road layout. In a town, for instance, having a central river crossing, all movement across the river inevitably passes through the middle. Road side counts, therefore, would show a widespread desire to go to the centre, which might very well be entirely at odds with reality. It is however, this very mistake which is still often made.

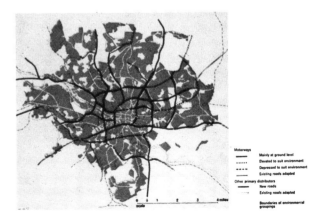

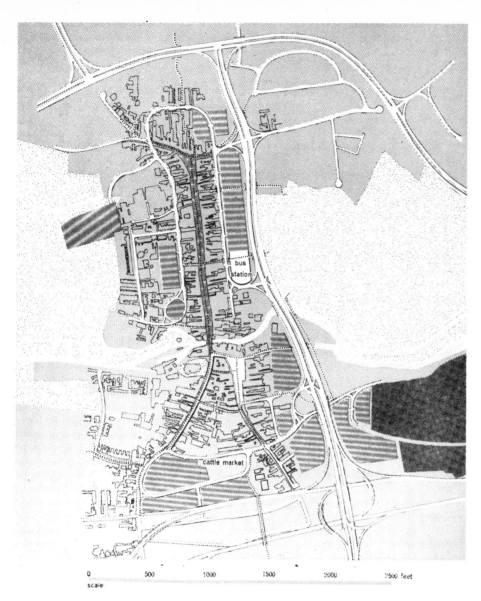

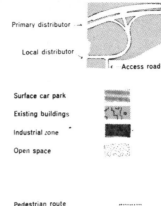

Primary distributor →

Local distributor →

← Access road

Surface car park

Existing buildings

Industrial zone

Open space

Pedestrian route

Pedestrian precinct

bus station

cattle market

| 0 | 500 | 1000 | 1500 | 2000 | 2500 feet |

scale

129 Newbury: minimum redevelopment:
South of the river, complete vehicle/pedestrian segregation
is prevented by the retention of existing buildings, but
'cost-benefit analysis' favoured this scheme.

applies to the existing town, mainly on the assumption that its future pattern of land use and other factors were given. Buchanan concedes that it may on occasion be necessary to plan for *'the rearrangement or regrouping of environmental areas'* but this is regarded as something in general to be avoided. With a new town, of course, it would be possible to designate land uses and social groupings in such a way that optimal conditions were obtained for both environment and access, as subsequent new town planners have (as we shall see) been well aware.

In making predictions about future traffic patterns, Buchanan makes use of techniques evolved by traffic engineers (mainly in America). Chief among these is the use of a 'gravity model,' which he describes as follows:

'We divided the whole city into zones, and then estimated the inter-zonal movements that would be likely to take place having regard to the resident and/or employed population in each zone, the amount of floor space devoted to particular land uses in each zone, the distances between zones, and the travel habits of people in given circumstances.'[122]

The technique was used mainly because direct evidence was at the time not available, but spot checks confirmed that the results were not far out. These methods have since been elaborated and extended into other aspects of planning.

In the case of Newbury, it was found entirely possible to arrange new roads in such a way that a decent environment was retained, while everyone who wanted to, was able to run around in cars. But Buchanan's 'law' allowed that environmental standards could vary, and the amount of money available could be a limiting factor. Accordingly, four schemes were investigated: one, *minimum redevelopment,* retained the old centre more or less in its entirety on 'environmental' grounds and restricted access accordingly. The second — *partial redevelopment* — allowed some rebuilding in the centre at the expense of less-important historic buildings, and a corresponding improvement in vehicle/pedestrian segregation and in vehicular accessibility. The third — *comprehensive redevelopment* — threw caution to the winds and allowed the wholesale reconstruction of the centre, resulting in a layout which combined the highest standards for both pedestrian and motor vehicle. Finally, they considered,
'what would be the result if the local authority, while accepting that nothing could prevent the eventual build-up of private cars to the maximum,

117

nevertheless decided that it could not face the cost of anything more than a modest network with conventional roundabouts for intersections. We assumed that the environmental standard for the shopping and business streets could not be seriously departed from, and that it would still be necessary to clear all or most of the traffic out.' [123]

Only 60% of the potential demand for the general use of cars could be met with such a *'restricted network,'* and this might result in loss of retail trade vital to a market town.

Another relatively new technique was introduced by Buchanan in order to effect a choice among these possibilities: *cost-benefit analysis.* In an appendix he translates into comparable terms all the social gains and costs involved in the 'restricted', 'minimum' and 'partial' schemes. The calculations tended to favour the 'minimum' scheme.

The Newbury study allowed that the existing urban fabric could be rearranged to some considerable extent. In Norwich this was not so. Here,

'any general policy of widening the existing streets . . . must be ruled out because this would destroy the historic character . . . Similarly, to remove large numbers of buildings in the centre to make way for car parks, would destroy the traditional compactness . . .' Thus:

'the main principle is abundantly clear — if the environment is sacrosanct, and if no major reconstruction can be undertaken, then accessibility must be limited. There can be no question about this. Once this simple truth is recognised for areas of this kind, and future attempts to cater for the whole future demands of traffic are put aside, then planning can be started on a realistic basis. It becomes a matter of deciding what level of accessibility can be provided and how it can be arranged, and then it is a question of public relations to ensure that the position is clearly understood.

'The problem resolves itself into an exercise in environmental management on a big scale, with the whole of the old city forming one potential environmental area. The steps required to establish an environmental area are as follows:

(i) Numbers, types and speeds of vehicles to be kept down to a level compatible with environmental standards.

(ii) Circulation of essential traffic to destinations to be contrived, but not necessarily by the shortest route nor even with any choice of route.

(iii) Streets and areas which are used predominantly by pedestrians to be converted for pedestrian use only.

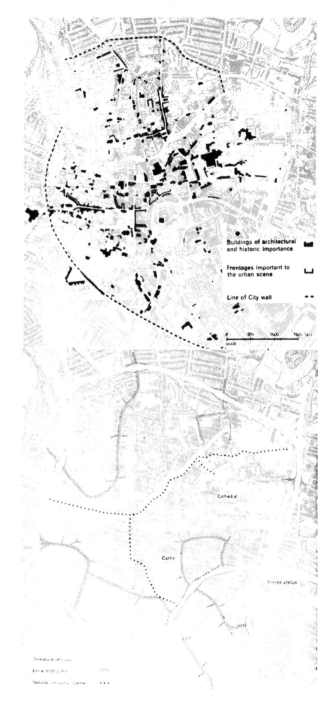

130 Norwich: '. . . if the environment is sacrosanct, and if no major reconstruction can be undertaken, then accessibility must be limited'.

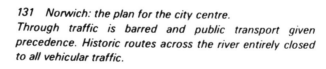

131 Norwich: the plan for the city centre.
Through traffic is barred and public transport given precedence. Historic routes across the river entirely closed to all vehicular traffic.

(iv) **All through movements to be prevented.**

(v) **Internal movements to be reorganised to eliminate the conflict of criss-cross journeys.'[124]**

On the assumption that a primary network for the city as a whole would bring traffic as far as the vicinity of the old city wall, within the centre itself the solution adopted envisaged closing to vehicular traffic historic N-S links across the river, and restricting the use of city centre streets almost exclusively to essential traffic and buses.

Thus in Norwich, the built environment dictated the accessibility — the traffic levels which could be permitted. In the Marylebone study, the opposite is found to apply.

Since to prepare a plan for the whole of London was clearly out of the question, it was necessary to make some assumptions, especially about a future 'primary network'. In view of the 'obvious' characteristics of Central London, an orthogonal grid was thought to be appropriate. Although the realities of the study area were adhered to, the study itself then became to a large extent abstract: the *'study of an area bounded on two adjoining sides by primary distributors.'[125]*

It was first of all possible theoretically to show that an orthogonal grid of primary roads, and the 'super-blocks' they enclosed, had certain measurable relationships. If the grid were widely spaced, too much traffic might be generated by a super-block for it to accept, and traffic within the super-block would itself begin to demand roads of primary standard. If spacing were too close, it would not be possible to provide sufficient junctions. Also traffic which ought to remain within the superblock would be using the primary grid. Calculations shewed that a grid 4,500 ft. square permitted the highest level of generation per hour. It follows from this that no matter what redevelopment was considered appropriate from other points of view, in terms of its capacity to generate traffic, it would have to be kept within definable limits (estimated as equivalent to 12,200 cars per hour). Effectively, therefore, it is shown that no matter how ambitious in terms of high-capacity roads a planner was prepared to be, there is an upper limit somewhere, and this had implications for the type and intensity of development he might wish to propose. The limitation arises mainly from the fact that, in any route system, it is not the route itself, but the junctions (in that they cannot be too closely spaced) which ultimately determine its capacity.

		A	B	C	D
1	Grid dimensions (feet)	3000 × 2150	3000 × 3000	4500 × 4500	6000 × 6000
2	Area enclosed (acres)	148	208	467	832
3	No. of ramps	2	4	8	12
4	Possible traffic exodus rate p.c.u./hr.	6,000	12,000	24,000	36,000
5	Additional internal generation p.c.u./hr.	1,200	4,700	14,000	24,000
6	Total permissible generation for the grid area p.c.u./hr.	7,200	16,700	38,000	60,000
7	Study area as % of grid area	100	71	32	17
8	Total permissible generation for study area p.c.u./hr.	7,200	11,850	12,200	10,200

133 *Marylebone: grid capacities and maximum permissible traffic generation for four possible arrangements.*

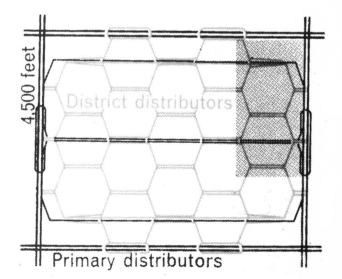

132 *Marylebone: the study area: 'an area bounded on two adjoining sides by primary distributors'.*

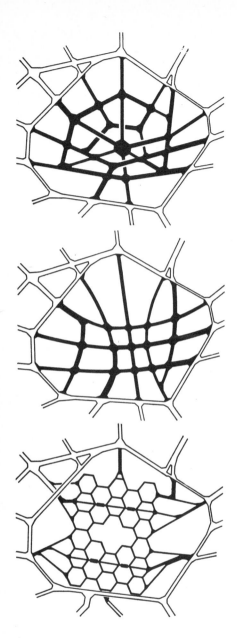

134 *Leeds: three alternative arrangements for roads within the city centre.*
The first is a ring-and-radial system. The second is based on an orthogonal grid. The third is a two-tier hexagonal system. All three would be impracticable.

We have reserved until last the study of Leeds, since it is from this that the Buchanan Report's most significant conclusion emerges. Before attempting to fit in a primary network big enough to cope with the maximum foreseeable demand, Buchanan thought it well to look at the city centre, where it was likely that it might be difficult to insert all the car parks and the roads necessary to distribute the traffic that would be arriving there. After looking at every possibility, it was found

134 *'. . . the network which is needed would be quite impracticable. In theory, the area . . . could be served by a series of cul-de-sacs. Six would have to penetrate as far as the central business area, and a further eight would be needed to serve the densely developed belt around this. Such a system would however throw an additional load onto the cross-links, which would then be quite unmanageable. Three possible arrangements have therefore been examined which provide direct access to all parts of the centre. The first is based on a conventional ring and radial system; the second is based on a grid-iron plan with a bias towards the area of greatest traffic generation in the centre. Both of these would be quite impossible in practice, because the distance between the intersections of the network is so small that there would be little or no opportunity to provide access to the very area it sets out to serve. The first also produces the greatest concentration of traffic at the very heart of the centre where new road works would be the most difficult and costly to construct. The third scheme is based on a two-tier system of one-way hexagons, the inner system being more tightly-knit and made independent of the outer by means of connections direct to the network. It is considered that this would be just about feasible, but only if it were possible to redevelop the whole of the area covered by the hexagons, some 2,000 acres.*

'It is thus concluded that there is no possibility whatsoever, in a town of this size and nature, of planning for the level of traffic induced by the unrestricted use of the motor car for the journey to work in conditions of full car ownership.'

Bent on pursuing his initial intention, which was to see how far the motorist could be satisfied before there was any talk of restriction, Buchanan looks at the possibility of an 'intermediate' solution for Leeds, putting onto buses as small a proportion of the load as possible. The best he can do results in well over half the total having to go by bus or some means other than the motor-car.

Buchanan had backed his written findings with copious illustration, many of them pictures of ambitious 'traffic architecture', with roads and car parks at various levels. 135 Because these were much easier to assimilate than the text, it has since been popularly supposed that he was advocating the universal remodelling of our cities in the interests of Standard Oil and General Motors. As our summary shows, this was very far from the truth. While throughout he uncritically reiterates his belief that the motor-car (with its present inadequacies) is here to stay, he advocates policies a long way from complete surrender to its more unreasonable demands. His field studies — especially those of Newbury and Leeds — shew in considerable detail how new high-capacity roads could be inserted into towns without wrecking them. He had shewn that there was considerable scope for the precision of measurement in town planning, and gave those opposed to the blindness of much that had been done in the name of traffic engineering, the rudiments of a scientific answer. He had proved that, beyond a certain size, it was impossible to design for mainly 'private' transport, and that for our larger cities at least, we had to continue to place considerable reliance upon a public service. In the practice of urban renewal, regrettably little understanding has been shewn of the principles he was urging — in spite of much lip-service. Regrettably also, he misleadingly pursued his discovery concerning public transport in terms of still trying to please the motorist. But others — especially designers of new towns — have developed his conclusions and his methods in more promising directions, as we shall see.

As if to underline the fact that it had been Buchanan's task to consider motor traffic in isolation, at about the same time as he was preparing his report, others were preparing a vast reduction in the only purpose-made national route system Britain had — the railways. Co-ordinated transport planning, advocated by every town planner at least since 1920, continued to receive verbal support, but in practice was deliberately undermined.

135 *Marylebone: an impression of a scheme for complete redevelopment.*
Pictures of ambitious 'traffic architecture' have misled many to assume that Buchanan was advocating complete surrender to the automobile.

● *Group 1 New Towns*

■ *Group II (Cumbernauld)*

□ *Group III*

△ *Town Expansion (Group III)*

As a result of all-too-apparent shortcomings, and especially the continued despoliation of the urban environment, planners and planning itself began to come under attack. In 1961, Jane Jacobs wrote her *'Death and Life of Great American Cities'* in which she set out to refute every shibboleth of planning as she understood it. Against Le Corbusier's rejection of the corridor-street, she acclaims its virtues, especially in terms of its role as the social focus of a locality. Against the division of the city into 'use-zones', she advocates the richness which variety brings. Against the desire for open spaces, she upholds the wisdom of every American mother, who knows a child is much safer on the 'sidewalk', silently watched by a hundred anonymous eyes, than in the park, where the peace is only broken by *'the occasional sound of someone being mugged'*. Instead of the attrition of the city by automobiles, she advocates the attrition of automobiles by the city, i.e. making the footpaths wider, slowing the traffic down, discouraging traffic intrusion where it was not needed. In place of the destruction of older areas in the name of 'comprehensive redevelopment', she urges the banding together of the local citizenry to fight 'City Hall,' and force the retention of a multitude of old buildings wherein could flourish small businesses, and all the intricacy and richness of truly urban life.

While American experience would suggest that mugging is by no means confined to the parks, and the sidewalks themselves are not as safe as she proclaims, there was none-the-less in her criticism sufficient sense for it to cause some reappraisal of aims and methods among town planners. A loss of certainty begins to characterise current thinking on every aspect of the subject. The disciples of Ebenezer Howard were old men, and regarded as old-fashioned. CIAM proclaimed its mission accomplished, disbanded itself and allowed its *avant garde* mantle to fall on new shoulders: notably the Smithsons in England, Buckminster Fuller in the United States, and Doxiadis in Greece. Means begin to

attract more attention than ends. Throughout the whole of architecture, there is a growing vogue for 'design theory' which, especially in terms of 'systems analysis' begins to turn town planning away from socio-political objectives towards an almost total preoccupation with technique.

The tendency continues, but has not been without positive results. The first of these in Britain, was a reappraisal of statutory planning procedures. In future, a sharper distinction was to be made between *strategic* long-term objectives or 'structure plans,' which were to be less precisely formulated than hitherto, and *tactical* 'action plans' for localities. By the middle of the decade, regional studies concerned especially with local economy were in hand, and 136 alongside these arose a crop of proposals for yet more new towns.

As a portent of the new approaches these were to evince, and as an able illustration of the kind of thinking then in vogue, a proposal for new towns (prepared under the patronage of a firm interested in promoting its products in the building industry) by two architects — Gordon Cullen and Richard Matthews — is worth noting. *'A Town Called Alcan'*, published in 1964 demonstrates how completely dominant was the current concern with traffic and how the answer was seen in the *linear form*.

All zoning is abandoned. The whole town is disposed along 137 a linear route which combines all modes of transport. The 138 linear route is closed into a circle — largely to facilitate public transport. Everyone lives, works, shops and goes to school within a few yards of the transport system. The centre of the circle is given over to the public open space, the approach to it passing over or under the traffic routes. The monorail is introduced as a device especially well adapted to permit unobstructed pedestrian movement at ground level. Pristine agricultural land is not encroached upon: rather it is the derelict left-overs of previous urban exploitation which are chosen as sites. While each 'circuit-linear town' is a

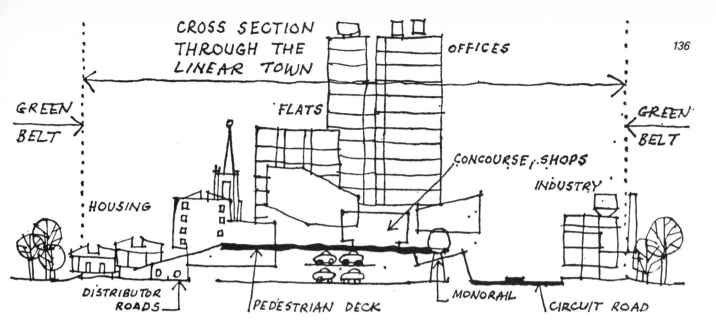

CROSS SECTION THROUGH THE LINEAR TOWN

OFFICES

FLATS

CONCOURSE; SHOPS

INDUSTRY

GREEN BELT

GREEN BELT

HOUSING

DISTRIBUTOR ROADS

PEDESTRIAN DECK

MONORAIL

CIRCUIT ROAD

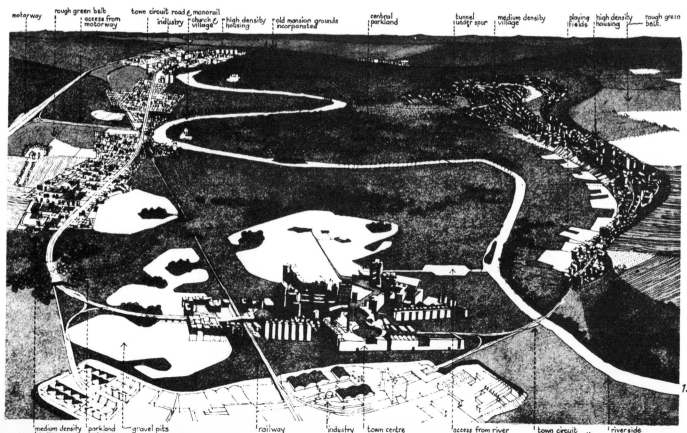

motorway | rough green belt | access from motorway | town circuit road & monorail | industry | church & village | high density housing | old mansion grounds incorporated | central parkland | tunnel under spur | medium density village | playing fields | high density housing | rough green belt

medium density housing | parkland overpass | gravel pits | railway | industry | town centre | access from river | town circuit road & monorail | riverside parkway

137

distinct entity, an evolving series can be linked by a regional motorway.

During the 'sixties, something which more far-sighted town and regional planning had long been aware of, began to demand official attention: population growth. Mankind became aware that his numbers were increasing at such a rate that 'population explosion' was considered by many almost too mild an expression. For Britain, Buchanan had described the position thus:

'Where, in this small island, within the next 45 years, are we going to find accommodation for a further 20 million people, or even more? Where are they going to work, and what work will they be doing? Where will they find their recreation, and what kinds will they want? Where and how are they all going to move about? How are we going to build all the necessary accommodation — the equivalent of a new Bristol every year for forty-five years — when we already carry the burden of a vast legacy of obsolete development from the industrial revolution? These are desperately difficult and urgent questions. They concern essentially the form and organisation of urban areas which is now coming into perspective as the supreme social problem of the future.'[128]

Population explosion was also urban explosion, and especially the explosion of the largest cities — of the metropolitan areas. The United Nations organised a symposium in Moscow in 1964 to see what light might be thrown on those aspects of the problem which most concern us here: the *'Planning of Metropolitan Areas and New Towns'.*[129]

A preparatory meeting of experts had been held in Stockholm in 1961, and the symposium itself brought together economists, geographers and planners from most European countries. The main concern was population growth in cities (which was said to be at least twice as fast as in the world generally) and which was bringing to the fore the question of the optimum size of towns and the pattern of their future development.

New towns were discussed, mainly as having a role to play as satellites within metropolitan regions, rather than as pioneering settlements intended to promote the opening up of new areas (although — especially within the USSR — they still had that role also). There appears to have been a general acceptance of the large complex city as having advantages which, potentially at least, outweighed the difficulties it was creating.

Salvation was seen in *cellular form*: in breaking down the city into viable sub-divisions, into a *'confederation of neighbourhoods'*. The Greek planner Doxiadis gave his classification of 'communities' and their populations:

Community Class	Population	Economic Function
I	30-80	—
II	500	local shops, newspaper stand, etc.
III	2,000-2,500	neighbourhood shopping, handicraft shop
IV	6,000-10,000	self-contained commercial shopping
V	30,000-60,000	transport centres, controlled industry, central markets
VI	150,000-300,000	specialised functions serving large areas
VII	900,000-1,500,000	do.
VIII	4,500,000-7,500,000	do.

Doxiadis was also emphatic in his advocacy of *'cellular growth'*

'When an organism changes size, its cells do not also change in size. What allows the organism to grow is multiplication of the cells.'[130]

Thus, whether one accepted his figures or not, the problem was seen as one of identifying and understanding the *'urban cells'*. Other estimates of size, and other criteria of classification, were made. The residential 'neighbourhood' was discussed, and it was said that estimates of its population varied from 3,000 to 20,000, with a norm around 6,000-12,000. P. N. Blokhine (USSR) gave 100,000-250,000 as the optimum size for a town capable of sustaining the main branches of industry, and described, as a basis for its planned sub-division, a hierarchy of community groupings based on *'public amenities'*, not unlike the first British new towns (which, however were criticised as not being big enough to act as counter-magnets to the 'mother city'). In the USSR, policy was to build satellites with populations in the range of 50,000 to 100,000.

A topic inevitably associated with the arrangements of the larger settlements under discussion concerns location of industry. Here, there were many references to the desirability of dispersal. C. A. Wissink (Holland) described the loosely-knit complex of Holland's principal cities — *Randstad* — as a unique example, in which the aim would be to preserve its decentralised and 'multi-nuclear' structure, as this combined the minimum of 'commuting' with the maximum of 'opportunity'.

In the larger city also, as Buchanan had shewn, the problems of transport are acute. Thus, this inevitably came into the discussion. From Stockholm it was said unequivocally that public transport would have to be independent of the overloaded road system if it were successfully to compete with the automobile. Others asserted that the emphasis would have to be upon public transport, with the automobile severely restricted to exceptional journeys and for family recreation. The aim in the USSR would be to ensure a maximum journey to work of 30 minutes duration, and public transport would be free.

The most sophisticated contributions came from Poland. Julius Gorynski believed it was possible *'through complex economic analysis to determine the optimum size of a town'* Boleslaw Malisz proposed a costing technique to determine a city's plan from given local characteristics and other criteria. For him, the journey-to-work was all-important in the definition of a settlement's 'catchment area', and he talks not only in terms of desirable maxima, but also of 'threshold size', below which a population is not adequate economically to sustain the facilities it requires.

Ideas such as these have since advanced considerably our understanding of urban structure. They have come in the main from economists, geographers and others whose interest has been analytical rather than creative. But they were to influence professional planning to an increasing extent thereafter, as we shall see. For architecture and civic design in general, a potent influence came from a fellow designer and pioneer in 'design theory': Christopher Alexander. Applying the fast-developing techniques of cybernetics and computer science to urban problems, Alexander attacked the concepts of urban form which had dominated the recent past as over-simplifications. In an article *A City is not a Tree*[131] he added considerable weight to those who were rejecting the neighbourhood and the branching hierarchies of the first new towns. He argued instead, that urban structure was a 'semi-lattice', with **139** overlapping sub-divisions associated in complex ways.

139 'A city is not a tree': Alexander argues that urban structure is better viewed as a 'semi-lattice' (left) and not a 'tree' (right).

The critical interest that town planning was arousing in architectural circles was sufficient for the Royal Institute of British Architects in 1967 to devote its annual conference to the theme. There it was said that the consensus was that the first new towns, in spite of some success, had failed to affect in a major way the distribution of work and people in the regions where they were placed. They had had no significant effect on the growth of London. They were too small, too slow and put too near the metropolis. They were designed to improve the lot of a static population, not to resist a population explosion. They had had (albeit successfully) to increase their population targets. They had not achieved their planned rates of growth. There was a failure to keep work and homes in balance in the early years, and there had been imbalance also in the provision of social facilities. The causes of all this were to be found in the plan form

'which, as it was concentric and hierarchical, made it almost impossible to produce a viable community structure during growth . . .'

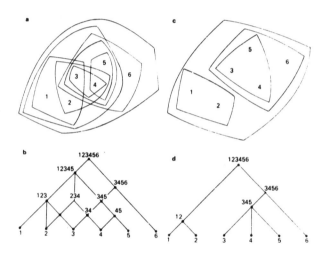

Government economies and unco-ordinated official policies relating to industrial location were also blamed, as was the lack of financial and other control over their own destinies. Above all, the new towns prior to Cumbernauld had failed *'to anticipate and adapt to the increase in private car ownership and use that has followed increasing wealth.'* Cumbernauld was approved as *'the first attempt to capture the cohesion, tightness and urbanity of the historical towns that was lost in the earlier models'*. But it too had its failings. Nearly half its people had to live in flats (which no one any longer could pretend were popular). In spite of the best intentions in separating vehicles and pedestrians, *'people still walk over the roads at night because they do not like using the dimly-lit subways.'* The concentration of industry was uneconomic in terms of road usage. The centre, which could not be built as a whole until the population was there to justify it, resulted in their still (in 1967) being *'a great vacuum in the centre of the town.'* There were also problems of growth inherent in the form chosen.

The post-1961 new towns

'developed out of a series of regional studies conducted by the Government, prompted by forecasts of dramatically rising population and the need to generate economic growth to support it. It was also a renewed effort to relieve congestion in the existing conurbations by promoting new centres. The idea this time was to make these new centres sufficiently big and active to be real counter-magnets rather than satellites of the existing centres of economic activity. There was also an interesting new move — the appointment of planning consultants to make designation proposals and to follow these up with the development plan. Previously it had been the practice for the Government to make a designation proposal, to draw a blue line on the map within which the new towns had to be, and then it was up the planners to fit the town within the line as best they could. Now we have the opportunity to study the town structure that may emerge before the line is drawn on the map, and there is therefore a better chance of the ultimate development plan being more logically related to all the relevant factors.'

For the most part, this new batch of 'new towns' were based on existing settlements of considerable size, and had target populations into the hundreds of thousands. They were also expected to grow at a faster rate.

In reviewing the proposals as they had been developed at that time, it was noticed that there was an emphasis on open-endedness; a tendency towards a dispersal of land use; *'a consensus in favour of residential densities of between 30 and 75 people to the acre';* an assumption of much higher car-ownership levels, and

'an attempt to strike an economic balance between allowing complete freedom for the car on the one hand, and producing a viable public transport service, that will be competitive because it is attractive, on the other.'

But there seemed to be *'considerable uncertainty'* about urban structure, and the tendency — rightly — was to keep the options open.[132]

In the regional studies referred to at the 1967 R.I.B.A. Conference, there had been a more sophisticated application of some of the techniques of survey and analysis than Britain had seen before. New procedures involving computers, aerial photography, systems analysis and cost/benefit studies were also beginning to find a place. If, for the most part, all that resulted was more 'trend planning', technically at least, much was learnt and achieved.

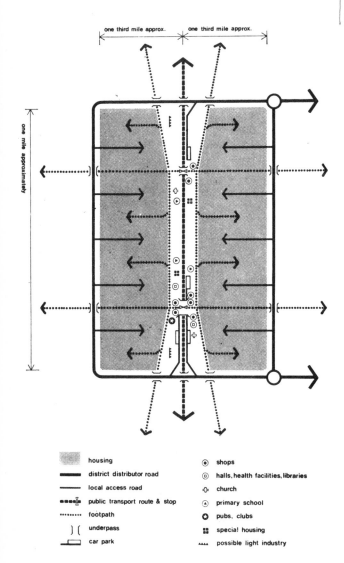

140 *Redditch: basic residential district: symbols represent community facilities along a public transport spine. Footpaths bridge over at shopping places, and both footpaths and the public transport route are separate from the roads.*

one third mile approx. | one third mile approx.

one mile approximately

	housing	⊙	shops
▬	district distributor road	◉	halls, health facilities, libraries
—	local access road	✛	church
▪▬▪	public transport route & stop	⊙	primary school
⋯⋯	footpath	⦾	pubs, clubs
)(	underpass	▪▪	special housing
▭	car park	⋀⋀	possible light industry

Diagrams such as 140 do not reflect how people think, act, and feel in the non-commercial emotional parts of their lives. The individual and small group levels of analysis are really ignored. City planners simply don't understand people.

A comparable situation would be a field of medicine where studies and remedies focused on organs but stopped there, no knowledge of cells. Or a clinical psychologist doing family therapy who could/would not talk to individual people, e.g., in an abusive family.

Livingstone, in Scotland, was the first new town to be designated in the 'sixties, but, largely as a penalty for being first, displays less well than its successors the new currents in planning theory. The Master Plan (by Peter Daniel) was produced at much the same time as the Buchanan Report, and reflects the same influences. Skelmersdale was being actively considered at the same time. The planners here were Sir Hugh Wilson (who had been responsible for Cumbernauld) and others. Skelmersdale was to be for Wilson (now in partnership with Lewis Womersley) the first of a series of similar commissions, and it will be instructive to follow the development of his ideas during a decade in which ideas about planning generally have changed with bewildering rapidity.

In an interim report on Skelmersdale, in 1963,[133] Wilson sets out his 'general approach'. Much that he says confirms his thinking at Cumbernauld. 'Master Plan' is too finite a concept: one must allow for changes as things develop. One must have regard for a high level of car-ownership. There must be segregation of vehicles and pedestrians. In coping with the motor car, one is led towards the concept of a compact town, with the population within walking distance of the centre. Apart from corner shops, local centres are therefore unnecessary except for those who are more than ten to fifteen minutes' away from the centre of the town. A multiplicity of industrial sites would ease traffic congestion. There should be a contrast between town and country, and the town should have a readily understood, coherent structure. One should aim at a good balance in age, family structure and employment, and the programme should ensure good facilities at each stage.

A more mature proposal for an urban form, appropriate to the problem as he saw it, begins to appear in Wilson's report on a regional study of Northamptonshire, Bedfordshire and North Buckinghamshire.[134] Here, he talks unequivocally about *'a public transport spine'* linking together new urban development. What he has in mind can be seen most clearly in the proposals for Redditch,[135] for which he was commissioned in October 1964. He was now able to elaborate his approach, and sets out some *'principles we believe applicable at the present time'*. There should be flexibility to allow for changes, especially in population targets. Allowance should made not only for the car, but for public transport as well, and public transport would increase in relative importance. Town growth should be related to traffic growth, and a change in emphasis from the motor car to public transport would have to be planned for. The safety of pedestrians is talked of now in terms of *fast vehicle/pedestrian segregation*, and Buchanan's concepts of 'environmental areas' and hierarchy of roads are explicitly adopted. Land uses with high traffic generation should be dispersed to achieve balanced peak flows, and he reiterates the other desiderata noted above. Since it was likely that Redditch could not be counted upon to stop growing at the intended 90,000, and since any increase would invalidate a road network designed for motor-cars, there was added ground for a greater reliance on public transport.

Any town with a high degree of reliance upon public transport would find in the public transport stops a natural focus for pedestrian activity. An appropriate town structure would therefore be

'in the form of a series of districts based upon walking distance from these foci, containing residential, industrial or recreational development and related uses, connected to each other and the town centre by a public transport line as well as by roads and footpaths.'   140

Such a plan form could be likened to a necklace, having the public transport system as the string. Its fundamental feature would be the road for public transport, unimpeded by other vehicles. Community facilities (shops, schools, meeting halls, health centres, churches, playing fields, etc.) would be around the stops, and everything else within seven to ten minutes (¼-½ mile) from the public transport spine.

Wilson and his partners design the town accordingly. For the time being, the public transport route serves as an all purpose road. Eventually, other routes are provided for cars, but the strategy is flexible and can allow for different solutions as circumstances demand.

The most recent fruits of Wilson's thinking may be seen in the new town of Irvine, a Scottish coastal town to the south-west of Glasgow. His first proposals, put forward in 1965, follow directly from Skelmersdale and Redditch. Nearly three years were to pass before any real progress was made, during which time certain detailed facts came to light which invalidated some of the proposals, and a further plan [136] was prepared. By this time also, experts in systems analysis and computer programming were commissioned to work alongside the architects, the intention being to compare the costs and benefits of alternative possibilities.

While the first plan had marked 'linear' characteristics, the second came closer to an orthogonal grid. But the *cardinal feature* which persists throughout is the concept of *'community routes'*, and along these we still have the *'string of beads'*. As the proposal now stands (1973) it is for a new town with an ultimate population of 120,000 (by 1986), with the possibility of growth to about 140,000.

The *'principles of development'* are clearly stated:
'One of the main objectives of the New Town plan is to provide easy movement at all times by various modes, pedestrian and vehicular, public and private. A hierarchy of routes has therefore been proposed ranging from pedestrian pathways at the lowest level to regional motorways at the highest level. It is a principle of the plan that movement about the town is by progression through the hierarchy. Easy movement by car is no longer possible on multi-purpose roads and to avoid congestion it is necessary to provide for regional, town, and local traffic by accommodating each on fast or slow roads designed to permit through movement or to give access to development.

'Public transport will also require a separate route to function efficiently and advantage has been taken of the extensive network of existing roads which might in time be used exclusively as bus ways. Main pedestrian movement generated by local shops, schools and bus stops will be segregated from vehicular movements. This will be encouraged by locating local facilities along the bus way which then becomes the focus of community activity or the "community

route". Certain sub-regional facilities which will attract people from a wide area might best be located where the community route crosses distributor roads making them highly accessible by bus and car.

'Development is so arranged that the community route runs through the centre of each residential area. Distributor roads located on the periphery of each area draw vehicular traffic in the opposite direction from pedestrian traffic. To reinforce the effectiveness of this system further and to provide a choice of dwellings accessible predominantly either by car, or by bus, or on foot, densities have been increased around the community route.' [137]

The planning strategy must be flexible, must allow for growth and uncertainties in long-term forecasting. Building should proceed comprehensively, and so that at each stage *'a part of the town is established that would support a reasonable range of facilities.'*

The community routes can conveniently and economically utilise existing roads and country lanes as public transport routes.

'The community routes are seen as the focus of the surrounding development, with social, educational and other facilities located at public transport stops. Housing will be at higher densities adjacent to the community route and lower densities further away. The community routes provide the basic method of linking housing communities in a way which has not been achieved in previous new towns. The high density housing adjacent to these routes could provide a pedestrian system to allow residents to move from district to district with maximum weather protection.

'Distributor roads will be developed in parallel to the community route as housing is built. Initially the community routes will continue as all purpose roads but it is important that they are not overloaded and damaged by high volumes of service or constructional traffic. Distributor roads providing access to new development will be built as soon as practicable. Rear access with a link to the new distributor roads will be provided wherever possible for existing property fronting directly onto the community routes. The general policy will be to allow no development from the existing roads unless provision is made for the future connection of vehicular access to the distributor road and the closure of access via the existing road. The community route which already contains many existing public utilities will also provide an economical route for gas, electricity, G.P.O. and other services.

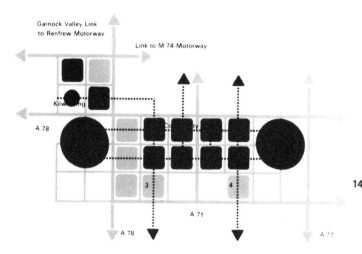

141 Irvine: diagrammatic proposals for the sub-region: solid rectangles represent urban development (mainly residential; some industrial). 'Community routes' are dotted.

141

142

'*Ultimately the community routes could carry public transport vehicles only and they are suitable not only for buses but also for any future public transportation system which may be developed, such as air cushion craft.*'[138]

The '*basic elements*' of community structure are the 143 primary school and local shop, which together require a '*support population of around 4,000*'. Taking 5-7 minutes walking time as the limit of their catchment area (i.e. 0.5 km.) '*a theoretical basic residential unit was evolved*' comprising 1,100 dwellings and capable of variation in density and form.

'*A number of these basic units grouped on both sides of the community route and related to a comprehensive school and local centre, define the community structure . . . The main development is in the form of a series of residential units based on walking distances, connected to each other and the central area and industrial areas by public transport routes and footpaths*'[139]

Schools were to have '*community wings*' and be available for use as community centres.

'*A structure has been evolved within which it is envisaged that the new residential areas of the town can be developed as a comprehensive entity in terms of built form and not as a series of unrelated developments or separate neighbourhoods. The community route will add strength to the form of the town. Owner occupied housing areas where car ownership is likely to be high, are located near to peripheral distributor roads while housing areas of higher density close to the community route will be based more on pedestrian needs and the availability of public transport. The build-up in density and form towards the community route will emphasise its significance and create a higher density spine of development punctuated by centres containing social, educational and shopping facilities.*

'*A series of residential units located along community routes results in a town structure capable of expansion in various directions by the addition of further units and the improvement or construction of associated distributor roads necessitated by the increase of traffic.*

'*Within the basic development and circulation principles, units are capable of independent design thus allowing variety to be achieved in population, density, urban form and layout by the exploitation of the natural landscape characteristics of each site.*

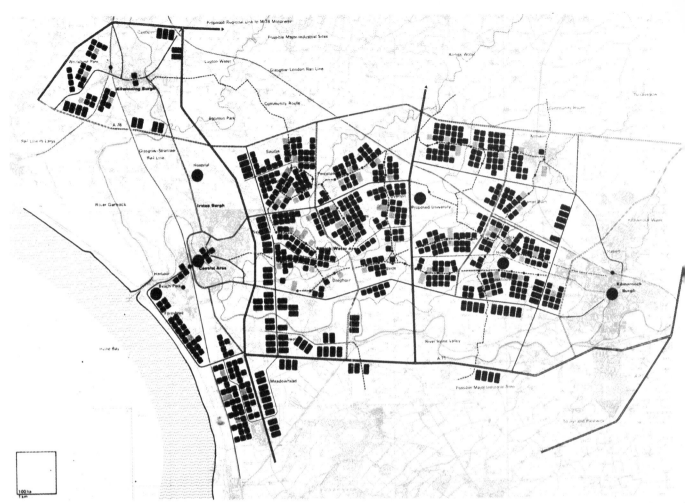

142 Irvine: the sub-region showing 'modular' form to allow flexible growth by stages.

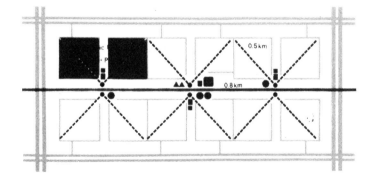

143 Irvine: a residential unit built up of basic cells with 4000 + people with their local facilities around a community route. Everyone within half a kilometre of a bus stop.

'The location of community facilities adjacent to the public transport system induces a strong pedestrian movement towards and along community routes in new areas. Pedestrian routes will be located alongside but separate from the community routes, either as raised footpaths, on banking, or as part of a covered pedestrian way associated with the higher density housing. Pedestrian crossing will take place principally at the local centres and at bus stops and building form may be utilized to effect this . . .

'The bulk of the new housing will be in low rise development in net densities ranging from 30-160 persons per hectare. As long as the present indicative cost system remains unchanged, it will be necessary to design to a net density of up to 235 persons per hectare for rented houses. This higher density housing will be located closest to the community routes and local centres, including primary schools, with the lower densities, including private housing, on the periphery . . .'[140]

Of employment it is said:

'It would be unrealistic to suppose that even if labour supply and demand within the town are kept in balance at all times, all those who live in Irvine will work here or that all those who work here will live in the town. Even with a well balanced town of 120,000 there will be thousands who, for special reasons, travel out or in to work. It is a great advantage to the industrial firm, particularly if it is seeking rare and specialised skills, to be located in the centre of a large labour catchment area. This situation already applies in Irvine and will apply increasingly as the town and region develop.'[141]

The development of Irvine was indeed being undertaken as part of a regional plan, and the idea of the 'city region' is characteristic of contemporary theory. It is also noted that

'the future economic success of the New Town is not only dependent upon the quantity of jobs attracted to it, for quality is equally important if an economic imbalance is not to be created. In particular, there must be provision within the employment range for people wishing to work in service industry, as well as in manufacturing industry, and while it is probable that the latter will be more significant in the earlier years of the town's growth, care will be taken to ensure that this early growth does not lead to a later imbalance.'[142]

A growing awareness of the significance of 'service industry', and the relative decline in terms of manpower of factory employment, also characterise current thinking throughout Britain. But, lacking power to direct employment

location, the Irvine plan provides for an extensive belt of factory sites adjoining the principal road from Glasgow to Ayr, and tacitly accepts Clydeside's role as a stronghold of the 'blue-collar' proletarian. In spite of public transport, planning proceeds on the assumption that *'75% of the journeys to work in the New Town will in future be made by private car'*. The city centre builds on that already existing in Irvine, and follows in essentials the now fashionable Cumbernauld 'indoor' pattern.

An appendix to the latest (1971) report on Irvine describes a procedure of cost-benefit analysis by computer which was tried in order to facilitate planning decisions. It was believed that the application of computer analysis to the strategic problems of urban and regional planning would enable a better plan to be produced more quickly, economically and accurately than would be possible by traditional methods. The objective of the town planning process is defined as being to determine for each unit of land its designated use and the intensity of this use for each future time period.

The problems are complex, and many solutions are possible. There were physical and geographical constraints (such as the total area available, the structure of land, etc.); social and economic environmental constraints (such as the forecast demand for housing, transportation, industrial, commercial, entertainment activities); norms to be maintained (e.g. provision of open space and parking requirements); value constraints (e.g. preservation of landscape and amenities, design preferences); political constraints (e.g. desired size of the town) and many others. Within the framework of these constraints lay the field of possibilities within which the planner was free to propose his solutions.

To compare proposals, it is necessary to express all their comparable characteristics in measurable terms, and this poses problems. Many can be measured in money, but some cannot. Thus, the best a computer can do, is to find alternative solutions which are efficient but not necessarily optimal. There exists in fact an infinite number of feasible plans that conform with the requirements for open space, community facilities, phasing, population mix, land suitability, housing standards, etc. The selection of the optimal plan requires the deep consideration not only of planners but also most importantly, of the public authorities. Data will have been produced, however, which would allow initial decisions to be looked at afresh in the light of the effect they were having, and rational modifications made.

The technique used, involved the division of the total

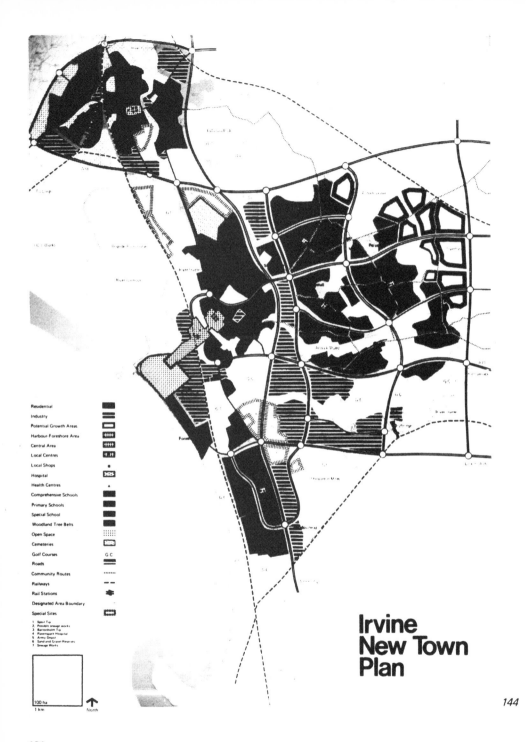

Residential
Industry
Potential Growth Areas
Harbour-Foreshore Area
Central Area
Local Centres
Local Shops
Hospital
Health Centres
Comprehensive Schools
Primary Schools
Special School
Woodland Tree Belts
Open Space
Cemeteries
Golf Courses   G C
Roads
Community Routes
Railways
Rail Stations
Designated Area Boundary
Special Sites

1 Spoil Tip
2 Possible sewage works
3 Bartonholm Tip
4 Ravenspark Hospital
5 Army Depot
6 Sand and Gravel Reserves
7 Sewage Works

Irvine
New Town
Plan

144

100 ha

1 km

North

designated area into reference areas. to which could be allocated significant characteristics concerning land use. traffic, etc. It was then possible to devise a 'computer model' which allowed the interactions of these characteristics to be evaluated. Several possible arrangements were compared on this basis, and one chosen for further elaboration.

While the use of the computer in this way was a major step forward in that it takes account of certain financial implications of alternative plans and it had the added benefit of bringing together all the major professional disciplines at the planning stage and the interim revised outline plan was produced more quickly, in a number of respects the study was less valuable than had been hoped. It was not capable of optimising all factors simultaneously and even if the criteria could have been measured in financial terms, it could not, as claimed, have produced an optimum plan. In phase three of the study it was necessary to adopt the industrial sites and the basic road network and drainage pattern already prepared by corporation technical staff as constraints and vary only the location and density of housing sites.

In other ways, too, the technique was lacking, and these factors, together with the questionable emphasis placed on socio-economic grouping and travelling time, cast serious doubts on the value of the computer model as a suitable method for assisting in the detailed planning of the New Town.

Bearing all these considerations in mind it was not intended to continue to use the model for updating the plan at regular intervals as had been suggested. There is still some hope, it seems, for the human brain.

There were others working at the same time along similar lines. A regional study for mid-Lancashire[143] resulted in proposals for a new linear city based upon the existing centres of Preston, Leyland and Chorley, which it was proposed to **148** link with a 'triple strand' of routes: the central one being similar to the 'community route' we have just been discussing, and both the outer ones being roads for automobiles. The form arises quite straightforwardly from **145** combining the requirements of residential development on both sides of a public transport route with those of the 'Radburn' layout. Applied to a new 'city region' of 500,000, there are complications and, instead of deriving the whole structure from the bus-stop, the community structure is organised to conform with the catchment areas of groups of **146** facilities. Given that the populations of the 'neighbourhood', the 'district' and the 'township' are known, as well as the

KEY

Existing urban area

General residential area

Industrial area

Town centre

Special ownerships

Open space and landscape features

Land over 600 feet

High speed road

Railway

Public transport route

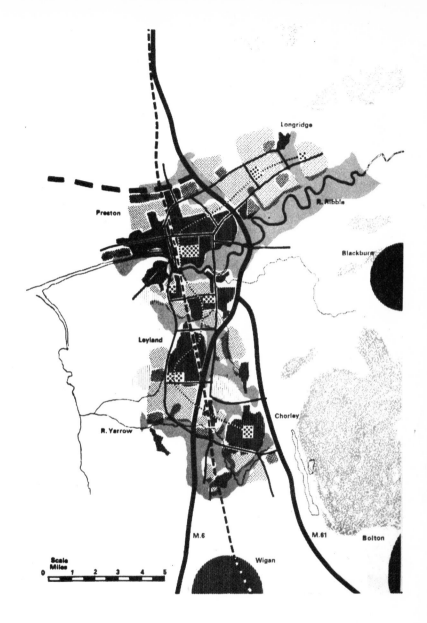

148 Central Lancashire: the 'three-strand' structure applied to Preston-Leyland-Chorley.

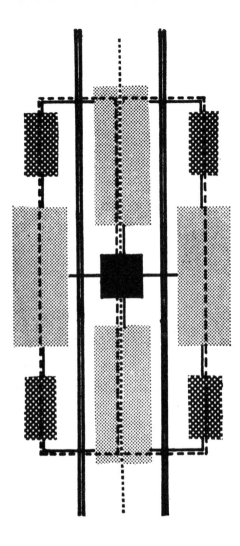

High speed road

Express public transport

Low speed road

Local public transport

Centre

Residential

Employment

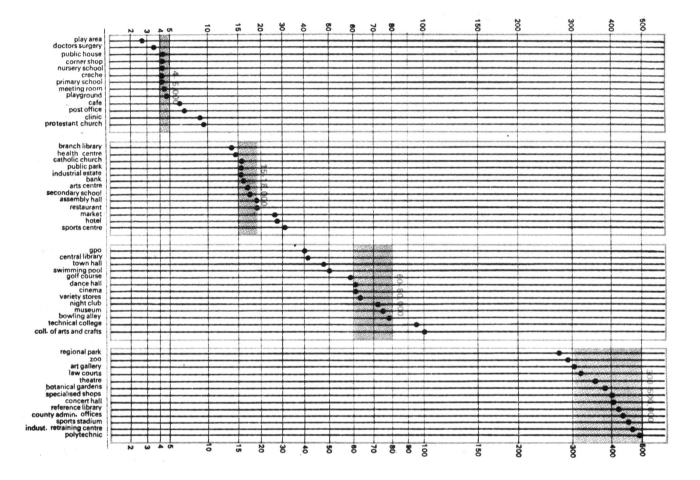

146 Andrew Derbyshire's diagram relating community facilities to size of population served. The shaded areas indicate greatest coincidence of catchments. The logarithmic scale shows population in thousands.

145 The 'three-strand' structure.

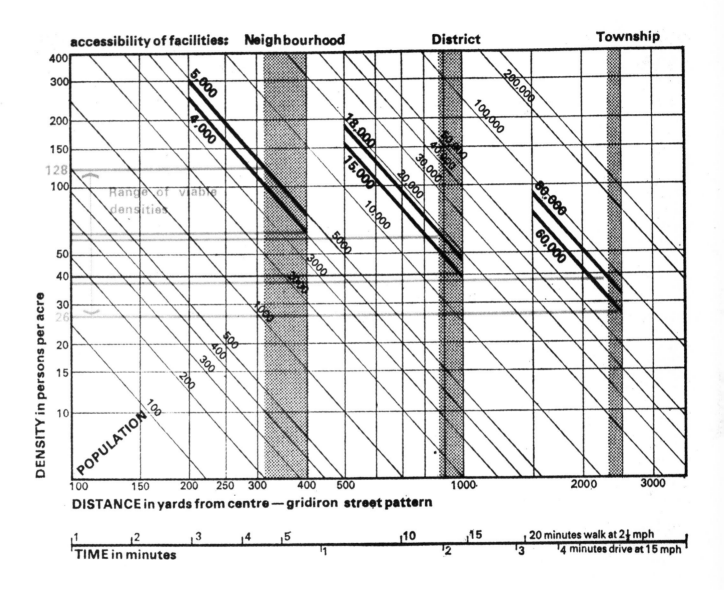

147 *Population, density and time/distance relationships. If two variables are given, the third may be determined.*

maximum distance people should have to walk or ride to get
147 to the centre, then the range of viable residential densities can
be calculated. The advantage of dispersing *'major city
functions'* is argued at length. It results in *'a distributive
rather than centralised transportation system'* and suburbs
'can now become identifiable districts or townships' with *'a
city sense to the whole structure without prejudicing the
dominant role of the centre.'*[144] We thus have something like
a marriage between Soria y Mata's Linear City and Mark I
New Town, with the added upward steps in the hierarchy
from 'township' to 'city region'.

It remained for Arthur Ling, who had had a hand in both
the Abercrombie and Mars plans for London, to 'go the
whole hog' and propose a solution based without reserve on
public transport.

Runcorn is in Cheshire, a part of the Merseyside
conurbation. The proposed new town is based on existing
development having a population of some 30,000, as well as
considerable industrial development. The intention is that
the town's population shall eventually approach 100,000, but
while it is conceived as part of its region, the concept is more
that of an entity complete in itself.

Development which had already taken place made a
compact town impossible, but to design for full reliance on
the motor car would be wasteful and would result in the
deprivation of those unable to command the use of a car. A
'planned balance' between the use of the private car and
public transport therefore became the basis of the proposals,
and

*'A linear arrangement of the new residential
communities, on either side of a spinal public transport
route, has been evolved so that the majority of people will be
within five minutes walking distance, or 500 yards, of a route
which is especially reserved for buses.'*[145]

By a process of elimination, a theoretical town diagram is
arrived at. This is similar to the circuit linear form we have
already encountered, except that it is twisted into a figure-of-
149 eight and bounded by an expressway. The figure-of-eight
resulted from local considerations, but allows the town centre
to take up a focal position. The expressway results from a
decision to divorce the public transport route from other
traffic. This decision is argued thus:

*'The problem is how to provide economically for the socially
satisfactory movement of people and goods without the*

*environment being dominated by vehicles and
communication ways. It is necessary to look ahead to the time
when the national average saturation level of car ownership
predicted for the year 2010 is reached. It has been assumed
that even with this level of ownership at least 15% of the
journeys to work, together with a significant proportion of the
shopping, social and school journeys will require some form
of public transport, as this proportion of the population will
be without the use of a car at a particular time.*

*'When public transport such as the train, or monorail, uses
a fixed line means of conveyance, the problem of congestion
and hindrance to other traffic is automatically eliminated.
The tram, it is true, was usually routed along existing roads,
but this form of transport originated when other traffic was
proportionately negligible. This other traffic, however,
became so dominant in its demand for more road space, that
it became a contributory factor in the elimination of the tram
in Britain. With a network of separate tracks, they probably
would have survived. Later, for the same reasons, even the
trolley bus was superseded by the motor bus, which had been
developed to a comparatively high standard and was able to
show economy in running costs. In this process public
transport became subject to all the inefficiencies of out-of-
date road layouts and the mounting congestion created by the
vastly increased number of private cars. As a consequence,
the speed of bus journeys has been reduced below that of the
private car and in the centres of many cities averages only
about 8-10 miles per hour.*

*'In many post-war new towns and suburban extensions, the
tendency has been to design the road layout for private
vehicles and then to route buses along the most appropriate
roads. This has led in some instances to a minimum use of
public transport which has made it uneconomical to provide
socially convenient services. It is considered that the
contribution of public transport to a new town is of such
importance that it is essential to plan for it as an integral part
of the town structure and not to provide it as an afterthought . . .*

*'The solution adopted provides the buses with a separate
track so that they are not subject to the delays of traffic
congestion and at the same time provides other vehicles with
a road system which is free of the delays occasioned by buses
which stop and start at frequent intervals. With such a system
it is possible to plan on the assumption that there is no
discouragement to the use of public transport on grounds of
delay and inefficient service. The maximum use of private
cars would require additional expenditure on road works and*

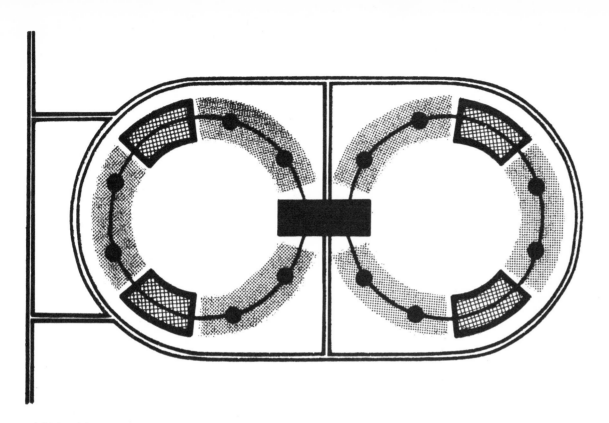

Residential.

 Industry.

Centres.

═══ Expressway

━━━ Public Transport Route

149   Runcorn: theoretical town diagram.

Might work for higher-level units, esp. re food production in the centers. for I-20 in Madison parish?

car parks. *If an efficient public transport system could be provided, taking people to their destinations in a much smaller number of vehicles at less cost or even at the same cost and without the necessity of providing vast car parks, it would provide a new town with the economic means of moving people to and from their destinations. A public transport system of some kind must be provided for the people who are unable to use cars. Although they are relatively few in number, there is still a need to consider the provision of an efficient public transport system. It is desirable that this system should be of maximum efficiency so that the maximum number of people will want to use it, thereby helping to make it economic.*

'*A conventional form of public transport, such as buses using the normal roads, for the level of car ownership ultimately envisaged, would result, for a town of 100,000 population, in high fares, a poor frequency of service or a public subsidy. To provide an acceptable economic level of service for the non-car owners and to make a significant saving in parking provision, a "modal split" between the use of private cars and public transport of 50:50 for work journeys has been taken as an objective. This means that a proportion of workers having the use of a car must be attracted to public transport and to achieve this, the service must be cheap, fast and frequent, giving as near to a "door-to-door" service as possible. A separate rapid transit track has therefore been provided linking the communities, the town centre and the industrial areas, with walking distances kept to a minimum, so as to keep door-to-destination journey times by public transport favourably competitive with those by private car. The separate track will enable the buses to maintain higher average speeds than normal as they will be free from delays caused by traffic congestion. The directness of the routes will also ensure that operating costs will be at a minimum . . .*'[146]

Buses operating on major all-purpose roads passing through the residential areas would, furthermore, be detrimental to community life, and people would find themselves living on either side of a main traffic artery.

In detail, the theoretical ideal had to be modified to suit local peculiarities, but the broad intention still underlies the plan. As with Central Lancashire, the living areas are sub-divided into a hierarchy: *groups* of 100-200 persons (30-60 houses) which '*experience shows will allow a reasonable choice of contacts*'; *neighbourhoods* of 2,000 (right for a 1-form entry primary school); and *communities* of 8,000, who, at 70 persons per acre, can all live within five minutes walk of

Pedestrian Routes.

Distributor Roads.

Rapid Transit Route.

Pedestrian underpass.

Pedestrian crossing at grade.

Traffic signal controlled intersection.

Car Parking and Garaging.

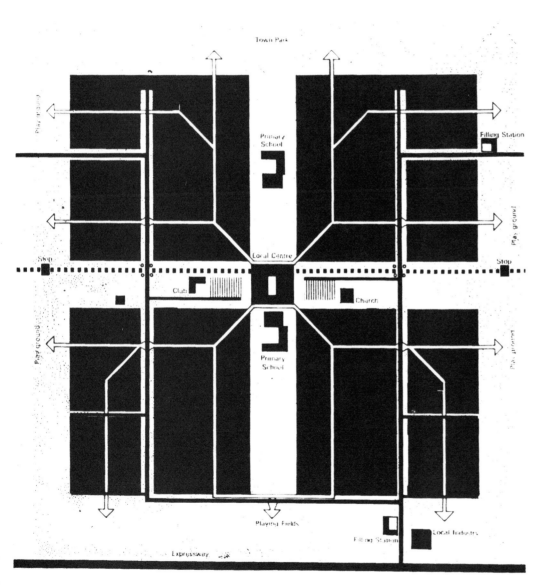

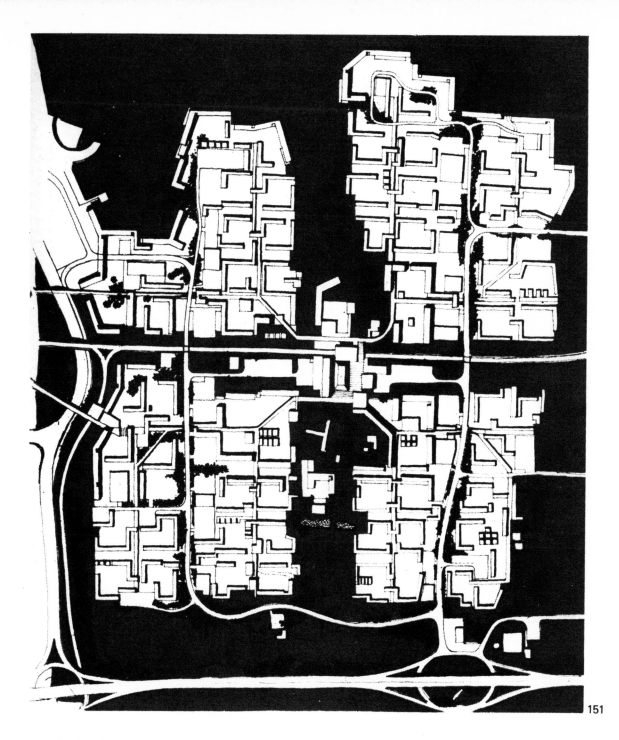

151

a bus-stop. Densities are graded from centre to periphery, and a choice of locations for the supporting social facilities is allowed. On one side is the expressway, on the other the town park.

Considerable detail is given concerning the internal arrangement of residential areas. Of particular interest are the local distributor roads. They form a continuous system, but their tortuousness is intended to prevent unnecessary infiltration.

Before buses were decided upon, other possibilities were considered, and these are reviewed. The choice fell on '. . . *single-deck buses, operating on their own track, except in part of the western section of the town. This track has a design speed of 40 m.p.h. The bus has flexibility of movement as compared with the monorail and can readily be used on multi-purpose roads either in the existing town or in the new parts of the town during the early stages when the road network, including the reserved track, will not be complete. The reserved track will cross the distributor roads at some 23 places. These crossings will either be at grade, controlled by traffic signals giving right of way to the buses, or grade-separated where the topography allows them to be constructed economically and/or the traffic volumes demand them . . .*

'*The basic off-peak frequency of 15 minutes on each service will provide a 7½ minute or 5 minute frequency where there are two or three services operating over a common section of the route. These common sections will pass through the new residential communities so that some 63% of the population will have a 5 minute off-peak service in each direction, and a further 23%, a 7½ minute service. These services will be augmented at peak periods so that the frequency of service will be considerably higher . . .*

'*The type of bus envisaged for the rapid transit system is a low-floor single-deck type with accommodation for up to 80-90 persons, including standing passengers. The vehicle will be approximately 8 ft. 9 in. high with . . . a high rate of acceleration in the vicinity of 3.2 ft./sec.² from 0-30 m.p.h. These buses will demand a minimum height clearance considerably less than the normal 16 ft. 6 in., and this will show substantial savings in bridge construction costs. It is assumed that the vehicles will be one-man operated with automatic fare collection. They will have multiple sets of doors to give quick access and egress. They should also provide for the access and carriage of prams and pushchairs.*

Runcorn new town

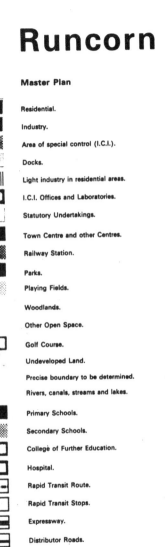

Master Plan

- Residential.
- Industry.
- Area of special control (I.C.I.).
- Docks.
- Light industry in residential areas.
- I.C.I. Offices and Laboratories.
- Statutory Undertakings.
- Town Centre and other Centres.
- Railway Station.
- Parks.
- Playing Fields.
- Woodlands.
- Other Open Space.
- Golf Course.
- Undeveloped Land.
- Precise boundary to be determined.
- Rivers, canals, streams and lakes.
- Primary Schools.
- Secondary Schools.
- College of Further Education.
- Hospital.
- Rapid Transit Route.
- Rapid Transit Stops.
- Expressway.
- Distributor Roads.

Prepared for the Runcorn Development Corporation by
Arthur Ling, BA, FRIBA, MTPI,
of Arthur Ling and Associates, Nottingham.   1967

This could be facilitated by the provision of automatically dropping ramps at the entrances and exits of the buses. Further possible developments of the vehicles include the provision of doors on both sides permitting the use of central island platforms at the picking-up points.'[147]

The other aspects of the town have also been worked out in considerable detail, but propose nothing fundamentally different from what we have already encountered elsewhere. In the detail of housing areas there are approving references to Scandinavian practices, especially in the use of combined pedestrian and vehicle ways. With so finite a form, there are clearly difficulties regarding growth. Beyond the ultimate size intended, this is impossible, but it is claimed that growth up to the total form can be developed gradually by 'pincer movements' from the centre.

At Runcorn, and in other proposals deriving from the linear theme, it will be noted that adjoining routes tend to have differing uses. Motor road alternates with community spine, cul-de-sac with walkway. Something similar was originally proposed for Dawley (Telford)[148] with a town walkway sandwiched between primary and secondary roads. A proposal for Caersws — a new town in Mid-Wales[149] — envisaged the stringing together of 'villages' of 2,500-5,000 in a linear form beside a new high-capacity road linking Newtown with Llanidloes. This road would pass under a new city centre, but elsewhere would be a by-pass, parallelled by local roads joined to the primary route at junctions a mile or so apart.

Developed in detail over an area, the linear form may also begin to assume some of the characteristics of the orthogonal grid, and this venerable device of town planning must now be examined in its modern guise.

152

153

154

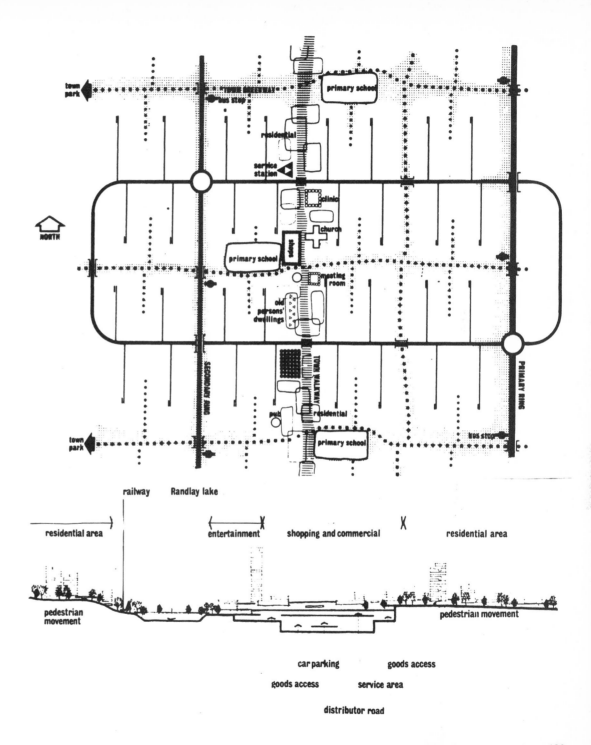

152 Runcorn New Town: the master plan.

153 Telford: diagrammatic structure as originally proposed.

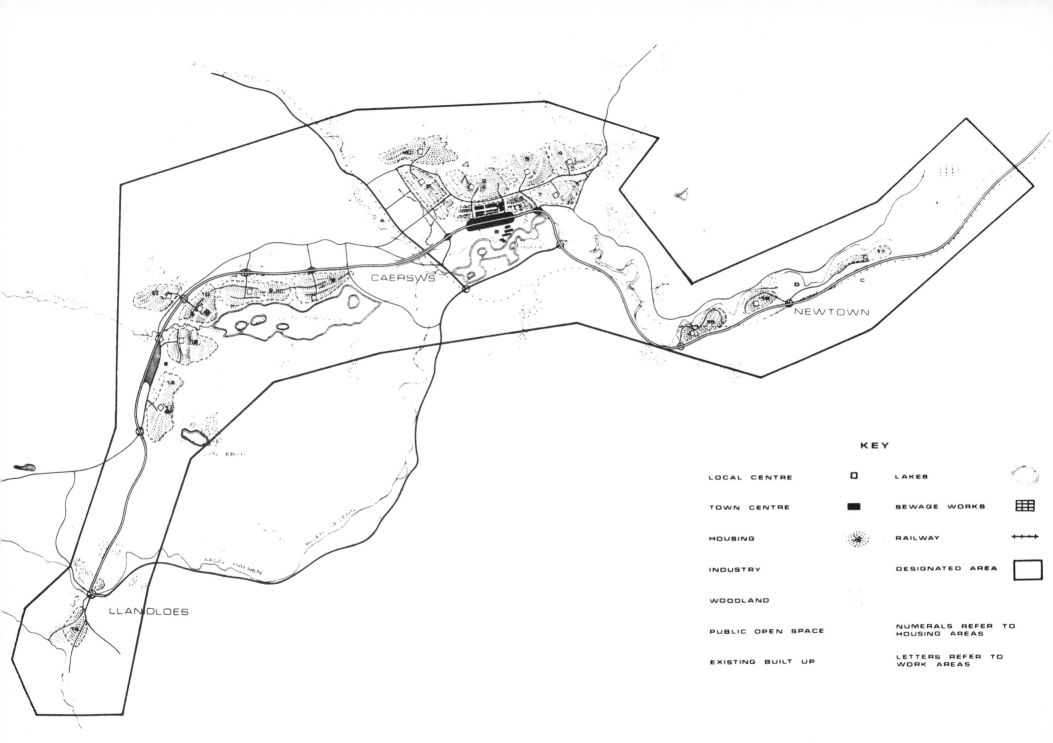

CAERSWS

NEWTOWN

LLANIDLOES

KEY

LOCAL CENTRE   LAKES

TOWN CENTRE   SEWAGE WORKS

HOUSING   RAILWAY

INDUSTRY   DESIGNATED AREA

WOODLAND

PUBLIC OPEN SPACE   NUMERALS REFER TO HOUSING AREAS

EXISTING BUILT UP   LETTERS REFER TO WORK AREAS

155 Washington: the interim proposal based on a half-mile grid with access to 'villages' mid-way between cross-roads.

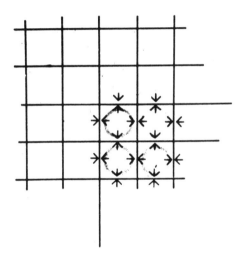

154 The master plan for Caersws, a new town in Mid-Wales:

'Villages' of 25,000-50,000, each with a local centre, linked to each other, a city centre and an industrial zone with an express-way by-pass.

The orthogonal grid had, it will be recalled, been proposed by Buchanan in his theoretical study based upon Marylebone. Since access to a high-speed road must be limited to a few junctions, a system intended to distribute traffic over a wide area may quite logically be arranged as a gridiron, and this, in contrast to the linear form, has been exploited in recent years by planners more concerned with achieving an even spread of traffic over a town than with concentrating public transport along a limited number of routes.

The first systematic investigation in terms of a British new town is at Washington, County Durham, where initially another attempt was made to derive from first principles the ideal answer to an urban form appropriate to the age. New towns *'should be now seen as forming part of a regional or metropolitan complex'* not as *'separate self-contained entities'*. Daily movements would be on a regional scale. It was necessary to find *'a form of urban development which provides the right balance between independence . . . and interaction with the . . . urban region.'* In a region which had been allowed to decline economically, one of the objectives should be *'to provide a focus for high quality living and thus help the whole region to reach higher standards.'* Since the days of Letchworth, social and economic aims may have remained much the same, but the method of attainment must now be different. A prime objective was to accommodate growth and change, and this was especially a problem where items of major investment such as roads were concerned. The neighbourhood concept is again questioned, and a *'looser and freer'* structure sought as appropriate to the motor age. A town should not be conceived as *'industrial

estate, housing estate, central area, etc.'* but more as a complex, overlapping structure.

In spite of this fashionable condemnation of 'neighbourhood', the development of the plan posits a settlement pattern not unlike that proposed at Runcorn. The key grouping is a 'village' of 4,500 — the population required to support a primary school. These villages are found to require an area ½ mile square, and the first proposals suggest that this should be a pedestrian area, bounded on all sides by roads. The object was quite simple: a uniform coverage of the whole town by a uniform primary road system should provide the best possible basis for an even spread of traffic. Prevent local concentration of 'traffic generators', and the resulting traffic volumes everywhere would be compatible with planned capacity and decent environmental standards.

It is necessary, in such an arrangement, somewhere to join to the primary road grid the local roads which are to distribute traffic within the villages. It was decided to place these junctions mid-way between the main cross-roads. The question then arises: should these minor roads themselves be continuous, or should they be arranged so that one always enters and leaves by the same junction? It was decided that local communication demanded a degree of continuity (imagine otherwise how tortuous local distribution door-to-door might become), but to prevent the infiltration of unwanted 'through' traffic, the local system (as at Runcorn) is made unattractive as a short cut, and is arranged to link 'nodes' with the primary system diagonally. A system of footpaths converge to the village centre, where, with the provision of 'bus only' links in the secondary system, a public transport service could penetrate.

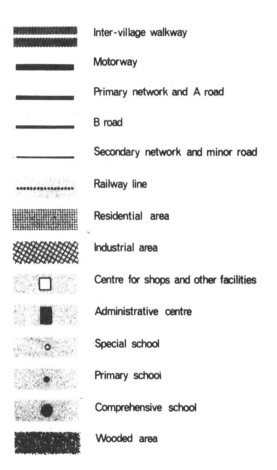

Inter-village walkway

Motorway

Primary network and A road

B road

Secondary network and minor road

Railway line

Residential area

Industrial area

Centre for shops and other facilities

Administrative centre

Special school

Primary school

Comprehensive school

Wooded area

*160 Communications networks within the Master Plan.
Vehicular and pedestrian networks connect to all routes
around the Designated Area. The evenly balanced service
given by these networks over the New Town provides the basis
for the land use plan.*

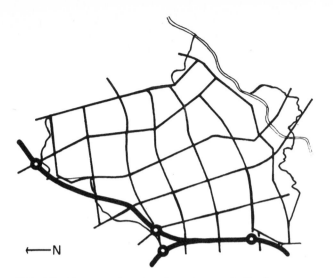

156 Washington: the plan based on a half-mile square grid.
157 Washington: the hierarchy of roads.

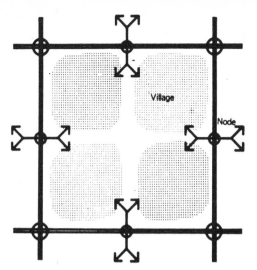

158 Washington: the revised proposals based on a one-mile square grid. Four 'villages' in a 'super-block'.
159 A town walkway system links village focal points.

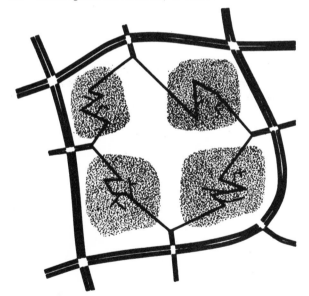

Primary roads
Secondary spur roads
Secondary distributor roads
Development roads

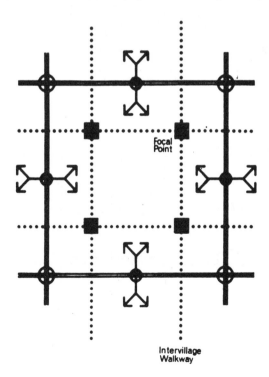

A traffic analysis of these proposals shewed that they were less workable than had been supposed. The primary system had to join into the regional roads at a limited number of points, and this would inevitably result in some elements of it being much more heavily loaded than others. There would also be junctions to negotiate every ¼ mile — much too close for comfort. The scheme was accordingly revised, and something much more like a hierarchy of roads substituted, with the primary grid at approximately 1 mile spacing. There were now four 'villages' in each grid square. The pedestrian routes linking their centres are developed into a continuous town walkway system, passing under or over the main roads, approximately midway between 'junctions' and 'nodes', and forming village focal points where they intersect. It is claimed that a clear frame of reference is achieved giving the desired 'clarity of structure', which at this time was becoming an explicit aim in town planning.

With this schematic layout in mind it was possible to summarise the planning principles which were being pursued as follows: For next-higher units —evident

'i. Village centres and local centres should be situated either where the inter-village walkways intersect, or near the nodes on the primary network.

ii. Industrial areas should be fairly close to nodes on the primary network.

iii. The secondary road layout must not provide short cuts across the square which might divert traffic from the primary network.

iv. A secondary road should pass through, or else close to, all centres.

v. All centres within the square should be connected to one another by the secondary road network although these connections may be less direct than connections by the pedestrian routes.

vi. All centres should have connections to adjoining centres in nearby grid squares by passing across the primary network, through a node.

vii. Buses will pass through each square and will use the secondary road network together with bus only links wherever needed, so that they can pick up all centres by reasonably short routes.'

Within a grid square, other uses like industry could replace one or more villages. In the development of detail, the nodal points on the grid become of particular significance as they provide major accessibility for appropriate traffic. But the truth Buchanan had propounded concerning the limit to development imposed by the selection of a road system is underlined and accepted as a strongly formative feature of the plan.

The town as a whole is elaborated in detail and, in spite of considerable mutilation, much of the original intention comes through. But the planners of Washington have since elsewhere achieved greater maturity in working out their chosen solution, as in due course we shall see.

It is of interest to note how this orthogonal grid solution also tends towards the alternation of routes for different purposes. If we except the MARS plan as a somewhat tentative essay, perhaps the earliest purposeful combination of alternating routes in a gridiron belongs (like so many pioneering notions) to Le Corbusier. In his elaboration of the development plan for Chandigarh (the new capital of the Punjab) he sub-divided superblocks bounded by major roads, with minor streets running in one direction and green ways for pedestrians and cyclists in the other.

For the most complete and elaborate exposition of the orthogonal grid we have to return to Buchanan. Commissioned in 1964 to look at South Hampshire, he produced on a regional scale proposals not for new towns, but for the systematic growth and redevelopment of an already intensely urban area, in terms which have universal application.

He begins with an able analysis of urban form, contrasting the radial-concentric with the grid, and showing how each should be developed to serve modern road traffic, public transport being separated from other traffic onto separate networks. The radial-concentric form is less able to accommodate growth and change than the orthogonal or linear, and he argues his way eventually to a preference for a 'directional grid' which combines the virtues of the lattice and the line.

He also makes a pioneering attempt to apply 'systems analysis' to urban structure. He describes the kind of hierarchical groupings we have become familiar with, many of which have a branching structure. Corresponding to each step in the hierarchy, there is a communications link: from home to school, a footpath; from local centre to district centre, a minor road; from district to town, a bigger road; from town to city, a bigger road still; and so on, up to national — and even international — level. Such a system put together would have *nodes* where a lower category of route intersects with a higher, and it is at these that, for good accessibility, would be sited those facilities approached via

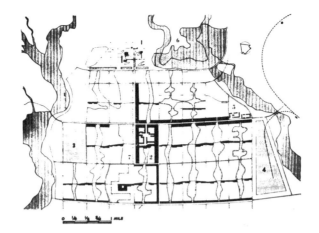

161 Chandigarh: alternating categories of route in a gridiron plan.

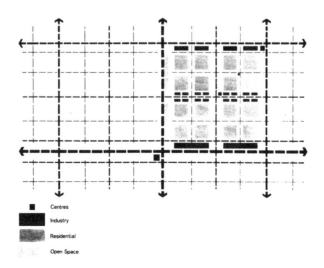

162 An 'idealised diagrammatic centripetal structure': the radial-concentric form is less able to accommodate growth and change.

163 An 'idealised diagrammatic grid structure' . . . 'a grid with networks of different categories to accommodate nodes of urban facilities related in category to the scales of the grid, and dispersed evenly over the grid.' Better than the centripetal form, but still insufficiently flexible. Not suited to public transport. Invites car usage.

the intersecting routes. Thus a primary school, could be appropriately sited at the junction of a footpath (used by its pupils), with a minor road (used by service vehicles).

Combined with the 'directional grid' this reasoning leads to an arrangement wherein the lowest category of routes are the most closely spaced and run parallel to one another. They are crossed at right angles by the next lowest category, running parallel at a wider spacing. At right angles again, and still more widely spaced, comes the next higher category of road, and so on.

Above a certain level, however, it is necessary to distinguish between traffic moving longer distances or at random, and traffic having a specific origin and destination within the locality. Alternate routes within each category are accordingly designated for these two purposes. The 'green' routes are for 'through' or 'random' traffic, and do not provide frontage access. Along the 'red' routes are located those facilities requiring road access. Although Buchanan studiously avoids commitment, 'green' and 'red' routes (in the lower categories at least) could be seen to imply greater emphasis on 'private' and 'public' transport respectively.

Buchanan next shows how the scheme could be applied to South Hampshire. He demonstrates how well adapted to growth it is, and how it can be implemented to facilitate higher or lower rates of growth.

166

167

168

'The structure is not fixed or static in its size. This was a basic factor in our whole approach to the study of the growth of urban structure, that it should be a structure capable of growth in the future and should never be seen as a complete unit. This structure allows growth in many directions; it can be applied on many scales, from a town to a whole region . . .'

'Its development is not governed by a preconceived rate of growth. It can develop under different conditions and be influenced by these conditions, which will probably be changing over different phases of growth. It does not result in a fixed static plan of development, but suggests a framework on, and within which, changing trends and strategies of growth towards different goals are possible. The method of using this structure as we visualise it is not one of drawing up a "development plan" and requiring private developers to conform to it. It is much more a matter of drawing up a general strategy within which private enterprise will have considerable freedom to operate and to make their own judgements, but where a pattern of strong market forces will be created by public sector investment

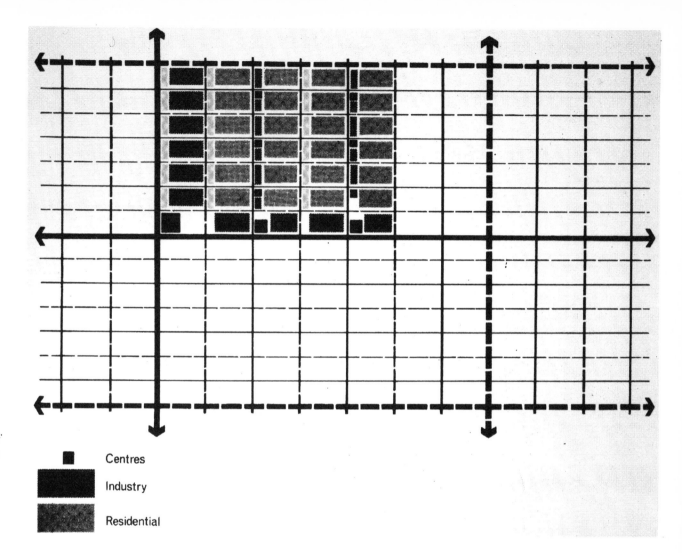

■ Centres

Industry

Residential

164 An 'idealised diagrammatic directional grid structure'. Evolved from a linear form of growth depending on 'a basic communication spine along which the dominant elements are located.' Allows flexibility in transport policy; change; modular growth; good accessibility. Compare the three-strand structure (fig. 145).

145

within which private developers will find it advantageous to operate. Conditions can be created in which they will be only too anxious to play a part.'[151]

Buchanan had indeed invented what he intended as little less than a matrix for the whole future development of mankind. *Yes, this is the answer for the next-higher unit. See Unwin pp.82-83.*

165   Education: a typical urban 'sub-system'.

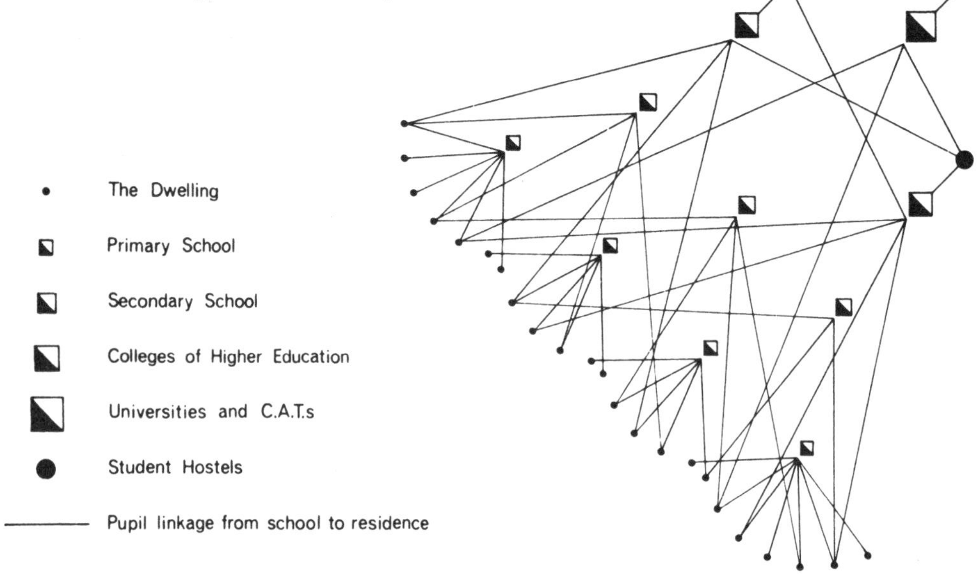

- ● The Dwelling
- ◪ Primary School
- ◪ Secondary School
- ◪ Colleges of Higher Education
- ◪ Universities and C.A.T.s
- ● Student Hostels
- —— Pupil linkage from school to residence

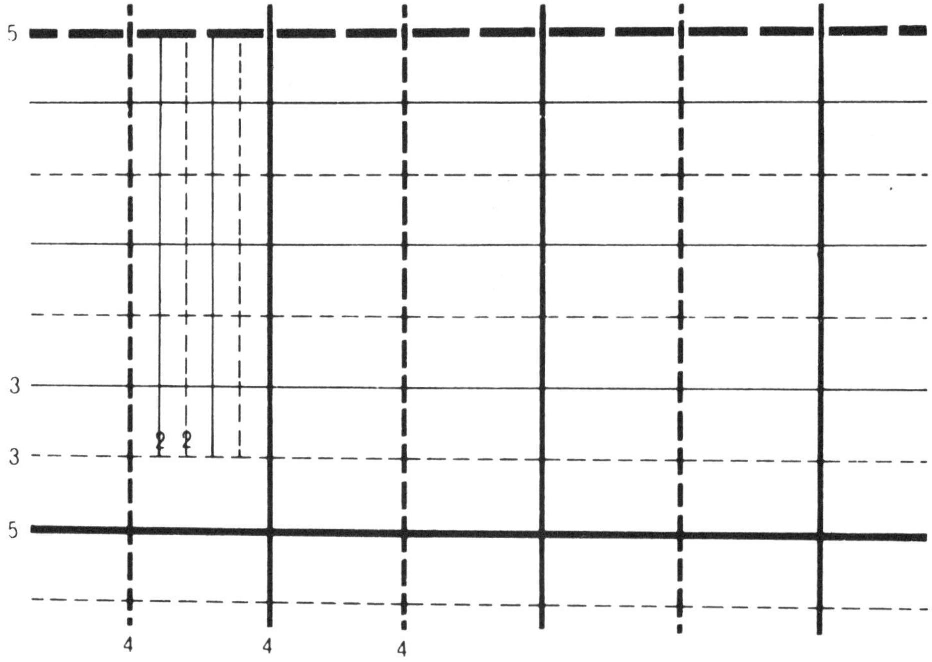

166   A grid of routes of various categories. Footpaths (the lowest level) and category 6 (national and regional routes) are not shown. The broken lines represent 'green' routes for through or random movement, alternating with 'red' routes (firm line) of the same category, along which most facilities generating traffic are sited. Intersections or 'nodes' are especially significant: they provide locations for facilities (e.g. factories, shops, offices) which draw employees or customers via lower categories of route, and require regional or national linkage via a higher category.

167 The 'directional grid' in detail. Arrows indicate potential growth. The 'residential models' are various combinations of dwelling types, and size of symbol indicates size of facility proposed. The theme is the concentration of facilities which generate movement along 'spines of activity' ('red' routes) related in scale to the facilities they serve.

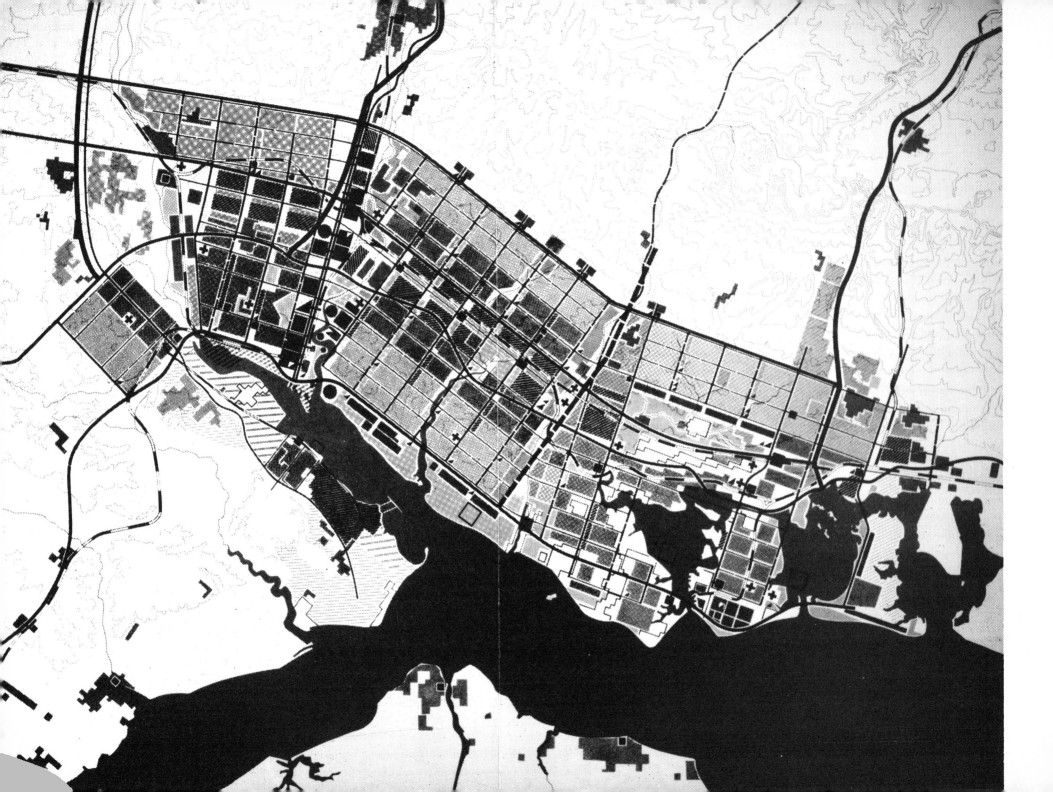

One of the new towns of the 'sixties has a history which extends over the whole decade, and from it many lessons can be learnt. Already in 1959, the County of Buckingham was looking at its problems with an eye to coping with a considerable increase in urban population. If every little market town and village were allowed to grow haphazardly, then their existing structure would become overloaded, with disastrous results. A possibility was to allow them to grow as dormitory suburbs of one or more new 'out-of-town' centres, which would draw workers, shoppers and others, with their motor-cars, away from the existing historic centres, leaving 169 these to continue in a relatively minor role. But this was felt to be wrong: a city needs a heart, and such a solution relies too much upon the motor car. The alternative was to build a new city, a term used advisedly from the outset to emphasise the much larger scale intended than in previous new 'towns'. By 1962 the basic features of a plan for a new city to accommodate 250,000 had been produced. 170

The argument for it ran as follows:

'A.   That it was impossible at reasonable costs to produce a satisfactory city plan designed for 100 per cent motor car use and that public transport should be seriously investigated.

'B.   That, following A, all development would be planned around four loops of public transport which would be linked together at a city centre.

'C.   The running costs of the public transport system — a monorail — would be rate-borne. Costs of the system as a rate-borne service were assessed on figures then available as the equivalent of about three shillings per week for a typical three-bedroom dwelling.

'D.   Housing would be high density alternating around the loops with areas of industry to give a more even distribution of traffic on the public transport system.

'E.   The areas within the public transport loops would be the city's areas of open space and would contain schools, hospitals, etc.'

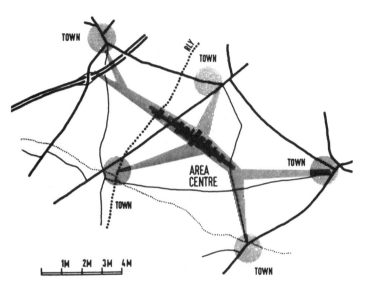

169   Urban expansion based on existing market towns with a new external centre.

168   A diagram showing the directional grid structure fully exploited for Southampton-Portsmouth. Higher densities in darker grey. Diagonal hatching: industry etc.
A matrix for the future development of mankind?

Later the same year the circuit linear form had been investigated, and it had become clear that development [P17 →]

'*should take place within an area around the stopping places, the radius containing the development being determined by such factors as:*

'*A. Acceptable walking distance to station, assumed at not exceeding 7 minutes;*

'*B. Spacing of stations on the route;*

'*C. Capacity of the system;*

'*D. Community size accepted as between 5,000 - 7,000 and known as "townships".*

'*All dwellings would have garages and access to city roads. There would be a completely segregated pedestrian access to the public transport station, located in a building which would also contain shops, clinics, primary schools, etc. There would also be traffic free access to the public open space within the public transport routes and to adjacent areas of housing and industry.*'[152]

Various forms of public transport were considered, and the choice fell between the underground railway and the above-ground monorail. The higher construction costs associated with the former resulted in the selection of the monorail. Subsequent costing showed that although the initial cost of such an installation would exceed that required for a 100% car usage system, the cost per passenger mile would be much less than travel by car, and a modest rate charge would allow the system to be paid for, operated and replaced after 60 years for much less than the alternative high capacity road system which would be needed. **171**

The overall density of the 'townships' was to be 50 persons per acre. These could be mainly in housing of the patio type (a fashionable device for achieving high density without going above two storeys) but it was assumed that there should be a build-up involving taller buildings and flats towards the transport stop. Within each township there would be **172** supporting facilities sufficient for 5,000-7,000 persons, and it could include some industry. At the stop itself there would be local shops etc. An independent road system gave access *à la* Radburn to ample car parks and garages, and linked to the city's roads.

170 North Bucks New City — diagrammatic form.

171 Public transport systems compared.

METHOD	CAPABILITY FOR AUTOMATION	BAD WEATHER OPERATION	SAFETY	PEDESTRIAN CROSSING	VEHICLE CROSSING	ROUTE FLEXIBILITY	PRESENT PRACTICABILITY	CAPITAL COST	SUMMARY
UNDERGROUND	✓	✓	✓	✓	✓	✗	✓	HIGH	GOOD, NO FLEXIBILITY OF ROUTE. HIGH COST MAKES FOR IMPRACTICABILITY.
ON GROUND A. TRAM	✗	FAIR	FAIR	✗	✗	FAIR	✓	FAIR	FAIR COST, DOES NOT MEET REQUIREMENTS.
B. BUS ON SEPARATE ROUTE	✗	✗	✗	✗	✗	FAIR	✓	LOW	LOW COST, FAIR ROUTE FLEXIBILITY, DOES NOT MEET OTHER REQUIREMENTS.
C. GUIDED ROAD	✓	FAIR	FAIR	✗	✗	✗	✗	HIGH	NOT AT PRESENT PRACTICABLE.
ABOVE GROUND	✓	✓	✓	✓	✓	FAIR	✓	FAIR	GOOD, COST FAIR, BEST COMPROMISE.

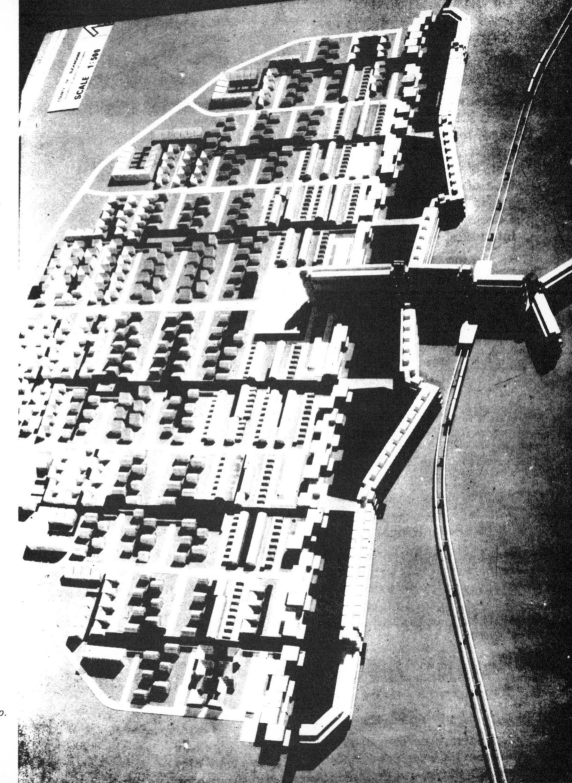

172　North Bucks New City: a typical township.

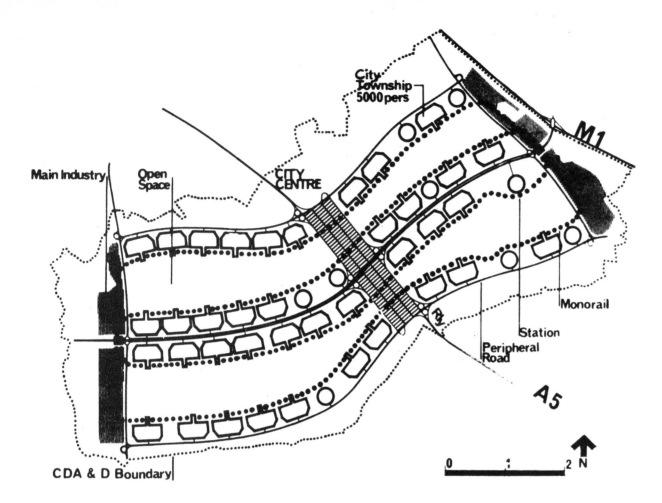

City Township 5000 pers

Main Industry

Open Space

CITY CENTRE

M1

Monorail

Station

Peripheral Road

A5

CDA & D Boundary

0   1   2   **N**

173 A new city for 250,000: the plan.

* Principally, F. Pooley and B. Berrett, of Buckinghamshire County Council.

The whole
'consists of four basic circuit linear groupings which join at
the city centre. The groupings are connected by two
interlinked circuits of a public transport system which joins
home, work, recreational and central zones together. It is
planned in such a way that every dwelling and important
building is within a maximum walking distance of seven
minutes from a transport point. Most of the walk ways from
dwellings and shops to the transport points will be under
cover . . .

'To make the (monorail) service attractive to the public and
to make considerable savings in administration, it was decided
that travel should be fare free and the running cost met from
the local rates. The service which it is proposed to provide
would be adequate to meet the most difficult peak traffic
conditions and at the same time be frequent and
comfortable.'[153]

As their work progressed, the architects* became more and
more enthusiastic about its possibilities. The monorail system
provided, in effect, a series of 'ring mains': the most
economical form for distributing services of all kinds to a
predetermined pattern. Since they were also concerned with
the planning of the whole county, they were aware that a new
city such as they were proposing would require not only new
schools, shops and factories, but also new engineering
services — especially electricity. Why not put a new power
station at the heart of the city, and circulate power via the
ring mains? Why not do the same with district heating? Why
not combine both functions, and generate electricity and heat
from the same plant? Why not at the same time burn the
town's refuse and recover the heat?

Unable with their own resources to investigate these
possibilities, they enlisted government support, and found it
in the person of a former colleague largely responsible for
Coventry's pioneer planning, then a senior civil servant: Sir
Donald Gibson. A working party of engineers and others was
set up to look into these matters. There were both technical
and administrative difficulties which would have to be
overcome to achieve everything which had been suggested.
They noted how much easier it would be with nuclear power,
and commented on the new town of Farsta near Stockholm,
where it was possible to bury a nuclear power station under
rock and thus place it close enough to the town for its waste
heat to be used. The possibility of burning refuse was not
pursued. But the conclusion emerged

'... *that there is a distinct possibility that district heating for the city in North Buckinghamshire might well provide an economic supply of heat to domestic, commercial, public and industrial buildings ...*'

and further studies were advised on matters of detail. The cost of heat to householders, for all space and water needs throughout the year, would be less than could be achieved using the cheapest fuel in a domestic installation, and in addition,

'*The availability in the new city of a supply at low cost of hot water from the district heating mains could open up new possibilities for a standard of amenities at present considered impracticable.*'

These could include:

'1. *Road heating for frost and ice prevention.*
2. *Walkways and shopping arcades to be similarly heated.*
3. *Patio heating.*
4. *Central Rotunda, or Piazza heating.*
5. *Sports facilities: all the year round availability.*
6. *Swimming pools.*
7. *Playground heating.*
8. *Food production*
9. *Refrigeration*[154]

Buckinghamshire County Council's proposal to build a new city in North Buckinghamshire was confirmed after a governmental investigation of the region. The new town site was designated in 1967, but, to their regret, the Council's architects were not allowed to proceed with their scheme. Instead, consultants were appointed. The choice fell upon Llewellyn Davies and Partners — the planners of Washington — who now proceeded to plan the town which has since become known as Milton Keynes.

The thoroughness with which the work has been carried out, the declared intention to involve as much public participation as possible, and the resolve to evolve solutions over a period of time, rather than impose a master plan preconceived in detail: all this has already resulted in a mass of published material, which makes a summary account difficult.

An interim plan, produced in 1969, was submitted to the criticism of all concerned. There were some changes as a result, but the basic strategy remained unchanged.

The 'brief' required that transport should be a prime factor; that at least half the dwellings should be for 'owner-occupation'; that at each stage in the development, there should exist a '*viable community*'; and that the new city should take account of the region in which it was placed, for which it was destined to become a '*major sub-regional centre*'. Population targets were 150,000 newcomers by the early 'nineties, which would result in a total by about that time of 250,000. The city was to be a '*balanced community, mainly self-contained, as regards shopping, public services, recreation and other amenities.*' Six broad 'goals' were identified, as follows:

'i. *Opportunity and freedom of choice*
ii. *Easy movement and access, and good communications*
iii. *Balance and variety*
iv. *An attractive city*
v. *Public awareness and participation*
vi. *Efficient and imaginative use of resources*'[155]

In order to find an appropriate physical framework for the realisation of these somewhat pious objectives, nine alternative possibilities were compared. These took account of three possible residential densities; three levels of employment concentration; and three transport principles. It was quickly found '*that only those plans offering the potential for low concentration of work places and low residential densities, were likely to meet the goals*'. A kilometre square grid of main roads was found to be efficient from a traffic point of view, and of the seven possible types of public transport system examined, the choice fell upon the conventional bus — at least for the time being.

A basic 'module' of one kilometre square having been decided upon, the remainder logically follows. The low densities proposed, and the ample road network, results in modest traffic flows both within the 'environmental areas' bounded by the main roads, and on the main roads themselves. There is thus no need for more than traffic signal control of crossroads, and except for a length of urban motorway linking with the regional system, nothing more elaborate than more-or-less conventional 'dual carriageways' is called for. It is also possible to combine public transport with other main road traffic. Bus stops are at one kilometre

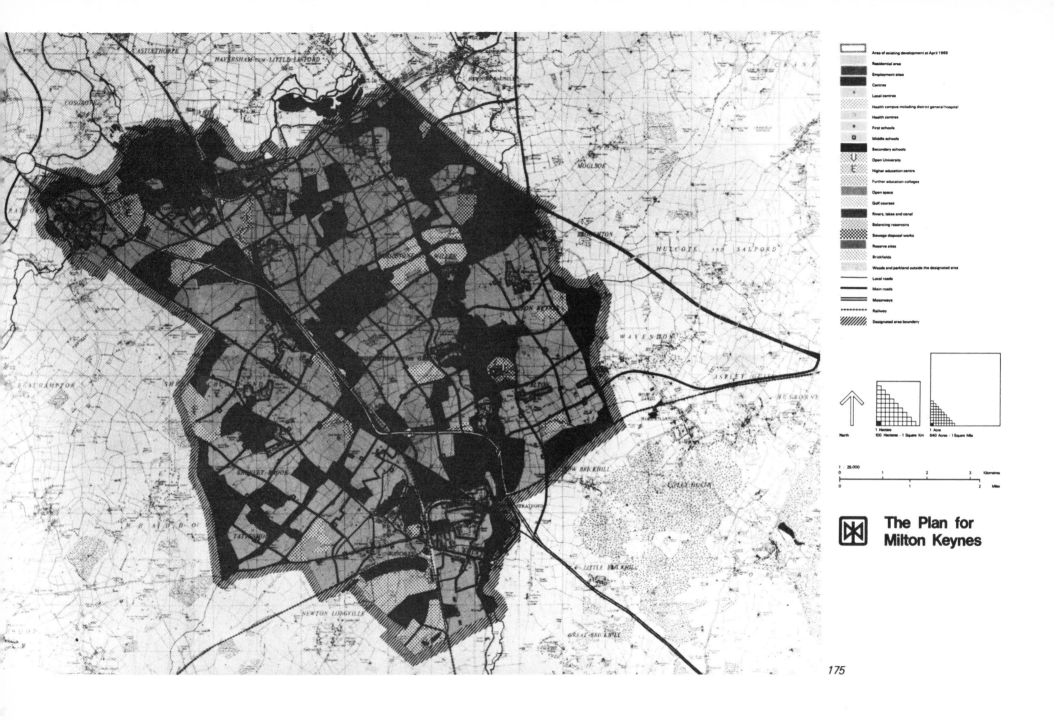

The Plan for
Milton Keynes

	Area of existing development at April 1969
	Residential area
	Employment sites
	Centres
	Local centres
	Health campus including district general hospital
	Health centres
	First schools
	Middle schools
	Secondary schools
	Open University
	Higher education centre
	Further education colleges
	Open space
	Golf courses
	Rivers, lakes and canal
	Balancing reservoirs
	Sewage disposal works
	Reserve sites
	Brickfields
	Woods and parkland outside the designated area
	Local roads
	Main roads
	Motorways
	Railway
	Designated area boundary

North

1 Hectare
100 Hectares · 1 Square Km

1 Acre
640 Acres · 1 Square Mile

1 : 25,000

154

175

177 Milton Keynes: an impression of part of the city. The secondary local roads connect to the main kilometre grid at the third points between main cross-roads. 'Activity centres' occur at pedestrian underpasses midway between main cross-roads.

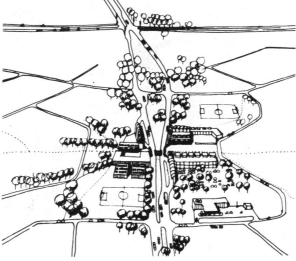

176 Milton Keynes: aerial sketch of a typical 'activity centre' associated with a pedestrian underpass below main dual carriageway (Housing not shown).

spacing, equipped with slip roads and underpass. For ease of pedestrian access over a radius of half-a-kilometre, these stops are placed midway between cross-roads. 175

The stops themselves are designated *'activity centres'*. Around them are grouped appropriate community facilities, and upon them a footpath system converges. The footpath system also has 'grade-separated' links near the cross-roads, and in this way it becomes possible to move on foot easily from super-block to super-block. The goal of variety and choice is thus achieved: there is no rigid separation into 'neighbourhoods' or other sub-divisions. Instead, throughout the town as a whole there is created a series of overlapping catchment areas in such a way that a choice of facilities is never difficult to achieve. 176

The secondary road system giving access into the super-blocks is spaced at approximately 300 metres: i.e., at the third points between cross-roads. Traffic on them will be slow, and there is need neither for elaborate junctions nor for Radburn layouts. To facilitate short journeys, the secondary system is continuous, but contorted to discourage improper use. 177

There is a city centre. It is planned in some detail, but avoids the Cumbernauld solution as unsuitable for speculative development. There are some concentrations of shops, etc. in local centres, and some other concentrations of particular 'land uses'. But, as far as possible, concentration is avoided. 178

The strategic plan is thus very straightforward and simple. It allows for the unforeseen. It can grow without difficulty, and without wholesale expenditure on a costly 'infrastructure' years in advance of its being needed. New technical devices such as 'dial-a-bus' and computer control of traffic lights can later be incorporated. Everyone who wants to, can go about by car; and for those who do not, a bus service (which would *'compare favourably'* with those currently available in other towns) would be available. The strategy lends itself to tactical adjustments, and a computer programme will be used to effect these as development proceeds.

In producing their plan for Milton Keynes, its authors collaborated with many of the nation's leading experts. A formidable array of professors of everything from agriculture to art history is listed on the title page of their report. The mountain has laboured. The Greeks, the Romans, the colonists, pioneers and land speculators of every age would no doubt applaud so authoritative a confirmation of their practice.

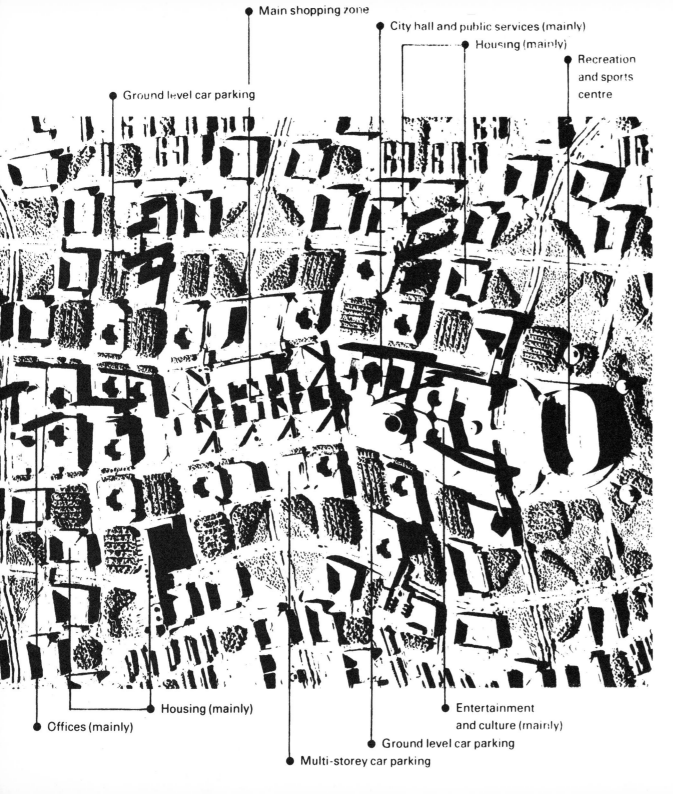

Main shopping zone

City hall and public services (mainly)

Housing (mainly)

Recreation and sports centre

Ground level car parking

178 Milton Keynes: an impression of the new city centre.

Housing (mainly)

Offices (mainly)

Entertainment and culture (mainly)

Ground level car parking

Multi-storey car parking

These two tales of one city eloquently contrast tendencies in modern British town planning and represent the latest state of controversies which have long been with us. But already some common ground appears, and it will be useful to explore this more fully.

Today the tendency is to accept the 'super-city' as unavoidably typical of the age. This is the more surprising, in that a decade or two ago, the consensus was the other way. The root cause, it seems, is in economic realities. The giant scale of modern industrial organisation is today inescapable. One large factory replaces a host of smaller ones. 'Economies of scale' are claimed for undertakings wherein the entire production of a nation's (or even a continent's) requirements for this or that commodity is undertaken more or less under one roof. Complex interlocking and mutually dependent networks develop. There are advantages in diversifying production within one organisation. A computing centre, a research laboratory, an administrative headquarters, is inefficient below a minimum 'threshold' size, and uneconomic unless involved in the servicing of a giant organisation.

There clearly must be upper limits beyond which costs outstrip gains. But it would be reactionary as well as Utopian to dream of reversing this trend in favour of the small-scale industry of the past. Modern communications make it possible, of course, to scatter the parts of industrial combines. But they sub-divide most readily 'horizontally' rather than 'vertically': that is, in such a way that were each part to be placed separately in a different small town, the employment available would be restricted in one place to research, in another to administration, and in another to 'blue-collar' work. The evils of the one-industry town (which all recent town planning has set out to avoid) would be resurrected.

Thus from the point of view of the modern economy, the super-city is justified. Advantages are also claimed in the range of facilities it can support — from Olympic stadia to universities — although here it could be argued that Athens, Florence and Venice in their time, with comparatively small communities, enjoyed a richer culture than does modern London, Tokyo or New York. And even today, our greatest universities are not in our largest towns.

But however matters may be economically, socially the super-city is certainly suspect, and we have seen how for at least thirty years, planners, unable to arrest its growth, have been trying to break it down into socially-viable units of limited size. In doing so, they may have been guilty of over-simplifying the complexities of urban society into neat branching hierarchies, adapted to the requirements of planning rather than those of real life. But they have been motivated — although perhaps not too clearly — by the same logic which led Aristotle, Owen and Howard to place in the forefront of their argument the question of optimum size.

How the city should be divided, how big the parts should be, and how they should be related to each other, consequently becomes a key problem in modern town planning. It has long been customary to conceive the city as comprising a variety of elements, like market places, streets and buildings. Today we have long (and uncritically) become used to the idea of numerous types of buildings: offices, schools, banks, shops, libraries, apartments, cottages, etc. — all separately devoted to separate uses at separate times. Ever since Owen, the factory has dominated the arrangement of the city. In that it requires the congregation of large numbers in a specific place at specified hours, it has had, and continues to have, profound consequences. And these are no longer confined to workshop and assembly line. Today, indeed, vast acres of manufacturing industry can function automatically with very few workers. But, to some extent as a

* Definitely not so. Research is imperative about individuals, families, +(other) small groups. But these elemental units are ignored by the planners.

consequence of this, 'white-collar' workers now daily throng the office zones in what in many respects are fast becoming the factories of tomorrow.

Without exception, the recent plans we have reviewed, have placed the factories in a separate part of the town — usually in an industrial *zone*. Originally the reason was that factories were dirty, noisy and generally obnoxious. This is no longer necessarily so, but the practice of zoning industry continues, and has extended to all 'land-uses'. Today, there are some who advocate mixing them all up again in the interests of variety and liveliness, and this may to some extent be possible. But in that large centres of employment generate traffic out of scale with residential surroundings, there is still a strong argument in favour of segregation.

Thus alongside the factory grows up the practice of the division of the town into zones, for this use or that. In recent planning practice, this has sometimes approached the level of absurdity. Central areas have been subdivided into 'cultural', 'entertainment', 'shopping' zones and the like: the intention being that a block of theatres should stand apart from another of libraries, museums and art galleries. Even working men's clubs have been assigned a quarter of their own. The practice no doubt owed much to planning legislation, which through zoning alone was able to have some control over the use to which privately owned land could be put.

After factory towns grew to unmanageable sizes, sub-division by zoning, difficult in any case to achieve, did not in itself seem enough, and for Howard the answer lay in the disintegration of the city itself. In practice, what happened was universal sub-urbanisation: the wholesale spread of the residential suburb. Thus the city could now be regarded as having a central core, industrial zones, and suburbs. Out of the suburb grew concepts of cellular structure, neighbourhood theory, and the notion of a city divided into a hierarchy of social groupings.

In spite of recent attempts to re-think social structure, much of the neighbourhood argument still persists. Groupings based on the population required to support a primary school and other facilities with a pedestrian catchment area, are still a basic ingredient in design. There is also today the wish to give the urban environment a 'meaningful image'* This, in a forthright utilitarian spirit, attempts to tie 'aesthetic' matters in civic design down to questions of intelligibility, and it is argued that a sense of 'belonging' to a definable location is necessary to the enjoyment of urban life. A citizen is bored, bewildered,

rejected and alone in an amorphous urban jumble. It is argued that if the large city is inevitable, some sub-division into intelligible parts is necessary to facilitate its comprehension, no less than its design and its management. For this reason, some designers are concerned to break down the neighbourhood itself into even smaller sub-divisions, beginning with the houses grouped around close or green.

The *district*, which in the first new towns embraced the population of a group of neighbourhoods, is less explicit. Concepts of total form are tending towards a looser structure wherein larger residential neighbourhoods (sometimes now called 'townships') are directly associated with 'whole-city' facilities: factories, offices, supermarkets, secondary schools, etc. A comprehensive totality is still usually aimed at, and to this end, the concept of the city centre persists. But there are signs that this is being questioned. With a tendency to design cities in such a way that they form continuous regional conurbations, the whole begins to assume a federated form, with 'neighbourhoods', 'villages', or 'townships', interspersed with major facilities, all more or less accessible from any part of the region and not specifically associated with any part. This, at any rate, is the pattern which would suit industry and employment generally, but it may yet prove desirable that secondary schools and some of the things previously thought of as appropriate to district centres, should provide the basis for a still larger, denser neighbourhood, or for groupings intermediate between neighbourhood and city.

Thus, in planning the structure of the modern city, we have elements of two *schemata*: *zones* based on land use, and *neighbourhoods* based on residential groups. In the latter, an element of social organisation is always present, and there is in town planning a praiseworthy tradition of positive community planning, which dies hard. This tradition has always contained a strong undercurrent of socialist egalitarianism, and, as a consequence, the examples we have studied obscure the third and most obvious element of sub-division in the modern town: that based on social class. If under euphemisms like 'density', 'car-ownership', and the like, separate provisions for different 'socio-economic groups' are customarily made, these have usually (so far) been *within* the residential cells. At Milton Keynes, however, in an area where the white collar is as common as the blue, and where market forces are to be given wide scope, we may expect an outcome not unlike that in established cities, where today every rank in society — and every race — knows its own place.

Another common theme today, is the anticipation of continued *growth*. Thus the design is required to be open-ended and admit of variation. Most importantly, it must facilitate *growth by stages*.

The device hit upon to achieve staged growth, is one long familiar in architecture: the *module*. The city is conceived as a multiplicity of *basic cells* or modules, each independently viable up to a point, and connected to the whole via an efficient transport system, which must also be capable of staged growth. We are led once more in the direction of the neighbourhood.

The anticipation of growth is also, for most, the acceptance of *uncertainty*. This results in a preference for plans which divorce a permanent 'infrastructure' of roads and engineering services, from a 'superstructure' of buildings, which at any time are free to take a variety of forms.

Associated with the acceptance of growth is another remarkable characteristic common to all recent proposals: the total rejection of the radial-concentric form. In its place, we have for the streets of the town, three typical *schemata*, based respectively on what may briefly be characterised as the *line*, the *loop* and the *grid*.

The linear form facilitates movement and expansion. Since however (as we have noted) access to any route must be confined to specific points along it, and since these may be elaborated into cross-roads, the linear form translates most readily into the grid. From the standpoint of traffic, the choice in the examples we have reviewed has rested principally upon the intention concerning public transport. There is, *prima facie*, an advantage in having buses (or what-you-will) concentrated onto a limited number of linear routes, where they can follow one another at short intervals: i.e. *to concentrate the demand*. With the automobile in the town, on the other hand, the advantage is all the other way. To keep roads and junctions uncongested and to modest dimensions, it is better *to spread the demand*. The loop is a finite elaboration of the linear form, and as such does not so readily permit expansion. The examples we have reviewed show, however, how their designers have proposed to overcome this limitation, which they have regarded as a minor one compared with the assets of the 'ring main' or 'circuit linear' form. With it the performance of public transport is still further improved, and it is better adapted to engineering economy.

The radial-concentric city is not only unable to grow. It also promotes traffic congestion. And traffic congestion

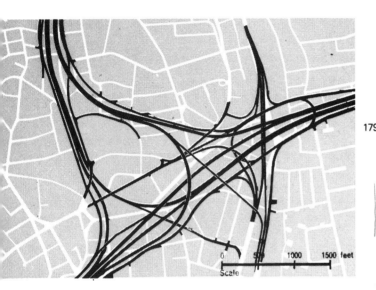

179   The motor car demands space: an urban motorway junction superimposed on the map of part of Boston, USA. It occupies about 100 acres.

* The recent work of Kevin Lynch, whose *Image of the City* pioneered experimental investigation here, has stimulated renewed interest in this topic.

† Or train, or tram, or cushion craft, or travelator, or monorail or . . .

brings us to the problem of *internal communications*, which for modern times has dominated technical aspects of town planning in much the same way as, in previous ages, did defence and public health.

Enough has been said to remind us that hitherto most journeys in towns were on foot. Le Corbusier's opprobrium was misplaced: it was men, not donkeys, who made the city's tracks. But now, for the first time in history, the automobile has made it possible seriously to consider the disappearance of the city. With it, we can live miles from our work, we can collect supplies of food and fuel from distant markets. With the kind of engine it uses, we can even generate our own electric power to pump our water, light our homes and power our television sets. The 'new nomadism' proposed by contemporary futurists is no idle dream.

The motor-car, indeed, not only promotes the dissolution of the city: it virtually demands it. It demands space, and its use is facilitated by *dispersal*. A city designed for its uninhibited use would be spacious indeed. But problems arise when grandparents want to go out, or children go to school. Unless automobiles can be made safe and manageable for everyone, irrespective of age, the price of universal mobility for the able-bodied will be the social life of the young and the infirm. It goes without saying that this deprivation, with our present inequalities, will extend also to those too poor to own a car. So there has to be some kind of public transport. Those who cannot drive themselves have to be driven. But here arises the fundamental dilemma: the efficiency of public transport is promoted by *concentration*. Unless every bus †is to be a taxi, or services are to be run at intervals of several hours, there must be potential passengers in large numbers near to every bus stop. Thus the public transport solution militates against the car, and the automobile solution is unacceptable on social grounds.

But one is reluctant to lose the advantages of the car. We have seen that the size of a settlement has an influence upon its traffic, and it may be that a solution lies that way. Small towns, however, are unacceptable on economic grounds. Thus another way out is sought: the city is broken down into areas small enough for them not to be suffocated by their own traffic, and these areas are connected together and to the city as a whole by main road systems external to them. This is the direction taken by Buchanan in his 'Traffic in Towns'. But for both Leeds and London he had eventually to assume a heavy reliance upon public transport. Ever since, the solution has been sought in more-or-less the terms he proposed, with a greater or lesser reliance on public transport, which is now

found to have a logic of its own.

A significant characteristic of a public transport system, is the station or stop. This has certain measurable qualities, which can be exploited in planning — especially in residential areas. The efficiency of the system, as we have seen, depends upon the number of passengers within easy reach of it. Theoretically these can most efficiently be contained in a circle, the radius of which is the maximum acceptable walking distance from the stop. From this quite logically arises the 'string of beads' principle. The number of passengers potentially available at each stop, furthermore, increases as the density of the residential area rises, and this argues compactness. It also argues discouraging the motorist from using his car, and the layouts we have examined show how it is proposed this should be done.

We are thus led once more in the direction of the neighbourhood, and the logic of public transport has begun to affect basic decisions concerning residential groupings. The pattern which most clearly emerges, is that of a community having as its focal point a public transport stop and probably also such local facilities (a primary school, etc.) as it requires. Towards this a footpath system converges. Non-public transport is distributed within the neighbourhood by a system of minor roads which, in order to dissuade unnecessary use, often become bewildering in their complexity. These minor roads are connected to the town's primary road system, which by-passes the built-up areas.

The most significant differences arise from the relationship of the public transport system to the primary road network. Buchanan had assumed the two would coincide, and the same still holds good for Milton Keynes. But at Runcorn there is, as far as possible, complete separation, and as an ideal it is not hard to justify.

Just as we have seen that the automobile and the bus pull the town in contrary directions, so do they require totally different 'primary networks'. The car is best served by the motorway, on which pedestrians are not allowed, waiting is prohibited, speeds are high, and junctions few. The bus route must be readily accessible and crossed on foot, and permit a vehicle to weave in and out of the traffic stream at close intervals. It would most usefully pass right through the heart of the locality it serves, whereas, at least since the time of Tripp, every planner has sited motor roads on the periphery. It is possible to use the same road for cars and buses only when traffic densities are low. And this, as we have seen, argues low density all round and an indifferent bus service — as at Milton Keynes.

There are problems associated with the Runcorn solution, however. Extended over a city region, the public transport system would itself begin to assume formidable dimensions. It might be difficult to pass, through the middle of all the residential areas, express services linking localities with regional centres far away. They could of course go underground, but, however arranged, the different kind of service required argues a regional system, with stops more widely spaced than on the more local network. Thus in a city region planned for public transport, there may again be a hierarchy, this time relating to stops on the local system, and to those more widely dispersed points where the local and regional transport services interconnect. This is the kind of problem Buchanan was beginning to tackle in his South Hampshire study, and foreshadowed decades ago by the MARS group. With regional facilities dispersed to nodes on the regional transport system, the whole city dissolves again into a federation of 'villages' interspersed with employment zones, hospitals, supermarkets, colleges and the like.

Another problem associated with the public-transport-only route, arises from the need to serve every premise in the town with vehicles of some sort. Allowing that most people can walk to the bus-stop most of the time, there are still those who cannot. There are still goods (and babies) to be delivered, buildings to be built, refuse to be collected, furniture to be moved, and — at the end of it all — coffins to be carried away. For all of this, there have to be roads, and we have seen how at Runcorn and elsewhere these are provided for. The scale upon which they are designed, however, has so far always assumed a high residual use of the privately-owned motor-car, which is kept at the home or near it. Perhaps beyond this current preference, there lies the possibility that the use of the car within the town will diminish to the point where the town-dweller will consider its ownership unnecessary and content himself with the hire of a car, a cab or a van on the rare occasion he needs one. Perhaps when he goes out in the countryside he will ride in comfort to a remote destination and then proceed in a vehicle hired on arrival. Perhaps then, the amount of traffic seeking to circulate on the streets of future residential communities will be such that it can easily be accommodated on the 'community routes', and the duplication of systems which characterize most recent plans will, as far as residential localities are concerned, become unnecessary. Perhaps, too, if the vehicles used, and their speeds, numbers and other characteristics are brought down to the scale acceptable and safe in a pedestrian environment, then the fashion for footpaths à la Radburn will also largely disappear. But for this to happen, planning for public transport, which is now in its infancy, and the design of public transport systems, will both have to be mastered.

The probable future strategy which emerges from our review is thus clear: whatever else persists alongside it, the city region is typical of the age. Decisions as to its location and growth are primarily issues of national policy. Socially, it should have a federated, rather than a hierarchical, structure, the basic modules being residential cells, interspersed with regional facilities, and linked by an efficient transport system. This system should comprise two principal components: one for local, one for regional travel. In each basic 'module' should live a community large enough to be socially viable and manage its own affairs, but not so large that traffic and other big-city problems begin to appear within it. The regional facilities should be easy of access, and comprise everything that would allow everyone, in every part of the country, to enjoy the fruits of big-city living without its drawbacks.

Where does this lead us tactically? Our examples have been drawn from new towns, where reason is less inhibited by the residue of the past. But our typical and most pressing problems lie in existing cities, which are the starting points for the new city regions, and which, in the older industrialised countries like Britain, are in urgent need of attention. It goes without saying that, if the new towns are to serve as models for the old, the rejection of the radial-concentric form raises (in many European cities at least) acute problems.

The first — and long-overdue — tactical step, is to reverse the present policies which are based on trying to cope with as many automobiles as possible, bringing in public transport only as a regrettable afterthought, in favour of policies based upon *absolute priority for public transport.** In most cities, there still remain the essential elements of the route systems which served public transport in the past. These can be revived as the basis for the local network. Usually this will be the more appropriate in that a short time ago public services performed exactly the sort of function aimed at by the 'community route', and the roads along which they ran were the lines along which the city grew. They will usually be found to comprise the old main road system of the town, which, for twenty years or more, engineers have been trying to convert into automobile expressways, with enormous consequent damage to public transport and local communities alike.

180 An American urban motorway.

Instead of turning the city inside out, as Tripp was trying to do, it is necessary to restore it as it originally was, and to remove all traffic which in any way impedes public transport from the main roads of our cities.

The community routes thus re-established, it would be necessary to plan the communities — the string of beads — along them. Here again, advantage could be taken of much that survives from a recent past, when schools, pubs, and shops 'naturally' sited themselves at nodal points on the public transport system: exactly the pattern aimed at in many new towns.

In technical terms, what is immediately necessary, is to define the centres of pedestrian activity, and then devise a public transport system to link them as efficiently as possible. All other traffic will have to be confined to times and/or places where there would be conflict neither with public transport efficiency nor with safety and a civilised **181** environment. The implications for car ownership and usage in towns is profound, but will have to be faced. Profound too, is the need to rethink public transport in all its aspects so that movement in towns becomes once more a stimulating social experience instead of a selfish free-for-all.

It will be necessary to effect some redistribution of land use, to ensure that city-region facilities are dispersed to locations on a regional transport network. Much present zoning practice is little more than a confirmation of existing land use, and has aimed at the concentration of offices, shops and industries in as few places as possible. The new strategy requires their dispersal, and the location most critically affected in this will be the city centre. For years developers have been tearing the guts out of our cities in order to fill them with office blocks. The result has been to place the intolerable traffic load generated by the most densely-populated employment provision, precisely where it causes the most disruption. Offices, like factories, should as far as possible be dispersed from central areas — and so should warehouses and wholesale markets. The city centres appropriate to our age should offer a range of cultural facilities which, since they require the support of a region, should be dispersed throughout it to places accessible from the regional transport network. In place of an urban hierarchy (which in Britain is on the national scale and has gone to an intolerable extreme), headed by one West End, one National Theatre, one Festival Hall, one National

Gallery, all clustered in one corner of the land, we should plan to have, throughout every city region, theatres, concert halls, sports stadia, department stores, giving to every locality in every city region a share in the excellence of the nation's culture. Might it not be possible in this way to move towards a situation in which a federation of communities, each of them in size and excellence comparable with the Athens of Pericles, the Florence of Alberti, or the London of Newton and Wren, extends throughout the length and breadth of the habitable globe?

* Which must include everything from taxis and car hire to trains, express goods and emergency services.

In Britain today, town planning is directed to the extension of established cities like Peterborough and Northampton, to which some of the new town lessons are being applied. Elsewhere — and nowhere more than in London — the goal of comprehensive redevelopment over large areas has been achieved. But instead of the new neighbourhoods and precincts of the Abercrombie plan, wholesale clearance is followed by office blocks and road works. Even under the guidance of able architects, and in spite of their best intentions, the results are much the same, and the human scale of the past is supplanted by the mammoth size of the modern economy and its attendant structures.

Outside Britain too, the more typical lessons are now to be learnt in terms of urban expansion and renewal. In the United States, computer programmes are run to monitor the likely outcome of present trends, and, in spite of professions of *laisser faire*, there is an awakening to the consequences of uncontrolled development. Throughout Europe there has been progress, especially in those countries where, as in Britain, a few major centres are growing at the expense of the country as a whole.

The Swedish experience is especially of note, and, as we have seen, has been acknowledged as an influence in Britain. The expansion of Stockholm has been affected by two important factors: first, the acquisition by the City itself of large rural areas for future development; and, second, the planned extensions of the City's underground and other railways since 1944. Satellite settlements have thus grown around suburban railway stations, under much the same stimulus that characterised similar development in London. But around Stockholm this growth has been more deliberately organised into 'new towns', of which the best known are Vallingby and Farsta.

183 Vallingby centre: a pedestrian deck over a railway below.
184 Farsta: a new town in Sweden. Combined way for pedestrians, cyclists and buses.

182 *Underneath an urban 'freeway'*

The centre of Vallingby we have already noted as being one of the earliest to create a new pedestrian level above the existing ground, which was given over to vehicular transport 183 of various kinds. A pedestrian 'deck' spans the railway line, and on it are built shops and offices. The pedestrian routes flow directly into the residential areas, and Vallingby claims to be the first to achieve vehicle/pedestrian segregation on so large a scale. At Farsta, this segregation is less complete, and the combination of access road and footpath in residential areas is accepted as a more desirable solution, provided the design is such as to make sure that vehicle speeds and numbers are kept to a low level compatible with a predominantly pedestrian environment. At Farsta also, there 184 is talk of the need to create combined pedestrian and bus routes as a main element in the design, combining the roles of footpath and busway even more emphatically than Ling had proposed at Runcorn.

For Stockholm as a whole, the plan now envisages a population of some 2-2½ million. There will be a discontinuous urban structure, with the outer residential areas organised as a string of suburbs, linked by rail to the centre, with a motorway by-passing between them. Industry and appropriate social facilities will be distributed throughout the whole, but offices will retain a central location. A new major recreational area is proposed at Grimsta, concentrating in one area a variety of activities. The earlier attempt to provide a job for everyone close to his home is in practice abandoned, and extensive 'commuting' accepted as inevitable. But the plan is for three-quarters of commuters into Stockholm proper to be carried by public transport — especially underground. And as we have seen, in Sweden it is said that for public transport to work on this scale, it must be independent of the overloaded road system.[156]

Also of note are recent developments in the USSR. We have seen how in the early 'sixties their experts were talking in terms which in Britain were beginning to sound a little old-fashioned. Their main pre-occupation was still the housing of 25 million homeless from the last war. Town planning objectives at that time were conceived in terms of decongesting existing cities, and distributing urban development as evenly as possible throughout the country, so that nowhere was there a shortage of urban facilities, and the distinction between rural backwardness and city life was eliminated. This policy carried over from the earlier period

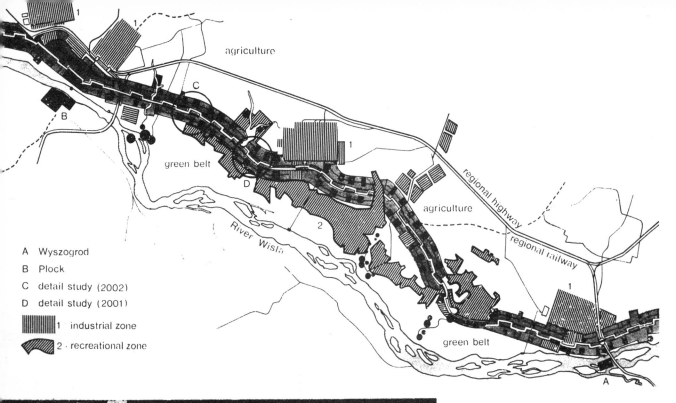

A Wyszogrod
B Plock
C detail study (2002)
D detail study (2001)

▦ 1 industrial zone
◩ 2 recreational zone

185—186
Proposal for a linear city near Warsaw.

(reviewed in Chapter 9), and it had achieved much. Since 1917, 800 new towns and 200 other urban settlements had been created. In 40 years the number of towns had increased by two-and-a-half times.[157] New life had been injected into previously backward areas, like Siberia, where recently a notable cultural centre has been built near Novosibirsk.[158] But by 1969 the same features observed elsewhere were gaining recognition. The big cities had increased their populations sixfold, and the biggest, tenfold since the Revolution. Modern production was demanding concentration, and even if there were hidden social costs, there were advantages in the super city which had to be reckoned with. There was need for research, and there was renewed interest in the pioneering efforts of the 'thirties.

There were population forecasts also. While in so vast a land, there did not appear to be any need for panic about over-population, there would be up to 350,000,000 Soviet citizens by 2000 AD, of whom about 240,000,000 would be town-dwellers: 70% as compared with 18% in 1917. The British experience was being repeated on a mammoth scale.

Current reports from the USSR suggests that policy will now be directed towards the creation, by the end of the century, of some eighty big city agglomerations in place of the present twenty-four. Within each of these there will be in excess of 1,000,000, grouped in towns with populations of about 100,000, and having a central city as a nucleus. Industrial zones will be dispersed throughout these 'urban galaxies', and innocuous industries may be integrated into residential areas. In Leningrad the city's computing facilities may be used to plan and manage all aspects of the city's future development.[161] In Poland also there are moves towards concentration of new urban growth in linear forms similar to those advocated by Miliutin in the 'thirties.[162] From China, on the other hand, reports speak still in terms of dispersal and a strategy similar to that of the 'De-urbanists' of the 'twenties.[163]

In the past we have seen how potent an influence have been fantasies concerning the 'city of the future'. The last decade has been especially fruitful in this way, and a continuing stream of projects, from the pens of students and others, has formed a vivid background to the more sober professional work we have reviewed. In a small way, some of it has come before the public in projects such as 'Habitat' at the Montreal Exposition in 1967, but most is less well known. A recent publication[164] has made an extensive review, and it is necessary only to summarise the main features below.

187 Paolo Soleri: Babel II B: a cross-section through a city in one building.

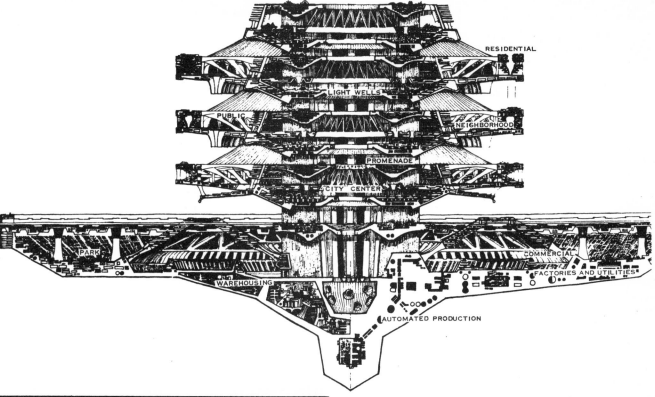

RESIDENTIAL

LIGHT WELLS

PUBLIC

NEIGHBORHOOD

PROMENADE

CITY CENTER

PARK

COMMERCIAL

FACTORIES AND UTILITIES

WAREHOUSING

AUTOMATED PRODUCTION

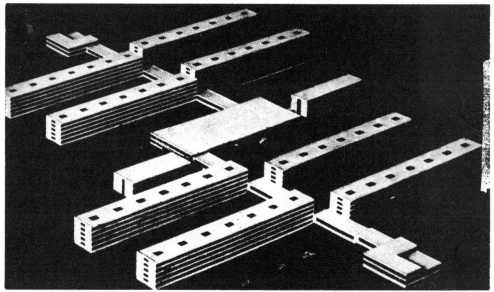

189 Aikhal: a model of part of a new town in Siberia. Social facilities are centrally placed and approached via enclosed air-conditioned streets as in Fourier's Phalansteries.

At one extreme we have proposals, such as those put
187 forward by Soleri, for vast complex structures — virtually a
city in one building, with all its energy supplies and other
'life-support systems' fully integrated into a pre-arranged
whole. The inspiration comes partly from the same source as
had inspired Le Corbusier — the ocean liner — brought up-
to-date with space technology. There is also the influence of
an outstanding inventor and romantic — Buckminster Fuller
188 — whose geodesic domes have been proposed as roofs over
whole cities, wherein the need for buildings as we know them
would largely disappear. There have recently been reports of
189 proposals for such towns in the Soviet Arctic.

At the other extreme, taking its cue from the caravan and
191 space capsule, is the notion of 'Instant City'. Using the latest
in tents, inflatables and 'packaged' buildings of all sorts —
and exploiting what is already observed in caravan parks,
where whole communities can live in homes completely
190 independent of each other, and of all main services — the
advocates of this solution emphasise the virtues of mobility
and impermanence as being especially appropriate to our
mass-production age. Carried to extreme lengths, a house
becomes no more than a space-suit, and every man an
individual in space.

Between these two extremes, and more in accord with the
192 thinking we have already encountered, is 'Plug-in'. The most
vivid developments here have come from a group called
'Archigram', who have developed their ideas over a period of
ten years or so. Essential to the proposal is the separating out
of what are regarded as the more permanent elements of a
city: the services, communications network — and their
combination into an 'infrastructure', including perhaps also
a structural framework for the 'buildings' themselves. The
argument broadly derives from a current theme in
architecture, where the same kind of division is made within
multi-storey buildings, divorcing 'structural frame', 'service
ducts' and 'service cores' as a predetermined 'grid', in which
can be accommodated a variety of rooms as circumstances
demand. The designer is able to plan for unforeseen
eventualities, and a great deal of choice is left to the
consumer. As technical innovation out-modes a 'living cell', it
can be discarded like a piece of furniture, by simply
'unplugging' it from the 'mains supplies' and replacing it
with the latest model. As families grow, they can add new
units, and when they move they can take their houses with
them. On a more modest two-dimensional scale, the influence
of 'Archigram' can be seen at Milton Keynes, with its
'infrastructure' of dual carriageways.

191 'Instant City 1969': travelling cranes and tents: a
mobile city drawing its inspiration from the caravan site and
the 'pop' festival.

190 A caravan suburb.

166

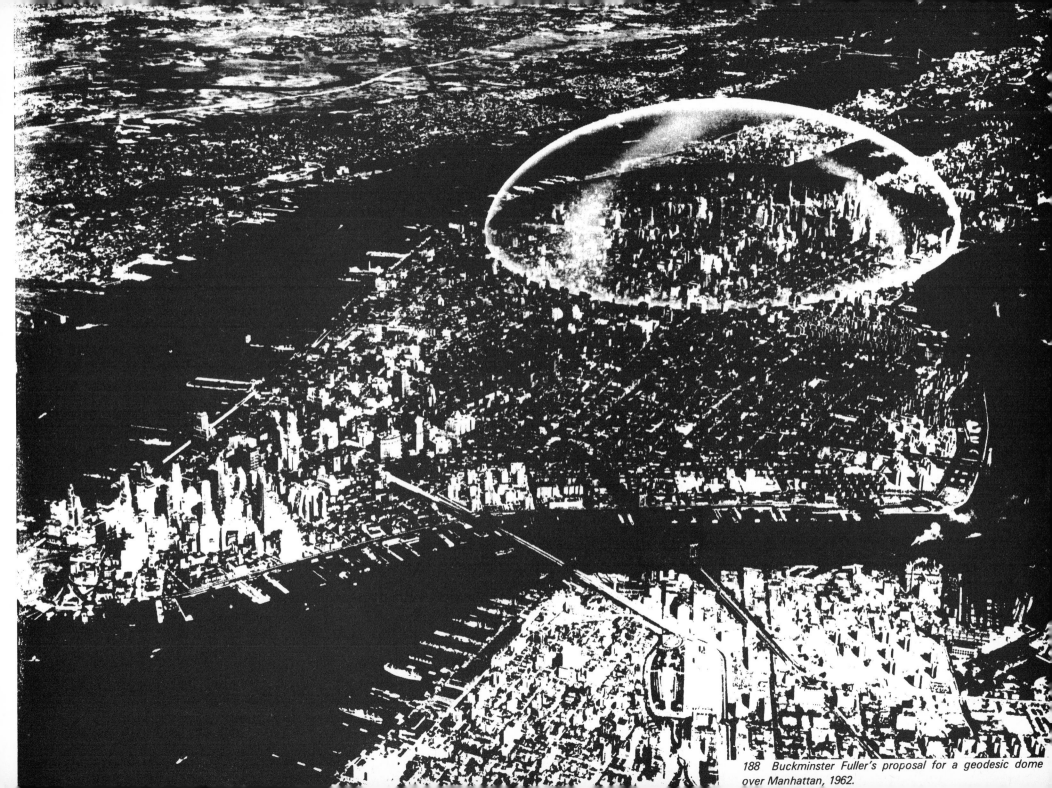

188 *Buckminster Fuller's proposal for a geodesic dome over Manhattan, 1962.*

Fantastic schemes now multiply as technology offers more and more opportunities for innovation. We have long passed the stage where we are to any significant extent limited in what we *could* do. From the engineers themselves — more competent, but less prone, to dream — we have occasional glimpses of what might be achieved if we were to use our technical potential in regional planning. Engineering has scarcely yet been used creatively in the design of towns (the nearest we have seen was in the earlier project for Milton Keynes by Buckinghamshire County Council) and we may be a long way yet from moving mountains and irrigating deserts. But the absence of creative intent in the use of our modern resources does not mean that they are not being used. The scale of modern operations in agriculture, in mining, in forestry, in waste disposal, in sewage, in consumption of energy and raw materials of every kind, is already on a gigantic scale. And voices are already heard reiterating the warning that Nature may at this moment be preparing her counter-attack upon a mankind recklessly bent on undermining the delicate mechanisms by which she manages her resources. We may have to resort to 'global engineering'[165] sooner than we think.

The control of the city — especially the large city — today emerges as one of the most significant theoretical problems of the age, and this finds reflection in a growing literature. Much is concerned exclusively with describing, from the standpoint of geography, sociology, economics or engineering, what are regarded as salient facts and trends. Much again is devoted to the elaboration of techniques of planning. What is of interest to us here, however, are those works which attempt to develop a general theory.

In the United States the best known writer on the theme is Lewis Mumford, whose *City in History* published in 1961, is the culmination of a lifetime's work. Broadly, he subscribes to the views of Howard, and throughout there runs a fundamental dislike of large cities, of bureaucratic centralisation which runs counter to *'free human association and autonomous development'*. He looks forward to a future *'world city'* which would have a *'reciprocal relation between smaller and larger units, based on each performing the sort of task for which it is uniquely fitted.'* He sees in modern industry a tendency to diffusion which could result eventually in a general *'etherialization'* of the city, and suggests a future in which new urban constellations will develop on the basis of a *'functional grid'* of power distribution and communications

systems. Writing at the height of the 'Cold War', however, he saw the ominous prospect of *'a massive extension of our present mechanical-electronic facilities, without any change in social purpose, or any attempt to translate the product into higher terms of human association . . .'*[166] and called down curses upon both the USA and the USSR.

Another distinguished American writer, E. A. Gutkind, whose *International History of City Development* runs to seven volumes, published in the 'fifties a work which comes to similar conclusions. In his *Expanding Environment: The End of Cities — the Rise of Communities* he argues that the division of town and country and the hierarchical arrangement of settlement belongs to the past. He wants instead numerous small communities as *'organic entities . . . of regional unity.'* and sees *'the centreless region as the final goal of development'*[167]

Paul and Percival Goodman elaborate a similar theme. They argue that the key relationship in town planning is that between the arrangements for working and those for 'living': broadly equivalent in their eyes to that between *production* and *consumption*.

On this premise, they erect three 'paradigms'. One — a *'City of Efficient Consumption'* — emphasises consumption; another is based on efficient production; and another — which they prefer — on the elimination of the difference between the two. This preferred solution would unite, within a region, farms and factories around small urban centres of 200,000. Within the built-up areas there would be little 'zoning' — only *'nuisance factories'* being sited apart. To ensure relative autonomy for each region, there would be located within it some facilities necessary to the national economy. Local balance, local self-government, and the integration of home and work, are the desired aims.[168]

The architect Victor Gruen, whose radical proposals for Fort Worth in the USA we have already noted, published in 1965 *The Heart of our Cities: the Urban Crisis: Diagnosis and Cure*, in which by a route which mainly criticizes recent US experience, he eventually arrives at his *'Metropolis of Tomorrow'*. Unlike Mumford, he does not shun the idea of a metropolis, and unlike Gutkind, he retains a hierarchy. His cellular structure derives from the analogy of the city with all other living things. His metropolitan area has a population of 3,300,000 (about the median figure in the

193

194

195

196

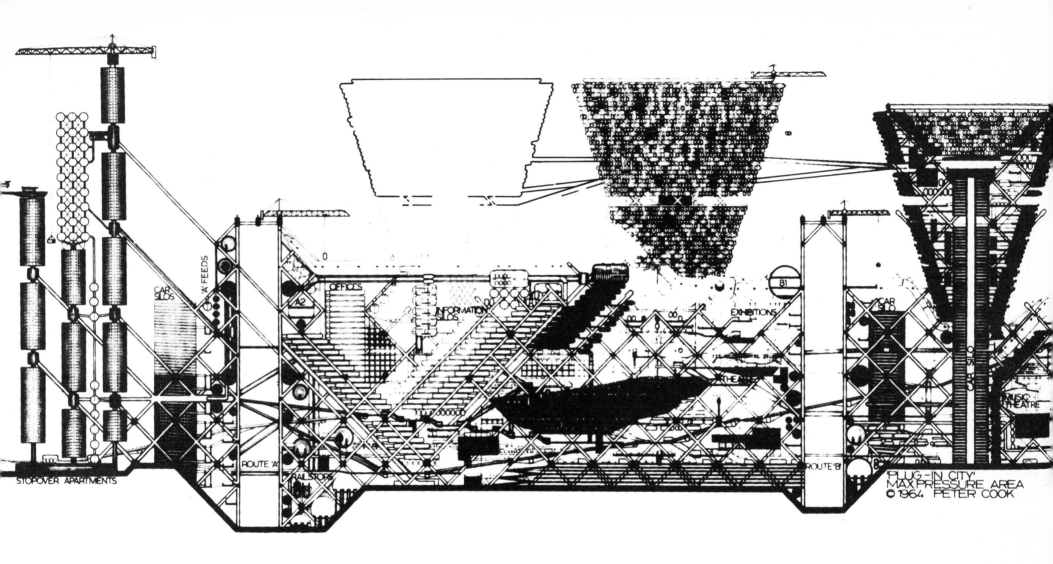

Labels within the image:
STOPOVER APARTMENTS
CAR SILOS
'A' FEEDS
ROUTE 'A'
RAIL STORE
OFFICES
INFORMATION SILOS
EXHIBITIONS
THEATRE
CAR SILOS
ROUTE 'B'
MUSIC THEATRE
PLUG-IN CITY
MAX PRESSURE AREA
© 1964 PETER COOK

192 Plug-in City: Peter Cook, 1964. A basic extensible 'infrastructure' accommodates 'plug-in' dwelling and other units, which may be changed at will.

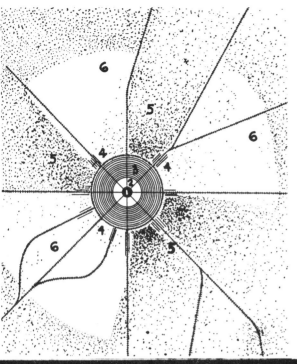

193 A 'city of efficient consumption' centred on the market place and entertainment.

1. Market, light industry, offices, entertainment, hotels, and terminals 2. Culture, universities, museums, zoo 3. Residences, schools, hospitals 4. Heavy industry, terminals, long distance airports 5. Forest preserves, vacationland 6. Agriculture.

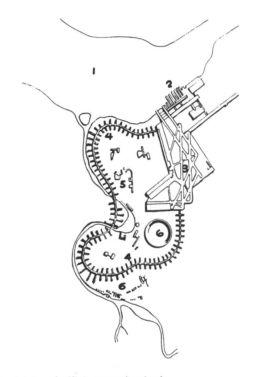

194 A 'city of efficient production'.
1. Harbour 2. Docks 3. Airport and factory 4. Housing 5. Community buildings 6. Sports

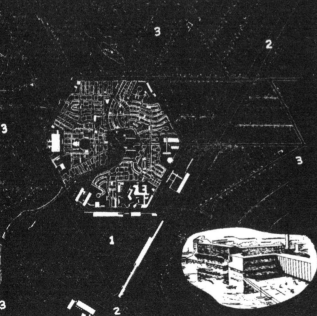

195 The Goodmans' preferred solution:

1. Airport and interregional market 2. Express highways, green belt, and nuisance factories 3. Four-acre farms, urban parents' dwellings and elementary schools. The peripheral roads, bordering the hexagon of city squares and serving the local automobile and truck traffic, pass under or over the express roads or connect with them by ramps.

USA). He has 500,000 living in the 'metrocore' and 280,000 in each of ten planetary 'cities'. Each city comprises ten 'towns' of 25,000, around a centre with 30,000. Each town has a centre with 3,400 and four 'communities' of 5,400. Each 'community' has a centre of 900 and four 'neighbourhoods' of 900. Each neighbourhood consists of 'groups', and each group of families, and each family of individuals. From top to bottom the hierarchy is complete. Cells are separated from their neighbours by open space, and there are wide green belts throughout. The gross overall density is 7.42 persons per acre, varying from 216 p.p.a. in the central area to 50p.p.a. in the neighbourhoods. There are five industrial zones. There is pedestrian priority within the cells and mechanised transport is segregated, either peripherally or underground. He acknowledges his debt to Howard, from whose proposals he differs in the main only in terms of detail and size.[169]

We have already encountered Jane Jacobs, whose *Death and Life of Great American Cities* makes short work of architects like Gruen, whose outlook she saw as a root cause of the damage being done to American cities in the name of progress. She condemned equally the cataclysmic approach of Le Corbusier and the anti-city bias of the Garden City Movement. In a recent essay she attempts an historical justification for her attitude, and on this basis advances some elements of a general theory. On the evidence of recent archaeology, which has revealed large Stone Age settlements, she argues the primacy of settlement to agriculture, and goes on to assert the primary and necessary role of the city in all economic development. The city is specially significant in that it promotes 'new kinds of work', as incidental off-shoots from the established economy. It would be 'profoundly reactionary' to limit the sizes of great cities. On the contrary: it is necessary that government should intervene against the dead hand of vested interest as a 'third force' to promote the growth of healthy young industries, within them. She concludes:

'. . . cities will not be smaller, simpler or more specialized than cities of today. Rather they will be more intricate, comprehensive, diversified, and larger than today's, and will have even more complicated jumbles of old and new things than ours do. The bureaucratized, simplified cities, so dear to our present-day city planners and urban designers, and familiar also to readers of science fiction and utopian proposals, run counter to the processes of city growth and economic development.'[170]

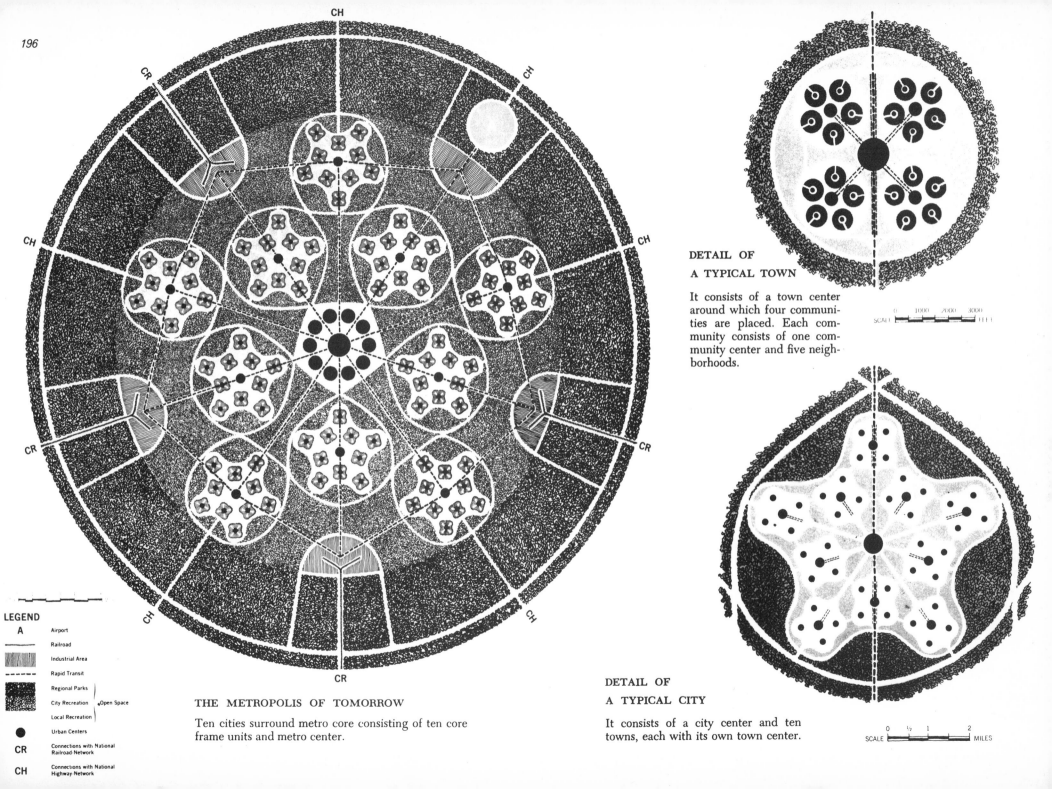

LEGEND

A	Airport
	Railroad
	Industrial Area
	Rapid Transit
	Regional Parks
	City Recreation
	Local Recreation
●	Urban Centers
CR	Connections with National Railroad-Network
CH	Connections with National Highway-Network

Open Space

THE METROPOLIS OF TOMORROW

Ten cities surround metro core consisting of ten core frame units and metro center.

DETAIL OF A TYPICAL TOWN

It consists of a town center around which four communities are placed. Each community consists of one community center and five neighborhoods.

SCALE 0 1000 2000 3000 FEET

DETAIL OF A TYPICAL CITY

It consists of a city center and ten towns, each with its own town center.

SCALE 0 ½ 1 2 MILES

The distinguished French writer, Robert Auzelle, writing in 1968, recapitulates recent French experience. He regards the present as a transitional stage in 'urbanism', the history of which he divides into three main periods: autocratic and efficacious; technocratic and speculative (beginning under Napoleon III and characteristic of the present day); and 'community and aleatory' urbanism: the urbanism of the future, necessarily open-ended and offering an element of choice.

He cites Hippodamos' perfect city (10,000 citizens — with women, slaves and foreigners, 100,000 in all) as his precedent for the belief that there is an upper limit to acceptable size. *'The industrial town, having destroyed almost all reference to the cycle of seasons or the passage of hours, is about to destroy, through the excess of its density, the human time-scale.'* The whole fabric of everyday life, of birth and death, is negated by it, and it threatens the unity of *being* and *form* which is the very essence of the urban *milieu*. Excessive quantity will destroy the very quality of the town, and abolish its essential roles as a setting for material and spiritual exchanges; as a school of life; and as the living embodiment of the past. Present inadequacies extend to transport, sewers and water supplies. Pollution becomes intolerable. Citizens are deprived of the right to be involved in the running of their city, as control passes more and more into the hands of central government and technocrats.

Auzelle poses the question whether the town has already passed its heyday, but his belief in mankind leads him to look for its metamorphosis into forms which will allow a man to be a citizen of the natural world *and* a citizen of the man-made city. He quotes Balzac: *'To saunter is a science; it is the gastronomy of the eye';* and pleads for what he regards as two basic human needs: to meet in familiar places, and to walk.

Auzelle's solutions are sketchy, but are in the same spirit as most of what we have recently encountered. He wants public participation. He wants to reform social and economic administration. He wants a city in which a preponderant and prestigious centre is federated organically with *'heterogeneous and complex localities'*. He wants flexible solutions — ones which leave most room for the initiatives of posterity.[171] *so what does HT leave for posterity? Open space, parks, a lot.*

The most recent and comprehensive attempt to build a theory of town planning comes from the pen of Constantine Doxiadis. He regards the present epoch as one of urban explosion which, within the foreseeable future, will result in a continuous *'Ecumenopolis'* throughout the world, covering all those areas where topography, water supply and climate permit. He sees this mainly as a consequence of population growth. His arguments are almost entirely a-political and unhistorical, although he adduces to them numerous historical examples. He classifies settlements primarily with respect to their size, and quantitative aspects loom large throughout his whole approach. CIAM had proposed an analytical 'grid' based on the four elements of *dwelling, recreation, work* and *transport*. Doxiadis replaces this with a five element system: *nature, man, society, shells* (buildings), and *networks* (communications etc.). His analysis leads to the advocacy of urban forms which permit growth, in consequence of which two significant conclusions emerge. Growth of the city, should be as with all living things, by the multiplication of cells which should themselves remain static in size. And, to avoid the problem of the embedded centre, growth should be unidirectional and not circumferential.[172]   197

Doxiadis elaborates his theories with a wealth of detail, and his *Centre for Ekistic Studies* in Athens has added much since. His approach is empirical and concerned more with quantitative and technical matters than with the political and economic. He devotes much of his effort to the development of planning techniques, and in this comes close to much that is currently developing in Great Britain, where recent theoretical work has been characterised by the development of techniques of analysis and prediction.

Outstanding is the work of McLoughlin[173] and Chadwick.[174] Alexander's work[175] has lately been in the U.S.A., and in England the most promising recent developments come from the London *Centre for Environmental Studies.*[176] There is a rapid growth of 'systems analysis' in planning. This makes much use of mathematical modelling and the computer. Much of value has been and will be learnt, and in town planning, systems analysis is a timely antidote to unrealistic Utopianism. But there is a tendency to go too far. We have seen at Irvine how the planners could find no substitute for their own original thinking. There is a strong analogy to the situation which has for nearly a century attempted to substitute engineering science for architecture, in the mistaken belief that all architecture can be reduced to building technics — and even then, to those things which engineers can quantify. The collection of data and its processing is a necessary part of all design, but so also is the choice and definition of objectives

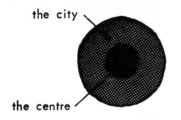

the city

the centre

a. the static city of the past

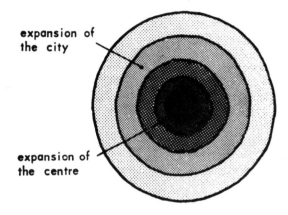

expansion of the city

expansion of the centre

b. the static city which now grows into a Dynapolis

and the conception of hypothetical solutions. It is also necessary to have a guiding theory which distinguishes between the essential and the inessential: there is a tendecy otherwise towards a blind empiricism which does not distinguish good from evil, better from worse, important from trivial, transient from permanent. In current planning theory there is a tendency to emphasise complexity to the point where clarity is lost, and to regard planning not so much as a purposive activity in its own right, but as a response to external pressures and *a priori* goals, over which it has little control and about which it has little to say. The constraints imposed by the existing socio-economic framework are accepted as more-or-less unchangeable, and 'trends' largely replace overt political objectives. The whole thus becomes the basis for 'scientific' fortune-telling, in which various prognostications are translated into algebra and compared, to see which is the least undesirable. One is reminded of Hogarth's comment that Durer, *'who drew mathematically, never so much as deviated into grace'*. The art of town planning as of all architecture, has ample use for all the science it can get. But it needs no less values and objectives of its own: a *purpose* as well as a *method*.

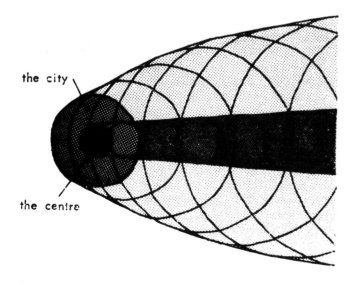

the city

the centre

197 Doxiadis' Dynapolis.

198 St. Mark's Square, Venice: the timelessness of good civic design.

Is any consistent theory of town planning possible? Should we be content merely to pursue pressing technical problems, providing immediate answers to each as it arises? Should we follow the Utopians who seek to impose ideals upon a hostile world? Should we follow the 'trend planners' who regard men as the puppets of fate?

The first course is unprincipled opportunism, which everywhere must blunder from crisis to crisis and, in the long run, is the very antithesis of planning. The second exaggerates the potency of ideas, the last belittles them. But somewhere between the extremes represented by Utopianism and trend planning, a solution must be found.

Our historical survey has shewn us that the city may be variously regarded. At different times and in different places, it has been shelter, refuge, workshop, market. To the priest-king it was a holy place, to the warlord a stronghold, to the slave a prison. Today, with our divided culture, it has one significance for the geographer, another for the sociologist, the economist, the historian, the political scientist, the engineer, the architect. For an adequate understanding, nothing less than a 'synoptic' view is, as Geddes argued, vital. For those who wish to change it, to plan its future growth, this understanding must highlight the essential characteristics of human settlements and of those processes whereby they may be controlled.

However obvious a truism it may be, we must recognise that the purpose of every human settlement is at root the creation of favourable conditions for human life. With the possible exception of the most primitive circumstances, it is remarkable how little in essentials these have changed. In spite of all the vicissitudes in urban form we have reviewed, rooms, buildings, courtyards and streets retain most of the characteristics they have had since the beginning of civilisation. Dimensions within buildings still remain much as they have always been and only within living memory have the skyscraper and the motorway begun to overwhelm our

senses. A modern man would not be uncomfortable in a house of ancient Egypt, and we would still agree with Herodotus in finding the walls of Babylon huge, as he would still find Red Square immense or England's village greens confined and intimate.

The reason is not far to seek. If we limit our enquiry to our basic physical attributes, we find that, in spite of stunted growth and shortened life-span which, from time to time, have resulted from malnutrition and disease, we are still the same species which dim ages ago first evolved as *homo sapiens*. We have much the same propensities, and they still provide us with the measurements against which we judge the size of our surroundings, and they set limits beyond which we can no longer see or hear clearly, or 'feel at home'. When, in the daily round of social life, we put aside telecommunications and supersonic speeds, we still walk the same distance before tiring, find the same hills too steep to climb, and feel lost among a crowd of strangers. If we are lucky, we sleep at nights, and (like all living things) roll round in Earth's diurnal course. We respond in the same way to heat and cold, sunshine and shade, as have men since the beginning of time. In spite of millenia of change in other ways, the best our modern athletes can do, is to knock hundredths-of-seconds off long-established records — demonstrating perhaps how much more precisely we can measure, than how much faster we can run.

In the city, it may be argued, we are dealing not with individuals, but with societies, and here there have certainly been changes. But in many essential respects, there are constancies also. The number of friends one can know intimately; the number who can sit down and discuss a problem together; the number who can watch a 'live' performance on the stage; the number who can participate in a game or in deciding their own affairs: these have not changed. It is this that still gives weight to Aristotle's teaching that there are dimensions to community life that

cannot be exceeded.* In spite of television and electronic brains, the maximum length of an act in a play today is set by the same human physiological limitations as governed Aeschylus. For us, as for him, a theatre needs to be much the same size, and so does a footpath or a public forum.

Thus in town planning, and throughout architecture generally, we can agree with the Renaissance that *'Man is the measure of all things'*, and find considerable justification from this fact for the opinion we have constantly encountered that there is a proper human scale for the city. We can equally reject as false doctrine the mistaken zeal which in his day led Le Corbusier to condemn Paris as inadequate because it was allegedly 'out-of-date', and which still gives support to those who seek the mindless destruction of our towns. Wherever the trouble has been taken to retain and re-equip them, most older buildings and the older quarters of our towns, are not infrequently found to serve as well as new ones, with the added virtue that they perpetuate with a tested human scale the memory of things past.

From our relatively timeless physical attributes, therefore, we can derive a general principle concerning size and scale in town planning. Its elaboration still stands in need of further investigation, and it can be extended to all our social institutions: to schools, factories, universities. In all of these, the issue of optimum size is becoming a major problem of our age.

It is no less a truism that every settlement must be created out of the natural environment, and will be constrained by it. Here, the whole history of mankind is one of gradual conquest, until today we have the potential to create our cities

---

* See especially *Politics* vii, 4.

Dead wrong. Most modern settlements have been built to make money primarily.

almost anywhere. Yet, in so far as climate, water supply, and accessibility are natural phenomena, most of those locations favoured throughout history retain their intrinsic advantages, and we are unlikely in seeking new places for urban growth deliberately to choose difficult terrain or hostile climes. We should note again our own characteristics as an earthly species, and how these have an enduring influence in such matters as exposure to weather and sun. Thus aspect, sunlight, wind and rain, exert a continuing influence both in the siting and the detailed design of towns.

Until recently, the principal limitations imposed upon a city by its site, we may perhaps summarise as those related to defence, external communications, and natural resources. To what extent do these still apply?

Defence in recent times has been used as an argument in favour of dispersal*, and there may be still some advantage in locations where deep atom-bomb-proof shelters (if there be any) may be excavated. It is quite conceivable that policies in countries with vulnerable border areas will continue to reflect traditional caution. In the light of their recent experiences, we should not expect Germany's neighbours to site major cities on her doorstep. But, except in so far as it gives additional ground in favour of dispersal, defence today appears to exert little influence upon urban location or growth.

External communications are nowadays apparently less pressing than those within the city itself, and would not appear any longer to play a decisive role. Those sites most favoured with natural approaches by sea, river or land still offer obvious advantages, but sites less-favoured in this way have for some time presented civil engineering with tasks well within its capacity. In a country with a developed overland communications system, it would clearly be folly to ignore its potential usefulness in servicing new urban growth. It will also be necessary in a relatively undeveloped region to plan towns and their external communications together. And with both existing and new route systems, it will be necessary to remember Buchanan's rule that there is a measurable limit to capacity. If, at junctions every two or three miles along a motor-way, a large new town were to be built, the road would quickly become overloaded. But by the same logic, the existence of spare capacity in an already developed region, argues against dispersal into relatively undeveloped areas.

A new and rapidly developing factor in external communications is air transport. It is now possible for a town to thrive with no links to the outside world other than by air,

* Most recently in China, whence it is reported that the dispersal of resources is advocated on many grounds, including defence.

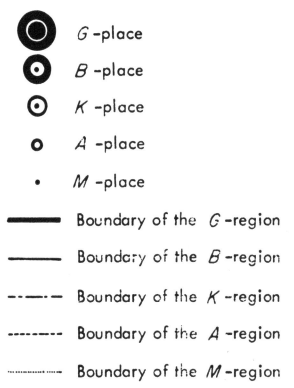

199 A theoretical distribution of a hierarchy of settlements in a featureless plain according to Christaller. 'G' is the largest settlement, 'M' the smallest.

G -place

B -place

K -place

A -place

M -place

——— Boundary of the G -region

——— Boundary of the B -region

-·-·- Boundary of the K -region

------- Boundary of the A -region

·········· Boundary of the M -region

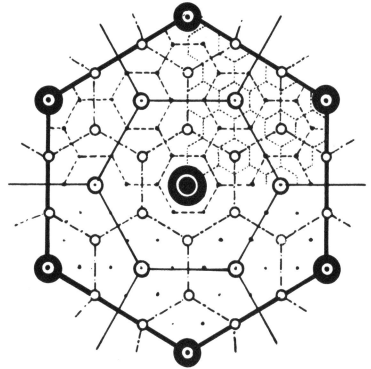

and reasonable access to an airport is today as necessary as access to rail transport used to be. Technical limitations in aircraft have hitherto required large flat landing grounds, but current changes towards vertical and short take-off airplanes may alter this. The location of airports *vis-a-vis* cities poses also the question of nuisance and danger to the citizens themselves. The noise of aircraft taking off, landing and circling overhead, and the heavy flows of surface traffic associated with them, give rise to great difficulty in current town planning. But in so far as their influence upon the location and growth of cities is concerned, it is well to remember that all journeys by air begin and end with a trip by road or rail. Provided this is appropriately catered for, and well-integrated with air travel facilities in a regional transport plan, there is no necessity for a city to be so close to the airports serving it that these become a nuisance to it.

In considering communications, we should finally note the most rapidly developing form of all: telecommunication by radio and telephone. Both within cities and between them, these are capable of having a profound effect, especially in that they could drastically reduce the need for movement. But their significance as an influence on the planning of cities lies mainly in that they bring greater freedom from an age-old constraint.

The development of cities with reference to *natural resources* today poses problems of a different sort from those which influenced earlier civilisations. Even before the coming of modern industry, the limitation imposed by a city's walls and defensive works had already been superseded by that imposed by the market. As Christaller[177] has shewn, a market economy based on local agriculture tends to impose upon
199 settlement a hierarchical order in which larger towns are spaced well apart, each with a subsidiary constellation at such a distance that the return journey to market could be made within a day. Since the total population would (as with all of Nature's species) be limited by the available food supply, this pattern also determined the size of settlements. The 'pure' form of course was modified by many factors, but in principle it was there. Only those cities engaged in trade on an international scale could significantly outstrip the limitation. With the first development of industry in association with water power, coal, or other resources having a limited local source, similar natural limits were set. But such constraints are today of little significance. There is
200 instead a tendency for the most successful cities to grow to enormous proportions. Raw material, food and other bulk

supplies are now customarily distributed world-wide and only after the most basic operations are performed at source. There seems, in many cases, more to be gained by shortening distances entailed in the final distribution of manufactured goods, than is lost by carrying bulk raw material over thousands of miles. There are some technical reasons for this: many different raw materials are today of necessity brought together in manufacture; and raw material can often be handled mechanically and with less care than can finished goods, which may be bulky, easily damaged and perishable. But we should also bear in mind the economic inequalities which have placed, and continue to place, those regions and countries which produce raw materials at an unfair disadvantage, and this situation might change. If it did, there might again be some advantage in siting manufacturing cities nearer the sources of key raw materials, thus easing the distribution of both raw material and finished article. But, technically at any rate, there is today no pressing need to plan cities with regard to sources of raw material.

Water as a natural resource poses a more complex problem. Although it is not unusual for a city to obtain its water by pumping it uphill over a watershed from a neighbouring valley, it is clearly folly to do so unnecessarily. Water is also involved in many aspects of urban life — especially in drainage and sanitation generally — and an abundant supply is at least as necessary today as it ever was.

There can be few places blessed with a more reliable and consistent rainfall than Great Britain, and yet as a consequence of her intense urban development, there is today a real threat of water shortage. Apparent abundance has encouraged bad management. The traditional practice of collecting run-off from roofs and pavings, and storing it *in situ* for washing and other non-drinking purposes, has been abandoned. As a result, not only after every heavy downpour does the rapid run-off from impervious urban areas cause rivers to flood, but nine-tenths of the water purified at great trouble to make it fit to drink, is used for non-culinary purposes. Having been passed through factories, baths, water closets and sinks, it finally arrives in sewage works, where the treatment consists essentially of taking the water out of the water-borne sewage, and returning it to the natural water-courses from which it originally came. In many situations, this process is then repeated in other cities further downstream.

The 'hydrological cycle' still presents difficult technical problems but these, being technical, are capable of technical

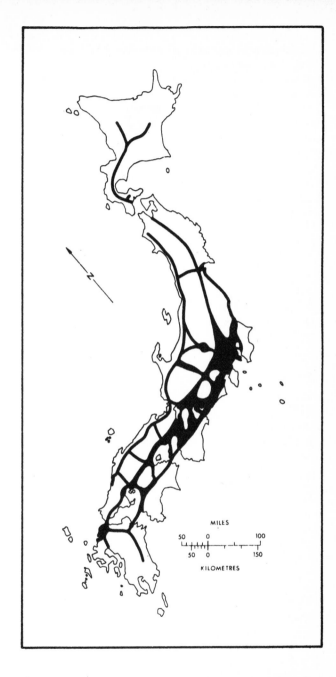

200 A forecast for Japan: a 'megalopolis' extending the length of the country.

solution. From the point of view of the limits imposed by water on urban development, there is still much to be said for Geddes' view that the river valley should be taken as basic, and comprehensively developed as a natural resource.* The total requirements of new urban development are entirely calculable, as is the quantity of water supply which could be made available by natural means. That this calls for planning on the largest scale goes without saying, and it should also be realised that in dealing with water in this way, we inevitably deal also with every aspect of 'land use' and economic life over large areas. More water could be taken from the Thames for consumption in London, if navigation were reduced. More storage reservoirs could be built, if land required by agriculture or for airfields, mineral extraction or building were to be taken.

201 The wider ramifications of water conservancy and supply have recently led to proposals such as those for estuary barrages. These derive partly from the proposition that the river estuaries themselves are the obvious place to impound the total run-off from a river system without encroaching on valuable dry land. It is argued that the barrage itself (especially in tidal waters) could produce energy — including that needed to pump supplies back to settlements upstream, in an endless process of re-cycling. There may be places where the reasons for urban development make it worthwhile to expend considerable energy in transporting, pumping, distilling or other means of obtaining water. Recent advances in still design — some of them using solar heat — and in the osmotic filtration of sea water, offer the prospect of freeing the city from its oldest natural constraint, but so far it is one we still have to reckon with.

Water as a natural resource has also historically been significant as a source of power. More recently, coal has greatly influenced the location of cities. Does the availability of natural sources of *energy* any longer have significance for urban location? At present the position is tied up with that we have noted for raw materials. It is easy to transport modern fuels and to distribute electricity. Also, as we noted for external communications, new urban developments will have to be planned regionally, in scale with the provision of power from new or existing gas and electricity 'grids'. As we saw with Buckingham County Council's scheme for Bletchley, there is much to be said for planning the energy of a new city as an aspect of its total design. And as we are now becoming aware, the next technical crisis facing mankind may be shortage of energy. But as an over-riding constraint on future

* In this respect, it is noteworthy that the French 'Departments' are based on the catchments of major river systems.

201 *Barrage across the estuary of the Rance in France producing electrical power from the tides.*

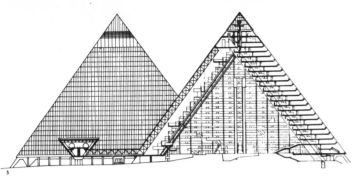

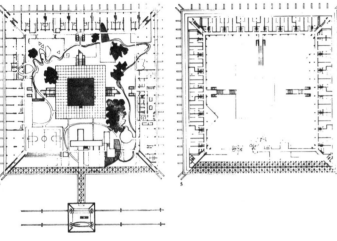

202—203 *Siberia: an imaginative proposal for pyramidal structures for 2000 people, totally enclosed with an artificial climate. Dwellings on three sides, daylight admitted through the fourth to a central 'winter garden'.*

urban growth, the *location* of natural sources of energy does not appear to be significant.

What natural constraints are there, then, upon the siting of cities and their growth? Most of those which have operated in the past are now found to have at most a limited significance. We may not wish to avail ourselves of the freedom given to us by modern technology — it may be folly to do so — but it is there for us to use if on other grounds we deem it worthwhile.

In detail, of course, some age-old considerations still operate. Like Vitruvius and Alberti, we should wish to avoid unhealthy sites, although here again there is little we could not do by way of drainage and construction to ameliorate most natural conditions. Topography and climate so far retain much the same significance they have always had. In Britain, planners continue to avoid north-facing and steep slopes, fog hollows, and areas too much exposed. In most lands, it will be unusual for settlement to be on sites above an altitude at which natural conditions are considered too harsh, and in some, lowland areas will be avoided for similar reasons. But even here, we are reminded by our contemporary 'futurists' that the totally-enclosed city, with its own controlled environment, could be planted at the South Pole, in outer space, or on the bed of the sea.

202

203

From recent town planning practice in Great Britain, we
204 have seen what 'natural' factors are most commonly taken into account in choosing sites for urban growth. The desire to avoid areas valued agriculturally, or for their landscape, is today perhaps the most significant. It arises from one or more of a variety of motives. There is the universal desire to maintain the distinctiveness of town and country. Unwin, it will be remembered, regretted the passing of the walled city with its clear-cut form, and, to take its place, modern town planning has invented the 'green belt'. There is still the desire to protect valuable agricultural land in the interests of food production, coupled with the wish to maintain the rural landscape as something to be enjoyed by the town dweller as a recreational resource.

In Britain it is probably true that agriculture has survived in urbanised regions only because planning legislation has prevented land from being taken out of farming. While local agricultural self-sufficiency is now rarely aimed at, and Howard's wish to unite town and country economically is almost wholly forgotten, there is widespread concern that world-wide food shortages should not be exacerbated. It is, however, factory farming and modern food technology,

179

neither of which necessarily rely on green fields, which are now setting the pace. From the point of view of food production *per se*, the cherished notion of the green belt is difficult to sustain, and it is on the grounds of its value as a recreational resource that the protectionist approach to Britain's countryside increasingly relies.

Here again, much is taken for granted. It has long been remarked that, in England especially, there is a deep-seated anti-urban sentiment which first strongly emerges at the time of the industrial revolution, and finds expression equally in nature poetry, landscape painting, architecture and town planning. We too easily forget that previous ages found all they wanted of grace and beauty within the city, and regarded all outside it as, in every sense of the word, uncivilised. Even as recently as 1802, Wordsworth could stand in the middle of London and pronounce it fair. But modern industry and its consequences have now, it seems, left us with nothing to admire in the city, and relief from daily toil amid its ugliness is sought mainly beyond it — in the countryside. To the extent that the desire for rural surroundings close at hand persists, the planning of cities will be influenced by a desire to preserve the countryside 'unspoilt'. But already it is clear that a passive preservationist attitude to landscape is not enough. The Victorians themselves, with their town parks, made notable advances in creating oases of green within cities. The pressures upon the countryside, now that the motor-car makes it everywhere easy of access, raise more sharply the need to plan town and country together, in the interests of both. It is difficult to see how a genuinely rural landscape can be maintained without a viable agriculture, and we are thus led from a selfish concern for the citizen to a concern for the proper planning of the whole region of which the city is inevitably a part. Near to towns, patterns of farming will probably have to change to cope with urban pressures. Modern agriculture has become an industry, and as such, makes the lowest demand of all for workers per acre. There is therefore no adequate basis in agriculture alone for the old pattern of rural settlement. Present tendencies suggest that hamlet, village and market town will survive as appendages of big cities — either as dormitories or week-end refuges. It may be that some encouragement of urban migration (including urban industry) into rural areas could provide a basis for overcoming in our modern conditions the age-old handicaps of farming life. It could at the same time provide new urban environments with the countryside close at hand.

Town planning thus merges into regional planning, among the advocates of which are those who point to the long-term damage likely to result from *producing* in one place, and *consuming* in another. In spite of artificial fertilisers and factory farming, they argue that those who live *off* an area should also live *on* it. They point out that the development of the city has gone hand-in-hand with the ever-increasing transport of food and other resources, so that today mono-culture and intensive local concentration is fast becoming the rule throughout the world. In this, it is said, is the root cause of the 'ecological' damage that civilisation does to Nature's economy. They point out that it is folly to foul the rivers of the world with valuable organic waste, to sink the fertility of steppes and prairies into oceans, to bury the mineral wealth of the world in municipal refuse dumps.

While there is no doubt that in this and other 'ecological' matters, our understanding of all the factors involved falls far short of our practices, sooner or later it will be necessary to use and re-use all the world's resources in an endless process of re-cycling, to regulate the human population at a level related to those resources, and to restore the equilibrium between Man and Nature that the city from the outset has disturbed. It will be necessary for all artefacts — including buildings and the towns themselves — to be designed for long life, or with easy reclamation and re-cycling in mind. Whether we shall require the maximum *in situ* consumption of food and other resources, will presumably in the last resort depend upon the availability of the energy required to move and process them. We know already that the fossil fuels, which have kept us going so far, and which cannot be re-cycled, will one day be exhausted. The difficulties associated with the use of atomic and other sources of power, such as the winds and tides, have yet to be overcome.

Thus there is still a considerable constraint imposed by natural resources upon our freedom, but it may be said to diminish with our understanding and control of natural processes themselves. This control today demands, however, that we treat as a whole the many-sided process in which we are inevitably involved as a species, at once a part of Nature and her potential master.

204 A 'sieve' map showing the significant natural constraints analysed in selecting sites for urban growth in an area west of London. The white areas merit further consideration.

Combined physical constraints

Main settlements

Motorway line fixed

Motorway line to be determined

Major roads

Major railway lines

Agricultural land of well above national average value   Class I

Landscape areas of great significance

Areas liable to flood

Areas containing gravel deposits

Crown lands and special areas

Extent of London Metropolitan Region

0   5   10 Miles

0   5   10   15 Kilometres

Thus far in our search for a consistent theory, we have established the significance of the human scale and the natural environment. We have been looking at what Geddes would have recognised as aspects of his categories *folk* and *place*. Pursuing his classification further, we can now introduce the vital middle term which relates these two: *work*.

Mankind's physical attributes may be relatively constant, and the natural environment may change on the time-scale of Darwinian evolution and geology. But through his activity — his work — man demonstrates qualities which make him unique as a species. All other living things — even the higher social mammals — can make little more than instinctive responses to such stimuli as their surroundings and bodily processes provide. Thus (if it were not for the interference of men) they change in themselves or in their circumstances only as Darwin has described. But when men work upon their environment, they do so with a unique capacity for learning from experience — a capacity magnified thousandfold by exceptional powers of mental abstraction and the ability to communicate through speech and other means the experience of previous generations. They also act consciously: they have definable objectives in view. They can *plan:*

'Primarily, labour is a process going on between man and nature, a process in which man, through his own activity, initiates, regulates, and controls the material reactions between himself and nature. He confronts nature as one of her own forces, setting in motion arms and legs, head and hands, in order to appropriate nature's products in a form suitable to his own wants. By thus acting on the external world and changing it, he at the same time changes his own nature. He develops the potentialities that slumber within him, and subjects these inner forces to his own control. We are not here concerned with those primitive and instinctive forms of labour which we share with other animals . . . We have to consider labour in a form peculiar to the human species. A spider carries on operations resembling those of the weaver; and many a human architect is put to shame by the skill with which a bee constructs her cell. But what from the very first distinguishes the most incompetent architect from the best of bees, is that the architect has built a cell in his head before he constructs it in wax. The labour process ends in the creation of something which . . .already existed in an ideal form. '[178]

Mankind is able to progress consciously, purposively, and thus to some extent is independent of those natural laws which govern the evolution of other species, and the changes man has made, and continues to make, in adapting the natural environment to his own purposes, proceed on the time-scale of human history, and today at an ever accelerating pace. It is in the *work* that men have done that we can detect the principal dynamic factor which has propelled mankind forward from the palaeolithic to the atomic age, and from this therefore we may hope to learn some of the fundamental reasons for changes in his settlements.

If first we consider the changes in technique which men have employed in converting their material environment into settlements — in *building* — we shall find that these have (at least until very recently) been much less than may be supposed, and it would be difficult to explain changes in civilisation or in cities as arising from his cause. We still for the most part build from stone, wood and mud* in various forms as have men from time immemorial, and many of our building processes are remarkably similar to those used in ancient Egypt. Throughout the millennia of history, cities have come and gone while building techniques have remained the same. True, the introduction of iron and rolled steel in the nineteenth century began to change things, and we may now be on the verge of a technical revolution in building. Already we see the effects, in the drab monotony of much modern building, of the impact of the age of mass production, and we may perhaps have further to travel in this direction. It may also be, however, that building, having for the most part for so long resisted conveyor-belt technology, may, by over-leaping this stage, be one of the first industries to exploit newer techniques now made possible by cybernetics and automation: mass-producing 'one-offs' by the use of computer design programmes linked to automatically-controlled production plant.

But, as with human physique and natural environment, changes in building processes have had so far a limited effect upon changes throughout the history of urban development. To see how *work* has affected settlement, we must extend our investigation to embrace a wider field.

If we look at the city not so much as a *product* of labour, but as an *instrument* intended to facilitate it, we find immediately much to account for changes in its development and form. We have seen already the role of granary, harbour and market. For each stage in the development of modern industry our review revealed a typical urban arrangement: first, the industrial village associated with the isolated mill; then the single-industry town and the company town; then the industrial city and the industrial conurbation, together with its administrative and other ancillary areas. It is the role which the city plays in facilitating the social processes which are an essential and evolving characteristic of human production, which is of the greatest significance.

We now arrive at an aspect of human experience which can be shown to evolve from stage to stage, and which, in its ramifications, involves every aspect of economic, cultural and
205 political history, including the city and city planning. To an ever-increasing extent, men have worked together by a *division of labour*, the account of which is economic history, and its study the substance of the 'dismal science' itself. At a very early stage in its development, this division is found to be facilitated by settlement, and the city itself we have defined as one element of an economic division fundamental to the whole of past history: that between town and country. Within the city there also develops from the earliest times, a division of labour of increasing complexity, together with its necessary concomitants: specialisation and exchange.

Every aspect of the city is affected by these circumstances. Firstly, it should be noted, that the division of labour is the division of what must, from the point of view of society as a whole, operate as a whole; and that the greater the division, the more necessary it becomes to make sure that all sectors are harmoniously combined. History reveals not a few calamities arising from failure in this respect, which are outside our present concern. What is clear, is that the social organisation of production as a whole is facilitated by proximity and communications, and from this it follows that a city should be sufficiently compact, and have good internal and external communications.

Until recently, the division of labour between town and country resulted in a relationship which was everywhere one of open or veiled hostility. The division of the world into imperial power and colony bears much the same character. Historically, this hostility was revealed in the total form of the city, which with its defensive walls held the countryside at bay. Today the town is dominant, and local self-sufficiency has been replaced by interdependence on the national and international scale. The division of labour now extends to the towns themselves, and each to some degree plays a specialist role in the national and international economy. Hierarchical relationships are established, which result in the growth in size and importance of some cities and some regions and the decline of others.

It is abundantly clear that any plan for a city today would have to have regard for its destined role in the national and international division of labour. We have seen how in recent years excessive specialisation has resulted in 'depressed areas' and how a prime objective of town planning (in theory, if not in practice) has been the restoration of a better balance in the economy of each town. Most recently, the same ends have been sought with the aid of good communications on the regional rather than the city scale. We encounter here again a perennial theme in contemporary town planning: concentration *versus* dispersal. The excessive concentration of populations with high levels of production and consumption in a few selected areas, and the corresponding lack of these things elsewhere, has long passed the stage where it can be accepted without serious questioning. Although it has played, and continues to play, a vitally necessary role in the development of mankind, the division of labour is now reaching levels which pose for town planning, and for every aspect of individual and social life, problems we are ill-prepared to tackle and barely yet understand.

* I include brick and concrete under this term.

DIVISON OF LABOUR — DIVISION OF SPACE *

Society and space are profoundly linked. Today's spatial arrangements are the product of today's society, but they are also the product of all previous societies. We must understand how, in parallel with the evolution of the means of production, towns were formed and the countryside became depopulated. This account is divided into two parts: on the left is depicted a succession of societies, on the right, the corresponding spatial organisation. It applies only to certain western countries, such as France.

Antiquity

With the increase in population and the growth in external relations, wars of conquest appear. The prisoners of vanquished tribes become slaves. Then the slaves, once the common property of the tribe, become private property, and thus the forms of property in antiquity are born. The fusion of several tribes gives birth to cities, which surround themselves with an agricultural territory which they dominate. Thus appears the separation of town and country.

Feudalism

Invasions occur. Agriculture, artisanry and trade decline. Existing populations are scattered throughout a vast territory. Consequently, unlike antiquity, feudal society appears over a much more widespread terrain. The *seigneurs* own great domains which they exploit through *serfs* — a new subservient class. The principal source of wealth is agriculture. Local production, both peasant and artisan, is matched by local consumption. Farms are isolated, roads unsafe, and trade weak.

*after G. Darris: a pictorial account by a French writer showing in broad terms the influence upon the town of changing economic conditions. Like all summaries, it contains questionable over-simplifications. The translation is my own.

Tribal Society

Let us begin with the historic origins of humanity. Men distinguish themselves from animals as soon as they begin to produce their means of existence. The first form of the division of labour is based upon sex, and is essential to the family. Little by little, families unite and form *tribes*. At first, tribes have little contact with each other: each is content to remain within the limits of its own hunting territory. The primitive level of productive forces and limited consumption allows tribes to ignore, or to live on good terms with, each other.

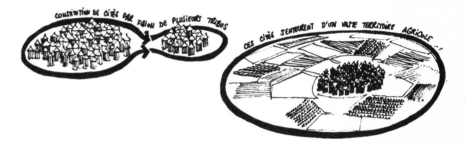

With social development, new classes appear. Division of labour straightway develops between farmers and citizen-artisans; then, within the towns, between artisans and merchants. Slavery remains the basis of all production.

The uneven development of cities and the incessant warfare which they unleash, promotes the domination of a single city. Rome, in particular, never became more than a city: the bonds tying her to the provinces which she dominated remained almost exclusively political. Rich and poor were already deliberately separated within the city.

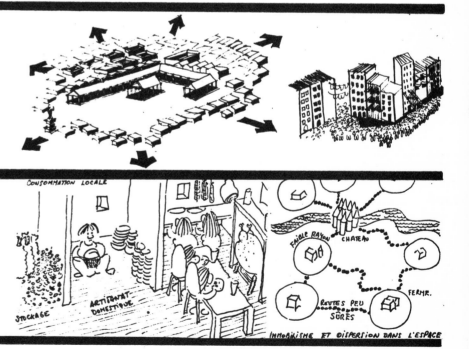

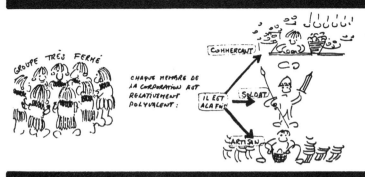

GROUPE TRÈS FERMÉ

CHAQUE MEMBRE DE LA CORPORATION EST RELATIVEMENT POLYVALENT:

COMMERÇANT

IL EST À LA FOIS

SOLDAT

ARTISAN

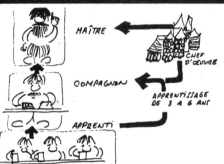

MAÎTRE

CHEF D'ŒUVRE

COMPAGNON

APPRENTISSAGE DE 3 À 6 ANS

APPRENTI

Each guild remains a closed group. Patriarchal and contractual agreement, a long and difficult apprenticeship, ties the apprentice and the journeyman to their masters.

This hierarchy, embedded in production, finds expression in the dwelling, with the shop at ground level, the master's quarters on the first floor, and those of the apprentices above.

(CORRESPOND AU PREMIER TEMPS)

D'ABORD COOPÉRATION SIMPLE   TÂCHES INDÉPENDANTES

... SPÉCIALISATION   TOUS FONT LE MÊME TRAVAIL PARCELLAIRE (CORRESPOND AU DEUXIÈME TEMPS)

LE DÉVELOPPEMENT DU ... CE CRÉE DE NOUVEAUX BESOINS QUI NE PEUVENT PLUS ÊTRE SATISFAITS PAR LA CORPORATION: C'EST ALORS QUE NAÎT LA MANUFACTURE.

Manufacture

But progressively, growing demand, linked to increasing production, promotes links between guild towns, and then trade. In the 13th century a special class emerges which devoted itself to commerce. On this basis, manufacturing industry is born in the 15th century. Weaving, from its origins in peasant practice, is the first — and remains — the principle manufacturing activity.

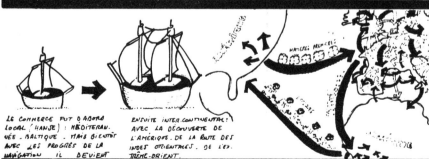

MATIÈRES PREMIÈRES

LE COMMERCE FUT D'ABORD LOCAL (HANSE): MÉDITERRA- NÉE - BALTIQUE. MAIS BIENTÔT AVEC LES PROGRÈS DE LA NAVIGATION IL DEVIENT

ENSUITE INTER-CONTINENTAL: AVEC LA DÉCOUVERTE DE L'AMÉRIQUE. DE LA ROUTE DES INDES ORIENTALES. DE L'EX- TRÊME-ORIENT.

The Guilds

To escape the oppression of the *seigneurs*, more and more serfs find refuge within the towns. At the height of Feudalism, the division of labour was in fact little developed. The hierarchical structure of landed property is matched by the urban hierachy of the *Guild*.

At the end of the 12th century, certain towns set themselves up as 'free' towns, in spite of opposition from feudal overlords, but with the support of the king — whose role in this respect was progressive. Little by little, the surrounding countryside, then the neighbouring nobility, came to rely on these towns for their rare products. Commercial ties thus gradually became established — first on a regional, then a provincial, scale.

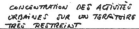

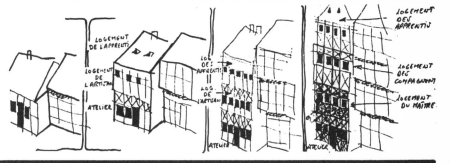

In order to escape from guild law and be in a better position to compete with artisan production, manufacture has to develop outside towns, in agricultural areas where there was a sufficient density of population. Thus in Italy and in Flanders, within *manufacturing* towns, appears a new class of weavers. Towns without guild organisation rapidly become the most flourishing in each country.

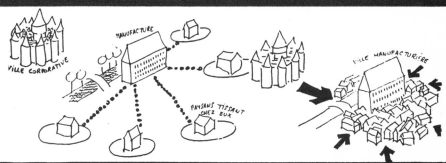

By the 15th century, progress in navigation led to the great discoveries. Competition develops between nations. With manufacture, the towns take precedence over the countryside. In the 18th century, merchant cities — in particular, the ports — acquire supremacy. Certain towns specialise, each one exploiting one branch of production.

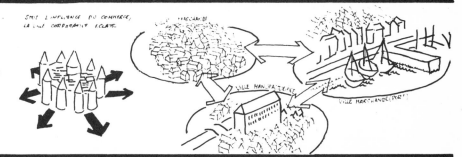

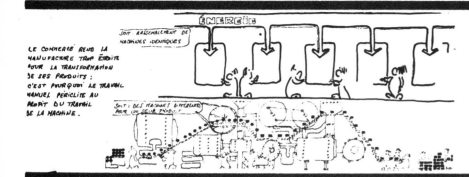

Capitalism (Free Trade)

Concentration of commerce and manufacture in one country — England — progressively creates for her a relatively world-wide market and, consequently, demands which the former productive forces cannot satisfy. Technical progress — the invention of the steam engine, spinning and weaving machines — at the end of the 18th century permits a new form of production: *large-scale industry*. Machine tools begin to replace human skill. Man becomes merely a motor. Then, after the harnessing of energy, he himself is transformed into machinery.

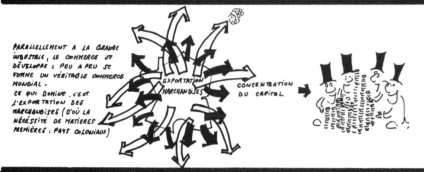

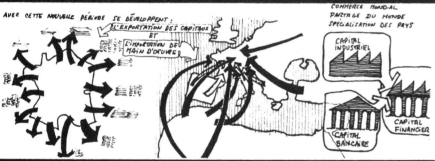

Monopoly Capitalism

At the outset of the 20th century, a new stage appears: trade has become universal, the partition of the world is achieved. Export of capital supplants export of merchandise. Great international monopolies are formed. There is specialisation of countries, and their separation into dominant and dominated. Finance capital (fusion of bank capital and industrial capital) becomes all-powerful.

The concentration of capital and labour, combined with the unequal development of regions within the one country, provokes the phenomenon of *metropolisation* and the increasing decay of rural areas for the benefit of a handful of great towns.

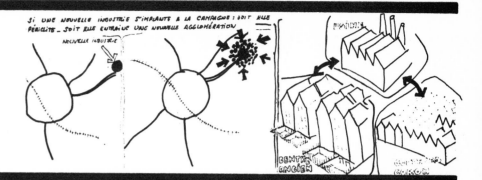

Large-scale industry consolidates the victory of the town over the countryside. In place of towns naturally born, it creates the great modern industrial town. The massive influx of peasants into towns ruins the petty artisan, and gives rise to a new social class — the *proletariat*. The housing of this class in the 19th century takes two principal forms: on the one hand, new homes and new towns created by employers; on the other, ancient city centres abandoned by the moneyed classes.

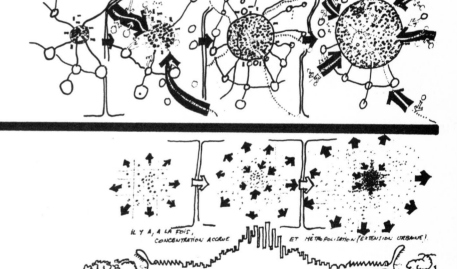

With large-scale industry appears a new dominant class: the *bourgeoisie*. Great colonial empires are formed, with their corollary: the concentration of wealth and capital in very few countries. Industry, at first planted near sources of energy, is soon to some extent liberated from this constraint. It is thus able both to become reintegrated with existing cities, which it modifies, and to create new industrial towns. In either case, it promotes concentration in important agglomerations.

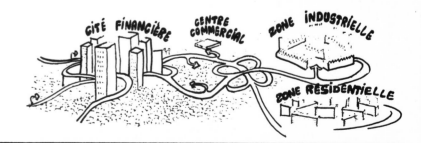

At this new stage of production, division of labour is pushed to its limit, and the contradiction sharpens between the entirely *private* appropriation of surplus-value, and production, which is more and more *socialised*.

In parallel with the concentration of activities in large urban units, appears their dismemberment into well-separated functional groupings. 'Zones' are created, and activities are systematically separated. The division of labour thus finds its most extreme spatial expression.

189

Division of labour, at the various stages of its development, has required also the division of society. Implicit in the town-country dichotomy there is already the division between town-dweller and countryman, which still carries its political and cultural overtones. There are then, among the town-dwellers especially, divisions based on craft and trade, between skilled and unskilled, literate and illiterate. These overlay, and to some extent may coincide with, divisions based on age and sex, but should not be confused with them. 'Family' and 'household' nonetheless are far more involved in the economic organisation of society than much modern town planning allows, and these concepts should not be handled unhistorically as if they were now set in perfect forms which will endure for all time. Many of the difficulties modern housing policy faces, arise from recent changes in the characteristics of households, and present social tendencies severely threaten long-accepted notions of family and marriage.

But these issues are peripheral to our theme. We have said that the division of labour requires also its unity: that what is divided in detail must be organised as a whole. It is this requirement which gives special significance to that division within society which separates out the tasks of organisation, direction, leadership — including the control of town-planning itself. In pre-history it is doubtful if the roles of leadership were more than *ad hoc* or carried more than modest privileges, but with the birth of civilisation they acquire unique characteristics of an enduring and fundamental kind. Not only has the task of organisation become more complex, in that it requires the keeping of records, calculation, and reliable predictions of natural phenomena. Not only does it carry with it responsibility for military, political, cultural as well as economic leadership. By the time civilisation has arrived, it carries privileges as well, and one privilege in particular: that of *ownership*. Since with civilisation, more is produced by society than is necessary for subsistence, and since the distribution of the surplus would dissipate its usefulness and raise insoluble problems concerning the rights of individuals, the surplus remains at the disposal of the leaders themselves, who use it to consolidate the society they govern, and consequently their own position as a propertied class. The history of past civilised society thus becomes the history of the production of wealth which is owned by a governing class and produced under its control by other, less privileged, classes.

Wealth accumulates in the hands of the rulers and consolidates their power. Its earliest form is in the possession of land, cattle and slaves. Its latest is in the possession of power over all things given by vast financial resources. It begets the laws of inheritance, the institution of legal marriage and of legitimate birth. It provides patronage for the artist and funds for the maintenance of science. It provokes envy and greed, and more or less perpetual war. It brings with it the institution, concept and law of *property*, and there is no aspect of the city and civilisation which does not in some degree reflect either the reality of property or its effects upon the lives and ideas of men.

That the institution of property has affected town planning and the form of cities is apparent in many ways. The right to 206 enjoy (or to share with the group to which one belongs by virtue of kin, age, sex or other characteristics), the use of a room, a building, or a plot of land, carries in pre-history no greater right of ownership than is claimed by every child who calls his home 'my house'. But with civilisation, the practice grows of dividing the settlement into separately-owned parts, fenced off from the public domain, and entirely at the disposal of individuals. Occasionally, history presents us with the spectacle of a settlement planned and administered under one ownership. It was to this that the best Baroque examples and the first British new towns aspired. Recent new town planning, as at Milton Keynes, on the other hand, does little more than define the difference between the public and the private domain, and does so in the manner used since the days of Hippodamos. Within existing cities, established property boundaries represent a formidable condition for town planning, and not infrequently delay or frustrate entirely the achievement of worth-while ends. For this reason, the advocacy of some form of public ownership of all the land is also one of town planning's perennial themes.

We need not look far either for evidence of the way propertied ruling classes throughout history have shaped the city to fulfil their political and ideological objectives. We have seen something of the significance which has been given at various times to fortresses, palaces, temples, processional ways, lawcourts, senate houses and stock exchanges; and the significance of prisons, barracks, and places of execution speaks for itself. We have seen also how these things weighed in the opinions of Aristotle, Alberti and Wren. Much of what is customarily discussed in aesthetic terms has a lot to do with how the city is arranged in order to underline ideological aims. Thus, windowless walled enclosures bespeak the mysterious power of theocracy; battlements, the might of tyranny. The royal palace at the centre of a spider's web of routes epitomises monarchy; ostentatious variety, the

206 Throughout history the division of the city into privately-owned plots affects its form.

207 independence of the merchant and the rights of the individual. It is usually outside the city that the friendly huddle of dwellings around a common, tries to proclaim the brotherhood of man. → Home town, yeah.

At each stage of its development, the city has mirrored contemporary divisions in society and the concomitant property relations. The propertyless poor have for countless centuries lived as best they could on the streets, in shanty towns, or in the cellars or attics of the better-off. We have seen how modern town planning was largely born out of the campaign for better living conditions, without which things in Britain's older towns would be worse than they are. But in spite of town planning, there is still the contrast between slumdom and suburbia, east end and west end. The better-off move into new homes, and their outworn cast-offs are meanly adapted for multi-occupation by the poor. Twelve decades of state intervention have not changed fundamentally a situation in which millions of the poorest still live in conditions officially condemned as sub-standard, and as long as private property and the law of the market are allowed to dominate planning, this situation is inevitable.

A society divided into classes, one of which enjoys exceptional privileges and power, inevitably provokes hostility and a desire for change among those less-privileged. Thus, in addition to external wars against the uncivilised or against rival civilisations, there is within such societies themselves a perpetual tendency to civil war. This also finds reflection in what Alberti had to say, and the work of Haussmann in Paris was, as we have seen, largely prompted by the threat of continued insurrection. Even as recently as the 'thirties, blocks of flats were looked at askance in British Government circles, as being potential 'hotbeds of red intrigue'. Today, 'owner-occupation' is for similar reasons preferred and regarded as a device to inculcate in Everyman the conservative outlook of the proprietor. At the same time, the role of the city itself, especially in recent history, has been that of the promoter of change. Urban conditions are the most favourable for the rapid and continual innovation in social production which characterises our epoch. They are the most favourable also for the resolution of the conflict between rulers and ruled, which over the centuries has been moving to its climax.

Capitalism now advances to the stage where the entire life of a city, a region, a nation or even a continent, is effectively controlled by a few men whose decisions rest on one criterion — profitability. Yet at the same time, social production has

Likely The syndicates in U.S.

advanced to unprecented levels. Skilled and unskilled workers, salaried managers, technicians, scholars, designers and planners, make decisions, divide their tasks and carry them out with no need of direction from those who own controlling shares in the office blocks, factories, machines and raw materials with which they work. These anonymous proprietors in many cases do not even know what work is being done on their behalf, let alone how to do it. The historic justification for a ruling class — that it was necessary in order to direct and organise the work of society — is gone. Left to themselves, those who do the work could now be freed to make their own plans about what society needs to produce, how, and where. If they were, their decisions, no longer directed towards securing the profits of an oligarchy, could pursue the goals sought by the pioneers of modern town planning: social well-being, care of the under-privileged, and a more equitable distribution of the fruits of social labour.

Now also, the potential always implicit in civilisation, that one day mankind would turn *surplus* into *abundance,* and remove as a consequence the last excuse for private ownership of wealth and the division of society into classes, is no longer a distant prospect. Mankind stands on the threshold of the destiny towards which the creation of cities was the necessary first step: the conscious, compassionate, deliberate and truly democratic control of all the circumstances of his life: of himself, his activity and his surroundings, in town and countryside.

We have seen how even before the full tide of modern industrial capitalism began to flow, men like Owen and Fourier boldly foresaw this end, and how, throughout two centuries, town planning (in its intentions, at least) has never been far from socialism. No matter how these and other pioneers would have differed on matters of detail, for all of them socialism in essence meant the ownership and control by society as a whole of the land and all the means by which wealth is produced. Today we are in the midst of the most gigantic transformation of society, which is rivalled in significance only by that which took place when cities were first created. In the thousands of years since then, mankind has staggered painfully to his present level. We see in the emerging socialist societies some indication both of the triumphs and difficulties he has yet to face. In them, the process of transformation is now coming out of its most critical stage, when town planning could do little more than repair the destruction of war, prepare to stave off fresh attacks, and cope with the most pressing needs of rapid

207

economic growth. The achievement of socialism is. still, in countries like Britain, the essential prerequisite for humane town planning, as for every worth-while social endeavour. Without it, there can be no lasting progress, and the best we shall achieve will be tainted by the imperfections of an obsolete, demoralised and demoralising social system. What is technically and socially possible, today more than ever before, looks for its achievement to the necessary political changes. Without them, what is achieved stands always at risk of being perverted to ends contrary to those that were intended. Slum clearance and comprehensive redevelopment — both, in their time, battle-cries of progressive town-planning — are in Britain today the excuse for urban destruction, on a scale which outstrips the Blitz, in the interest of property speculators and the motorways lobby. The division of the city into healthy communities becomes in practice the excuse for class districts and racial ghettoes. Urban renewal and the rehabilitation of homes, forces rent up and the poor out.

The city then, (or whatever we should henceforth call human settlement) should be planned so as to be in scale with mankind, individually and collectively. It should be fashioned with due regard to natural constraints. It should be conceived as part of a regional plan. It should fulfil an appropriate role in, and facilitate, social production. It cannot outstrip the limitations imposed upon it by the prevailing production processes and property relations, but when production (and consequently town planning) is frustrated by an obsolete social system, this frustration has to be removed before significant progress can be made. ⚹

But neither townsmen nor town planners can simply fold their arms and wait for political change. It is not (as Geddes hinted) a question of concerning oneself with affairs of state *or* affairs of the *polis*. Today, every pressing problem in town planning is rapidly becoming an affair of state, and the defence of human standards, humane environment, and the very planet on which we depend for life, is itself a necessary condition for humanity's further progress. This progress

demands of town planning that it defends the advances it has already made, and that it debates, discovers and, as far as possible, creates for the world to see, the possible Utopias within our grasp.

⚹ Not necessarily. Politics since 1975 in Britian says socialism + capitalism wax & wane, w/ capitalism generally stronger, socialism curbing its excess. The better solution is a human-scaled settlement based on values reflecting human needs of individuals, families, + neighborhood groups — from the "parish pump" [p.53, here, Geddes] on up harnessing the economic power of capitalism.

208   Hook: a possible Utopia.

192

REFERENCES

1. WISSLER, *An introduction to social anthropology*, quoted HAWLEY, Amos H. *Human ecology*, New York, 1950.
2. HAWLEY, Amos H, op.cit.
3. HALL, Peter, *The world cities*, London, 1966.
4. FRENCHMAN, M. *Blueprint for megalopolis* in *The Times*, London, 24 April 1973.
5. FRASER, D. *Village planning in the primitive world*, London, 1968.
6. HAVERFIELD, F. *Ancient town planning*, Oxford, 1913.
7. BERNAL, J. D. *Science in history*, London, 1954.
8. Ibid.
9. LAVEDAN, P., *Histoire de l'Urbanisme, I*, Paris, 1926.
10. Ibid.
11. Ibid.
12. HAVERFIELD, F., op.cit.
13. CHILDE, V. G., *What happened in history*, London, 1947.
14. LAVEDAN, P. op.cit.
15. HAVERFIELD, F. op.cit.
16. Ibid.
17. Ibid.
18. LAVEDAN, P., op.cit.
19. Ibid.
20. DERRY & WILLIAMS, *A short history of technology*, Oxford, 1960.
21. DOBB, M. *Capitalist enterprise and social progress*, London, 1925.
22. MUMFORD, L., *The city in history*, London, 1961.
23. ARISTOTLE, *Civics*, quoted HIORNS, F. R., *Townbuilding in history*, London, 1956.
24. VITRUVIUS, *de Architectura*, trans. GRANGER, I, IV-VI.
25. BERESFORD, M. *New towns of the middle ages*, London, 1967.
26. ALBERTI, L. B. *Ten books on architecture*, trans. LEONI (fac. edn) London, 1955.
27. WREN, C., *Tracts on architecture*, Wren Society, XIX, Oxford, 1942.
28. BELL, E. MOBERLY, *Octavia Hill*, London, 1942.
29. ENGELS, F., *The housing question*, English trans., Moscow, 1970. (p.53).
30. Ibid. (p.169).
31. Ibid. (p.54).
32. Ibid. (p.53).
33. REPS, J. W., *The making of urban America*, Princeton, 1965.
34. OWEN, R., *Report to the Committee for the relief of the Manufacturing Poor, London, 1817, in A new view of Society and other writings*, London, 1966, (p.161 et seq).
35. Ibid. (p.265).
36. Ibid. (p.285).
37. Ibid. (p.268).
38. Ibid. (p.264).
39. FOURIER, Chas., *The establishment of a trial Phalanx*, in BEECHER AND BIENVENU, *'The utopian vision of Charles Fourier'*, London, 1972.
40. BENEVOLO, L., *The origins of modern town planning*, (trans LANDRY) London, 1967.
41. MORRIS, W., *News from nowhere*, Collected Works, XVII, London, 1912.
42. HOWARD, E. *Garden cities of tomorrow*, London, 1946.
43. CHOAY, F., *The modern city: Planning in the 19th Century*, London, n.d.
44. WIEBENSON, D., *Tony Garnier: the cité industrielle*, London, n.d.

45. GARNIER, T., *Une cité industrielle. Preface* trans. WIEBENSON, op.cit.
46. WIEBENSON, D., op.cit. (p.14).
47. GEDDES, P., *Cities in evolution.* London, 1915, (3rd edn. 1968), (p.198).
48. Ibid., p.393.
49. Ibid., p.49.
50. Ibid., p.132.
51. Ibid., p.142.
52. Ibid., p.107.
53. Ibid., p.97.
54. ASHWORTH, W., *The genesis of British town planning,* London, 1954, (p.178).
55. Ibid., p.183.
56. Ibid., p.196.
57. DERRY and WILLIAMS, op.cit. (p.196).
58. CRESSWELL, H. B., in *Architectural Review,* London, December 1958, quoted JACOBS, J., *The death and life of great American cities,* London, 1961.
59. *LE CORBUSIER, (pseud. JEANNERET) trans. ETCHELLS, The city of tomorrow and its planning,* London, 1971, (pp.300-301).
60. LE CORBUSIER, (pseud. JEANNERET) *The radiant city* (Paris 1933; English trans., 1964), (p.8).
61. Ibid. (p.301).
62. LE CORBUSIER, *The city of tomorrow,* (op.cit.), (p.54).
63. LE CORBUSIER, *Towards a new architecture,* Paris, 1925; (English trans., London, 1971).
64. LE CORBUSIER, *The city of tomorrow,* (op.cit) (p.102).
65. Ibid.
66. Ibid. (p.87-98).
67. Ibid. (p.160).
68. Ibid. (pp.160 et seq).
69. Ibid. (p.220).
70. ENGELS, F., op.cit. (pp.94-95).
71. Ibid. (preface to 2nd. edit.).
72. Ibid. (p.6).
73. Ibid. (p.18).
74. Ibid. (pp.41-42).
75. Ibid. (pp.38-39).
76. Ibid. (p.54).
77. Ibid. (pp.59-60).
78. Ibid. (p.12).
79. Ibid. (pp.22-23).
80. Ibid. (p.69).
81. Ibid. (pp.24-25).
82. Ibid. (p.96).
83. Ibid. (p.49).
84. Ibid. (p.49).
85. LE CORBUSIER, *The city of tomorrow,* (op.cit.) (p.302).
86. KOPP, A., (trans. BURTON), *Town and revolution,* London, 1970, (pp.197-8).
87. Ibid. (p.172).
88. Ibid. (Appendix 4).
89. LE CORBUSIER, *The radiant city,* op.cit., (p.187).
90. Ibid. (pp.91 et seq).
91. Ibid.
92. GROPIUS, *The new architecture and the bauhaus,* trans., P. M. SHAND London, 1935, (p.105).
93. Ibid. (p.57-58).
94. UNWIN, R., *Town planning in practice. An introduction to the art of designing cities and suburbs.* London, 1909, (Facsimile Edn. NY. 1971), (p.2).
95. Ibid. (p.289).
96. Ibid. (p.140).
97. Ibid. (p.138).
98. UNWIN, R., *Nothing gained by overcrowding.*
99. UNWIN, R., *Town planning in practice,* op.cit. (pp. 375-385).
100. Ibid. (pp.149-150).
101. OSBORN, F. J., and WHITTICK, A., *The new towns,* London, 1969, (p.85).
102. Ibid. (p.45).
103. Ibid.
104. WRIGHT, F. L., *The living city,* N.Y., 1958, (p.104).
105. KORN, A., *A new plan for Amsterdam,* in *Architectural Review,* 1938.
106. ASHWORTH, op.cit., (p.190).
107. Ibid. (p.213).
108. Ibid. (p.230).
109. BUCHANAN, C. D., *Mixed blessing: the motor in Britain,* London, 1958.
110. HIORNS, R., *Town building in history,* London, 1956.
111. ABERCROMBIE, P. Town planning, London, 2nd Edn. 1944.
112. FORSHAW, J. H., and ABERCROMBIE, P., *County of London Plan,* London, 1943.
113. OSBORNE & WHITTICK, op.cit. (p.100).
114. STEIN, C., *Towards new towns for America,* Cambridge, Mass. 1966.
115. BOYD, C., et al, *Homes for the people,* London, 1945, (pp.140-141).
116. KORN, A., & SAMUELY, F. J., A master plan for London, In *Architectural Review,* June, 1942.
117. WILSON, H., *Cumbernauld new town — preliminary planning proposals,* 1958.
118. WILSON, H., *Cumbernauld new town — 1st Addendum Report,* 1959.
119. BENNETT, H. et al, *The planning of a new town,* London, 1961.
120. BUCHANAN, et al, *Traffic in towns,* London, 1963.
121. Ibid. (pp.41 ff.).
122. Ibid. (p.84).
123. Ibid. (p.77).
124. Ibid. (p.119).
125. Ibid. (p.131).
126. Ibid. (p.94).
127. SMEED, R., *The traffic problem in towns,* Manchester Statistical Socy. 1961.
128. BUCHANAN et al, op.cit. (pp.7-8).
129. UNITED NATIONS, *Planning of metropolitan areas and new towns,* N.Y., (1967).
130. Ibid. (p.55).
131. ALEXANDER, C., *A city is not a tree,* in *Design,* London, Feb. 1966.
132. DERBYSHIRE, A., *New Town Plans* in *RIBAJ,* October, 1967.
133. WILSON, L. H. et al, *Skelmersdale new town — Interim report on planning proposals,* 1963.
134. WILSON, L. H. et al, *Report on Northampton, Bedford and North Buckinghamshire study,* HMSO, 1965.
135. WILSON, L. H., et al, *Redditch new town: Report on planning proposals,* 1966.
136. IRVINE DEVELOPMENT CORPORATION, *Irvine new town plan,* Irvine, 1971.
137. Ibid. (p.75).
138. Ibid. (p.86).
139. Ibid.
140. Ibid. (pp.87-88).
141. Ibid. (p.98).
142. Ibid. (p.101).
143. MATTHEW, R. et al, *Central Lancashire: Study for a city,* London, 1967.
144. Ibid. (p.57).
145. LING, A. et al, *Runcorn new town master plan,* Runcorn, 1967, (p.18).

146. Ibid, (pp.66-67).
147. Ibid. (pp.72-73).
148. MADIN, J. et al, *Telford development proposals*, 1969.
149. HALL, P. et al, (Economic Associates Ltd.) *A new town for mid-Wales*, Welsh Office, HMSO, 1966.
150. LLEWELLYN-DAVIES, R. et al, *Washington new town master plan*, 1966.
151. BUCHANAN, C. D. et al, *South Hampshire study*, HMSO, 1966, (p.103).
152. POOLEY, F. *North Buckinghamshire new city*, Aylesbury, 1966, (p.3-4).
153. Ibid. (p.92-95).
154. Ibid. (pp.79-80).
155. LLEWELLYN-DAVIES et al, *The plan for Milton Keynes*, Bletchley, 1970 (p.45).
156. *Regional plan for Stockholm*, Stockholm, 1966.
157. PENG, G. T. C. & VERMA, N. S., *New town planning design and development; comprehensive reference materials*, Lincoln, Nebraska, 1971.
158. SHVARIKOV, V. A., et al, *Pattern and form of new towns in the USSR*. (Report to UNECE, Holland, 1966), Moscow 1966.
159. OSIN, V. *Cities: Today and tomorrow*, in *Uchitelskaya Gazeta*, 7 Aug. 1971, (trans. N.P.A.).
160. KUDRYAVTSEV, B., *Man-dwelling-city*, in *Stroitelnaya Gazeta*, 3 March, 1972, (trans. N.P.A.).
161. ZUBAREV, B., *Cybernetics of a big city*, (trans. N.P.A. no source).
162. MORRIS, A. E. J., *A city of the future?* in *Built Environment*, Aug. 1972, (p.300 et seq).

163. TOWERS, G. *City planning in China*, Jnl. R.T.P.I. 59(3), March 1973 (p.125 et seq).
164. DAHINDEN, J., *Urban structure for the future*, London, 1971.
165. ADABASHEV, I., *Global Engineering*, Moscow, 1966.
166. MUMFORD, L. op.cit. (p.563 *passim*).
167. GUTKIND, E. A., *The expanding environment: the end of cities — the rise of communities*, London, 1953.
168. GOODMAN, P. & P., *Communitas: means of livelihood and ways of life*, New York, 1960.
169. GRUEN, V., *The heart of our cities: the urban crisis: diagnosis and cure*, London, 1965.
170. JACOBS, J. *The economy of cities*, 1970.
171. AUZELLE, R., *Ou en est l'urbanisme?* in *Lumiere et Vie(90)* 1968 reprod. in *Bulletin SADG* 178(18) 1973 (pp.5 et seq.).
172. DOXIADIS, C. A., *Ekistics: an introduction to the science of human settlements*, London, 1968.
173. McCLOUGHLIN, J. B., *Urban and regional planning: a systems approach*, London, 1969.
174. CHADWICK G., *A systems view of planning*, Oxford, 1971.
175. ALEXANDER, C. *Notes on the synthesis of form*, Harvard, 1964.
176. COWAN, P., (Ed.) *The future of planning: Centre for environmental studies*, London, 1973.
177. CHRISTALLER, W., (trans. Baskin 1966) *Central places in South Germany*, 1933.
178. MARX, K., *Capital*, I London, 1970.

ACKNOWLEDGEMENTS

A principal objective of this work has been to bring together essential texts and illustrations necessary to the understanding of town planning. I am grateful to the many publishers, authors and others who have given permission for reproduction. While every effort has been made to do so, it has not been possible in every case to trace everything back to its origins. Some illustrations have had to be copied from other publications, with less than perfect results.

Quoted passages are from the following works:

Fraser, D., Village planning in the primitive world, London, STUDIO VISTA, 1968 (ref. 5); Haverfield, F., Ancient town planning, OXFORD UNIVERSITY PRESS, 1913 (refs. 6 & 15); Lavedan, P., *Histoire de l'urbanisme,* Paris, LAURENS, 1926 (refs. 10 & 14); Derry & Williams, A short history of technology, OXFORD UNIVERSITY PRESS, 1960 (refs. 20 & 57); Bell, E. Moberley, Octavia Hill, London, CONSTABLE, 1942 (ref. 28); Engels, F., The housing question (English trans.) Moscow, PROGRESS PUBLISHERS (refs. 29-32, 70-84); Owen, R., A new view of society and other writings, London, EVERYMAN, 1966 (refs. 34, 35, 36, 37, 38); Beecher & Bienvenu, The Utopian vision of Charles Fourier, London, JONATHAN CAPE, 1972 (ref. 39); Geddes, P., Cities in evolution, London, ERNEST BENN, 1968 (refs. 47, 48, 49, 50, 51, 52, 53); Cresswell, H.B., *in* Architectural Review, London, December 1958, ARCHITECTURAL PRESS (ref. 58); Le Corbusier *(trans.* Etchells) The city of tomorrow and its planning, London, ARCHITECTURAL PRESS, 1971 (refs. 59-69); Kopp, A. *(trans.* Burton) Town and revolution London, THAMES & HUDSON, 1970 (refs. 86, 87, 88); Le Corbusier, The radiant city, (English trans.), London, FABER & FABER, 1964 (refs. 89-91); Unwin, R., Town planning in practice, London, T. FISHER UNWIN, 1909, facs. edn. New York, BLOM & Co. 1971 (refs. 94-100; Ashworth, W., The genesis of British town planning, London, ROUTLEDGE & KEGAN PAUL and HUMANITIES PRESS (USA), 1954 (refs. 106-108); Boyd, C. et al., Homes for the people, London, PAUL ELEK, 1945 (ref. 115); Korn, A. & Samuely, F. J., A master plan for London *in* the Architectural Review (June), London, ARCHITECTURAL PRESS, 1942 (ref. 116); Buchanan, C. et al., Traffic in towns, London, HMSO, 1963 (refs. 120-128); IRVINE DEVELOPMENT CORPORATION, Irvine New Town Plan, Irvine, 1971 (refs. 137-142); Ling, A. et al., Runcorn New Town Master Plan, RUNCORN DEVELOPMENT CORPORATION, 1967 (refs. 145-147); Llewellyn-Davies, R. et al., Washington New Town Master Plan, WASHINGTON DEVELOPMENT CORPORATION, 1966 (refs. 150); Buchanan, C. et al., South Hampshire Study, London, HMSO 1966 (ref. 151); Pooley, F. North Buckinghamshire New City, Aylesbury, BUCKINGHAMSHIRE COUNTY COUNCIL, 1966 (refs. 152-154); Llewelleyn-Davies, R., et al. The plan for Milton Keynes, Bletchley, MILTON KEYNES DEVELOPMENT CORPORATION, 1970 (ref. 155); Jacobs, J., The death and life of great American cities, London, JONATHAN CAPE, 1961 (ref. 170); Marx, K., Capital, English trans., London, LAWRENCE & WISHART (ref. 178).

Figures are from the following:

Aerofilms Ltd., 28, 36; Messrs. Alcan Industries, 137, 138; The Architect & Building News, 189; The Architectural Press, 63, 100, 101, 102, 103, 104, 111, 15, 99, 161, 153, 71, 72; Edward Arnold, 92, 13, 42; Athlone Press, 14; British Road Federation, 180; Buckinghamshire County Council, 169, 170, 171, 172, 173, 174; Cie des Arts Photo Mécaniques, 201; Faber & Faber, 59-61, 73, 74, 75, 76, 78-85; Greater London Council, 27, 88, 95, 112-122, 208; Airviews Manchester, 22; Viewpoint Projects, 11; A. F. Kersting, 45, 37; J. Allan Cash, 106; HMSO (Buchanan et al. Traffic in Towns, 1963) 93, 107, 125-135, 179; (Matthew, R. et al. Central Lancashire: A Study for a City) 145-148; (Economic Associates, A New Town for Mid-Wales) 154; (Buchanan et al., South Hampshire Study) 162-168; (Llewellyn-Davies et al. A new city — Newbury, Swindon and Didcot) 204; Walter Bor, 94; Historic City Plans and Views, 26, 43; Messrs. Hutchinson, 197; Irvine Development Corporation, 141-144; Cecil Stewart (A prospect of Cities, Longmans Green) 31, 32, 35, 48, 51; Lund Humphries, 10, 25, 77, 91, 98; Milton Keynes Development Corporation, 175-178; C. Stein, 96, 97; Oxford University Press 8; Mrs. Hattula Moholy-Nagy, 33, 47; Prentice-Hall, 199; Wilson & Womersley and the Redditch Development Corporation, 140; Andrew Derbyshire, 136; John R. James, 200; Arthur Ling and the Runcorn Development Corporation, 149-152; The Scientific American, 1; Thames & Hudson, 196; Washington Development Corporation, 155-160; City Librarian, Sheffield, 57; British Museum, 89; *Architecture, Mouvement, Continuité,* (Sept. 1973), and G. Darris, 205; H. M. Ordnance Survey, 12; A. E. J. Morris, 185, 186; Science Museum, 68; *Office de la Recherche Scientifique et Technique Outre-Mer,* 2; Journal of Egyptian Archaeology, 4; John Maltby, 181; Moholy-Nagy, S., Matrix of man, London, Pall Mall Press, 3; Wycherley, R. E., How the Greeks built cities, London, MacMillan, 1949, 5, 6; Wiebenson, D., Tony Garnier: the Cité Industrielle, London, Studio Vista, 7, 64, 65; Paul Hamlyn, World Architecture, 9, 22, 105; Korn, A., History builds the town, Lund Humphries, 14; RIBA, 16; Saalman, H., Mediaeval cities, Studio Vista, 21; K. Smigielski, 20; Argan, G. C., The Renaissance city, Studio Vista, 21; Burke, G., Towns in the making, Edward Arnold, 23, 89; Hiorns, F., Town building in history, 24; Mumford, L., The city in history, Secker & Warburg, 29, 40; Vitruvius (trans. Granger) X books on architecture, 30; Rosenau, H., The ideal city in its architectural evolution, London, Routledge, 34, 44; B. Berrett, 49, 50, 123, 124; Choay, F., The modern city: planning in the 19th century, Studio Vista, 52, 53, 54; Pugin, A. W. N., Contrasts, 1836, 58; Howard, E., Garden cities of tomorrow, Faber, 1965, 59, 60, 61; Cherry, G. E., Town planning in its social context, London, 1970, 62; Pevsner, N., The sources of modern architecture and design, London, Thames & Hudson, 1968, 66; The 'Observer', 69; Creese, W. L., The search for environment, New Haven, 1966, 86; Unwin, R., Town planning in practice, London, T. Fisher Unwin, 1909, 87; Wright, F. L., The living city, New York, Horizon Press 1958, 90; Cumbernauld Development Corporation, 108, 109; Jencks, C., Architecture 2000, London, Studio Vista, 1971, 110, 139, 191; Architectural Forum, 1963, 182; Gruen, V., The heart of our cities, 183; Dahinden, J., Urban structures for the future, London, Pall Mall, 1972, 187, 188, 192, 202, 203; Goodman, P & P, Communitas, New York, Random House, 1960, 193, 194, 195; R. Bryant, 206, 207; E. Daniels, 198; Bell, C & R, City Fathers, Barrie & Jenkins, 67.

INDEX *(figure nos. in italics)*

Aachen *18*
Abercrombie, Patrick *8,* 88, 91ff., 99, 134, 162
accessibility 6, 9, 14, 15, 17, 55, 115, 118, 127, 144, 158, 160, 172, 176
acropolis 9, 13
administrative centre *see* central area
Aeschylus 175
agora *6,* 9, 11, 24
agriculture, countryside, 4, 6, 8, 9, 12, 14, 22, 34, 37, 39, 47, 55, 67, 68, 93, 103, 122, 153, 168, 170, 178, 179
Aigues Mortes *13*
Aikhal *189*
Akroyd, Akroydon 32, 66
Alberti, L. B. 24, 41, 49, 161, 179, 184
Alcan 122 ff.
Alexander, C. 123, 172
Alexander of Macedon 11, 24
Alexandria 10, 24
almshouses 17, 82
altitude *see* constraints
Amarna *3, 4,* 8, 10
America 15, 20, 36, 42, 55, 58, 59, 86, 94, 103, 117, 122, 162, 168, 170, *188*
Amsterdam 22, 88
Antwerp 22
Aosta *8*
Archigram 172
Aristophanes 24
Aristotle 24, 157, 175, 184
Ascoral 103
Asshur 8
Athens 10, 161, 163, 172
Austria-Hungary 54
automobile *see also* traffic, transport, communications, pedestrian 51, 58, 64, 72, 87, 91, 102, 103 105, 108, 113ff., 122, 125, 126, 134, 149, 158, 160, 180
Auzelle, R. 172
Averlino (il Filarete) 26

Babylon 7, 8, 175
Baghdad 14
Barlow Report 88, 92
Baroque 19, *21, 25,* 26, 29, *42,* 184
Basildon 95 *infra*
basilica 11, 13
bastides *13,* 14, *17,* 31
Bath 31
bath-houses, thermae 13, 68, 82
Bauhaus 80
Bellamy, Edward 42
Berlage 88
Berlin 66, 106
Berrett, B. *123, 124,* 152 *infra*
betterment 90
bicycle *see* cycle
Birmingham 22
Bletchley *see* Buckinghamshire, Milton Keynes
Boston, USA *179*
bouleterion *see* public buildings
Bournville 32
Bracknell 95 *infra*
Brazilia 103, *106*
Bristol 123
Broadacres 87, *90*
bronze age 7
Brunelleschi *20*
Buchanan, C., Buchanan Report 113ff., 123ff., 141ff., 159, 160, 176
Buckingham, J. S. 47, *57*
Buckinghamshire *see also* Milton Keynes 149ff., 168, 178
building societies 66
building technique *9,* 13, 17, 18, 30, 50, 51, 64, 68, 70, 72, 76, 87, 166, 180, 182
burial ground *see* cemetery
Byzantium (Constantinople) 13

Cabet 42

Caersws (Newtown) 139

capitalism, capitalist 18, 32, 36, 38, 42, 59, 65, 66, 191

cardo 12

carparks, garages 62, 74, 77, 103, 108, 114, 115, *119,* 120, 135, 150

Carthage 5, 11, 13

Cassiodorus 24

catchment area, hinterland 17, 55, 120, 124, 128, 131, 143, 150, 158, 159

cellular structure *(see also* hierarchy, module, neighbourhood, suburb) 17, 114, 124, *143,* 157, 158, 168, 172

cemetery 6, 10, 26, 160

central area 6, 16, 24ff., 47, 60, 64, 65, 79, 81, 84, 93, 102, 105, 106, 108, 111, 114, 119, 120, 125, 129, 134, 140, 152, 155, 158, 161

Cerda 48

Chadwick 23, 65

Chandigarh 144

Charlemagne 14

Chicago 87

Chichester *12*

Childe, V. G. 8

China 5, 7, 13, 164, 176 *infra*

Christaller, W. 177

church, chapel *see* temple

CIAM *see* Modern Movement

civic centre *see* public buildings

class districts 23, 25, 39, 84, 85, 92, 93, 108, 131, 158

class, social 59, 64, 67, 81, 83, 184

classification of settlements 5, 15, 18, 23, 25, 124, 172, 175, 183, 184

climate *see* constraints

clusters of towns, constellations *(see also* conurbation) 47, 124, 141, 158, 160, 161, 164, 168, 172, 177

Cole, G. D. H. 92

college, collegiate form 15, 82, 184

colony, colonisation *5, 8,* 9, 11, *14,* 14, 20, 31, 32, 37, 56, 66, 123, 155

commerce, trade, shops 17, 22, 29, 32, 47, 64, 70, 74, 81, 85, 87, 93, 94, 100, 105, 115, 122, 126, 150, 155, 157, 160, 161, 163

communications, transport, traffic 9, 12, 17, 23ff., 32, 36, 38, 39, 48, 50, 52, 55ff., 59, 60ff., 70, 76, 91, 92, 95, 100, 103, 113ff., 124, 126ff., 135, 143, 144, 153, 157ff., 160, 168, 172, 176, 177, 180, 182, 183

community centre, facilities 34, 38, 41, 47, 68, 70, 74, 79, 81, 86, 87, 92ff., 103, 116, 122, 125ff., 141, 144, 150, 155, 158, 159, 161, 175

community route 127, 161

Constantinople 13

constraints *(see also* drainage, energy, water supply, region) 6, 24, 25, 32, 52, 172ff., 192

conurbation *(see also* clusters, region) 53, 158, 164, 183

Corby 95 *infra*

Cordes *17*

Costa, Lucia 103

cost-benefit analysis 53, 125, 129

countryside *see* agriculture, town and country

Coventry 88, 91, *93,* 152

Crawley 95 *infra*

cremation *see* cemetery

cul-de-sac, close 84, 111, 120, 139

Cumbernauld 103ff., 125, 126

Cwmbran 95 *infra*

cycle-ways, cyclist, bicycle 96, 101

Darwin, Charles 182

decentralisation, dispersal, decongestion *(see also* De-urbanists) 26, 43, 47, 62, 87, 93, 134, 140, 157ff., 168

decumanus 12

defence 6, 9, 14, 15, 24, 25, 159, 176

density of population 12, 39, 61, 62, 72, 73, 76, 79, 80, 87, 92, 93, 100, 101, 102, 108, 111, 125, 127, 128, 134, 149, 150, 153, 157, 159, 170, 172, 184

Derbyshire, Andrew *146, 147*

de-urbanists 68ff., *76,* 164

dispersal *see* decentralisation

Dinocrates 24

Diodorus 8

Doxiadis, Constantine 122, 124, 172, *197*

drainage, sewerage 7, 9ff., 15, 20, 23, 25, 26, 31, 34, 53, 56, 168, 172, 177, 179

Dravidian cities 7

Dublin 88

Dürer 24, 173

East Kilbride 95 *infra*

economy, economics, economic systems 5ff., 15, 18, 20, 30, 34, 36ff., 53, 56, 66, 122, 124, 125, 129, 159, 162, 168, 173, 177, 179, 180, 183ff.

education, schools, etc. 26, 36, 37, 47, 64, 74, 81, 85, 87, 93, 94, 102, 111, 115, 122, 128, 141, 145, 149, 150, 157, 160, 161, 172, 175

Eesteren, van 88

Egypt *3, 4,* 7, 8, 11, 175, 182

employment *see* industry

energy production, distribution 15, 22, 29, 30, 32, 43, 51, 53, 56, 57, 68, 70, 88, 152, 159, 168, 177ff.

Engels, F. 65ff.

engineer, engineering 24, 29, 30, 48, 60, 68, 87, 88, 103, 116 *infra,* 120 *infra,* 160, 168, 176, 178

engineer, military 18, 24, 29

engineer, traffic 103ff., 172

engineering services 48, 127, 152, 158, 166 *(see also* drainage, heating)

environmental area 113ff., 126

environmental capacity 114

environmental management 118

environmental standards 118·

Escorial 39

Etruscans 6, 11

factory *see* industry

family, household 5, 17, 36, 41, 68, 82, 87, 182, 184

Farsta 152, 162, *184*

fascism 72, 86, 88

fauborg 15

feudalism 14, 81

Filarete, il (Averlino) 26, *33*

fire station 95

flats *(see also* housing, unite d'habitation) 41, 50, 62, 64, 68, 73, 74, 80, 85, 92, 115, 125, 150, 157

Florence, *20,* 29, 157, 161

Forshaw, J. H. 92, 93, 99

Fort Werth 106, 168

fortification *(see also* acropolis, wall) 14, 15, 17, 19, 24ff., 29

forum 11, 13, 175

foundling homes 17

Fourier, Chas. 37, 67, 191

France, 88, 172, 178 *infra, 201*

Fuller, Buckminster 122, 166, *188*

futurism *see* science fiction

garages *see* carparks

garden, small-holding, allotment 16, 36, 38, 39, 62, 66, 80, 82, 85, 86, 108

Garden City Movement 5, 47ff., 52, 60, 61, 62, 72, 80, 83, 85, 92, 94, 96, 102, 170

Garnier, Toni 49, 52, 68, 79, 108

gate, town gateway 15, 24ff., 80

Geddes, P. 52ff. 65, 80, 103, 175, 178, 182, 192
Germany 15, 54, 86, 176
Gibberd, F. 93, *99*
Gibson, Donald 91, 152
Giorgio, Francesco di 24, 26, *32*
Glenrothes 95 *infra*
Godin, J. B. 37, 41, *54, 55, 56*
Goodman, P. & P. 168
grand manner *(see also* monumentality) 29
gravity model 117
Greece, Greek civilisation *5, 6, 7,* 24, 25, 55, 122
green belt 36, 47, 62, 64, 70, 79, 80, 89, 92, 93, 108, 170, 179
green wedge 36, 53, 92, 102
gridiron plan *5,* 6, 8, 10, 14, 20, 24, 50, 56, 60, 64, 79, 87, 91, 101, 105, 119, 120, 127, 139, 141ff., 153, 184
Grimsta 163
Gromatici 12
Gropius, W. 80
Gruen, V. 158
Guernica 88
Guise 37, *54, 55, 56*
Gutkind, E. A. 168
gymnasium 10

Hampstead Garden Suburb 48, 81, 83ff., *86*
Harappa 9
Halifax 32
Harlow 96, *98, 99,* 103
Hatfield 95
Haussmann 32 *47,* 56, 66, 191
health centre 36, 51, 74, 102, 111, 150
heating, district 82, 86, 152
Hemel Hempstead 95 *infra*
Herodotus 8, 175
hierarchy of settlements 48, 95, 96, 100, 122, 124, 134, 144, 157, 158, 160, 161, 168, 177, 184, *199*
hierarchy of spaces 111
hierarchy of roads 91, 95, 114 *infra,* 126, 127, 143, 160
hinterland *see* catchment area
Hiorns, F. 88
Hippodamos 24, 172, 184
Hogarth 173
Holland 5, 103, 124
Hook 103ff., *208*
Horsfall, T. C. 54
hospital, infirmary 17, 36, 93, 114, 149, 160
hotel 36, 62

houses, housing *(see also* flats, residential area) 8, 17, 22, 26, 31, 36, 41, 47, 50, 57, 62, 65ff., 67, 72, 73, 74, 84, 87, 92ff., 100, 102, 115, 128, 149, 150, 157, 164, 191
household *see* family
Howard, E. 43, 47, 52, 83ff., 93, 122, 157, 158, 168, 170 179
Hungary *see* Austria-Hungary

India 7, 13, 144
industry, factory, employment, production 5, 17, 22, 29ff., 32, 34, 36, 38, 47, 49, 51, 56, 62, 79 83, 84, 87, 88, 92, 93, 95, 100, 108, 115, 123ff., 129, 143, 150, 157, 161, 163, 166ff., 172, 175, 182
industrial revolution 23, 52, 54, 67ff., 177, 179
insulae, street block *(see also* super-block) 11, 13
Irvine 127ff., 172
Italy 5, 15, 54, 86

Jacobs, Jane 7 *infra,* 122, 170
Japan *200*
Jefferson, Thos. 31, 87
Jerusalem, New 34
Jones, Inigo *38*
journey-to-work 72, 100, 116, 124, 134, 159

Karlsruhe *23*
Kahun 8
Knossos 9
Krupp 66

Lagash 8
Lanark, Lanarkshire 34
land, landscape *(see also* agriculture, constraints) 5, 74, 111, 172, 179
Laufenburg *15*
lawcourts *see* public buildings
Le Corbusier 51, 59ff., 67, 70, 72ff., 83ff., 102, 103, 105, *105,* 113, 122, 144, 157, 166, 170, 175
Ledoux 30, *44*
Leeds 22, *46,* 66, 85, 116, 120ff., 172, *181*
legislation 12, 52, 54, 55, 66, 83, 88, 179
L'Enfant 20, *25*
Lenin, V. I. 67
Leningrad (St. Petersbourg) *26,* 48, 67, 68, 164
Leonardo da Vinci *see* Vinci
Le Play 52
Letchworth 48, 52, 83ff., *87,* 141
library 10, 82, 95

linear cities 48, 70, *77,* 79, 101, 103, *140, 144, 149, 154, 170, 185, 186*
linear *growth* 58, 122, 126ff., *138,* 140, 144, *145, 149, 150,* 158, 164
Ling, Arthur 134, 163
Lisbon 22
Liverpool 66, 86, 102
Livingston 126
Llewellyn-Davies and partners 153
London 5, 12, 22, *27,* 30, *42, 45,* 47, 53, 55, 56, 59, 64, 66, *69,* 84, 86, 88, *88,* 91, *95, 99, 100,* 103, 108, 114ff., 119ff., 125, 150, 157, 159, 161, 162, 178, 180
Lynch, K. 158 *infra*
Lyons 50
Macadam 56
Madrid 48
Magnitogorsk 70
Manchester 22, 53, 65
market place *(see also* agora, commerce) 6, 13, 15ff., 19, 24
MARS group, *see* Modern Movement
MARS Plan 99ff., 134, 144
Marseilles 103, *105*
Martini *see* Giorgio, Francesco di
Marx, Marxism 65, 67
May, E. 70
Memphis 7, 8
Mesopotamia 7, 8
metropolis, central city *1,* 5, 12, 47, 60, 70, 88, 123, 125, 141
middle ages, mediaeval town *13,*14, *14, 15, 16, 17,* 31, 55, 56, 81
Middlesbrough 31
Milan 22, 26
Milton Keynes 149ff., 159, 166, 168, 185
Miliutin 70, 164
mineral extraction 178
modal split *see also* public transport 135
Modern Movement 51, 52, 59ff., 68, 70, 85, 88, 99, 103ff., 122, 129, 160, 172
module *(see also* cellular structure, neighbourhood, residential area) 8, 13, 128, 135, 139, 141, 150, 153, 157, 158, 160
Mohenjo-Daro 9
Monastery, abbey *14,* 15, 26
Montreal *207*
monumentality 8, 19
More, Thos. 34, *51*
Morris, Wm. 42, 48, 49, 80, 87

Moscow 67, 70, 88, 123
motor-car *see* automobile
Mulhausen 66
Mumford, L. 168

Naples 22
Nancy *19*
Nash, John *45*, 56, *67*
natural resources *see* contraints
neighbourhood (*see also* cellular structure, module, residential area, suburb) 68, 82, 92, 93, 94, 103, 108ff., 113, 124, 128, 131, 141, 155, 158, 162, 168
Newbury 116, 120
New Earswick 32
Newton, Isaac 37
Newton Aycliffe 95 *infra*
new towns (*see also* colony) 5, 15, 19, 20, 22, 43, 103ff., 114, 117, 124, 125, 134, 160, 162, 176, 191
New York 5, 62, 88, 157
Niemeyer, Oscar 103
Ninevah 7, 8
Northampton 162
Norway 53, 54, 103
Norwich 116, 118
Nuremburg *16*
nursery, kindergarten 68, 74, 82

objectives, aims, principles 23, 24, 31, 34, 36, 37, 52, 53, 60, 61, 68ff., 80, 92, 93, 99, 108, 112, 113, 115, 124, 126, 141, 143, 146, 149, 153, 157ff., 166, 172, 175, 191
offices 48, 62, 87, 91, 92, 117, 157, 161, 162, 163, 191
orientation, aspect 8, 12, 24, 25, 61, 76, 82, 111, 164, 179
orthogonal plans *see* gridiron
Ottoman Empire 14
Owen, Robert 34, 41, 47, 60, 67, 157, 191
ownership, tenure 6, 8, 15, 32, 60, 80, 88, 90, 93, 128, 153, 158, 184

Palermo 22
Palma Nova 26, 29, *36*
Paris 22, *41*, *47*, 56, 59, 64, 66, 78, 175
parish 17, 43
Parker, Barry 52, 80, 84, *87*, 94
pedestrian, footpath 10, 13, 50, 58, 72, 76, 77, 96, 101, 143, 175
pedestrian, segregation 26, *34*, 39, 55, 56, 73, 74, 76, 91, *92*, 94, 96, *97*, 108, 117, 118, *120*, 125, 126, 150, 153, 163, 170, 183

pedestrian range 94, 126, 127, 141, 144 150, 155, 159, 161, 163, 172
Pemberton's Happy Colony 42
Pergamom *7*, 10
Perry, C. 94
Persia 11
Peterborough 162
Peterlee 95
phalanstery 37
Philadelphia *24*
philanthropy, paternalism 32ff., 37, 47, 66, 85, 86
Phoenicians 11
Plato, platonism 24, 26, 34
playground 74, 82, 86, 158
plot (houseplot) 8, 13, 31, 81
Plug-in 166, *192*
Poland 124, 164
police 74
pollution 23, 26, 31, 36, 56, 72, 158, 172, 180
Polo, Marco 5
Pompeii *11*, 11, 13
Pooley, F. 152 *infra*
population 5, 16, 52
population balance 37, 108, 126, 129, 153
population growth 5, 15, 16, 22, 25, 113, 123, 125, 149, 164, 172, 180
Port Sunlight 32
Portsmouth *168*
postal services 100, 128
precinct 91, 93, 114, 162
pre-history 6, 170, 184
Preston-Leyland-Chorley 131, *148*
Priene *5*, 6
procedure, planning technique 6, 12, 52, 53, 80, 81, 83, 88, 99, 116, 125, 126, 129ff., 144, 146, 153, 168, 172, 179, *204*
processional way 8, 10, 16, 184
public buildings (*see also* community facilities, restaurant, theatre, etc.) 10, 11, 13, 17, 19, 23, 26, 29, 31, 32, 34, 48, 50, 62, 81, 87, 93, 94, 184
public health 23, 31, 60, 67, 158
public open space, parks 16, 24, 36, 39, 48, 62, 73, 78, 84, 85, 87, 91, 92, 96, 99, 102, 111, 121, 122, 149, 180
public transport (*see also* communications, railways, traffic) 12, 48, 56ff., 78, 87, 93, 100, 108, 111, 119, 120, 122, 125, 126, 128, 135, 141, 143, 149, 153, 158, 159, 160, 163, *171*, *181*, 184

Pugin, A. W. N. 42, 80
Pullman, Ohio 32

Quarry Hill, Leeds 85

Radburn 94, 105, 108, 131, 150, 155, 160
radial plans 16, 24, 48, 56, 91ff., 101, 103, 120, 125, 144, 158, 160, 184
Radiant City (Ville Radieuse) 72ff.
railways, railway station 32, 47, 55, 57, 60, 62, 65, *70*, 72, 79, 84, 85, 94, 100, 111, 120, 134, 150, 160 *infra*, 162, 177
monorail *(see also public transport, communications)* 122, 134, 149, 150ff.
Randstad 124
rapid transit *see* public transport
recreation 36, 48, 73, 82, 102, 123, 153, 179
Redditch 126
redevelopment *see* urban renewal
refuse disposal, collection 10, 15, 16, 23, 51, 86, 152, 160, 168, 180

refuse recycling 180
regionalism 26, 52ff., 88, 90, *91*, 108, 122, 123, 125ff., 127, 134, 141, 144, 160, 161, 168, 176ff., 184, 191
Reith Committee 93ff., 108
renaissance 19, 24, 42, 175
residential area (*see also* housing, neighbourhood, suburb) 105, 108ff., 112, 127, 128, 134, 139, 158, 159, 160, 163, 170
restaurants, canteens, kitchens 34, 38, 41, 64, 68, 70, 76, 82, 87
retail trade *see* commerce
Richardson's Hygeia 42
Richmond, Yorks. 6, 15
roads, streets 6, 7, 10, 12, 13, 17, 24ff., 36, 48, 72ff., 80, 84, 95, 134
roads, streets enclosed 39, 55ff., 74, 91, 94, 101, 105, 111, 113ff., 144, 150, 153, 155, 157
roads, **corridor street** 15, 61, 65, 159, 160, 162
Roman planning 6, *8*, *10*, 11, *11*, *12*, 24, 55
Rome 5, 12, *21*, 22, *37*, *39*, *40*
Rotterdam 91, *94*
RIBA 125
Runcorn 134ff., 141, 159, 160, 163
Ruskin, J. 80
Russia *see* USSR

St. Augustine 34

St. Petersburg *see* Leningrad

Saline de Chaux 30, *44*

Salt, T. Saltaire 32, *48, 49, 50*

sanitation *see* drainage, public health

Sant 'Elia 51, 59

Sao Paulo 4

scale, proportion 26, 64, 74, 105, 158, 160, 162, 172, 175, 182, 192

Scamozzi 26, *36*

schematic plans, *schemata* (*see also* objectives, strategy, urban form) 19, 36, 88, 94, 101, 143, 158, 172

schools *see* education

Schneider 66

science fiction, futurism 49, 51, 59, *66*, 159, 164, 170, 179

Scott Committee 90

Seville 22

sewerage, sewers *see* drainage

Sheffield 22, 53, *111*

shops *see* commerce

site, choice of (*see also* constraints) 6, 9, 14, 17, 24, 25, 37, 50, 52, 55, 68, 88, 111, 160, 176ff

Sitte, Camillo 36 *infra*, 49, 60, 81

Sixtus V, Pope 19

size of settlements (*see also* catchment, territory, population, scale) 5, 8, 12, 16, 20, 22, 24, 26, 34, 36, 37, 39, 47, 48 *infra*, 50, 61, 67, 68, 73, 80, 83, 87, 92, 93, 94, 102, 103, 105, 111, 114, 123ff., 134, 141, 149, 150, 153, 157ff., 160, 163, 164, 168, 170, 172, 175, 177, 180

Skelmersdale 126

Smith, Dr. Southwood 31

Smithson, A. & P. 106, *110*, 122

socialism, communism 34, 36, 42, 47, 49, 53, 59, 65, 81, 158, 191, 192

Soissons, Louis de 85

Soleri, P. 166

Soria y Mata 48, 134

Southampton *168*

South Hampshire 144ff., 160

Spain 5

sports facilities 62, 74, 79, 82, 87, 93, 108, 153, 157, 161, 175

Stalingrad (Volgograd) 70, *77*

Stein, C. 94

Stevenage 103, 108

stoa 9

Stockholm 123, 139, 152, 162

strategy (*see also* objectives, procedure schemata, urban form) 72, 113, 121, 127, 146, 155, 157, 159, 160, 164

streets *see* roads, gridiron, radial

suburbs (*see also* cellular structure, neighbourhood, residential area) 23, 32, 47, 54, 55, 57, 60, 64, 72, 80, 82ff., 92, 94, 100, 131, 149, 158, 163, 191

superblock (*see also* insulae) 62ff., 78, 94, *96*, 111, 119, 141, 144, 153, 155, *158*

surveys (*see also* procedure) 52, 80, 83, 172

Sweden 162

systems theory (*see also* procedure) 122, 125, 127, 144, 172

technological determinism 53ff., 60, 172

Telford (Dawley) 139

Telford, Thos. 56

temple, chapel, church 6, 8, 10, 11, 14, 17, 19, 24, 26, 31, 81, 82, 93, 184

TVA 88, *91*

Theatre 10, 11, 42, 87, 93, 158, 166, 175

Thebes 7, 8

Theodoric 14, 24

thermae *see* bath-house

threshold size, etc. 124, 157

Timgad *10*, 12

Tokyo 5, 157

topography *see* constraints

town and country (*see also* agriculture) 5, 14, 18, 34, 36, 47ff., 67, 68, 108, 126, 163, 168, 179, 183, 184

town hall *see* public buildings

Town Planning Institute, the Royal 52

trade *see* commerce

traffic *see* communications, journey-to-work

traffic capacity 115, *133*

traffic generation 116, *133*

transport *see* communications, automobile, public transport roads, journey-to-work

trend planning 53, 125, 162, 172, 175

Tripp, Alker 91, 92, *92*, 114, 159, 161

Tudor-Walters Report 84, 86

unite d'habitation (*see also* flats, phalanstery) 37, 64, 103, 166

Unwin, Raymond 52, 80, *86*, 94, 179

Ur 7

urban form (*see also* gridiron, radial, cellular, linear, hierarchy, schemata) 6, 8, 12, 14, 15, 18, 19, 24, 25, 26, 29, 30, 34, 36, 42, 47, 48, 50, 53, 55, 61ff., 68, 70, 79, 84, 87, 93, 95, 103, 108, 114, 124, 126ff., 134, 141, 144, 146, 149, 152, 157, 159, 160, 168, 183, 184, *205*

urban renewal, redevelopment 32, 48, 52, 64, 65, 67, 73, 85, 91, 92, 103, 113, 114, 117ff., 120, 122, 144, 160, 162, 168, 175, 192.

urban sprawl 58, 68, 72, 81, 88, 91, 158, 159

Urbanists 68ff.

USA *see* America

USSR, Russia 59, 65, 87, 124, 163, 166, 168, *189, 202, 203*

Uthwatt Committee 90

Utopia, Utopianism 34ff., 37, 42, *51*, 53, 65, 67, 72, 157, 170, 172, 175, 192

Vallingby 106, 163, *183*

Vauban 19, 30, *43*

vehicles *see* automobile, communications

Venice 157

Versailles 19, *22*, 38

Victoria 42, 47

Vienna 66, 86

villa 15

village *2*, 5, 14, 22, 34, 41, 49, *52*, 68, 82, 141, 149, *154, 155*, 180, 183

Vinci, Leonardo da 26, *34*, 42

Vitruvius 24, *30*, 49, 179

Voisin Plan 59ff

wall, circumvallation, fortification 6, 8, 10, 12, 16, 18, 19, 24, 25, 29, 80, 119, 177, 179, 183

war (*see also defence*) 6, 18, 184,

war civil 19, 25, 12, 191, 192

wards 43, 47

Warsaw *185,186*

Washington, D.C. 220, *25*

Washington, co. Durham 141, 153

water supply 8, *9*, 12, 16, 20, 23, 31, 37, 53, 172, 176, 177

Wells, H. G. 48

Welwyn Garden City 48, 85, *89* 95

Wilson & Womersley 126

Wissinck, C. A. 124

Wordsworth, Wm. 180

Wren, Christopher 29, *42*, 161, 184

Wright, Frank Lloyd 86, 88, *90*

Wright, Henry 94

zones, zoning 17, 23, 25, 38, 47, 50, 54, 62, 79, 92, 93, 99, 108, 114, 116, 117, 122, 129, 141, 149, 155, 157, 160, 161, 168, 169